The Heart Is Unknown Country

The Heart Is Unknown Country

LOVE IN THE CHANGING ECONOMY
OF NORTHEAST BRAZIL

L. A. Rebhun

STANFORD UNIVERSITY PRESS
STANFORD, CALIFORNIA

Stanford University Press
Stanford, California
© 1999 by the Board of Trustees of the
Leland Stanford Junior University
Printed in the United States of America

CIP data appear at the end of the book

For My Parents

☞ Acknowledgments

If I have seen further it is by standing on the shoulders of giants.
Sir Isaac Newton. Letter to Robert Hooke, February 5, 1675

I could not have carried out the research upon which this book is based without the hospitality and patience of the people whose stories and opinions form its subject matter. My debt to them is enormous, and I thank them. In addition, a number of Caruaruenses helped me to find people to interview. I am especially grateful to Lucivanda Maria Leite, Jerónimo Teutónio de Melo Neto, Sandra Lúcia Silva Lima, Maria das Graças França, Valdelice da Silva Mendonça, and Luiz Alexandre de Menezes for their assistance in introducing me to interviewees and finding my way around Caruaru, as well as for their hospitality in welcoming me into their homes. Caruaruense anthropologist Iván Brandão provided enormous help, from setting up a bank account to introducing me to local college students studying anthropology, for which I am most grateful. In Recife, Russell Parry Scott facilitated my affiliation with the Universidade Federál de Pernambuco, and in addition Maria do Carmo Brandão provided guidance in my research. Both generously aided me with many details of getting along as an anthropologist and offered advice on both personal and academic matters. I thank them profusely.

The staff of the United States Consulate in Recife, especially Carmen and Marilene, were enormously helpful in my various interactions with the Brazilian bureaucracy and in facilitating my Fulbright fellowship. Martin Adler of the United States Information Agency also provided advice and support at the consulate. For that I am grateful.

My first fieldwork experience in Brazil was conducted as an assistant to Marilyn Nations, who had first introduced me to medical anthropology years earlier and who encouraged me to go to graduate school to study the subject after I had spent two aimless postgraduate years in Charlottesville, Virginia, wondering what to do with my life. Under her tutelage, I first considered questions of love, in that case maternal love under conditions

of high infant mortality. Dr. Nations also introduced me to popular healers like the Catholic faith healers I have continued to study, and set me on
the path that eventually led to this study. For her guidance and example I
am grateful.

My intellectual debt to my dissertation supervisor, Stanley Brandes, is
enormous. Dr. Brandes guided me as my academic advisor during my
graduate training, and both his published work and his comments on my
work have given me new insights into anthropology in general and my
own research in particular. Dr. Brandes also provided guidance and edit-
ing during the preparation of this manuscript. In addition, the other members of my committee, Alan Dundes, Joan Ablon, and Candace Slater,
have provided much-appreciated guidance. Dr. Dundes in particular introduced me to the field of folklore studies and encouraged my sometimes
eclectic interests. Any errors I may have made are despite their excellent
guidance.

Several graduate school colleagues have given me support and advice
for which I am grateful: Nancy Abelmann, Michael Gallo, Lisa Hand-
werker, Valerie Kaalund, Eunshil Kim, Misha Klein, Molly Lee, Randall
Millikin, Michael Nunley, and Holly Tannen. Maria Laura Massolo provided encouragement and assistance in the preparation of the manuscript,
as well as friendship since graduate student days. In addition, Donna
Goldstein has served as a sounding board and idea-exchanger, and has
helped my understanding of Brazil to grow.

During the process of converting the dissertation into a book, I was
supported by my employment at Yale University. Several colleagues here
have given me advice and comments on the developing manuscript, especially Angelique Hagarud, Eric Worby, and James Scott. Through
James Scott's program in Agrarian Studies at Yale, with its weekly collo-
quium series, I have learned about many aspects of agrarian societies and
agrarian transition around the world, greatly enriching my own work.
Like his cousin in Recife, Jim has become an intellectual guide and mentor,
and I thank him.

During final preparation of this manuscript I was supported on a Junior Faculty Fellowship from Yale University, for which I am grateful, and I
was a visiting fellow at the Getty Research Institute, which provided a
luxurious environment in which to work. I was guided in obtaining these
fellowships by William Kelly and Helen Siu of Yale, and by William
Christian, who was then visiting in the Agrarian Studies Program and

whose work has long been an inspiration to me. I am very grateful for their help and support.

The seminar on "Passions" at the GRI, under the leadership of Michael Roth, gave me much to think about, and fellow fellows Darcy Buerkle, Andreas Gailus, Elizabeth Liebman, Margaret Pagaduan, and Catherine Schaller, along with Michael Roth and Charles Salas, gave me useful comments and suggestions on chapter one. Thanks! The Getty also provided me with an excellent assistant, Zaia Alexander, who provided invaluable help with the preparation of the final manuscript, as well as doing the legwork of digging up references from UCLA so that I did not have to venture out on Los Angeles freeways in search of the books. I am most grateful for her help and encouragement.

I would also like to thank Donna Goldstein, Ruben George Oliven, and anonymous reviewers for their very helpful comments on the manuscript, and my editor, Muriel Bell, for her help and encouragement. In addition, two other Stanford editors, Martin Hanft and John Feneron, have provided invaluable assistance.

The research upon which this book is based was supported by grants from the Fulbright Foundation (International Institute of Education), the Social Science Research Council, the National Science Foundation, the National Institutes of Mental Health, the Tinker Foundation, a Hannum-Warner Travel Fellowship from Mount Holyoke College, and a Lowie fellowship from the Department of Anthropology at the University of California at Berkeley.

Finally, I could neither have survived the program at Berkeley, completed fieldwork, nor finished the dissertation and subsequent book without the support of my parents, Lionel I. Rebhun and Mildred Rebhun. It has been my great good fortune to have such interested and supportive parents. Their own professional achievements have been an inspiration, and they have given me constant encouragement, advice, and financial support. It is to them that this work is dedicated.

L.A.R.

⌒ Contents

10 pages of photographs follow page 86

The Heart Is Unknown Country

States of the Brazilian Northeast.

Introduction

Studying Love in Northeast Brazil

O coração, minha filha, é terra desconhecida.
("The heart, my daughter, is unknown country.")
Catholic faith healer (*rezador*)

This is a study of love in Northeast Brazil, or, more specifically, of the impact of rapid social and economic change on courtship, marriage, cohabitation, and infidelity, and their accompanying emotions. Rapid urbanization and the expansion of a cash economy have transformed this region, altering the relative importance of physical intimacy, economic intimacy, and emotional intimacy in conjugal relationships as people increasingly attach ideas of romance—once more associated with infidelity, concubinage, and courtship—to marriage itself.

My discussion responds to three main bodies of literature: the growing number of anthropological studies of weddings and marriage, the anthropological literature on emotion, and the historical literature on romance in European and Europeanate cultures. A number of studies have illuminated changes in marital ceremonies and relationships in local areas and the way in which they reflect the economic and cultural transformations of the world economy of the late twentieth century (Argyrou 1996; Cancian 1986; Collier 1997; Douglass 1992; Hoodfar 1997; Kendall 1996). In particular, these studies call attention to the balance among attraction, respect, economic cooperation, and love in marriages, and to the increasing worldwide adoption of the Victorian white wedding ceremony.

Like the people studied in these earlier works, the Northeast Brazilian working-class people whom I studied struggled to define the emotional and economic nature of their conjugal relationships. Their struggles reflect similar issues in earlier transformations studied by historians of romance in medieval and early-modern Europe, themselves responses to rapid social change of their day.

I also look at love as a kind of emotion. Research in diverse settings has shown the complexity of the combination of biological states, cultural constructs, social roles, internal experience, and interpersonal interactions that make up emotion, shifting not only from one setting to another but also among social classes and individual roles within particular cultures. By focusing on the various ways that the women and men of Northeast Brazil whom I studied used the word *amor* ("love"), I hope to illuminate theoretical issues in the cross-cultural study of emotion.

In addition, concepts of love form part of the historical development of traditions of romance. Historians of Europe, the United States, and Brazil have debated the relationship between shifts in ideologies of romance and such cultural changes as the expansion of cash economies, the growth of the state, increasing urbanization, the development of ideologies of privacy and individuality, the growth of medicalization, and increases in social, economic, and geographic mobility. In Northeast Brazil, where rapid urbanization and economic change have made people's lives dramatically different from those of their parents, ideologies of romance, their place in courtship and relevance to marriage, have changed in ways that shed light on historical debates about similar processes in other times and places.

So this is a study of contemporary history, of the old and the new and the relationship between the two. In regions like Northeast Brazil, people hold the concept of modernization self-consciously. They continually classify behavior and beliefs, as well as styles of dress, artwork, speech, morality, and sentiment, as being either traditional or modern, and they often remark on regional differences in style as if they indicated a kind of anachronistic coexistence of separate historical epochs. These kinds of distinctions have become so commonplace in the late twentieth century that the idea of arranging them onto imaginary axes spanning the geography of city and countryside elicits little comment. This recasting of geographic, political, and economic relationships as historical difference reflects an attitude whose familiarity too frequently obscures its strangeness (cf. Fabian 1983).

People speak as if each city generates its own figurative temporal wheel, forming the proudly modern center of a circle that grows more old-fashioned the further out you travel from it (cf. Williams 1973). The countryside becomes transformed into an imagined space-time continuum, with the cities' modernizing wheels ranked against one another in size and degree of modernity. And yet, although styles do vary geographically, those parts of the landscape imagined to be backward do not in fact live in the past, nor are the cities building the future. Rather, the entire countryside displays what García Canclini calls "multitemporal heterogeneity" in which "traditions have not yet disappeared and modernity has not completely arrived" (1995, 1). Much of the discussion of contemporary marriage takes place within this imagined temporal geography.

This book also constitutes a story: the story of my voyage to what was to me a foreign land, of the companions I met there, and of what I learned from them. Although cultural anthropology takes its place among the social sciences, it also borrows strongly from the humanities in its form and sensibilities. The instrument of investigation in anthropological fieldwork is the researcher herself. Her data are formed by the places she visits, the people who befriend her (and those who merely tolerate her), and her observations of and reactions to her experiences. Collecting narratives and reporting data in the form of a narrative make ethnography as much a literary as a scientific endeavor (Clifford 1988; Clifford and Marcus 1986; Marcus and Fischer 1986). I find the idiom of storytelling especially relevant to the study of love, for love so frequently takes the form of a romance: a story of attraction, affection, passion, desire.[1]

My research took the form of a physical journey that was also an intellectual and emotional one. If there were times when, gazing at the unfamiliar Southern Hemisphere constellations, I felt I had traveled to another planet, there were others when the people I met seemed alien to me—and no doubt so I appeared to them. But more misleading were the times when everything seemed to make sense, when it seemed that all I needed were intuition and empathy to understand those around me. I had to learn to annotate, study, and puzzle over everything, even the seemingly familiar. Paradoxically, it was only when I got over my search for the comfort of the recognizable, when the foreign became commonplace and surprise prosaic, that what had seemed alien revealed itself as ordinary. Those who do fieldwork in their own cultures struggle with the dynamic between the intimacy of familiarity and the distance offered by the role of researcher (Argyrou 1996; Hayano 1979; McLaren 1991; Messerschmidt 1981; Powdermaker 1966; Preston 1994). The same tension informs cross-cultural research, which offers the advantage of not being able to take knowledge for granted and thus being forced to ask more probing questions, with its twin, the disadvantage of easy misunderstanding, of missing the broad picture because the details have been ignorantly misconstrued. However, foreigners can more easily get away with asking ignorant questions; a native researcher, even one working outside his or her home area or social class, may not be treated with as much tolerance.[2]

Patience and careful consultation with locals offer at least partial correctives to these disadvantages. I was lucky enough to receive funding for two years, and it took most of the first year to reeducate my sensibilities. It was only then that I began to catch hints and get jokes, to be able to follow what people tried to communicate indirectly, being unwilling or unable to state it out loud. Even then, I was careful to check my understandings and interpretations with my companions.

Traditions of Romance and the West

Conventional wisdom has it that romantic passion exists only in European and North American cultures, especially among elites living after 1650 or so. Cross-cultural and historical research has begun to dent the notion that desire, and not love, is the only purview of the poor, the non-Western, and the long dead (Jankowiak 1995b). But "romance" is not the sole part of the phrase "Western traditions of romance" that requires deconstruction. The category "Western" also needs investigating.

To some, anthropological deconstruction of "Western" seems paradoxical. Anthropology began as the study of the non-Western Other: tribal societies, the Orient, rural and poor people in Europe and the Americas. Early anthropologists invented hierarchies of savagery and civilization that we see as biased today; those researchers have been taken to task posthumously for their extensive involvement with colonial domination, as have their modern professional descendants (Clifford 1988; Fabian 1983; Said 1978, 1989; Young 1995).[3]

Attempts to create a more politically informed anthropology include considerations of the political and economic context of ideas and practices (Ortner 1995, 174), especially descriptions of the often painful process of modernization as local responses to the pressures of international capitalist transformation. This critical approach has itself come under criticism, for its rigidly materialist base (Ortner 1984), for its reification of the West (Carrier 1992), for its continued reliance on a temporal model of progress (Fabian 1983), and for its failure to deconstruct the imbrication of the categories "modern" and "Western" (Argyrou 1996).

The tension over reification of the category "Western" appears most strongly in ethnographies on the perimeter of that category, especially studies in the contemporary Mediterranean. While celebrating the ancient Greeks and the Renaissance Italians for their contributions to the accomplishments of Western civilization, European and North American formulations of "the West" tend to exclude modern Mediterraneans as tainted by too long an engagement with "Middle Eastern" Ottomans and Moors (Argyrou 1996; Faubion 1993; Hertzfeld 1987). The racist underpinnings of confinement of the prestigious sobriquet "Western" to the United States, Canada, nonnative Australia and New Zealand, and the countries of northwestern Europe, especially Germany, England, and France, go largely uncommented upon in contemporary considerations of "Westernization" and "modernization."[4]

Similarly, the national cultures of Latin America tend to be lumped, at least by anthropologists from the United States, into the "non-Western" category, despite their status as former European colonies with significant Mediterranean cultural influence. Whether this derives more from the exclusion of the contemporary Mediterranean from the "West," from U.S. racial categories separating "Hispanic" from "Caucasian," or from the perception of Latin America as located on the poorer end of the political-economic hierarchy, it displays the same difficulties as the exclusion of the modern Mediterranean from the "West."

E. Valentine Daniel, calling essentialism "the bad word of late modernity," points out that theorists are not the only people who construct essentialized categories, and that the fragility of cultural constructions is often apparent to "those who live in and with them" (1996, 14). Essentialist ideas of the Western, the modern, and romance exert a strong influence in places like Caruaru. The practice of romance reflects a prestigious involvement with the "West," its economic domination, its glorious cultural heritage, its prestige, and its modernity, especially regarding romance as expressed in marriages for love celebrated by women in white dresses and men in dress suits, attended by identically dressed witnesses and blessed by church and state ceremonies. In this work, I examine not whether romance is Western or modern, but rather what "romance," "Western," and "modern" mean to Caruaruenses, and how the reification of these categories affects the ways in which they live their lives.

Getting to Caruaru

Wait a minute, *Gringinha* (little North American). Let me get this
straight. You're saying that you came to a place you had never
visited before, without speaking the language fluently, unmarried,
alone, leaving your mother at home? You came to a city you did
not know, to live with people who were strangers to you, to find
out what anyone could tell you, and that the government of your
country paid you to do this? *Que mundo de maravilhas!* ("What a
world of marvels!").

A seventy-eight-year-old woman in Caruaru[5]

Anthropologists take for granted the normality of journeying to unfamiliar lands in search of answers to esoteric questions. My socialization into
the discipline after years of undergraduate and graduate course work
blinded me to the true strangeness of my situation. I found myself sitting
in the receiving room of Dona Maria do Monte, a Catholic faith healer in
Caruaru, trying to explain why she should tell me her life history. I had
come to Brazil, quite naturally I thought, to study the cultural aspects of
emotion among recently urbanized women.

I had previously worked as a research assistant for medical anthropologist Marilyn Nations, investigating the cultural aspects of infant
mortality in the Northeast Brazilian city of Fortaleza. Our investigations
into the nature of maternal attachment, caretaking behavior, and grief in
the context of Catholic folk beliefs about children's lives and deaths (Nations and Rebhun 1988) gave me insights into intriguing questions not
only about Northeast Brazil as a region but also more generally. I did not
question that I would return to the region for further investigation into the
nature of emotion: My concerns lay in picking the right field site, planning
the study, and financing the venture.

It wasn't until I sat waiting to board my international flight in Miami
that I began to feel the first symptoms of nerves. My dissertation advisor,
Stanley Brandes, had told me to be sure to carry at least one hundred dollars in cash on my person so that I could get a good hotel room when I arrived. That way I would be able to sleep well and wake up refreshed to
face what the next day would bring. I had the money in my pocket and a
reservation already made.

I reminded myself that I had read and debated books on fieldwork
methods in my seminars, passed my Ph.D. qualifying exams, studied the
history and culture of Brazil, taken intensive language training in the

Portuguese language, and completed a previous research trip to Brazil, during which I had had the opportunity to visit Recife, capital of the state of Pernambuco, my current destination. During that trip I had taken a bus for the two-hour trip up into the mountains to Caruaru, falling in love with the dusty town, its bustling market, leather-clad cowboys, and vivid popular art. That, I decided, was where I would do my dissertation research. Surely all this had prepared me well for my latest venture. Still, it took conscious effort to suppress the physical symptoms of anxiety.

My flight was uneventful, if lengthy. Humid heat smothered me in its exhausting embrace as we disembarked at Recife's international airport in the predawn darkness. After some initial confusion over unforeseen irregularities with my visa, I was processed, admitted, and allowed to take my luggage to the taxi stand, where I paid for the trip to my hotel. The taxi driver informed me that the hotel at which I had a reservation was not as good as another one, to which he insisted on bringing me.[6] I was too tired to argue, quickly completing negotiations with the hotel clerk and collapsing into a creaky bed.

Several hours later I awoke to full sunlight. Opening the shutters I gazed out on a bustling street scene. Vendors stood over piles of tropical fruits, shouting enticements to passersby, men scurried about with heavy bags of goods for sale, a man with a microphone stood amid a display of dead lizards, explaining the virtues of a medicine made of the finest snake oil, two teenagers faced off in a staged display of the martial art of *capoeira* while little boys expertly picked spectators' pockets. Women gracefully wended their way through the chaos, many of them balancing shopping bundles on their heads to leave their hands free for holding on to their children. Chickens, goats, and donkeys added their voices to the cacophony. "It's Brazil, all right," I thought, and went back to sleep. The next day, well rested, I was in better shape to enjoy the sights, sounds, and smells of the city.

The activities of the next few weeks distracted me from any worries. Registering with the U.S. consulate, visiting universities and research institutes in Recife to introduce myself, finding a better hotel, acquiring and recovering from dysentery, and finding a place to live in Caruaru took all my attention. My illness, the tropical humidity, and the strain of trying to communicate full time in a new language left me too weary to fret. It was not until I was settled in Caruaru, mercifully located at a cooler, drier altitude than Recife, mostly recovered, and beginning to penetrate the puzzles of the local accent that I felt free to speculate on my situation.[7] Sitting in Dona Maria do Monte's receiving room after being blessed to remove the evil eye from my hair, I could only agree with her: A world in which I could end up in her house is indeed a wondrous strange place.

The Interpenetration of Plural Realities

Among the responses to the moral and political dilemmas of fieldwork has been a more humanized view of belief and behavior, one that takes into account both the existence of multiple perspectives and the political dynamics of conceptions of reality.[8] I did not meet any typical Northeast Brazilians during my journey; rather, I met individuals who could debate the meanings of terms and concepts as cogently as any academic—and often with more insight and less pretension. I met people who consciously made choices in their lives, who debated passionately with family and friends over the right way and the wrong way to do things, who agonized over the propriety of their actions, who made mistakes (sometimes the same mistakes repeatedly), who searched for meaning in the events of their lives, sometimes finding it, sometimes not.

This does not mean that the concept of culture should be entirely discarded: Ideas, practices, economic institutions, and structures of society transcend individual lifetimes and organize individual experiences. It does mean, however, that we need to pay as much attention to how individuals go about understanding, interpreting, and reacting to the ideas and practices they inherit as we do to those ideas and practices themselves. Rather than see culture as a monolithic, static, and all-encompassing whole, we can see it as various, dynamic, and diffuse: an ever-changing, constantly reformulated, negotiated, interpreted set of ideas, practices, and manipulations of power.

This approach takes a view of culture as a series of ideas and practices among which members choose, and a conviction that local history influences which choices are available to members of a given culture. In the case of Brazil, the legacy of Portugal's conquest and reconquest by Moors and then Iberians, brought to Brazil in the context of its own conquest by the Portuguese, mingled with the inheritance of enslaved Africans and the syncretic practices they created in their new world. These mixed yet again with ideas and practices from native peoples, themselves engulfed by the European expansion into their territories. All get reflected in the language, folklore, religion, food, architecture, clothing, beliefs, and practices of Brazilians, along with the influences of more recent immigrants from Germany, Japan, and other countries.

Antonius Robben, in a study of Northeast Brazilian fishermen, describes Brazilian culture as "pluriform" (1989, 3). Richard Parker, examining sexuality in Rio de Janeiro, agrees, writing about the "multiple subsystems, recurring yet often disparate patterns, conflicting and sometimes even contradictory logics that have somehow managed to intertwine and interpenetrate the fabric of social life" (1991, 2). Parker's "many layers of meaning" (1991, 5) and Robben's "discursive contradictions" (1989, 9) both offer vocabularies in which to describe the dynamic tension inherent in contemporary understandings of culture. This dynamic view informs my approach. I believe that attention to the contradictions of people's lives, their triumphs, fears, and foibles, but also the assumptions and practices that make up their daily experience, serves as a partial corrective to dehumanizing stereotypes, whether contemptuous or romanticized. Taking local people seriously, not just as examples of the variables that make up theoretical postulates but also as complex human beings with important comments and insights to offer makes for both more respectful fieldwork and more faithful findings (cf. Wikan 1990, 282).

Approaches to Fieldwork

From December of 1988 to December of 1990, I conducted research in Caruaru and neighboring towns, as well as rural homesites and small farms.[9] Constant traffic wends between various rural locales and Caruaru, especially on market days. In Caruaru I worked with people primarily from four neighborhoods: (1) the working-class neighborhood in which I lived for most of my time there, (2) a former *favela* that had turned lower working-class upon official legalization,[10] (3) a poor neighborhood of both legalized and nonlegalized housing, and (4) a government housing project for former *favela* dwellers in which I lived for the last few months of my fieldwork. In addition, I held interviews in the *favela* on the slope of the Hill of the Good Jesus in the middle of Caruaru, and in a number of small *favelas* in the interstices between wealthier neighborhoods.

Although some *favelas* are clearly distinguishable from working-class neighborhoods, many are not. In general, nonlegalized status marks *favelas*, which are composed of shanties put up without permits. But, in actuality, many non-*favela* houses are also not legalized, even those of wealthy people. While newer, poorer *favelas* may contain shacks improvised of cardboard, mud, and found objects recovered from garbage, others boast cobblestone streets, cement and brick houses, electricity, and even piped water. Over time, the Caruaru city government has legalized a number of former *favelas*. In some neighborhoods, shanties of cardboard and junk abut brick houses; often the shanties have piles of bricks growing in their yards, their owners having begun the years-long process of collecting materials for home-grown housing improvement one brick and one stone at a time (see also Perlman 1976 on *favelas*).

I did not originally set out to study love, as such, but was led to the topic. When I first arrived in Caruaru, I set about collecting an emotion lexicon with which to map the cognitive structure of emotion concepts. My original plan was to do a linguistic study of emotion of the type then popular in anthropology. This involved collecting as many terms as possible and then using materials from in-depth interviews to analyze the meanings and relationships of the words. My innovation would be to include the vocabulary of folk medical syndromes as emotion terms: words like *nervos* ("nerves"), *susto* ("shock"), and *mau olhado* ("evil eye"). I was interested in how emotions became defined as causes or symptoms of medical disorders, as well as being medical disorders in themselves. However, I encountered a number of problems with this approach.

One was that the Portuguese words *emoção* and *sentimento* do not correspond exactly with similar English terms. That is, although *emoção* can be used to mean exactly what the English "emotion" means, its primary meaning is more like that of "excitement." Similarly, while one can speak of *sentimentos* and convey the same idea conveyed by the English "sentiment," the word also implies something corny or nostalgic, as does the English "sentimental." Asking people to name and describe all the words for sentiments in Portuguese therefore got me responses different from what I had expected, an interesting result in itself.[11]

Second, people found my questions boring, and frankly, so did I. Shortly after arriving in Caruaru, I began to look for people to interview by going to the homes of Catholic faith healers (*rezadeiras*) and chatting with the people waiting to be blessed as well as with the healers themselves. I found that when I asked people about their lives and problems, and especially about their problems with the opposite sex, even strangers were eager to tell me detailed, elaborate stories. But as soon as I got out my notebook to take down lists of emotion lexicons and folk medical terms, the room started to get quiet and empty.

There is nothing more entertaining than other people's love lives, except perhaps one's own, and gossip about them is one of the joys of social life in any society.[12] Focusing on vocabulary did not leave sufficient time to collect and contemplate the rich stories people wanted to tell about their lives, or their lively opinions on political and social issues. There seemed a particular preoccupation with issues concerning love in Caruaru. This corresponded partly to the Brazilian self-image as a hot-blooded, tropical people, the sexiest population on earth (cf. Parker 1991), and therefore as experts on love. But, in addition, many of the people I spoke with expressed confusion over the nature of love and about the changes they had seen during their lifetimes in the definitions of love. Both men and women differentiated among types and qualities of love, the sexes both expressing puzzlement over the other's definitions of, and behavior in response to, love.

I found myself discontent with my research methods, not only in terms of these practical concerns but also for deeper reasons. I was struck by emotion's slippery nature: now conscious, now unconscious, now openly expressed, now indirectly expressed, and always manipulated. While I retained an interest in how people describe sentiment, I expanded my concerns past vocabulary to discourse: what people talk about in relation to sentiment, how they communicate, what they say, as well as what they leave unsaid and what they act out in wordless practice.

Vocabulary remained important. Sentiments take form through language; words mold, describe, and communicate experience. Momentary impressions solidify into sentiments through linguistic description. Individual words used to describe particular sentiments have multiplex meanings, and particular terms illuminate constellations of related concepts and suggest culturally defined trajectories of experience. Any given emotion-word can serve as a lens through which to view the patterns of social interaction in a given society. In this study, I use the word *amor* and related terms to illuminate patterns of connection in urban Northeast Brazilian society and to show how these patterns have changed with the shift from a primarily agrarian to a primarily urban setting.

Words, however, are not the only form in which sentiments may be experienced and expressed. Music, dance, gesture, and facial expression all shape and convey emotion, as do some forms of illness and many forms of labor. A woman who washes her husband's shirts every day for years may define that labor as an act of love; a man who brings home his paycheck to wife and children loves them through the act. Social and economic change affects not only how people talk about love but also how they enact love, how their bodies feel and express love, how they practice love in daily life.

Methods of Research

I began to conduct in-depth interviews with selected key respondents, often tracing out women's network connections to find interviewees. These key respondents were women who had the opportunity and inclination to spend time in lengthy discussions, who had connections to other people they could introduce to me, and who had the ability to discuss their lives and opinions lucidly. I asked any woman I interviewed to introduce me to her sisters, mother, mother-in-law, neighbors, and friends, and I tried to interview them. I also interviewed men, although it proved difficult to interview the husbands of my interviewees, partly because working-class men are not accustomed to talking with unrelated women who are not romantic interests, and partly because couples were uncomfortable with the idea of their both confiding in the same person about issues that might be in contention between them.[13]

I used both informal conversations and formal taped interviews (about 120 of them). Taped interviews range from twenty minutes to two hours in length, with an average of one hour. Some individuals were interviewed more than once. Wherever possible, I carried out interviews with more than one member of a family. In addition, I noted stray comments, jokes, proverbs, song lyrics, posters, sayings written on truck bumpers, and other communications. I often learned more from informal interactions than I did from formal interviews. Informal interactions also served as an arena for testing the veracity of answers obtained from formal interviews.

In interviews with both women and men I sought information on marriage and marriagelike relationships, as well as definitions of love, experiences with the opposite sex, family relationships, and life histories. I also asked parents about child-rearing, especially differences in raising boys and girls, and I questioned people about their relations with parents, lovers, spouses, children, relatives, and friends, asking for comments on issues such as virginity and sexual propriety. I sought descriptions of how their marriages compared with those of their parents or their children. I asked women to discuss the nature of men and men to talk about women. I asked both sexes about prostitution, concubinage, and for their definitions of and opinions about promiscuity. I visited Catholic faith healers to question them and their patients about their ailments. I also asked people about the economy and national economic policy, their incomes, economic interrelationships with relatives and neighbors, and the details of their expenditures.

Reflecting Northeast Brazil's religious heterogeneity, about two-thirds of those interviewed were Catholic; the rest were mostly Protestants: Seventh Day Adventists, Jehovah's Witnesses, Baptists, and members of the Church of the Universal Reign of God. Two were recently converted to the Church of Jesus Christ of Latter Day Saints. Some of the Protestants were firm members of churches, others were nominally Catholic but went through periods of interest and participation in Protestant churches. In addition, two described themselves as Kardecist.[14]

The most useful interview information came from high-density interviews, those with friends, with friends of friends, and with family members of other interviewees, each giving me more details and different points of view on the same stories. Throughout my fieldwork I hung out with the people I studied: I ate meals with them, helped with the housework, went to parties, shopped, attended festivals, watched television, gossiped, ran errands, attended church, and visited.

Much of my best information came from these informal activities. Sometimes days would pass while I learned few new things to annotate: a proverb here, a comment there. But through just being present I came to understand the rhythms of people's lives, to watch them act out the situations they described in interviews, and sometimes I was present when dramatic events occurred that otherwise might not have been revealed to me.

Hanging out is also a major element of friendship formation. Trust takes time to establish, as does a comfortable presence. Once people were accustomed to seeing me daily, they incorporated me into their lives and relaxed sufficiently to act naturally in my presence. Through spending time over a long term and by cross-checking interviews with several family members or neighbors, I was able to catch discrepancies and disguised statements. There were a number of situations I was able to reconstruct by interviewing everyone involved and then comparing their statements. Sometimes I became aware of the presence of interesting situations by overhearing sarcastic comments. At other times these comments illuminated contradictions in the accounts of various situations.

At first research was difficult, but after several months and many mishaps I began to make friends, come to know them, and become integrated into their friendship and godparenthood networks. From the neighborhood young men who showed up to take my part in debates about car accidents or prices, to the families who competed to see which one could outdo the others in hospitality, to the woman who knelt at my feet, crossed herself, and said, *"Me bença, antropóloga, porque pequei* (Bless me, anthropologist, for I have sinned)"* before reciting her life history, I was drawn into the intense social life of working-class neighborhoods, small towns, and rural homesteads.

Because I was more interested at first in mapping the variety of ideas and experiences people in this region describe than in the statistics of which types of events and interpretations are most common, I did not attempt to build a stratified, representative sample. In general I used a snowball sampling method based at first on a convenience sample of key respondents: whoever would talk to me followed by whoever among their friends and family would talk to me, with an eye toward including a variety of types of people. After the first set of interviews gave me an idea of the opinions and experiences I would encounter, and after securing funding for a second year of research, I chose some individuals for reinterview on particular topics.

Plan of the Book

Throughout this book I am concerned not only with describing the shape and historical background of phenomena, along with my interpretation, but also with presenting people's stories in their own words. I was struck by how much the locals love their language, delighting not only in clever turns of phrase but also in the devices of drama inherent in storytelling. A fascination with both tragedy and comedy emerges in people's self-presentation and in how they choose to live their lives. As much as possible I have tried to present situations in the respondents' own words, translated into English. I provide a glossary for quick reference. I collected my data as a series of stories, and, to the best of my ability, I have attempted to present it as a series of interlocking narratives.

Each individual cited has been given a pseudonym. Brazilian names draw not only from Portuguese but also from native South American, German, English, African, and French names. In addition, parents invent names or think up creative alternative spellings. All of the pseudonyms I use are actual names, taken from *telenovela* characters, people mentioned in municipal birth registries or newspaper articles, or from the relatives of respondents. In the text individuals are identified only by pseudonym, but in the appendix a list provides the age, social class, marital status, religion, and town of residence.

In order to protect identities I have engaged in some minor fictionalization of these capsule biographies. While I have not created any composite characters, I have on occasion given more than one pseudonym to a single respondent so as to isolate some better known anecdotes about them from perhaps more troubling or scandalous information. I have attempted to balance the need for confidentiality with the reader's desire for accuracy. While I quote many people, I quote some more frequently than others.

The book is divided into two sections, one focusing on issues related to emotion and economy in general, the second focusing on the special characteristics of romantic passion in particular. I begin with a review of anthropological theories of emotion, using them to interpret one woman's particularly adroit emotional manipulations and the nature of the folk ailment called "nerves." This is followed by a chapter on the economic, geographical, and historical conditions of Northeast Brazil, focusing on the Agreste geographic region and the city of Caruaru in particular.

In chapter three I discuss the nature of social networks in Caruaru and the relationship between emotional and economic aspects of love, here discussing love as the sentiment proper to kinship and friendship, not in its sexual sense. This section lays the groundwork for part two, in which I consider romantic passion as a particular kind of love, its correlation with other kinds of love, and its role in social and economic relationships.

In chapter four I discuss current theory on romantic passion. Chapter five deals with ideas of proper male and female roles in Caruaru, with particular attention to concepts of honor and shame, reputation and respectability, and the differing spatial and conceptual domains of house and street. Chapter six details the legal structure and customary practice of courtship, marriage, and cohabitation in Caruaru, and chapter seven addresses how Caruaruenses and the people in neighboring towns and rural areas talk about love. In chapter eight I consider the impact of male infidelity in companionate and romantic marriage, and in chapter nine I present my conclusions.

Left out of this analysis is close consideration of certain theological aspects of romance, the relationship between romantic ideology and images of motherhood, the romantic nature of the mother-son bond as opposed to sexual union, and details on high rates of domestic violence, male drunkenness, and anxiety and depression among women, which were also topics of my research. These will be mentioned here but considered in detail in planned future publications. Here I concentrate on conjugal relationships in their economic and cultural context and on close consideration of the nature of love as an emotion or, perhaps more accurately, as a related cluster of sentiments. I hope that I have represented the variety of Caruaruense opinions and experiences in a form that will be recognized by those familiar with the region but that can be understood equally well by those who are not.

Part I

☞ Economy and Emotion in Caruaru

For many people, the first thing that springs to mind on hearing the word "love" is an image of romantic love, or, alternatively, of parental love. The word—both in its English form "love" and its Portuguese *amor*, however, has a much broader set of meanings in common usage. The words can also be used to refer to the sentiments proper to a variety of social affiliations: the emotions that bind kin; the paternalistic sentiments of patrons toward clients and clients toward patrons; the sentiments proper to relationships among God, God's representatives, and human beings.

Because love may be thought of as a type of emotion (although as we shall see that is not the only way to define it), I consider first the nature of emotions, using the case of a woman I will call Maria Imaculada to test the great variety of theories about emotion. Then, after an introduction to some of the geographic, economic, historical, and cultural basics of the region under study, I turn to a consideration of love in its generalized sense as a sentiment of social affiliation. Here I look at friendship, customership, social networks, and the intertwined nature of sentimental and economic connection. This section forms the basis for discussion of the thorny complex of emotional, economic, and social ties that bind and separate men and women.

The emotional and economic issues involved in courtship, cohabitation, and marriage form a subset of the general emotions of affiliation in a society. In many ways, sexual love mirrors parental love, with which it may be intertwined to varying degrees. In addition, the bonds of sexual love create a miniature society between lovers that mirrors issues in the broader society. Before considering the specific case of sexual and romantic love in Northeast Brazil, therefore, I will consider love in its wider sense.

1 ~ The Problem

On the Nature of Sentiment

Vemos a cara, do coração não sabemos.
("We see the face, of the heart we don't know.")
Brazilian proverb[1]

The mysteries of sentiment puzzle scholars as much as they do lay people. Despite generations of theories, the heart remains unknown country. This chapter examines what little is known of that mysterious country by considering emotion in the context both of theoretical debates and case histories from my research.

On the surface, others' emotions seem translatable into familiar terms: *Amor* means "love," and thus should be the same as "love." But this surface resemblance is deceptive. Although the ideas of love to the middle class in the United States and of *amor* to the working class of Northeast Brazil both trace their ancestry from the same European tradition of romance, and although both respond to similar concerns about the role of passionate desire in sexual relationships, *amor* and love are not identical. To understand how they differ requires comprehension both of how sentiments vary cross-culturally and of those factors in the United States and Northeast Brazil that affect how people practice love.

Anthropological theory on emotion has moved from the early work of Darwin, in which verbal and nonverbal expression constitute an organism's awareness of a biologically based, universal set of excitation states (1872; see also Ekman 1980, 1984; Hatfield et al. 1994), to the ethnopsychological school of Catherine Lutz (1982, 1988), Michelle Rosaldo (1980), and Lila Abu-Lughod (1987, 1990; Abu-Lughod and Lutz 1990).[2] Building on the earlier "Culture and Personality" approach, which posited that cultural differences produce local variants of universal sentiments, these writers go further, claiming that the sentiments described in the vocabularies of various languages differ fundamentally from one another: Not only does the manner in which people experience, label, and communicate sentiments vary, but the very concept of emotion itself is not universal.[3]

Ethnopsychologists show that terms denoting sentiments cannot be directly translated between languages.[4] For example, the Portuguese term *saudade* encompasses meanings found in the English terms "nostalgia," "homesickness," and "to miss"; it describes the mingled pleasure and pain experienced upon remembering people and places now distant in time or space. The word cannot be directly translated into any single word in another language.[5] *Saudade* thus offers a window into Brazilian concepts of interpersonal connection, the relationship between emotional pleasure and pain.

Rather than seeing words as having rigidly set meanings, ethnopsychologists accentuate how people use particular terms, with all their connotations and associations, to comment on social events (O'Nell 1996, 184–85). This emphasis, deriving from the general thrust of contemporary theory away from reified categories and toward a dynamic view of social process, has been strongly influenced by the work of Michel Foucault, especially his insight that power, rather than residing solely in the activities of large-scale organizations, percolates throughout society, being formed and re-formed through the details of interpersonal interactions (1978, 1979).

Foucault directed attention to shifts in worldview that accompanied the complex of changes in European society called "modernity": the separation of remunerative work, domestic labor, and leisure; the intensification of divisions between public and private; the creation of regimes of expertise such as medicine and the consequent de-skilling of the general population; the expansion of the state and its increasing intrusion into the lives of citizens; and the creation of new ways of seeing and of experiencing time, space, movement, value, and the human body, ways that emphasize the quantitative numeration of discrete units over a more qualitative, continuous, unbroken experience (1979). These changes continue to have profound influence over the lives of men and women and the ways in which they interact.

Following Foucault's lead, contemporary anthropologists direct theoretical attention to the role of contending multiple voices in social interactions. Rather than write about cultures as entities, they direct their attention to narratives, discourses, and webs of significance, emphasizing the dynamic process of interaction that creates and sustains social reality. However, as people strive to define what is happening in any given encounter and what it means, their voices do not carry equal weight. Class, gender, age, and social position all affect how authoritatively people regard any given voice (cf. Lamphere et al. 1997). People also vary in regard to their social position, how openly they believe they can voice their contestations; the methods they choose with which to express themselves, and how others receive their expressions (cf. Scott 1985, 1990).

In addition, people vary in their skill at expressing themselves and winning over others to their point of view. Emotion emerges in what social actors experience and intend to convey, or what they convey inadvertently as they work through their relationships. More a negotiation than an event, emotion constitutes a vocabulary "manipulated, misunderstood, reconstrued, and played with" (Lutz 1988, 10) as social actors attempt to understand and control both themselves and others. Trying to understand emotion in light of these insights, Catherine Lutz urges attention to the "intensely meaningful" in interpersonal interactions instead of to static concepts or rigidly defined words (1988, 8). In the same light, Uni Wikan writes of the "lived predicaments" in which people find themselves as generators of emotional meaning (1990, 12–13). In this view, sentiments, as acts of communication, constitute a part of social process rather than exclusively individual phenomena.

This view of emotion contrasts with other current theories, in which sentiments correspond to particular configurations of brain activity or metabolic excitation (Bard 1934, 309), fit into biologically based schemas of facial expression (Ekman 1980, 1984), or otherwise reflect individual internal experience. These approaches see sentiments as part of the universal biological heritage of human beings, and to the extent that they recognize cultural differences in emotional experience, they interpret them as variations around a norm (a middle-class European or North American norm). They see historical, social, and moral aspects of emotion as peripheral rather than central (Harré 1986, 2; Hochschild 1983, 208; Lyons 1980, 3; O'Nell 1996, 181).

I take a compromise position between the extremes of social construction found in some ethnopsychology and the biological determinism of the Darwinist school. Emotion is as much biological as social, but it is also as much interpersonal as psychologically individual. These aspects of emotion are not mutually exclusive, and more fluid concepts of both the nature of the social and of the biological can accommodate them both.

A number of stories that local people told me about their lives brought home the complex, contradictory nature of their emotional experiences and the dynamic tension between emotion as individual experience and as culturally constructed social act. For example, a story told by a forty-one-year-old woman in a small town near Caruaru illustrates the slippery nature of emotion.

Maria Imaculada's "Nerves"

Sometimes the best strategy when faced with an intellectual puzzle is to consider it from several different points of view. Such was the case with Maria Imaculada's *ataques de nervos* ("attacks of 'nerves'").

At the age of sixteen Maria Imaculada had made a customary marriage with her first cousin, and she was now the mother of two teenage daughters. She did piecework at home, stitching blue jeans, while her husband spent weekdays traveling the local market circuit, buying precut denim and selling the finished jeans for a profit of about ten U.S. cents per pair.

While she said that she had been good natured *desde o primeiro choro* ("since my first cry"), she complained of unpleasant fits during which she experienced trembling, dizziness, tiredness, and chest pains, as well as numbness, tingling, weakness, and partial paralysis of her hands. She described these symptoms as *ataques de nervos* ("attacks of 'nerves'"). She had had her first *ataque de nervos* when her father died, and the *ataques* became more frequent after her husband had a car accident. During an especially severe *ataque de nervos* she lost much of the use of her left hand. That *ataque* left her in a state of permanent *nervosismo* ("nervousness"). She said that this severe *ataque* had been sparked by a single traumatic event.

The trouble began with the arrival one Saturday of an anonymous letter detailing her husband's infidelity. Anonymous letters frequently appear on the popular evening soap operas (*telenovelas*) that dominate Brazilian television, and they also crop up occasionally in everyday life. Maria Imaculada and her daughters had just returned from church (they are Seventh-Day Adventists) when the letter arrived. Because of Maria Imaculada's illiteracy, her oldest daughter, Lindinalva (age eighteen), read the letter aloud. Maria Imaculada described the dramatic scene:

My girls cried a lot, were all upset . . . Lindinalva, Virgin Mary! Lindinalva didn't even want to look at him [when he came home later], because she is very *nervosa*. . . . She read the letter, she was trembling like this, with the letter in her hand [re]reading to him . . . I kept[6] crying, *ataque de nervos*, I fell down.[7]

When both mother and daughter began to scream, female neighbors came running, and by the time Maria Imaculada's husband came home, an angry crowd was waiting to greet him.[8]

My husband arrived, saw [the people], and asked: "Who died?" Lindinalva said: "It was your shame [*a vergonha do senhor*], which died a long time ago!" ... So Laura [the younger daughter], when this happened, Laura is very artless [*simples*], she spoke really very simply, so simply that it really touched his heart. My neighbor heard her talking, and cried.

Maria Imaculada collapsed in the excitement, and there ensued frantic attempts to arrange for a car to transport her to Caruaru (about a forty-five-minute drive) for medical treatment. She was diagnosed as suffering from high blood pressure, weak nerves, and a mild stroke. The doctor advised her husband to end his affair, asking him whether his sexual satisfaction was worth killing his wife and dishonoring his daughters. The husband cut off the affair, and to Maria Imaculada's knowledge he has not entered into any other serious affairs since—or at least has become more discreet.

The interview took another turn when I asked if Maria Imaculada knew who had written the letter.

It wasn't a secret. Everyone knew about the *concubina*, because people told me that he had another woman. ... .[9] But when I asked him, he resisted. He said that I believed everyone else and not him, that if I loved him I would believe him. It was the biggest mess [*a maior bagunça*], so I dropped it.

The "news" revealed by the anonymous letter was not news at all. Prior to the arrival of the letter, neighbors had gossiped that her husband was living with a woman in one of the small towns of his weekly market circuit. Maria Imaculada had told her daughters that during Carnaval she was going to visit a cousin who lived in that town. Actually, her visit had had another purpose: "I was following him. ... I arrived directly there, and I saw what was happening with my own eyes. ... He was really living with her, sleeping with her ... and then the anonymous letter arrived."

Suspicious, I asked her again about the letter. She confessed:

I knew, thank God, I knew about it and ... with the powers of God I dismantled it all. I was clever [*esperta*]. Really clever! ... He thought it was an anonymous letter, but ... it was I who ordered the letter written,[10] to be safer, because if not, he would have given me more problems.

I asked why she had used the letter instead of confronting her husband directly.

It was in order for him not to say that [the story of the mistress] was just me lying. Also I didn't want to say who told me about the woman, so I ordered a letter written and then he couldn't keep saying that he hadn't gone out with her if it was the letter saying everything, rather than me.

Despite her orchestration of the letter, she insisted that her *nervos* attack had not been faked:

It was a real *nervos* attack because it really hurt me very, very much. And since that time I can't use my left hand anymore because of the numbness of the nerves. It was the shock. . . . When Lindinalva read the letter, that was when it all descended on my head and I was left with numbness in my hands.

Interviewing other women, I heard similar stories of female suffering caused by male irresponsibility, especially in terms of sexual misbehavior, and of women's attempts to manipulate their men into behaving more in accordance with women's views of propriety. The drama of these stories reflects the intensity of emotion around infidelity in conjugal relationships. Maria Imaculada's story also points out the complexity of the term *nervos*, the relationship between the cultural-linguistic and the physiological aspects of emotion, and how emotional labeling fits into power struggles in everyday interactions.

Folk Medical Terminology as Emotion Vocabulary

When I first arrived in Caruaru, I intended to explore the ways in which people talk about their feelings, with a particular emphasis on the words they use to describe their medical problems when talking with popular healers. Not only has recent cultural research revealed how deeply the disparate vocabularies of different languages shape sentiment, but also how difficult it can be to distinguish medical and emotional concepts (Clark 1989; Davis 1983; Low 1989; Rebhun 1993, 1994; Tousignant 1984; Wikan 1990). Some folk medical vocabularies incorporate folk theories of emotion, as in the Andean *pena*, in which people say that protracted suffering slowly turns the heart to stone, causing chest pains, sadness, and erratic thinking (Tousignant 1984, 387). Others express sociomoral concepts, such as the belief that when jealous, envious, or angry, people cast the evil eye, causing sickness and destruction (Dundes 1980; Foster 1972; Hertzfeld 1980, 1984; Maloney 1976; Rebhun 1995).

As the interpretive nature of both medical diagnoses and emotional

labeling has become clearer, so has the power struggle underlying interpretation. Lutz's point about emotion as a "cultural and interpersonal
process of naming, justifying, and persuading by people in relationship to
each other" (1988, 5) is equally valid for medical diagnoses (see also Crandon 1983; Crandon-Malamud 1991, 10; Kleinman 1980, 378).

Given that the same cluster of symptoms can be diagnosed with a variety of labels, Libbet Crandon has suggested that researchers ask not
"What is *susto* (or any other folk syndrome)?" but rather "Why is *susto* diagnosed in any particular case?" (1983, 154). Similarly, it might be more
useful to ask "Why is anger (or any other emotion-term) applied to the
feelings of a particular situation?" rather than "What is anger?" as a general philosophical question. To return to our case, why did Maria Imaculada describe her condition as *nervos* rather than as some other folk medical syndrome? Why did she emphasize a folk medical diagnosis rather
than use the official medical diagnosis—that her hand was paralyzed because of a stroke?

Nervos, Nervosismo, and *Nervoso*

When Maria Imaculada described her problem as *nervos*,[11] she was referring to a multicultural folk syndrome called "nerves" by anthropologists.[12]
Although there are cross-cultural differences in the description of
"nerves," there are also many similarities (Finkler 1989; Low 1989). Anthropologists have described "nerves" in Europe, North Africa, and the
Americas as involving headache, dizziness, fatigue, weakness, and stom-
achache, and as being generally associated with sadness, anger, fear, and
worry (Davis and Guarnaccia 1989, 7). While some theorists discuss
"nerves" among men (Duarte 1986; Koss-Chioino 1989; Low 1985, 1989),
others see it as either a specifically female disorder (Barnett 1989; Davis
1983, 1989; Finerman 1989; Kay and Portillo 1989; Low 1989; Slutka 1989)
or more typical of females than males (Camino 1989; Davis and Low 1989;
Slutka 1989).

"Nerves" was a particular preoccupation of North American anthropologists in the 1980s, especially after Setha Low's 1985 review on the
topic. Brazilian anthropologist Luiz-Fernando Dias Duarte has critiqued
North American formulations of nerves on two bases: first, what he sees
as a failure to examine closely an overly individualistic focus and a related
overly psychological analysis of the syndrome; and second, a preoccupa-

tion with the medical aspects of nerves. In addition, he criticizes concepts of what constitutes "the West" and of history embedded in some North American anthropological discussions of "nerves" (1993).

Certainly, most North American characterizations of "nerves" fall under the rubric of medical anthropology. Theorists have seen it as a "culture-bound" or "culturally mediated" syndrome (Low 1989); an aspect of menopause (Barnett 1989; Davis 1983); a reaction to stressful family problems (Guarnaccia et al. 1989; Low 1981) or gender-based overresponsibility (Finerman 1989); a manifestation of hunger (Scheper-Hughes 1988, 1992); a folk model of anxiety or depression (Kay and Portillo 1989; Koss-Chioino 1989; Nations et al. 1988); and a means of expressing socially unacceptable emotions (Clark 1989; Lock 1990). More sociopolitical definitions of "nerves" have included interpersonal manipulation (Krieger 1989); an idiom of women's social relationships (Davis 1983); and a reaction to economic deprivation (Dunk 1989; Scheper-Hughes 1988, 1992). Duarte argues against medical, political, and gender reductionism in "nerves," positing that concepts of "nerves" indicate a nonindividualized view of the person. Rather than taking form as a pathology, or an expression of individual experience, the concept expresses difficulties in interpersonal relationships in societies that are not fully integrated into modern subjective individuality and that share a historical relationship to the lengthy development of concepts of the human person, body, soul, and mind, from the ancient Greeks and Arabs to modern European and Europeanate cultures.

My data tend to support the idea that "nerves" reflects sociomoral concepts, showing similarities to ancient Greek anatomical ideas, as well as the idea that while "nerves" has medical aspects it is not an exclusively medical phenomenon. In general, the people I spoke with told me that both men and women can be *nervoso*, although they tended to see it as more a feminine condition.[13] *Nervosismo* involves victimization, more characteristic of women than of men, although it may involve an irritability and combativeness more acceptable in men than in women (cf. Dunk 1989, 38). One man ventured the opinion that while women get "nerves," men get drunk, indicating that men may have alternative ways of dealing with interpersonal difficulties. A *nervoso* person cannot handle strain, reacting by crying, trembling, or flying into rages at minor provocation, whereas people tended to say that men should not cry in most circumstances.[14]

Modern concepts of *nervos* reflect the historical influence of Greco-

Arabic medicine brought to Latin America by Portuguese and Spanish clerics (Low 1989, 42). Healers, such as clerics and barbers, numbered among the first travelers to the New World. Doctors arrived in Brazil in the third decade of the sixteenth century (Santos Filho 1966, 79), bringing with them pre-Copernican science and Galenic medicine (Foster 1953, 1987; Stepan 1976).

Galen saw the nerves as physical organs carrying animal spirits from the brain through the body (Davis and Whitten, 1988, 1210). Caruaruenses update this image, describing the nerves as tiny wires carrying a kind of electrical energy of emotional impulses throughout the body. *Nervos* is caused by an overload of these little wires, like that caused by an electrical short, rendering them unable to function properly (see also Duarte 1986, 29–30).[15]

In Caruaru and neighboring villages, people said that *nervosismo* is caused either by a single large emotional shock or by the frazzling of the nerves through repeated small shocks. For example, one of Maria Imaculada's friends, a Caruaruense housewife I will call Fátima, began to suffer from *nervos* after she received sudden, terrible news:

We were already sleeping when my niece arrived saying that they had murdered her father [Fátima's brother-in-law],[16] so that the news took me by surprise. I stayed cold for five minutes without being able to speak, I lost myself. I felt my chins trembling, *né* [isn't it]? Now I'm always trembling, *nervosa*. . . . It's horrible! Whatever little thing, I start soon [crying], uncontrolled; I'm very insecure now.

Nervos may also be caused by a series of shocks or a prolonged stressful period. This was the theory of Fátima's mother-in-law:

I've been a long time with my nerves trembling; you know from what? Worry. Because we get angry at something, then we get upset with something, get upset with something else, work too much, stay with the nerves drained, *né*? . . . We get tired of everything. . . . We have lots of worries, we struggle a lot, we get suffering in the nerves. . . . It's already too much, we already can't stand it at all any more.

Worry causes *nervos*, and so does the prolonged stress of accumulated unexpressed anger. One housewife explained: "Sometimes I have a big anger that I can't avenge; it's crying with anger, locked inside of me. We get revolted. Any little thing I'm upset. It's *nervos*." Folk metaphors describe anger as a dangerous force that accumulates inside the body much like a fluid in classical hydraulics (cf. Solomon 1984) or leaps out through the eyes to enter others' chests and cause sickness (Rebhun 1994). Overloads of emotion can cause various kinds of injury, including bruising as the blood boils in the veins or damage to the nerves, which, once frazzled, can no longer carry even the mildest of emotions without overloading.[17]

Women described *nervos* as characterized by a feeling of being on the edge of disaster, the desperation of not having enough strength to cope. This desperation distinguishes *nervos* from simple anger. The *nervosa* woman has lost the ability to control or suppress her anger; she feels passive, *fraca* ("weak"), and *falta força* ("lacking in strength"). Many women said that after becoming *nervoso*, their *nervos* attacks were brought on by *qualquer coisinha* ("any little thing"), *qualquer raivinha* ("any irritation"—the literal translation is "little anger"), *bobagems* ("nonsense"), *besterinhas* ("foolishness"), or other unimportant things. They lacked the courage (*falta coragem*) to face the burdens of life.

The label *nervos* contains an analysis of painful events as emotionally destructive. It reflects the idea that people can stand only so much and will legitimately lose control under difficult circumstances. Prolonged sadness or despair, shock, anger, or repeated irritation all cause *nervos* and all reflect a state of exposure to harm. Applying the term *nervos* reflects a judgment or a claim about the endurability of the conditions of life, and a commentary on the moral character of interpersonal relationships—including the difficult vulnerabilities of deep emotional connection to fragile loved ones. Their deaths, their betrayals, the frightening or irritating things they do, the protection they fail to provide, all cause harm, all lead to *nervos*.

Emotion and the Body

Although viewing *nervos* as medical reduces its complexity, so does viewing it as simply a vocabulary or concept. How can "nerves" reflect both physical process and the socially constructed nature of sentiment? Simply to say that Maria Imaculada had suffered a stroke is not sufficient to describe the nature of her physical problems. As she tells the story, her sentiments and their physical manifestation form a seamless whole. Her "nerves," as part of her expression of sentiment, took on physical reality in the form of bodily dysfunction. This seems to support the idea that particular sentiments have their basis in bodily experience rather than social ideation—at least if you believe that body, mind, and society constitute separate entities.

Much biologically based emotion theory uses a limited concept of the body's nature, in which the body is a purely physical object.[18] However, the human body is not only a physical entity; it is also part of a symbol system expressing both the microcosm of self and the macrocosm of social world (cf. Scheper-Hughes and Lock 1987). The ways in which people think about, talk about, experience, and use their bodies reveal attitudes on a myriad of issues, including gender relations, illness, and concepts of self (Bourdieu 1977; Cowan 1990; Foucault 1978; Scheper-Hughes and Lock 1987). In addition, in Robert Desjarlais's evocative words, the human body is not some kind of a suitcase that individuals lug around everywhere they go; it is an identity, not a possession (Desjarlais 1992, 31).

The experiencing mind is embodied, an integral part of the physically existing, culturally interpreted system that constitutes the body. Conditions like "nerves" are part of embodied apprehension and the expression of certain types of emotional experiences. The concept of embodiment takes root in the view of mind as the functioning of brain but expands that concept to include the brain's awareness of conditions in the entire body, as well as the body's interaction with other minds and bodies in cultural settings.

This realization has two consequences. It means that approaches to sentiment that privilege discourse over experience erroneously ignore the important realm of bodily practice and sensation, falsely treating individuals as if they were separate from their bodies (Desjarlais 1992, 31). However, it also means that approaches that privilege biological process over social and cultural interpretation falsely treat sentiments as distinct from thoughts (O'Nell 1996, 182). It is possible for sentiments to be both physiologically based and culturally various. The visceral world of bodily desire, sensation, and experience, and the cerebral world of perception, communication, interpretation, and ideation, are the same world: a world in which bodies see, hear, feel, taste, speak, practice, experience, and interact, a world in which individuals *are* their bodies, and bodies experience both their individuality and their collectivity in societies made up of other embodied consciousnesses.

Playing with Emotion and Role

In the United States we tend to believe that sentiment is genuine only if it is spontaneous; conventional, required, manipulated sentiment seems false (Abu-Lughod 1987; Lutz 1988; Trawick 1990) and its falseness morally reprehensible. But deliberation and requirement are as much a part of emotion as spontaneity. Lutz has shown how social actors "play with" sentiments as part of social manipulations (1988, 10).

Emotion is playful both in the sense of spontaneity and in the sense that it is full of play: susceptible to manipulation and imitation, and capable of being performed, sometimes performed so well that the performer comes to believe his or her own act (cf. Hochschild 1983, 1985). The idea that sentiment must somehow be spontaneous is related to a generally passive attitude toward the sentiments as things that happen to a person rather than things that a person does.

This attitude is perhaps even stronger in Brazil than in the United States. Brazilian Portuguese, like English, distinguishes between passions, which engulf a passive consciousness (*paixão*), and actively experienced emotions (*emoção, sentimento*) (cf. Averill 1982, 3).[19] Feelings are most likely to be judged passions when they are experienced as submersion in a stream of impulses that cause consciousness to "fall in"—such as love (Averill 1982, 13–17).[20] The idea that sentiments happen to a person tends to absolve people of blame for the sentiments they experience. Presenting oneself as the helpless victim of an overwhelming sentiment (in other words, a passion) means not having to justify how one feels.[21]

However, even when people see themselves or others as the victims of overwhelming passions, they still believe that there is a time, a place, and a way to express those passions properly. Only tiny children who have not yet been fully socialized can get away with uncontrolled tantrums, and even they do not have carte blanche to behave as they please. Adults can get away with passionate behavior, including violence, but not every adult, not every action, and not in every situation.

Any named sentiment has an associated role. In addition to feeling anger, one acts angrily; in addition to feeling love, one acts like a lover. Presenting oneself in an emotional role can be hard work. It includes work in the Goffmanian sense of working at surface presentation in order to manipulate others' impressions of oneself (Goffman 1959), and in the Hochschildian concept of emotional deep acting in which a person tries to manipulate his or her own feelings. As Hochschild shows, both kinds of emotional acting are common in everyday life and do not obviate the genuineness of emotional experience (Hochschild 1983, 38–48).

Emotional manipulation of the self may respond to a desire to avoid pain or a cognitive appraisal that continuing to feel a particular way will lead to trouble. Thus a person may try not to feel grief when to surrender to it would be too painful; to swallow anger no matter how it hurts to do so; or to concentrate on not loving someone who is unobtainable or unresponsive. People may also try to work up a feeling: try their best to love their spouse even though deep down they don't, or try to be brave even though they really want to run away screaming. Such self-manipulation may respond to the need to complete a task or series of tasks before allowing oneself the luxury of releasing control over one's emotions.

I, at least, I am able to react to something. Let's suppose if someone of mine, of my family, dies, I do everything in that hour, I bury, buy flowers, and put them in the coffin, I do everything, you know, but from there, I can stay five, six days in bed, crying without stopping. (Fátima)

Just as Fátima's grief is no less real for being delayed until she finishes her funeral obligations, Maria Imaculada's emotional reaction was no less genuine for being delayed until she set up the dramatic letter.

However, she had a choice of what to call her emotional reaction. Was she angry? Was she hurt? Was she shocked? A number of terms could easily be applied. First, she described her reaction as anger (*raiva*) and she acted correspondingly, confronting her husband with angry accusations. But this did not work to change his behavior.

I did not get an opportunity to interview her husband, so I can only guess at his opinions. It is possible that, like many men I did interview, he thought his affairs were none of his wife's business. Many unfaithful husbands I interviewed construed their infidelities in the discourse of romance, male privilege, or escape, focusing on the adulterous relationship as a romantic story, a justifiable response to the exigencies of male sexuality, or a reasonable reaction to some defect in their wives.

However her husband may have seen his behavior, Maria Imaculada was able to enforce her construal of it as unjustifiable lust combined with selfish disregard of his family's needs. Whereas he previously got away with ignoring her anger, he could not get away with ignoring her hurt, especially in the face of communal exposure and condemnation. As a *nervosa* woman, Maria Imaculada was able to continually act out her hurt, reminding him of the necessity of protecting her from his misbehavior, and enlisting her doctor and the community in her campaign to control his sexuality. *Nervos* in this case was a more powerful label for her emotions than anger.

Maria da Paz: Unsuccessful Construal

At the same time that the *nervosa* woman tries to manage others' impressions of the meaning and legitimacy of her condition, others try to put their own spin on the situation. *Nervos* is so complex a term that many interpretations are possible. People judge cases of *nervos* according to the details of the situations in which they arise, the particular symptoms they exhibit, and their impressions of the character of the sufferers. Different factions may take different points of view.

For example, one day my neighbor, the husband of thirty-three-year-old Maria da Paz, returned home late and drunk. Furious, she chased him out of the house, letting loose with a remarkable string of profanity that summarized not only his dubious genealogy but also his personal resemblance to a number of virulent diseases and horrible things from another planet. While the neighbors peered out of their doors, Maria da Paz's brother, who lived nearby, commented loudly: "My sister always was a big-mouth, a really *nervosa* woman. Take a tranquilizer, darling, and resign yourself [*se conformar*] to your fate." In so doing, he effectively transformed Maria da Paz's anger from a justified comment on her husband's misbehavior into a personal failing on her part, best treated with medication. There were a number of differences between her case and Maria Imaculada's.

Maria Imaculada was *nervosa* before the "anonymous" letter, attributing her condition to the death of her father and the near-death of her husband. But with the arrival of the letter, she was able to substitute her husband's behavior as the precipitating shock. That made his behavior itself the problem and her *nervosismo* his fault. Maria da Paz had had a different precipitating shock. She was the only daughter in a family with twelve sons. Her mother said that she had been *nervosa* since childhood because of having so many big brothers to tease her. In addition she had been involved in a serious car accident, requiring surgery on her badly broken legs.

The accident had occurred when she failed to yield the right of way to a male driver at a busy intersection. Legally she had had the right of way, but in the informal system that actually determines how people drive in the Northeast, men take the right of way over women, and she failed to accommodate that fact. Driving itself is rare for women of her class (the working class). As far as her family were concerned, the accident was caused by her inappropriate gender behavior.

The street on which she lived was inhabited mostly by Maria da Paz's parents, brothers, sisters-in-law, and cousins, with only a few unrelated neighbors. They generally considered her husband to be a good man because he was very hard working and maintained his family in a house that boasted all the luxury features, such as plumbing, electricity, a gas stove, tile floors, and good furniture. Their standard of living was above that of the neighbors, who generally thought that Maria da Paz had little to complain about in her industrious, generous, and handsome husband.

On occasion, however, he would go out with her brothers and drink, returning home staggering slightly. To the neighbors, whose husbands were regularly carried home unconscious with drink or were jailed on drunk-and-disorderly charges, this was a minor infraction. Maria da Paz's husband was also widely believed to be faithful to her, since he never spent a night away from home and was visibly working most of the time. In the community's opinion, her *nervosismo* was a sign of her inappropriate, and therefore trivial, anger.

Maria Imaculada's husband had actually been misbehaving, and his misbehavior was in fact a threat to her family's well-being. Maria da Paz's husband, however, was not endangering his family with his behavior. Maria Imaculada's *nervosismo* may have been at least partly a ploy, but it was an appropriate ploy. Maria da Paz's *nervosismo*, in contrast, was not defined by neighbors as justified but as an overreaction to her husband's small infractions. It undermined any power she might have had to control possible major misbehavior on his part.

Emotion: A Synthetic Approach

The cases of both Maria Imaculada and Maria da Paz illustrate the isomorphism of emotion and folk medical terminology, and also show the complexity of the relationships among political, moral, biological, and psychological aspects of sentiment. Certainly, Maria Imaculada's case supports the view of ethnopsychology in which emotion takes its place as a tactic in the struggle over power waged by individuals in society. Both Marias were trying to use the medical sequelae of their emotion to control their husbands; their imitation of passivity allowed them to play in the limited emotional space allotted to women. Taking a Hochschildian perspective, we could say that Maria Imaculada deep acted the role of the shocked, betrayed wife so well that she convinced herself of her own surprise. Immersing herself in the flow of events, she could forget her role in precipitating them, taking advantage of cultural constructions of *nervos* to believe herself a properly passive, victimized woman. Neither feigned nor false, her emotion was delayed until the appropriate situation allowed her to release her conscious control over it and experience it passively.

We also see the moral message in these women's *nervos*. Both women use their symptoms to denounce male infidelity and to enlist community support to control it, one more successfully than the other. By engineering the scene at the reading of the letter, Maria Imaculada demonstrated her husband's position in a web of emotionally charged relations affected by his behavior. After the letter, he had to address his wife's, his daughters', and his neighbors' interest in his fidelity. Maria Imaculada's *nervos* graphically demonstrated that his infidelity was dangerous to his family. More than a verbal statement could have done, it demonstrated the cry "I hurt" and pointed the finger of guilt to him.

Both women manifested physical symptoms of their emotion, describing them in the terminology of folk medicine. The visible pain of their bodies spoke for them as much as did their words: Trembling, fainting, pain, and paralysis combined with verbal statements to communicate their distress. These symptoms were not feigned. Rather, they were part of the process of emotional experience.

Theresa O'Nell has critiqued ethnopsychological approaches to emotion as too political, pointing out that too great an emphasis on the politics of interpersonal emotion distorts the "moral essence" of sentiment and implies too strongly a "uniformly willful" social actor motivated solely by "rational self interest" (1996, 188). Her point is well taken. To say that Maria Imaculada is acting as if she were passive but really she is active, that her *nervos* allows her to present herself as a victim when really she is powerful vis-à-vis her husband, is not the whole story. People are not in complete control over themselves and others as they try to orchestrate events, and they cannot accurately predict every aspect of what will happen. Moreover, modifying one another's behavior is not the only thing that they are trying to do when they feel and express an emotion.

To the first point, Maria Imaculada could not have known in advance exactly what would happen when the letter was read, exactly how her daughters would react, how the neighbors would respond, or how the reading would affect her husband. Nor could she have known that she would suffer a stroke. But once the stroke had befallen her, she was able to weave it into the ongoing improvisation that constitutes social drama. Like children's play, adult social play is characterized by flow, in which actors are both immersed in, and also trying to affect, perceptions and events. Attempts at manipulation are forays that, if effective, bring forth further attempts on the new situation created; if not effective, they require regrouping for the consideration of new tactics. The actual social situation constructed is a fluid result of multiple, competing attempts at construal as well as competing points of view.

O'Nell is correct to say that interpersonal politics is not all that is going on here.[22] Maria Imaculada clearly wanted to control her husband and to convince him and others of the immorality of his behavior. She was also simply upset: angry, betrayed, worried, hurt. Maria da Paz was also upset, and that her distress was a less reasonable response to events than was Maria Imaculada's does not minimize its importance to her—although it does affect its political significance and social utility. People do not always manage to feel what it would be politically expedient to feel or what they think they want to feel. They may know their fears are baseless but fear nonetheless; they may desperately want to love their spouse but not manage to do so no matter how hard they try. The interpersonal politics of sentiment are significant aspects of their definition, expression, and consequence, but they are not the only important aspect of emotion.

Emotions have interacting biological, psychological, interpersonal, and cultural aspects that are both passively and actively experienced. Sentiments are experiential and interpretive, shift among levels of consciousness, are redirected, reinterpreted, denied, or manufactured. People can fake sentiments so well that they come to believe their own act; or, alternatively, they may unsuccessfully deny sentiments that they are forced to feel. Patterns of sentiment vary among cultures, within cultures over time, and among roles within a single culture. They are not only playful but also essential to patterns of power and influence in a society. They are deeply moral and deeply personal, and not entirely under the control of those who experience them.

I have not yet told the whole story of Maria Imaculada—why it was so important that her daughters know of the affair, or how the affair came to take place, or who else was involved. The story is actually more complex than it seems on the surface, and the image of passive woman victimized by shameless man is both more complicated and less accurate than it would seem. But for now, I want to shift my focus to the region in which Maria Imaculada and Maria da Paz live, and the factors that shape their lives and sentiments.

2   ⌒ The Setting

Caruaru, Capital of the Agreste,
Mouth of the Sertão

Those cliffs along the river are a meeting place where the different
kinds of plague and pestilence hold congresses and sign treaties . . .
the dysentery that carries off children and the old bubonic plague,
still in there fighting . . . and illiteracy, the patriarch and father of
them all—out there . . . epidemics have powerful natural allies: the
landlords, the *coronels* ["plantation owners"], the police . . . in short,
the sovereign government. The allies of the people can be counted
on the fingers of one hand. . . . If it weren't for smallpox, typhus,
malaria, illiteracy . . . and all the other plagues that do such fine
work out in the countryside, how could those *fazendas*
["plantations"], some as big as whole countries, be kept up . . . how
could fear be cultivated and respect imposed and the people duly
exploited? Without dysentery . . . and starvation too—did you ever
think of the hoards of children who would grow up to be adults . . .
grabbing all the land and dividing it up? Plagues are necessary and
beneficial. If it weren't for them we'd have to say goodbye to the so-
called drought industry, which yields such good profits. . . . There
would be no holding back the people, the worst plague of all. Just
think of it, all those people healthy and knowing how to read.

Jorge Amado, Teresa Batista Home from the Wars, pp. 241–42

Maria Imaculada and her family live in a village near Caruaru in the state
of Pernambuco in Brazil's Northeast, a region that forms the setting of
some of Brazil's most striking literature. For example, Jorge Amado's
novels, often set in the Brazilian Northeast, play with the region's melodramatic image. Peopled by cruel plantation owners, exploited peasants,
ravished maidens, and prostitutes with hearts of gold, the novels capture
an imagined emotional intensity in a suffering land. Several of his novels
have been made into successful soap operas or movies (*Gabriela, Cravo e*

Canela; Tieta do Nordeste; Dona Flor e Seus Dois Maridos), playing back images of themselves to *Nordestinos* ("Northeasterners").

Real life is neither a novel nor a soap opera, although images from such artistic forms shape the views of both insiders and outsiders to the region. Influenced by novels, popular media, and folklore, Northeast Brazil enters the national imagination as a tragic and exotic region. Popular impressions focus on spectacular scenes, spiced with hints of fervent religiosity. Here in a storied past, slaves toiled and bands of outlaws harassed locals, ostensibly stealing from the rich and giving to the poor. The Northeast, and especially Pernambuco, has been the setting of violent conflict over land and property ownership for centuries. On the contemporary coast, fishing villages nestle amid white sand dunes on some of the most beautiful beaches in the Americas. Inland, the beaches give way to sugar cane plantations in the former Atlantic forest (*Mata*) and then to the fruit and vegetable farms of the Agreste, fading into the semiarid cowboy country of the drought-ridden Sertão.

A lively market in tourist art from Northeastern states presents collectors in the South with images: brightly colored paintings of street scenes and Afro-Brazilian rituals sold in Bahia, or scenes of palm-strewn beaches created in Ceará out of colored sand in little bottles. These and Caruaru's famous ceramic figurines depicting idealized rural life, scenes from folktales, or victims of Sertanejo drought forced off their land vie with handmade lace, embroidered dresses, and leather cowboy hats to shape Brazilian views of the Northeast. These images have their origin in a reality that they reflect at a slant; closer association reveals more diversity and less exoticism than the images suggest.

The welter of images confuses as much as delights visitors. With tourism an increasingly important industry, and in response to an often deeply felt desire to present the beautiful in the region while downplaying the ugly, Northeast Brazilians actively participate in myth-making about their region. Caruaru is a major center of figurative art. The home of the figurine industry,[1] Alto do Moura, is just up the road, and a short distance in the other direction, in Bezerros, is the block-print workshop of the internationally famous J. Borges. Image is piled upon image, story upon story, with artists and narrators producing nostalgia as much for themselves as for others.

The poverty in many areas of the Northeast colors its image: hard-bitten farmers and malnourished children, urban slums and shantytowns awash in open sewers, dysentery, cholera, Chagas disease, leishmaniasis, schistosomiasis, a world of parasites transmitted by insect bites or passed from anus to mouth in polluted water. The poverty dramatized in popular presentations is very real. The largest concentration of poor people in the Americas live here (Levine 1978, 9), although this poverty is not undifferentiated. The poverty of urban areas is different from rural poverty: poverty in the sugar-cane growing Mata region differs from that in the food-producing Agreste, and yet again from that in the dusty cowboy country of the Sertão.[2]

Life is not, however, the endless round of misery that a cursory perusal of health statistics might suggest. While hardship, suffering both physical and emotional, privation, and struggle all color the lives of *Nordestinos*, so do warm friendship, family loyalty, the delights of music, dance and celebration, the excitements of infatuation, and the deep satisfactions of faith. Marked social and economic inequality cruelly burdens the lives of the poor. Love defies the depersonalization of an unjust system; the pleasures of company relieve the loneliness of inequity.

Three hundred years ago the Northeast was among the richest areas of the Americas, dominated by the few whose fortunes, based on monoculture of sugar produced by slave labor, gave them control over the masses of bonded workers. Today the region is among the poorest (Pereira 1997, 20). Differences in the relative fortunes of the sugar industry (in the Northeast) and the coffee industry (in the South) began to arise in the nineteenth century, combining with years of inequitable investment by the national government to intensify differences among the regions of Brazil, favoring the South (Leff 1997, 35). Although both rural and urban poverty remain endemic in the country as a whole, the South boasts the major universities, museums, and cultural resources, the largest cities and busiest airports, the most modern banking system, and the biggest shopping malls.

The South also has a better-established and broader urban middle class than does the Northeast, more extensive systems of paved roads, piped water, and electrical power, a greater per capita density of telephone exchanges, and other advantages of infrastructure.[3] The Northeast seems almost a separate country from the South, forming part of a sense of abandonment reflected in persistent rumors of its impending sale to Japan in return for national debt relief.[4]

Northeastern urban social classes range from the most abject of the indigent, through shantytown dwellers, the working poor, and a small middle class, to the remnants of a semiaristocratic class of landowners, today more likely to be businessmen than the masters of plantations. In addition, a class of nouveau riche has begun to rub shoulders with the traditional old-money families.[5]

Despite the deeply felt differences between classes, Brazil has undergone a number of periods of accelerated social mobility (Pastore 1979). Middle-class status, marked by the ownership of such things as tile floors and extra sinks or of household appliances, the cut and quality of clothing, the acquisition of higher education, the employment of servants, the ability to travel outside the country, or the adoption of a variety of mannerisms that reflect upper-class disdain for those of lower social status, represents a conceivably attainable goal for poor and working-class people, at least at some times. Economic instability and the changing possibilities for social mobility contribute to tension about class status, intensifying both the tendency of those higher on the social scale to make as many distinctions between themselves and the lower classes as possible—and the tendency of those lower on the scale to resent upper-class privileges (O'Dougherty 1992, 1995, 1996; Rebhun 1995).

In the countryside, the sugar plantations of the Mata employ rural workers at low wages; farther west the small farms of the Agreste struggle without the benefits of modern technological agriculture to produce viable crops. The farther west you go, the more crop cultivation gives way to animal husbandry as soils get progressively shallower and rainfall more scarce. In addition, the sense of independence from centralized control increases with westward movement: The semiarid Sertão region has supported outlaws and rebels since colonial times, and was too dry to support plantation slave labor (Garcia 1986).

Anthony Pereira has described Northeastern rural people as "peasantariats," without either the ideological commitment to land ownership of European peasants or the self-conscious commitment to an identity as wage laborers of proletariats.[6] Rather, individuals shift between wage labor (legal, illegal, temporary, and seasonal) on plantations and periods when they work small plots as squatters, tenants, sharecroppers, or owners. Most people who work for wages, whether in the countryside or in the small cities of the interior, have relatives who work small farms; a division between wage workers and peasants is impossible to make cleanly (1997, 60–61).

Before 1960 most of the population lived in rural areas, but between 1960 and 1970 one in five Brazilians migrated to cities (Perlman 1976, 5). By 1980, only 45 percent of *Nordestinos* lived in rural areas (de Araujo 1987,

167). Urbanization in Pernambuco was especially acute, with 70 percent of the population living in urban areas by 1980 (Pereira 1997, 11). Millions of *Nordestinos* have migrated South in search of a better life, only to find the same old slums, shantytowns, hunger, and disease in southern cities. Others went north to what they hoped would be opportunities in newly cleared Amazon land, discovering instead shallow, infertile soils, political violence, and again, slums, shantytowns, hunger, and disease.

Rapid urbanization has transformed *Nordestinos'* lives in a single generation. Women whose mothers married cousins through arranged marriages, bore twenty children, burying eleven and raising nine, and never met anyone from farther away than the next village, today choose their own unrelated husbands, bear only two children in the full expectation of their survival, and debate whether *Star Trek* or *ET* reflects a more realistic view of the world.[7]

Pernambuco: A State of the Northeast

Despite its small size, Pernambuco, the site of the first Portuguese colonies in Brazil, dominates the Brazilian Northeast (Levine 1978, 1). It was conquered by the Dutch in the early 1600s and became a haven for Jews and Muslims fleeing the Inquisition. Upon reconquest some non-Catholics fled to other Dutch colonies, such as New Amsterdam,[8] or to the interior, where traces of their cultures still remain, mingled with earlier Muslim influences upon food, architecture, and social relations stemming from Portugal's Moorish period (between the eighth and fifteenth centuries) (Brandão 1971; Sobreira 1988).[9]

Most Pernambucanos are Catholic, although Protestants have made major incursions, especially Seventh-Day Adventists, Jehovah's Witnesses, and other Pentecostals, as has the Church of Jesus Christ of Latter Day Saints. In addition, a minority practice Afro-Brazilian religions or Kardecist Spiritism. Local Catholicism emphasizes the saints, pilgrimages, and festivals of its European origins, but many self-described Catholics also revere the Afro-Brazilian deity Iemanjá and local, non-Vatican saints such as Padre Cícero.

Regions of the Northeast

The Northeast, constituting nearly 20 percent of national territory (Garcia 1986, 16), contains five distinct geographic-cultural zones, corresponding to the progressive dryness of the climate: moving inland from a narrow tidewater area (Litoral) through the Zona da Mata, Agreste, Sertão, and Meio-Norte (midnorth). Pernambuco has regions of the first four types. Each region has separate concerns, corresponding to its distinctive agricultural practices and industries.

The regions shade into one another; constant movement, especially between Sertão and Agreste, means that Sertanejos and their descendants people all three regions. A self-image as hard-bitten, thirsty, but hardy people, a staple of Sertanejo folklore, permeates all four regions of Pernambuco.

While the Zona da Mata, whose forests have long been cut down, has a tropical climate, the Agreste and Sertão are semiarid. In the Mata, heat and humidity support monoculture of sugar. As in other regions where single crops are grown for export, its people are mostly poor; chronic undernutrition is common. The staples—beans, manioc meal, rice, and coffee—are all imported from other areas, only sometimes supplemented with fish or dried meat. Cheese and vegetables are hard to find outside Recife in the Litoral and Mata (Levine 1978, 6).[10]

The Mata and Litoral are subject to floods, especially the capital, Recife.[11] Playing to their national strengths, Dutch builders reclaimed land from low-lying tidal swamps where the Capibaribe and Beberibe rivers join the Atlantic. Because of the bridges connecting its islands, Recife bills itself as the "Venice of Brazil," enticing tourists not only with the calm, reef-protected waters of Boa Viagem beach but also with museums, markets, and baroque churches.

The fertile Agreste forms a transition between the Mata's plentiful rains and the dry Sertão. Locals plant cotton, corn, beans, bananas, guavas, manioc, potatoes, vegetables, paprika, and pineapples, and raise cattle, sheep, goats, pigs, and fowl. *Agrestinos* supplement their basic diet with spaghetti, meat, fish, fruits, vegetables, and cheese, all produced locally (cf. Levine 1978, 6).[12] Inhabitants of the Agreste also eat a great variety of corn dishes, including the puddinglike *canjica, cuscuz* (steamed corn meal),[13] and *manguzá,* made with hominy, coconut milk, and cinnamon.

Not everyone, however, has access to this varied diet. Like people in the Mata, Agreste farmers are poor, and their small farms employ only rudimentary technology (Levine 1978, 6), producing as much for subsistence as for marketing. As the proverb has it, *Pobre só come carne quando morde a lingua* ("The poor eat meat only when they bite their tongues"). But the generally greater availability of food produced at home or sold directly by producers means that chronic undernutrition (marasmus) is less frequent in the Agreste. Kwashiorkor, the acute malnutrition produced in otherwise healthy populations when once-plentiful food is suddenly unavailable, is more characteristic of the region, with its unstable economy and unreliable climate.[14] Malnutrition of some kind affects 75 percent of the Northeastern population at any given time (Ward and Sanders 1980), concentrated especially in the Mata.

More than half of the Northeast and 70 percent of Pernambuco is Sertão, a drought-ridden yet starkly beautiful area where scrub trees cast little shade and grass lies sere on naked hills. In good years a semiarid climate permits agriculture, and Sertão farmers plant cotton, carnauba palms, sisal, castorbeans, and cashews, and raise livestock (cf. Levine 1978, 7–9). Both Sertão and Agreste are subject to periodic droughts that can last for years. Low rainfall combines with poor irrigation and worse conservation to create the great human misery that has most shaped the region's image. Droughts occur every eight to fifteen years (Wagley 1965, 127). Droughts of more than three years' duration occur approximately every twenty-six years (Garcia 1986, 64), and when they do, the Sertão's shallow streams vanish and the people are forced off the land.

An elderly woman who survived the drought of 1915 as a small child described how her father cut his animals' throats in a desperate attempt to slake his family's thirst with the blood.[15] She told me in the dramatic metaphors of folk speech that "the Lord picked up his paintbrush in those days and painted the Sertão, and the color he painted it was the color of misery." When months pass and rain does not come, the cattle die and people are forced to become *retirantes*.[16] Figures of the *retirante* family retreating from the land with their meager possessions balanced on their heads and their starving dog trailing behind are a staple of local tourist art, reflecting both the realities and national stereotypes of the region (cf. Wagley 1965).

Local folklore refers to the droughts as a *judiação* ("torment"), from *judiar* ("to torment, afflict"), from *judeu* ("Jew").[17] The anti-Semitic folk metaphor of *judiação* compares the suffering of the Sertanejo to the scourging of Christ. The popularity of Easter passion plays, with scenes of Jewish rabble eagerly beating the cross-burdened Savior with whips of thorn bush, feed the image. Like that of Christ, the suffering of the Sertanejo becomes heroically redemptive in folk metaphor.

This symbolism gives more than a hint of the cause of suffering—not only natural conditions but also human callousness: in Amado's words, the alliance between landlords, *coroneis*,[18] police, illiteracy, and disease.

Add to this a lack of investment in the kind of water-management technology that makes climatically similar regions (such as southern California) bloom, and the human face behind the suffering becomes clear.

By itself, the word *judiação* does not show local awareness that the terrible suffering caused by the droughts results as much from politics as nature. But in combination with other forms of folk speech, it offers clues to local awareness of the politics of suffering. For example, a popular joke repeated to me illustrates this theme. An Arab (in some versions) or an Israeli (in others) is invited by the local politicians to come to Pernambuco to show farmers how to make the desert bloom. He's still walking around, says the punch line, looking at the cane fields, tomato farms, and grasslands, and asking, "Where's the desert?"

"Where's the desert?" joked tellers repeat, laughing. "Where is it?" gesturing wide, shrugging, and rolling their eyes. "Do you see it?"

"President Collor sees it," one man exclaimed, "but I don't. And the worst part is, this desert that's killing me is invisible! It's not really there!"

The themes of life in the Sertão are hardship, hunger, a stubbornly heroic insistence on survival, and, above all, thirst, resonate throughout the Northeast (cf. Scheper-Hughes 1992). *Retirantes* escape to the Agreste, where some manage to build homes and find jobs, but others do not. In a prolonged drought the rural Agreste too becomes uninhabitable, and the population retreats to towns and cities, and, failing that, to the Mata. From there they flee to the capital cities or the South, bringing their thirst with them. Yet many retain a strong nostalgia for the Sertão, the sere beauty of the land, the pride people feel in survival, the deep religiosity.

This nostalgia also longs for the apparent simplicity of a remembered rural life in which the ambiguities of the city seem distant, the difference between honor and shame clear; where men and women know who they are and how they are supposed to behave. In the Sertão, I was told, people knew how to love one another. People often stressed to me a perceived difference between a society based on love in the Sertão, where hospitality and mutual aid ruled human relationships, and the impersonal society of modern cities. The *saudade* of Sertanejo descendants glosses over the physical and human difficulties of rural life, ignoring the frequent violence, retaining the heroism and emphasizing the sweetness.

The hardships of life in urban poverty compare with the hardships of life in the Sertão during drought. People describe life as a *luta* ("fight") or *batalha* ("battle"): in the Sertão against drought, in the city against poverty and disease, and everywhere against the indifference of the powerful. As the proverb has it, *A vida é dura p'ra quem é mole* ("Life is hard for whoever is soft"). Negotiating a balance between the emotional "hardness" necessary for survival and the emotional "softness" necessary for social life remains a major preoccupation, especially for women.

Capital and Interior

In the United States, a request for directions elicits complex instructions, but Brazilians tend to answer a similar request with the instruction to go either *lá em cima* ("there above") or *lá embaixo* ("there below").[19] The division of cities into above and below reflects as much socioeconomic as spatial realities. Spatial and social locations both occupy the same axis, extending from center to periphery and encompassing inclusion and exclusion (da Matta 1985, 27). Not only are neighborhoods of cities "there above" and "there below"; within states, cities and towns are arranged hierarchically. In much the same way that denizens of New York City dismiss "upstate," the small cities, towns, and farms of the interior have a distinctly lesser status. The largest city in any state is the capital; capitals have state governments, foreign consulates, major hospitals, universities, shopping centers, factories, and businesses not elsewhere available.

In Brazil, the Northeast is "there below" in relation to the South, and more often than not resources are not available even in the capitals. Pernambuco is no exception. The wealth of Recife's seventeenth-century sugar industry has disappeared in the twentieth century, leaving behind only touches of its former glory. Although Recife remains a prime tourist destination and provides luxury beachfront apartments, restaurants, and nightclubs for the better-off residents, the Population Crisis Committee in 1990 ranked it as the fourth worst city in the world because of its extensive shantytowns, high rates of crowding, crime, disease, infant mortality, pollution, noise, and disrepair. In addition, the city suffers from low rates of education, electrification, and sewer service, making the quality of life for impoverished residents extremely low (Veja 1990, 64). Yet Recife continues to draw *retirantes* from the interior in search of a better life.

Residents of the interior are often acutely aware of the image their communities have as being backward. Certainly in Caruaru, the issue of who is a hillbilly (*matuto*) and who is a modern, city sophisticate is deeply felt. This concern is often revealed in unexpected ways. For example, one day, after I had been in Caruaru about a year, a UFO appeared in the sky. This bright light, visible for miles, hovered high in a cloudless sky. While many people ignored the apparition, others evinced concern. One of my neighbors, who was pregnant, hid in her house for fear that her unborn child might be marked by it.

The fourteen-year-old son of the family I lived with came running downstairs, chattering excitedly that the radio had announced that the Brazilian Air Force had sent up some planes to look at the object. It was reported that they did not know what it was, but they did know that "it was not from this earth." He wanted some filters from my camera to look through (I had shown him how to do this for an eclipse of the sun some weeks earlier).[20] We went out to look at the phenomenon, passing two women in the street. One, kneeling with her hands in the air, was praying excitedly. The other was pulling on her companion's arm. "Get up, Maria," she said. "God is bigger than that!" The light disappeared at sunset, and the next day's newspaper declared it to have been a fallen weather balloon, not an extraterrestrial visitation.

By then a joke was sweeping the city, a joke that all my friends thought absolutely hilarious but which I found merely puzzling. The one-liner went like this: "A UFO appeared over Caruaru, and that night it crashed in Sairé, killing five *matutos* (hillbillies)." Why was this funny?

Sairé, a tidy, small town farther into the interior than Caruaru, often figured in local humor as a home of backward *matutos*. People joked that the name of the town derived from *sai só de ré* ("leave only in reverse"), a phrase used to describe a dead-end street too narrow to turn a car around in. Sairé, then, was an emblem of outmoded, quaint, old-fashioned Pernambuco: the backward back woods from which modern, progressive Caruaru was to be distinguished by its economic development and the sophistication of its inhabitants.[21]

Perhaps it was the apparent anachronism of juxtaposing something as science-fictionally futuristic as a UFO with the "old-fashioned" hillbillies that gave the joke its kick. Jokers acted out the comic befuddlement of Sairenses trying to retrieve their crushed relatives from under the suddenly solid future that had fallen on top of them.

The hilarity of UFO jokesters in Caruaru reflected their tension over the clash of what they saw as the future and the past mingled in the present, and their anxieties over their own place in the hierarchy of time periods that they mapped onto the economic geography of the state. Their amusement reflected both their pride in Caruaru's economic and cultural achievements and their knowledge of how residents of the South regard Northeast interior cities like their own. Despite Caruaruenses' insistence that their city is a "minicapital," to Southern Brazilians Caruaru is but a large Sairé, no matter how hard Caruaruenses might try to convince them that it is a small Recife. And Caruaruenses know this, to their sorrow.

A Feira de Caruaru

Caruaru is the second largest city in Pernambuco (the population in 1989 was 210,000, 170,000 urban and 40,000 in the surrounding rural *município*). Located 130 kilometers inland from Recife, it sits at the *boca* ("mouth") *do Sertão*, the edge of the Agreste, where it begins to shade into Sertão. At 632 meters above sea level, its climate is both cooler and dryer than Recife's. Founded on the site of a *fazenda* whose owners built a church in 1781 in fulfillment of a promise to Mary of the Immaculate Conception, the Hill of the Good Jesus remains a holy site. Today, Caruaru styles itself as the "capital of the Agreste," boasting colleges, primary and secondary schools, public and private hospitals, major supermarkets, Catholic and Protestant churches, a Mormon worship center, Kardecist centers, and *terrenos de Umbanda.*[22]

Caruaru is famous for its open-air market (*feira*). The days of the week in Portuguese are numbers: Monday is *segunda-feira* ("second market"), Tuesday is *terça-feira* ("third market"), and so forth. Caruaru's schedule reflects the division of the week into daily markets. On Tuesdays and Thursdays the *sulanca* ("clothing") market dominates the fairgrounds. On Tuesdays there is also a livestock market. Mondays and Wednesdays offer the food and general merchandise markets. In Saturday's world-famous *feira* tourists shop for ceramic figurines, block prints, and baskets, while locals buy clay dishes, food, songbirds, shoes, toys, clothing, and whatever else they may need.

The market's geography divides space according to the type of items for sale: clothes near the bus station, food in the center, arts and crafts across the river. Vendors illegally sell songbirds in little cages alongside the Saturday-morning *troca-troca* ("trade-trade"), in which people barter items strictly without cash. To the rear, next to a library and a small museum commemorating important events in the city, a spreading area of covered stalls filled with lace, embroidered clothing, leather goods, pottery, ceramic figurines, block prints, straw hats, woven hammocks, shoes, toys, and paintings, each in its own section of the market, tempts buyers.

On Saturdays, strolling musicians sing such *forró* classics as *Feira de Caruaru* or make up humorous songs about passersby. *Repentistas* amuse the crowds with musical joke and insult contests, and the beggars are out in force. Bus service to outlying communities runs more frequently on Saturdays. Everybody wants to come to Caruaru to buy and sell. In addition, smaller daily food markets serve local residents in the neighborhoods throughout the week.

Along with the trade in agricultural produce, Caruaru's economy depends on the blue jeans industry. A few jeans factories operate in the area, and in addition mostly female pieceworkers assemble and topstitch blue jeans at home. In some of the outlying communities, such as Toritama, almost every household has at least one member employed in the blue jeans industry, most going to Caruaru to sell their goods in the *sulanca* market on Tuesdays and Thursdays.

Some of the small towns around Caruaru also have *sulanca* markets on other days, and men like Maria Imaculada's husband make their living on the market circuit, picking up cut pieces in one town, dropping them at home for the wife and daughters to stitch, and then taking the completed pants on to markets in towns like Santa Cruz and Caruaru in a weekly circle. Some make more elaborate circuits, stopping in towns like Toritama to get the jeans stone washed or to have designs painted or embroidered on them before moving on.

On the side of the river opposite the artwork and clothing and down the road a bit is the agricultural produce. An extensive area there is divided into sections for meat, vegetables, fruit, spice, and grain, making it the major agricultural market of the state. Whatever farmers grow in the interior they or their agents sell in Caruaru, and from there to Recife and beyond.[23] Like the rest of the marketplace, semipermanent stands and unlicensed interlopers hawking wares from blankets spread on the ground coexist in the food market. Permanent buildings house some of the meat vendors. The food market shades off into regions where stall vendors sell plastic goods, toys, clothing, tools, pots and pans, nail clippers, cosmetics, and watches. The streets on which the market functions are also lined with shops, and part of the market is housed in buildings alongside the stands. In addition, smaller food marketplaces function in neighborhoods outside the Centro.

Caruaru lacks the extensive blocks of *miséria* found in Recife. Its population derives mostly from rural migrants or their descendants. The poor and working class dominate the population, although some wealthier businessmen support families on large estates and a small middle class clings to precarious status. Brazilians count wages in fractions and multi-

ples of a minimum stipend, or *salário* ("wage"), approximately sixty-five
dollars a month during the time of my fieldwork.[24] According to most estimates, while people require at least two minimum wages for bare survival, many wage-earners bring in less than one. In practice, wage and
employment violations receive little attention. One factory worker explained:

> There in your country, people earn money. Here it is very disorganized. A
> man works a lot, earns little. Here no one values poor people's work. I went
> to work, they said they would pay one *salário mínimo*. When payday came,
> they said they'd pay only [less than half a minimum wage]. What can you do?
> Nothing. There's no union, there's only an empty belly and Mama wanting
> me to help [financially] at home. So I said, "Thank you," took my money, so
> there you go.[25]

Families survive by pooling resources and participating in social networks; survival becomes a collaborative rather than an individual enter-
prise.

Personalism in the Modern City

To understand the emotional life of any people requires comprehension of
the historical, political, and economic juncture at which they stand: the
situations to which their emotions respond and contribute, the discourses
in the context of which sentiments play out. Since love is a sentiment of affiliation, it responds to the general structure of human relationships in society. In Brazil, economic class and regional residence structure social relationships, along with socially defined physical characteristics such as
color and gender. This structuring has come into being over the course of
history.

The history of a place or people consists in a series of stories told and
retold, as much in the varied memories of contemporary peoples as in the
social and physical residues of past events. People-watching on any Saturday morning in Caruaru will tell a story of the encounters of civiliza-
tions: the shapes of faces, nostrils, cheekbones, eyes; the curl of hair and
shades of skin tell a story about migration, confrontation, and the intimacy
of conquest. The lovely old cathedral that used to stand near the town
center can now be seen only in photographs; in its place a concrete mon-
strosity bespeaks a people's yearning to join the sophisticated ranks of the
modern. Military police directing traffic while standing beneath lights
that rotate from red to yellow to green without affecting the flow of cars

similarly offer clues about the place of symbols of modernity in a society still based on the personal touch of authority.[26]

History displays as multiplex a character as ethnography: historians tell stories, often disagreeing with one another about both events and interpretations. Ordinary people also have their own varied sense of history, stories told about what happened, not so much to create an accurate view of past events as to justify what goes on now. Storytelling serves a purpose, then, not in the service of some impersonal Truth but in the service of the personal and political needs of contemporary storytellers. Historical metaphor also frequently expresses social status: Caruaruenses, like so many others, conflate geographic location and historical epoch, regarding the countryside and rural peoples as if they were somehow contemporaneously in the past. While it is true that the styles of the countryside, in dress, in mannerism, in mores, in religion, are often old-fashioned compared with those of the city, rural areas as well as urban trends have both been transformed by new technologies, state expansion, social and geographic mobility, and economic changes. Conservatism in style reflects more the scale of social life in small communities than rigidity in opinion or simplicity of thought.

The story I want to tell here about Caruaru focuses on the growth of cities and the increasing intrusion of urban values and lifestyles into the countryside. There exist many ways to tell the story of Northeast Brazil's past, but I believe that this offers the most clues to the crisis of contemporary romance, which will form the subject of the second half of the book. The expansion of cities has occasioned an expansion of the influence of the state over a greater number of people. In the past, rural workers on the Mata's large plantations and those who farmed smallholds in the interstices of grand estates turned to *coroneis* for services such as political protection and poverty relief, and for access to markets, medical care, and so on. The state's reach faded out farther west: Land ownership, political alliance, trade, medical care, care of the poor, and religious leadership all responded to locally based, informal systems in Agreste and Sertão. Contemporary city dwellers have their own informal systems, but they also use government-issued cash, state-funded medical care, state-provided poverty relief services, state-sponsored courts, state-issued identity documents, and so forth.

The Brazilian state has changed over time from its beginning as the only independent monarchy in the Americas,[27] then through the subsequent Republic, a revolution that brought the *Estado Novo* ("New State")

of President Getúlio Vargas, the 1964 military coup, and the return to democracy of the 1980s. State expansion has been marked by the relative
weakness of the center's control over local elites and by periods of marked
and destabilizing economic crisis.

Even when governments were elected by popular vote, those votes
were confined to the literate and collected in the Northeast by local landowners who got political support from state and national leaders in return
for the *voto do cabresto* ("bridled vote") of their workers,[28] until the dictator-
ship of Getúlio Vargas (1937–45) (Pereira 1997, 24–26). The Vargas government banned political parties and discontinued elections, and took
away the right of *coroneis* to private militias. The state took over police
forces, local military organizations were incorporated into the national
army system, and the federal government began to direct economic policy
centrally (Pereira 1997, 27). Still, local elites remained powerful, many
turning in the role of *coronel* for that of local politician. State expansion
gave them the incentives and the means to remove rural squatters and
tenant farmers. The size of estates in the Mata consequently grew as the
government began to modernize sugar production; the Agreste and
Sertão remain dominated by small farms.

Public Love

The word *amor* refers not only to the passionate intrigues that attract men
and women (or, as the case may be, men and men or women and women)
but also to the affections that unite kin. Love may be seen as a sentiment of
affiliation that allows societies to cohere. In addition to its nature as a personal sentiment, love in the sense of caring about and taking care of others
constitutes a social duty. In some societies, all social relations refer in some
way to kinship; in others, states take on obligations toward citizens. In this
sense, one may speak of public love or the obligations of governments to
take care of the needs of their citizens.

In Northeast Brazil, especially in inland communities such as Caruaru,
political relations explicitly follow a kinship model: Personal contact, patronage, and clientelism remain integral parts of the political system. Citi-
zen-clients expect care from patron-officials, and they discuss the responsibilities of the state more in terms of the obligations of love than of contractual rights. States intrude into citizens' personal affective arrangements by licensing marriages, determining legal fatherhood and custody,

and by supplementing parental care for children through the provision of medical attention, food, and legal protections.

In Northeast Brazil, local representatives of the state, especially mayors, public health workers, judges, and police chiefs, explicitly take on paternal roles toward their constituents, both of their own accord and in response to citizen demands. Caruaruenses frequently complained to me of what they defined as a lack of love in the public arena as being the cause of persistent poverty, health problems, poor public education, and lack of paved roads, sewers, and other facilities. "If the mayor loved us, he would take care of us," one young woman complained. "But Brazil does not love the poor."

To those accustomed to the legal protections of contractual relations, paternalistic personalism seems oppressive. But those accustomed to personalism find contractual relationships cold rather than protective. One man, returning to Caruaru after years of working in São Paulo, tried to explain to his younger siblings what it is like in the South: "Even if your own uncle owns a factory," he told them, "he won't give you a job unless you have the papers to show your qualifications. See," he said, turning to me, "write this down! There is no love today in Brazil. If he loved you, he would employ you. That is certain, here at home. There, a poor man can do nothing. No one has any power except the owners. Here, a man can do much, if he has family."

Under personalism, love as loyal service is the idiom of social relations. Those not born to power make their way through personal ties to the more powerful. While such a system of local protectorates sustains a rigid class structure, it also offers opportunities to those who, while lowborn, have a talent for making connections. The expansion of the state in Northeast Brazil has not superseded personalism. Redefined as corruption, personalism remains a way of life within the broader system of the state, allowing both unfair distribution of resources and the creation of spaces of moral obligation. Personalism and contractualism respond to different concepts of the moral nature of the individual. As Brazilian anthropologist Lívia Barbosa has written:

We want all the benefits of a system like the North American one, without the negative counterpart that is impersonality, vulgarly understood as "Anglo-Saxon lack of human warmth." We want to give a personalized treatment to all Brazilian citizens and maintain ourselves, at the same time, under the rule of universal laws. Theoretically, universal decrees do not combine with personal treatments, but it is exactly this that in Brazilian society we attempt to provide, by way of a social practice which incorporates the notion of the individual with its roots in two distinct totalities: one legal and the other moral, which permits . . . that the individual be the normative subject of institutions and [at the same time] of situations. (1992, 123; my translation)

The Miracle and Its Aftermath

The state intrudes into daily life through the regulation represented by the documents it requires of citizens, and especially through the provision of the cash that allows even strangers to engage in transactions. But this intrusion has been incomplete in the Brazilian Northeast, both in the large numbers of citizens who lack officially required documents (such as birth certificates and work-record booklets) and in the scarcity and instability of cash itself.

The contemporary poverty of the Northeast has been exacerbated by the aftereffects of economic policies during the past thirty years. In 1964, a military coup led by Castelo Branco overthrew populist president Joao Goulart. The new government engaged in widescale borrowing between 1968 and 1973. The economy grew by 10 to 12 percent per year during this time, in what has been called "one of the world's purest examples of inequitable growth" (Morley 1978, 244). Policies included suppressing labor unions, keeping down wages, enhancing production technology, attracting foreign investment, and investing large amounts of capital, especially in the South. Brazil's enormous economic growth during this period, often called the Miracle, left Brazil with the world's eighth largest economy and the world's largest foreign debt (U.S. $115 billion), sparking triple- to quadruple-digit inflation.

National policies contributed to economic mobility in some regions, especially in São Paulo, Rio de Janeiro, and Brasília. The Northeast, again, fell behind (Pastore 1979, 141). The devastating impact is reflected in health statistics. Let us take as an example the infant mortality rate (IMR), a particularly sensitive measure of economic status. An estimated one million children a year die before the age of five in Brazil (IGBE/UNICEF 1986), nearly 2,740 a day, mostly in the Northeast and mostly from combinations of infections and malnutrition.

From 1935 to 1940 the Northeast's IMR was 34.6 percent higher than the South's. But by 1980 the difference had risen to 104.4 percent, and by 1984 to 130.5 percent (IGBE/UNICEF 1986). Mean life expectancy at birth in the Northeast is 44.2 years (Soares 1978, 285); in the South it is 60 years

(Garcia 1986, 33). Clearly the Miracle has worsened living conditions for *Nordestinos*, who still have yet to undergo the health transition from conditions of high fertility and high mortality to a healthier pattern of low fertility and low mortality. Most of the mortality and morbidity in the Northeast is the result of old-fashioned killers long defeated in wealthier regions: dysentery, cholera, diarrhea, respiratory infections, measles, and malnutrition. Rates of more modern killers, such as heart disease, cancer, and AIDS, meanwhile continue to rise. But most *Nordestinos* lack access to primary health care, much less to the complex services required by heart, cancer, and AIDS patients. As long as provision of basic sanitation and health services remains off the list of priorities for the national government, *Nordestinos* will remain excluded from the benefits of the Miracle.[29]

Regional disparity also affects the nature of economic interactions. In the small towns and farmsites of the Agreste's rural past the economy depended not on the exchange of state-issued markers of value but on reciprocity, favors, and debts of gratitude owed for goods and services. Although the Miracle helped extend a cash economy through the Northeast through urbanization and investment in capital-intensive methods of agriculture, cash remains both scarce and unstable in Northeast Brazil. Although nearly a third of Brazil's population lives in the Northeast, only 8 percent of printed money circulates there (Garcia 1987, 28) and only 14 percent of national income is earned there (Patai 1988, 39).

The economic fallout of the Miracle affected intraregional disparities as well as differences between regions. From 1960 to 1980, income among the poorest 40 percent of Northeastern wage earners grew by only 0.66 percent, whereas income among the richest 10 percent of wage earners grew by 15.12 percent (Romão 1988, 137). By 1980, the poorest 20 percent of *Nordestinos* had an income share of only 3.8 percent, whereas the richest 1 percent earned 29.3 percent of all Northeastern income (Patai 1988, 39).

The new cash-poverty may well be worse than the rural poverty of the past. As one Caruaruense woman lamented:

It's so very sad. The financial situation is turning my Brazil very different, very violent, changing people, messing with them [*mexendo com eles*]. People today are poorer. In the past, the poor man on his little farm, he had his beans, his manioc meal, his corn, he was poor but he had sure [access to] food because he knew that by cultivating he would obtain it. Today not even cultivating do you have enough food. I think that the financial situation is destroying my beloved Brazil, my God in Heaven.

Living with Hyperinflation

Another fallout of the Miracle has been the effect on Brazil's economy of its national debt. For the past thirty years, the national economy has been characterized by cycles of inflation, currency devaluation, and recession that have been devastating to the poor. When the military seized power in 1964, inflation was 100 percent per year. It had dropped to 26 percent per year by 1973 (Baer and Beckerman 1988, 6) but surged to 1,500 percent per year by 1987 (p. 24). And in November of 1990, national news broadcasts put the inflation rate at 3,194.94 percent for the year.

During my fieldwork, prices rose daily. My friends joked, *Só que não sobe neste pais é pau de velho* ("The only thing that doesn't rise in this country is an old man's 'stick'"). The currency changed from cruzeiros to cruzados to cruzados novos and back to cruzeiros without halting its precipitous plunge in value. The actual value of the money was not what was printed on it but rather what was declared on the news, as the government regularly removed zeros from the values of large-denomination bills faster than they could print revised notes.

Figuring out what combination of bills corresponded to which value under hyperinflation required close daily attention to the broadcast news. A bill printed with the value of ten thousand, for example, might be later stamped with a ten, and people were as likely to call it ten thousand as they were one, ten, or one million —cruzados, cruzeiros, or mil-reis, or the slang *pão* (bread).[30] To understand prices, a buyer had to have a basic sense of what any given commodity was worth that day. Prices changed with such dizzying speed that this was trying indeed. Some examples: The 359 cruzados novos with which I bought a refrigerator in March of 1989 could buy only a slaughtered chicken one year later; what I paid for my stove in March 1989 bought two rolls of toilet paper in March of 1990, one roll in May of that year, and nothing more than a pack of chewing gum by June. In March of 1990 my water bill was 230 cruzeiros; by June it had risen to 1,670 cruzeiros, without any change in water use.

By the time I was back in the United States in 1991, my friends sent me letters in envelopes plastered with layers of stamps covering every square millimeter of surface area except for the address, because the government could not print money or stamps fast enough to keep up with hyperinflation. In a letter to me in 1992, a student colleague of mine living in Brazil, Misha Klein, complained of the difficulty of gaining what she called her "money legs," reminding me of my early difficulties. Like landlubbers at sea, newcomers had to learn how to negotiate the shifting waters.

During President Collor's first failed economic plan, I saw truck bumpers painted with the warning: *Cheque p'ra mim é papel higiênico* ("A check for me is toilet paper").[31] Under hyperinflation, checks diminished too rapidly in value between the time they were written and the time they were cashed to be worth accepting. No wonder people said, *Se corre o bicho pega, se fica o bicho come* ("If you run the beast gets you; if you stay, the beast eats you").

Bills were withdrawn from circulation when their value became too small. The printing of bills could not keep up with inflation, and the government was hard pressed to print bills large enough. When the five thousand cruzeiro bill was mandated by the legislature, a temporary, simplified version had to be hurried into circulation while the official version was being designed and printed. The five thousand cruzeiro bill came out in late 1990; by early December 1991 the Brazilian government was printing a fifty thousand cruzeiro bill.

It was common to find sarcastic graffiti, reflecting public disdain, scribbled on money. The inflation occurred mostly in Brazilian currency: When translated into dollars, prices remained comparatively steady. Investment in foreign currencies was a way for the middle class to accumulate capital, although it was illegal to have foreign bank accounts. The official price, the tourist price, and the "parallel" (black market) price of the dollar were all published on the front pages of major newspapers every day to facilitate investment.[32]

In 1985 the military government was replaced by an indirectly elected civilian government, and in 1989 the first direct elections for president in over twenty-five years were held, bringing to power the right of center Francisco Collor de Mello. President Collor moved immediately to seize bank accounts and freeze wages and prices.[33] Inflation, which had been over 100 percent per month, dropped to 3 percent per month within a few weeks because of the resulting money squeeze. Two months after the election, however, inflation was back in double digits, and the recession Collor created to combat inflation resulted in hyper-stagflation, in which wages stayed low and prices continued to climb.

During Collor's first year in office, the Brazilian economy declined by 4.6 percent while prices rose 400 percent (*San Francisco Chronicle*, March 20, 1991), despite price freezes. Collor's campaign promise to reduce infant mortality by 40 percent was never realized. Informants commented in sarcastic folk speech: *Quando a merda tem preço, o cú do pobre entope* ("If you could sell shit, the poor would get constipated").

President Collor was eventually forced from office in a corruption scandal, and his vice president, Itamar Franco, who took his place, was equally unable to stem inflation. More recently, sociologist-turned-president Fernando Henrique Cardoso instituted policies of monetary reform and of indexing the value of the new currency, the *real*, to the value of the dollar that have held prices at steady, if high, rates. In 1999 the real started to fail, when Brazil could no longer continue using foreign reserves to prop it up. In letters, my friends expressed the worry that the *real* might turn out to be *súrreal*, and in 1999 Brazil's inability to continue using foreign reserves to subsidize the real did lead to devaluation with a corresponding rise in prices in Brazil.

During my fieldwork, the unstable economy and low wage structure combined to make the working class especially insecure. Middle- and upper-class individuals had access to stable foreign currencies, but the working class had to scrounge every month to supplement wages that were not only inadequate to start but that also lost value daily with inflation. Those who lived in rented housing were especially vulnerable, and buying a house became more and more difficult each year because of the lack of access to credit and the impossibility of accumulating a surplus in local currency. Social networks became increasingly important to the economic survival of the working class, and therefore pressure to conform to norms of cooperative friendliness was high. This pressure was particularly intense for women, partly because women are customarily responsible for maintaining social ties, and partly because women depend more on the informal sector for income than do men. The connection between economic relationships and affiliations of affection is the topic of the next chapter.

3 ⌒ Love as Connection

Social Network and Emotion in an Ambiguous Economy

O amor é um substantivo que nem sabemos como conjugar.
("Love is a noun we don't even know how to conjugate.")
Branquinha

The small towns from which most Caruaruenses migrated over the last thirty years had economies and a style of interaction markedly different from that in the unstable cash economy of modern cities. The urban working class of the Northeast retains both an economic and an emotional style reminiscent of the rural past, but one that takes new forms in the urban present. Life in small towns and on rural homesites is also different from what it was yesteryear, increasingly transformed by new social and geographic mobility, cash-based transactions, and the contractual relationships supported by the state.

The Pleasures of Company

It is quite possible to reach old age in Northeast Brazil without once having been entirely alone; in fact, it is difficult to do otherwise. In Caruaru, when people are together, they touch. Women friends walk hand in hand, men drape arms over shoulders, people greet and send off acquaintances with kissed cheeks and carry, dandle, and rock infants to sleep. Children sleep three or four to a bed with siblings, cousins, or parents. People nuzzle children with affectionate *cheirinhos* or little sniffs, and most people use perfume in the expectation of being sniffed. Boys spend their days thronging with their friends in streets, workplaces, and schools. Girls are either in school with friends or accompanying female relatives on their daily rounds. People consider an experience not shared an experience not fully savored.

Speakers of Brazilian Portuguese, and especially Northeasterners, sprinkle their speech liberally with such tag questions as *não é?* and its contraction *né?* (isn't it?) or expansion *nao é não* (is it not?), and with *sabe* (you know), *não sabe* (don't you know?), *entendeu* (you understand), *viu* (you see), *pegou* (catch it), *capou* (do you get it?), and *veja bem* (look well), among others. These have the effect of drawing the listener in, forcing interactive responses, and referring to shared experience. Some people reach out to poke or pat the listener at every tag question; most use expansive gestures of hands, arms, shoulders, and face to embellish the spoken word.[1]

It's impossible to be able to live alone. The people feel this necessity to have someone together with them to exchange ideas, to converse, to love, to hug, to be able to cry on her lap, to be able to lament life, to be able to get things off your chest. To have a person to share with, because, sometimes, a happiness can turn into a sadness when you don't have anyone to share this happiness with, *né?* (Agostinho)

The smaller the city, the more togetherness is emphasized.

There in Recife there are so many people that we feel solitude in the middle of the multitude. Here in Caruaru, while surrounded by few people, we feel sheltered, accompanied, loved. And in Toritama or Brejo, small towns, where everybody really knows everybody, how much more. (Welington)

Brazilian Portuguese uses the words *amar* ("to love") and *gostar* ("to like") to describe positive feelings toward companions. It uses *saudade* to describe how bittersweet the memories of past companionship can be. Separation from loved ones is portrayed as dramatically tragic, not only in television and movies but also in the stories people tell about their lives.[2] Many of those I met in Caruaru had never been entirely alone. Most thought my strange practice of traveling alone, far from family, was inexplicable, terrifying, and an indicator of some tragedy in my background.

A number of writers have described societies in the grip of major disasters, whether hunger (Turnbull 1972), natural disaster (Erikson 1976), political oppression (Shkilnyk 1985), economic decline (Scheper-Hughes 1992), war (Daniel 1996; Nordstrom and Robben 1995), or some terrible combination of these. Watching dramatic rises in interpersonal violence, sexual abuse, alcohol and drug abuse, suicide, depression, and despair, charting the details of the disintegration of interpersonal bonds as compassion becomes a luxury no longer afforded, these authors describe a social world in which, in the evocative words of Shkilnyk, the poisons of self-interest and powerlessness have become stronger than love (1985, 242).[3]

Our horror at viewing social disintegration lies in compassion for those exiled from love, both the love that they might otherwise enjoy from their associates and all the physical and psychological consequences of being treated without love, and the emptiness of a life without the love one ought to but cannot feel. Horror lies also in the forced recognition of the power of anger, fear, hatred, jealousy, envy—morally condemned, antisocial sentiments all—over those sentiments regarded as the glory of moral humanity: compassion, generosity, forgiveness, courage, and love.

Love seems to be a kind of social glue that makes it possible for societies to cohere. But what is love? Is it really the case that in healthy societies some kind of steady state of loving-kindness binds members together in comfortable harmony dramatically different from relations under conditions of great stress? Or is that a fantasied image of idealized humane society? Is the social disintegration of societies under unbearable strain the result of some warping of the human spirit, or simply an intensification of the ambivalences of normal human interaction into a tragic burlesque, mocking our self-image of being nobler than the beasts? Love, even in the most benign of societies, is hard to define, hard to attain, hard to sustain. Self-interest and loving generosity are a tense pair anywhere, and often startlingly inextricable.

Communication of Love: Restricted and Verbal Codes

Love is not a singularity. The word and its variations can be used lightly to describe preferences (I love chocolate/*eu adoro chocolate*) or as a declaration of deep emotion (I love you/*eu te amo*). Its use as a gloss for deep emotion covers a great variety of sentiments bound together in the continuous stories of longtime acquaintance, interpersonal interaction, and mutual interdependence. A declaration such as "I love you" made between lovers might better be described as a characterization of a stance or attitude of the lover toward the beloved than as a description of a steady state of singular sentiment.

Among the definitions people gave me of the word *amor* was that love is the result of longtime intimate acquaintance. Some people described it in that way; others thought that familiarity destroys love, which they saw as a kind of idealization. To those who held the former opinion, love was a kind of intimate loyalty that might not include affection and that might encompass a good deal of conflict. For example, while discussing a recent, highly publicized murder of a woman by her live-in boyfriend, one older, rural man commented:

He killed her because he loved her. He maybe didn't like [*gostar*] her, he didn't approve of her, *né*, but she was his and he wanted her to be his. Being loved isn't always good for your health. Even the brutes also love, *sabe*?

Another man offered a proverb: "We fight because we love." Here love is more like affiliation than affection, but no less powerful an idea for all that.[4]

Love is, of course, more than a word. Like other sentiments, it is experienced and expressed in the acting out: something that happens within and between people.[5] In Christian countries, it is also an ideology in the sense of an articulated theory. Christian theology seeks to understand a God described as the ultimate expression of love itself. If God is love, and to be a moral person one must be godly, then to be a moral person one must behave lovingly.

Christian theology also posits a sharp distinction between those actions motivated by love and those actions motivated by economic interest. It is hard for the rich man to enter the kingdom of heaven, at least partly because of the suspicion that his wealth could not have been accumulated had he behaved in a generously loving fashion. It is not necessary to be a theologian to adopt Christian theological ideas in a Christian society: Theology underlies folk models of morality. Many scholars interested in the sentiments that both bind and separate members of social groups have unself-consciously adopted the same religiously based folk model as their Christian informants, by which emotion and economic interest are seen as conflicting, morally opposed forces (Medick and Sabean 1984b, 10), despite the importance of sharing and generosity to Christian concepts of love.

Much theorizing on love has come out of studies of the family in European history. Scholars are divided on the question of when love became an important aspect of family life, and on the relationships between ideologies of familial love and economic structures. One school posits an "increasing sentimentalization" (Shorter 1975) of family life accompanying increased life expectancy and prosperity (Ariès 1962; Shorter 1975; Stone 1977). Presumably, as parents had more certainty that children would survive and as conjugals could foresee a full life span together, people felt freer to commit emotionally to one another than they would under the specter of frequent early death.[6] Another view sees love-based relations as encouraged but not created by the effect of rising capitalism on interpersonal relationships and the concept of self (MacFarlane 1987).[7] Other scholars posit that the demographic transition and industrial revolution in Europe, while not dramatically changing family sentiments, pushed means of emotional expression toward the more verbal (Bernstein 1971; Cancian 1986; Gillis 1988).

Unlike the linguistically based models of sentiment used by Abu-Lughod and Lutz (1990), this model sees verbalism as a quality of emotion that emerges in some kinds of situations but not others. This school theorizes that material interest and sentiment are indistinguishable. Actions and statements form a code of communication within the family, expressing emotion without the need for direct declarations of the form "I feel." Economic behaviors that share, endow, or deny material goods can be seen as communicators as much of affect as of power (Medick and Sabean 1984b). Material and affective motives, rather than opposites, are indistinguishably intertwined.

In addition, economic systems and class status affect styles of emotional expression. Basil Bernstein (1971), for example, states that in societies characterized by shared understandings of history, face-to-face relations, and economic interdependence (such as peasant societies), verbal declarations of tender sentiment may be seen as threatening. Emotional connection is expressed instead through action or verbally through a combination of metaphoric folk speech and meaningful silences.[8] There is no need for verbal elaboration of explicit sentiment, partly because of the shared understandings presumed among those who live so closely together and partly because behavior is more important than internal experience in such societies.

Verbally restricted communicative codes are characteristic of working-class and peasant societies, while middle-class groups in capitalist societies tend to have elaborated verbal codes of emotional expression. In both types of society, emotional and material interrelations are interpenetrated, reflecting the multilayered nature of social relations.

In places like Caruaru, rural and small town people move to a cash-based, urban capitalist economy, a community of strangers and acquaintances very different from the world of cousins and face-to-face relations that make verbally restricted communications codes work. They live submerged in the cash economy, albeit frequently at its margins, where cash may wash over them leaving little in its wake. They must, in effect, code-switch between the different styles of emotional interaction.

Code-switching between two languages is different from code-switching between two distinct styles of experiencing and expressing emotion. Generally, bilingual speakers realize that two distinct languages exist, and they are able to switch consciously from one to the other as circumstances warrant. But emotional style is less explicitly existent than language. Emotion's nature as moral discourse makes code-switching among different emotional styles problematic. Emotional propriety becomes as ambiguously multifaceted as economic style.

Love in an Ambiguous Economy

Na feira de Caruaru faz gosto a gente ver/que todo que há no mundo nela tem p'ra vender ("In the market of Caruaru, it pleases us to see / that everything that exists in the world, they have for sale in it")
"Feira de Caruaru," *forró* song by Luiz Gonzaga

The economy of Caruaru's *feira* encompasses several types of exchange simultaneously. Vendors and buyers may confine themselves to one type, or they may negotiate shifts from one type of exchange to another, with the more clever finding ways to profit on the differences. In Caruaru's market you can use cash to buy whatever is for sale; indeed, with a little negotiating you can use more than one type of currency. Vendors recognize U.S. dollars, for example, as more valuable than Brazilian currency, and some are prepared to accept them, however quasi-legal that practice may be.[9] Some vendors accept personal checks drawn on Brazilian banks. A few are adventurous (or greedy) enough to risk a foreign draft, and some of the better established art vendors are prepared to accept credit cards from a variety of nations.

In the *troca-troca* ("trade-trade") area on the cobblestone flats across the street from the river, you can engage in barter. Your tape recorder might net you a nice blender; your television, a bicycle, especially if you throw in some batteries and maybe the odd spark plug or two. The vendors have a complex set of relationships among themselves, and, especially in the agricultural produce markets, vendors may buy and sell on credit, trading on the good name they have built up through long-term, trustworthy acquaintance with their partners rather than on government-regulated written contracts.

Some food vendors buy wholesale from farmers to retail at their market stalls in Caruaru. Others are small producers who come in to sell what they do not themselves consume for foodstuffs not locally produced, such as coffee, sugar, and cooking oil. Still other producers have long-term contracts with major buyers who can pick up produce at the *sítio* ("farm-site") or who buy predetermined batches at the market itself. The market is also the site for transfers, from the trucks of producers to the trucks of buyers, of produce that has already been paid for. The shift from political control by owners of large *fazendas* ("plantations") to government by appointed and elected officials has had a major impact on relations in agricultural markets like that of Caruaru.

In Northeast Brazil, political office has from earliest times been associated with patronage and family contacts (Graham 1990). Until the nineteenth century, *coroneis* controlled access to work, money, and markets (Eisenstadt and Roniger 1984, 104–5). Often generations of the same family would work on a single plantation for decades, trading work and loyalty for physical and economic protection and support. *Fazendas* often maintained their own private militias, and *coroneis* were extremely influential, even where they did not hold political office. Today, the *coroneis* have been largely replaced by politicians, lawyers, and large-scale merchants, the system of patronage by one of brokerage. Like the *coroneis* of old, they build power bases by maintaining networks of indebted clients, who in turn maintain networks of indebted clients of even lower status than themselves (Eisenstadt and Roniger 1984, 107; Martins Dias 1978). Unlike *coroneis*, politicians are not necessarily landowners and do not inherit their positions.[10]

It is rare today for *fazendas* to maintain the kind of long-term patronage with families that was common in the past. Those *fazendas* that still exist hire wage laborers on a temporary basis (Carvalho 1987), paying them either in cash or, like urban employees, in a combination of cash and standard portions of staple foodstuffs. As a part of the growth in the power of the state, workers seek benefits such as legal protection and health care from local governments in towns and cities, rather than from rural employers (Martins Dias 1978, 171).

The important patronage relationship increasingly is that between small farmers and town merchants. Rural to urban migration in the region has reduced the average size of farms in the Agreste. The *roça*, or small farm, is now a major rural establishment. While in 1920 the average number of workers per farm was 20.47 in Pernambuco's Agreste, by 1970 that number had diminished to 3.47 (Martins Dias 1978, 173). Small farmers can get ahead only by establishing a relationship of *freguesia* ("customership") with a merchant who extends credit to and establishes a marketing network for the farmer in return for political support and exclusive marketing rights.

Establishing a *freguesia* is not strictly a business endeavor, The farmer must show that he is *de confiança* ("trustworthy") and then work to establish an *amizade* ("friendship") with the merchant (Martins Dias 1978, 178–80). *Freguesias* are not usually guaranteed by any written contract. Indeed, asking for a written contract insults by its implication of distrust. What guarantees the contract is its long-term nature and the need for both buyers and sellers to retain a good name so that others will be willing to do business with them. *Freguesias* are generally established by men who engage in the same friendship-building activities as urban men: drinking together, serving as godfather for each other's children, or encouraging marriages between the sons of one and the daughters of the other. *Freguesias* have all the outward forms of affectionate friendship; the extent to which partners actually like each other varies.

In this system, ownership of the means of production (the farm) does not guarantee power. The ability to form social and emotional ties with powerful people does (cf. Martins Dias 1978, 182). Because the highly personalized concepts of honor, sentiment, and morality that underlie ties in this system are unstated, they are vulnerable to manipulation by reinterpretation (Roniger 1987, 316). Ideally, a clever operator could work the system to his advantage only to a point, because if his friendship proved false he would lose clients to more trustworthy patrons. However, some merchants are sufficiently ruthless or well connected to local politicians to enable them to eliminate their local competition, forcing *roçeiros* ("small farmers") into exploitative friendships in which the friendly sentiment is even more of a difficult act than usual.

Another complication of the *freguesia* system is that social actors at different levels in the political economic hierarchy operate according to different concepts of the composition and content of the economic domain. Antonius Robben's study of a fishing village in the Litoral of the Northeast Brazilian state of Bahia provides an illustrative example. He writes:

[E]ach principal economic group has a different conception of the fishing economy. Boat owners regard themselves as subject to an institutional conglomerate of banks, federal agencies, and large fish marketing corporations whose business decisions are guided by the impersonal forces of supply and demand. Boat fishermen, instead, perceive the economy as part of an interactional universe . . . [that] operates through such qualities as friendship, graft, favoritism, and manipulation, which . . . interlace the institutional links perceived by boat owners with other social ties. (1989, 3)

Like those of Robben's fishermen, the views of Pernambucan farmers and merchants regarding the nature of economic life are shaped by how well integrated they are into the national economy. Many of the urban poor, residents of small towns in the rural zone, and rural smallholders operate largely in an old-fashioned economy of tips, favors, debts, and gifts, whereas more established merchants work on the basis of the contractual relations of a capitalist commodity-driven economy.[11] Many inhabit an uncomfortable, ambiguous zone between the two types of exchange, each with its separate morality.

Small-scale vendors in the city also struggle with the meaning of *freguesia*. They need to build a regular clientele to survive, but building a clientele involves creating a set of friendships. And being a friend means generosity, here in the form of generous terms of credit. A Caruaruense shopkeeper explains the problem:

You have friends, and let's say you tell them that you won't sell anymore on credit or you're going to charge interest, and so suddenly in addition to losing a friend you lose a customer. There is a great connection between business and friendship here. But what kind of friendship is that? If they were a true friend they would always buy from you and not your competitors, and also always pay you on time and full price. But there are people who buy two, three thousand cruzados worth from me on credit, so a month from now, they don't have money, pay me one thousand. So afterward they come to pay me two hundred, three hundred more . . . or they don't complete it, or when they complete it the money has already lost value, with inflation every day. . . . What's to do? It's the Brazilian system. . . . Certain is this: Buy and pay at one time, if not, it's with interest. But you can't. Not and stay in business.

Vendors and service providers can neither fully charge friends nor avoid selling to them. The problem spans classes. A local veterinarian explained:

Look, when it's a friend, I have to give a discount. They pay only for the medicines, not for my work. The problem is that a customer who passes here two, three times turns into a friend and doesn't pay any more. I have to work on credit, and they always have reasons not to pay, and they never pay what the service really costs. I can't support myself on a small animal practice for this reason. At least the government pays me regularly to inspect farm animals.

These kinds of relationships may not be what immediately come to mind when one thinks of the meaning of the word *love*. But these statements, and discussions of commercially interested friendships and *fregue-sias*, came up in response to my question, "What does the word *amor* mean?" They formed part of a discourse on the topic "Why there is no love in Brazil these days," a topic that focused more on honest business practices, interpersonal respect, public obligations to support and protect the weak, and courtesy in general than on deep personal affection, intimate acquaintance, or sexual attraction—indicating the need to include these aspects of human interaction into the definition of *amor* in Northeast Brazil.

The two views of love form part of the contradictions between old-fashioned patronage in a system of reciprocal exchange and the norms of interaction in a cash economy. Surviving the moral, economic, and emotional contradictions of life in cities like Caruaru requires finesse. Some people are good at it, others are not.

Glória's Party: Investing in Emotional and Financial Debt

Caruaruenses switch among types of economic style in response to the situation, with varying degrees of success. For example, one day a woman named Glória decided to give a party. The party was ostensibly in honor of her mother's birthday, but there were other considerations as well. Two years earlier, Glória's father had died. Some years before his death, Glória's mother, Dona Magdalena, had discovered his long-term affair with a woman with whom he had been involved prior to his marriage to Dona Magdalena.

Dona Magdalena had made a vow to the Virgin Mary in response to this affair. She humbled herself by refusing to wear new clothing and became an expert in Marian religious folklore, leading small groups of women in rosary praying and the Ave Maria. She also kept small shrines to Mary and various saints about the house and prayed and carried out pilgrimages in behalf of relatives with serious health problems. Her family considered her a kind of living saint (cf. Gaines and Farmer 1986), and a number of people felt deeply indebted to her because of her prayers for them. For example, her uncle believed that she had cured him of alcoholism.[12]

When her husband died, suddenly and young during Carnaval, it was in his mistress's bed. The woman did not want to surrender the body, and friends had to go to retrieve it so that it could be laid out properly at home without Dona Magdalena's having to confront the other woman directly. In addition, he had left some gambling debts. Dona Magdalena and Glória did not know how much he owed, and they could not honorably go into the kinds of establishments where they might question his unsavory associates in order to make good. His friends paid off his debts and refused to tell the bereaved women how much they had had to pay. They also provided financial assistance to the pair until Glória was able to replace her father's support with a variety of businesses.[13] Dona Magdalena and Glória thus had a monetary debt of unknowable proportions, and a debt of gratitude for the considerate acts of these men during a time of hardship.

Glória had earned enough to pay off at least a portion of her cash debt.[14] But instead, she decided to give a big party, invite the people to whom she owed both money and love, and in that way pay off some of her debt. A rural cousin gave her a piglet, which she raised until it was big enough. She then hired a neighbor to slaughter the animal.

When she asked him how much he charged for the service, he asked her how the pig was to be used. If she were planning to eat the pig, he said, he would ask for a portion of the meat. If she were planning to sell the pork, he would ask for a portion of the money. Since she was planning to eat the pig, he opted for the meat. Here the negotiation over type of economic exchange was explicit.

On the appointed day the pig was dragged squealing from its pen, and Glória put on the radio loudly and hid in a bedroom while the butcher beat the pig over the head several times with a sledgehammer until it collapsed and its throat could be cut. Then she came out and, together with the butcher and some rural cousins who had come in for the day, she cut the pig up into portions, ground up some of the meat, salted and marinated other portions, and made the intestines into sausage. While they worked, the group cooked and ate portions of the fat from along the pig's spine. When the butcher left he neglected to take his portion of the meat, which had been set aside for him. Glória served it at the party.

The party was a big success, with lots of food and with live music provided by a cousin for whom Dona Magdalena had prayed, curing his skin problems. Glória told me the butcher and his family would probably come to claim a share of the meat, but they did not. I asked her how she would pay him, and she told me that it did not particularly matter because he was a good man and a good friend and anyway didn't I know that it was rude to talk about such things. I pressed her further on the matter.[15]

Glória, a seamstress, dress designer, and baker, mused that the but-cher's daughter was planning a wedding and maybe that had something to do with it. Sure enough, about a month later the bride came over for some fittings, and Glória made a smart white pantsuit for her out of mate-rial the bride's family provided. The day before the wedding, the bride's mother came over with sugar, flour, and other ingredients that Glória made into an impressive confection covered with curlicues and roses of blue and white frosting. She never charged for her labor and only reluc-tantly conceded that there might have been a connection between this service and the butchering of the pig.

Well, usually I know how much to ask for making clothes or a cake, and then I went over to the bride's before the wedding and put on makeup and did her hair. And I could figure out how much to ask for that too. But there are other things to think about, né? You have to think about whether it is more impor-tant to ask for cash or just to do it. Sometimes giving is worth more than re-ceiving, and sometimes it isn't. It's very complicated. (Glória)

For Glória, the party was a kind of investment, and much more profit-able than the liquidation of her debts in cash would have been. With the extravagant food and entertainment, Glória bought the goodwill of over a hundred guests to whom she now could turn if she ever needed another favor. As for the butcher, he had first inquired as to which economic sys-tem applied to the disposition of the pork. Assured that it was being used as a gift rather than a commodity, he opted to utilize his butchering serv-ices to gain a service from Glória, as part of an ongoing relationship, rather than to let it end with a bucket of meat.

Neither he nor she was willing to characterize their interactions as economic. Both claimed that an affectionate friendship existed between their two families and that people who like one another naturally take care of one another. They were simply behaving like decent neighbors. I told Glória my opinions on the economic benefits of giving the party rather than paying a debt in cash, and she agreed that there were benefits to de-cent behavior. Elaborating on the theme, she said that it was a good idea also to become the godmother to as many children as possible and always to keep an eye open for ways to help people. She sealed her discussion by telling me a story:

I had a friend once who thought she was better than other people. She always looked down on people who she thought weren't as well off as she was, you know what I mean? So she got married and moved to Recife and all kinds of things happened, and it ended up that she was widowed and she had to make her living selling sandwiches on the beach, *né*, who thought she was so much better than me who makes my living selling snacks from my home, you know? If you act obnoxiously [*chata*], and she was a bitch on wheels [*chata de galosha*, lit. "jerk in boots"], let me tell you, then you end up with no friends. She had to sell sandwiches to strangers, walking on a beach, carrying them all day and making them all night, whereas I have regular customers who come here to get what I make and buy from me every day without my having to leave the house or stay up all night or worry about whether anyone will buy tomorrow. Who laughed at me yesterday cries for help today.[16] That is to say, friendship is worth more than gold. Friendship is certainly worth more than cruzados—but then, so is toilet paper in this economy!

Being decent, being trustworthy, being generous, cultivating friendships, all have an economic value in a gift-exchange economy. In Caruaru, gift exchange and commodity exchange are interpenetrated, and those who wish to get ahead, or simply to survive, must be as canny as Glória in figuring out when to sell and when to give.

Parallel Economy, Street Rules, and the *Jeitinho Brasileiro*[17]

Quem tem boca vai arrumar todo.
("Who has a mouth will [be able to] arrange everything.")
Brazilian proverb[18]

One of the tasks of ethnography is to discover the basic cultural rules by which people live. However, Brazil is a society like a sieve, in which members are constantly escaping through loopholes. While many societies have developed means for their members to slip past institutional and economic barriers, Brazil has developed a whole vocabulary celebrating this process, which many of my informants took pride in (mistakenly) regarding as uniquely Brazilian.

One hears the terms *jeitinho, jogo da cintura,* and *lei de Gerson* constantly. Jeitinho means literally a "little way." To *dar um jeitinho* means to "find a way"; to *dar um jeitinho em* (in) means to "arrange, repair, manipulate, or swindle"; to be *jeitoso* is to be "resourceful, to have a way about one." *Jogo da cintura* literally means "waist game": It refers to the swaying of a samba dancer's waist (Nations and Farias 1990, 759) and to the complicated "dance" of manipulation in which the *jeitoso* individual engages.

To see my girlfriend I have to do a lot of *jogo da cintura* with my wife. I *dar um jeitinho* in her, I keep giving excuses, I keep making her be guilty for being jealous. "Oh, my passion, don't you trust me? You don't love me? Who loves has to trust!" I keep on saying, "I went to such and such a place, I have such and such an excuse," and so I do what I want.

Brazilians use the term *dançar* both to refer to the *jogo da cintura* and to describe the frustrated "dance" of those who have just missed out on something. A popular saying plays on the double meaning: *Quem não dança, vai dançar* ("Who doesn't dance, will dance"). Whoever does not enter the social dance of manipulation will be left dancing in frustration after unattainable goals.

The term *lei de Gerson* ("Gerson's law") is a reference to a popular soccer star known for his innovative seat-of-the-pants goal-making style. In a television advertisement he appeared boasting that while others live by the laws of the state, he lived by his personal law, the law of advantage: *Sempre gosto de levar vantagem, certo!* ("I always like to take advantage, right!").[19] This is the other side of the *jeitinho*, where innovative circumvention becomes exploitative fraud, and the *jeitoso* individual engages in *passando as outras pessoas por trás* ("passing or leaving other people behind"). The practitioner of the *lei de Gerson* tries to get ahead to others' detriment by the manipulations of the *jeitinho*.[20]

While people have always found ways to *dar um jeitinho*, the term itself is relatively recent, not extensively used until the 1980s (Barbosa 1988, 50–56), paralleling the decline of living standards.[21] The *jeitinho* is not necessarily viewed negatively, nor as something dishonest. *Jeitinhos* are often a means for disenfranchised, ignored, or prohibited populations to survive; they are among the "weapons of the weak" (Scott 1985), used as tactics by those on the lower end of the social scale. As such, they can be very satisfying. *Jeitinhos* are not confined to use by the lower classes (cf. Scheper-Hughes 1992, 473), although their moral valuation is different when used by the powerful.

The *jeitinho* is not unique to Brazil. In Argentina a similar concept is designated by the verb *enzafar*, referring to escape, which, like *jeitinho*, appeared around the same time as hyperinflation.[22] In southern Italy, the term *arrangiarsi* refers to the skill of finding the means to survive in a world full of economic and bureaucratic barriers (Berkowitz 1984, 85). Repressive and impoverished societies in Eastern Europe have their versions of the *jeitinho*, and it is well entrenched in Africa.

Anywhere poverty, discrimination, bureaucracy, and government control get in people's way, the clever find some *jeitinho* to get around it. But Brazilians believe that the *jeitinho* is their own invention, a testament to national ingenuity. Many call it *jeitinho brasileiro* with stubbornly patriotic pride. A Caruaruense shopkeeper put it this way: "We are like the best countries. The United States is a society of laws. Brazil too. Just that the law is the law of advantage."

Often the way around rules is to manipulate friendship and kinship networks to circumvent legal restrictions and economic shortfalls. A staple of the *jogo da cintura* is the action of *arrumando* ("arranging"). The *jeitoso* individual tries to *arrumar* ("arrange for") whatever is needed by whatever means necessary, be it a commodity, a service, or another person. People speak of arranging food, employment, housing, wives, husbands, mistresses, children, clothing—anything. It is not an activity for the shy. Arranging goes hand in hand with *agitando*, which is used in the Northeast to mean "prepare," "adjust," or "adapt." To *agitar* an individual means to manipulate him or her so that you can arrange what you need. *Agitando* is a staple of sexual interactions. Truck drivers like to paint often sexually tinged messages on their rear bumpers and dust flaps; one common message puns: *Mulher é como remédio: agita-se antes de usar* ("Woman is like medicine: shake up/manipulate before using"). Women also *agitar* their men:

He is very, very jealous. So I *agito* him, I do, I come close to him, give a little kiss, say, "No, little love [*amorzinho*], passion of my life, I wasn't at home because I went to such and such a place, to a girlfriend's house and so on and so forth." I start to kiss him, I stroke him [*alisá-lo*], so it ends up okay. It's the *jeitinho*.

Despite the sneaking pride many take in *jeitinhos*, some people regard them as immoral. Often the difference has to do with whether the speaker is *jeitoso* or a frequent victim of people who are still more *jeitoso*. In addition, *jeitinhos* used by the powerful to cement their exploitation of the weak, and *jeitinhos*, used by the poor to get around exploitation by the powerful have different moral characters. Nations and Farias distinguish between "survival *jeitinhos*" used to obtain needed goods and services and "power *jeitinhos*," used to amass capital and influence at the expense of others. The two have very different moral characters. While poor and working-class people may admire survival *jeitinhos* for their nerve and wit, they tend to recognize power *jeitinhos* as dangerously immoral, calling them corruption (*corrupção*) (Nations and Farias 1990, 760–61).

Government officials and police are themselves members of networks, using and abusing their institutional power and physical force to *dar um jeitinho* for their interests. While the personal nature of legal enforcement permits abuses and corruption, it also creates many loopholes for the *jei-*

toso. A sarcastic local joke points out the advantages of living in a disorganized society:

A Brazilian died and went to Hell. Arriving there, the Devil asked him if he wanted to stay in American Hell or that of the Brazilians. He asked the difference and the Devil explained: In American Hell you have to eat a spoonful of shit [*merda*] every day, whereas in Brazilian Hell you have to eat a whole bucket. He preferred, of course, that of the Americans. On his way, he met on the road another Brazilian, who asked where he was going and why. He responded, and the other Brazilian retorted: "Look, there they have to eat only one spoonful, but they have all the spoons in the world and as much *merda* as they need, so they eat it every day. Here in Brazilian Hell we never eat it, because when they have a bucket they don't have shit, and when they have shit they don't have a bucket, and when they have the shit and the bucket, they don't have a little demon to give it out! I've been here ten years and haven't eaten shit yet!"

The joke favorably contrasts Brazilian disorganization and underdevelopment with U.S. efficiency as a kind of freedom in which the condemned can find a *jeitinho* to avoid their punishment. But while the *jeitinho* allows for freedom of action, it denies protection from others' freedom to act. A Caruaruense lawyer observed:

This thing of not following the laws: You have a certain liberty to do what you want. But unfortunately, everyone also has the liberty to do what they want, and you don't have conditions to react. You don't have the protection of the law that is not being observed. You stay in a situation where who wins is either the most powerful, or, on the other hand, the most *jeitoso*.

Ideally, people include their friends and families as beneficiaries of their *jeitinhos*. Inside of friendship and kinship networks, moral obligations to share and not cheat prevail; outside, anything goes. One vendor complained:

Look, I'm an honest man, you know, I don't like this business of *lei de Gerson*, *né?* But it happens that everyone there on the street is corrupt. If I want to do business and everyone is passing the others behind [*passando os outros por trás*], so either I pass or I will be passed. It's like the people say, "In the land of the frogs, jump with them" [*Na terra do sapo pula com eles*]. Here at home I'm a respectable man. But in the street everyone's a dog, so I have to bark louder or die.

As she did with so many other things, Glória proved a good teacher, giving me a lesson in the importance of membership in social networks in the context of a society of *jeitoso* individuals. When President Fernando

Collor de Mello took power in 1990, the transition was marked by a closure of all banks, followed by a currency shift from cruzados novos to a new kind of cruzeiros. Among the shock treatment measures applied to the economy was the freezing of all bank accounts of over 50,000 cruzeiros (U.S. $1,592), including commercial accounts. Inflation dropped sharply as cash was removed from circulation. Money was in very short supply, and people were desperately *dando jeitinhos* to try to get some.[23]

It happened that fortunately I had bought a car before the bank accounts were sequestered, converting my cash into property just before it would have been seized. The car, a VW Bug described affectionately by my neighbors as being the exact color of diarrhea, ran fine except that the hand brake was not attached to anything. So I brought it to a mechanic recommended by a friend. He said to leave it there and a man would deliver it with a bill later in the week. While it was at the shop, most of the cash circulating in Brazil disappeared into the austerity measures. The family I was living with, no slouches in the *jeitinho* department themselves, immediately came up with some convoluted reason why I had to pay my rent again, and by some accident the electricity and water in my section of the house ceased to function until I finally gave up trying to understand why and forked over the extra rent money. Thereupon power and water were miraculously restored.[24]

That took most of the Brazilian cash I had, and no one could help me exchange dollars because cruzados novos had disappeared and cruzeiros were not yet in circulation. So I was in as much difficulty as everyone else, although people had trouble believing that. When the car came back, the mechanic's employee showed me some engine parts that he said had been replaced, along with a bill for quite a bit more money than I had in my possession. I was puzzled, since I had not ordered any work done on the engine, nor had I known that any was needed. I said I would get back to him.

I took the car parts to a friend, who took me to his cousin, another mechanic, who said that they were Chevette parts and could not have come from my VW. He looked at my Bug's engine, pointing out that to get at the equivalents of those parts you would have to remove the engine, and that the rust on the screws showed that my car's engine had not been removed in some time. He inquired as to the name of the *corrupto* who was trying to *dar um jeitinho* in me. When I gave him the name, he closed the engine compartment and said that he would appreciate it if I did not mention his name in connection with my car. He went on to say that he really couldn't help me, but that it had been nice to meet me. My friend later explained that the first mechanic I had gone to had "a certain reputation," and maybe it would be better if I just paid him.

As I spoke to various people, asking them to help me negotiate with the mechanic, a mysterious man came around, bothering the family that let me store the car in their garage. He said that some parts had disappeared from his Chevette at the mechanic's shop and that he had been told that some rich North American girl had stolen them. He hinted that he might come back armed. The family suggested that maybe I should just pay the mechanic what he wanted. No one believed that, even if I had not thought the situation terribly unfair, I did not have either the money or the means of getting the money until the crisis passed.

I took my tale of woe to Glória in search of some sympathy. She exclaimed at the number of men who had been fearful of helping me confront the mechanic, casting aspersions on the size and potency of their genitals if they were going to call themselves men and act that way. She asked me the name of the mechanic, and when I told her she grinned broadly and said, "Who doesn't have a dog, hunts with a cat. Let's go."[25] We went to the mechanic's together. On the way Glória asked me in excruciating detail exactly how much money I had access to.

When we arrived she went up to the mechanic with a big smile and greeted him with great pleasure. Turning to me, she said, "Luíz here was one of my father's best friends. Oh, the two of them used to get into so much trouble together!" Turning back to Luíz, she said, "Have you met my friend? Her name is Linda-Anne, but we call her Gringinha (little North American). She's a student who is studying Brazilian culture. She had a terrible time when she first arrived. Let me tell you, she studied Portuguese in school but the only Portuguese words she said that we could understand were *okay* and *bye-bye*. And she had the terrible misfortune to fall into a perfect den of snakes when she first got here, not knowing how things work." Glória led Luíz over to a table and gave some of my cash to one of his employees to have him get us some Coca-Colas.

For the next hour or so we sipped Cokes as she regaled Luíz cheerfully with exaggerated tales of the family I had lived with before, the ones who had stolen my first car, the one that this Bug was a replacement for, telling him how Fulbright (the international agency) had had to give me a special dispensation to buy it. Did he know that as a foreign student I was well connected at the consulate and had even received phone calls at her house from the federal police? She told him all about the trouble that ensued about the car—and wasn't it great that I had made such good friends with the police chief in the third district?—and oh, how scared her mother had been when a police prisoner transport van had pulled up in front of the house and then how relieved when Gringinha hopped out, since the police were being so nice as to ferry her around for protection because the family had threatened violence and had even fired off some shots, can you imagine? She talked about the bad impression I was getting about Brazil with all the *jeitoso* people and the corruption and all, and how I was going to go back to the United States and write a book about it. And she bemoaned the fact that Brazilians seem to think that all North Americans are rich, but you know students never have their own money, only scholarships, and they need to account to the government for every penny. Poor, poor Gringinha, everybody was trying to *dar jeitinhos* in her.

She then regaled me with tales of the mischief Luíz and her late father used to get into, the times they came home drunk and singing, the time her father had saved Luíz from drowning when he fell in a river, the great friendship that had obtained between the two men, how happy Glória had always been as a child to see Luíz coming around because his presence made her beloved father so glad. She also spoke of the great sadness in her house now that her father had died, not only the *saudade* they felt for him but also how she and her mother missed her late father's friends whom they never saw anymore, and wasn't that a pity.

After this masterful performance, she coughed delicately and allowed that some misunderstanding seemed to have arisen. Apparently one of Luíz's employees (and you can't get good help these days, can you?) had somehow confused a simple repair of the hand brake on Gringinha's Bug with some Chevette or something and there was a problem about the bill. Before Luíz could do anything more than look thoughtful, she suggested that a small sum like CR $4,000 might solve the problem, more than was usually paid for a hand brake job, a good deal less than what the benighted employee was making such a fuss about (and incidentally just about all the cash I had, which she did not mention but which I noticed). All in all, she went on, that was not a bad price for such a superior repair on the hand brake, which, after all, is an important part of the car (especially for poor U.S. students who don't know how to drive a shift car properly and tend to want to use the brake on hill stops instead of balancing between clutch and foot brake as a Brazilian would do).[26] Luíz and I were clearly in the presence of a master. We could do nothing but smile, nod, and complete the transaction as Glória had suggested, exchange *cheirinhos* and insincere promises to get together sometime, and then escape gracefully.

Glória had effectively told Luíz that whereas it was a perfectly honest mistake to think that he could morally *dar um jeitinho* in the Gringa, since she was rich and not part of any local network, in fact he had made an error. The Gringa was in fact well connected politically, not as rich as you might think, and besides, she was a member of a friendship network, to the members of which Luíz himself had emotional ties and therefore moral obligations to protect and not exploit. She gave him the excuse that it had been his employee and not himself who had made the error, preserving face for him, and also suggested a monetary transaction that gave Luíz more than he deserved but let everybody off the hook gracefully. She also later arranged to send back the Chevette parts and get Luíz's other customer-victim out of our way. Glória smoothly *deu um jeitinho* in Luíz's *jeitinho* by using the moral differences between the gift-exchange economy that obtains in social networks and the commodity economy that is present among unrelated people.[27]

Friendship and Patronage Networks

When I describe Caruaruenses as forming social networks, I am not referring to any centrally organized process. A network is what appears on paper when an analyst starts to draw a map of a given person's social relations. With the informant at the center, radiating lines on the paper indicate connections between an informant and friends, relatives, and acquaintances; lateral lines indicate the density of the network by showing how many of the informant's associates also know one another. Such a chart looks very solid, but in practice networks do not exist as objects in the world. Rather they constitute shifting series of events among social actors. Nonetheless, the metaphor comparing social relations to devices best used to catch fish is useful.

The kinds of social relations that translate on paper into networks are different in small towns and rural areas than they are in cities, and they are different among differing economic classes and different genders. In small towns and rural areas, networks tend to be dense: Everybody knows most everybody. In addition, members tend to have known each other over long periods and in a variety of capacities, and their emotional, social, and economic interrelations are multiplex.

Urban networks often connect a greater number of people than rural ones, but they are less dense. People tend to know each other less well, over a shorter term, and in fewer capacities. Networks provide social actors with companionship: people with whom to talk out problems, share confidences, and have fun—and also on whose shoulders to cry. In addition, people protect their friends and acquaintances, as Glória did for me in my automobile adventures, and they share cash, services, access, and commodities. Social networks can provide the ties that bring the bulk of resources into any household.

Both men and women construct social networks, although men treat women differently than women treat men, and male-male relationships are different from female-female ones in patterned ways.[28] Men form networks of friends and relatives (usually cousins and brothers) all at similar socioeconomic levels. This group of age-mates is called a *turma*. In addition, members of *turmas* may create alliances with one or more men at higher socioeconomic levels. These vertical alliances form part of chains of access to work or resources, repaid by political coalition or maintenance of availability. Women also form both horizontal and vertical alliances into networks, but the quality of the relationships as well as what people do when they are together is different.

Men promise or demonstrate loyalty and labor to vertical patrons in order to create and maintain their connection, whereas women's patronage relations have a higher openly affective content: Women offer compassion and affection in addition to their labor to their patrons. Women are also much more likely to be asked for sexual favors than are men.

Women frequently form patronage relationships to people they work for in a domestic capacity, which is structurally more similar to kinship than is male membership in, for example, a work gang. While men's vertical ties are mostly to other men, women make vertical ties to both men and other women. Women are also much more likely than men to receive charitable donations of clothing and household items from their patrons, although both sexes may receive gifts of food. This kind of charitable gift-giving allows people to live at less than subsistence wages, maintaining low wage structure (Gregory 1982, 117; Norris 1984, 23). The issue of maintaining face is harder for men than women in vertical relationships. Where masculinity is defined in terms of the ability to control oneself and one's subordinates, submissive behavior is more problematic for men than for women.

Male Friendships

When men get together to socialize, it is almost always over alcohol, unless they are practicing Protestants (and many ostensibly Protestant men do not actually observe the restrictions). They buy rounds of drinks for one another in bars;[29] go on picnics where they skinny-dip in local rivers, eat barbecue, and drink; or play penny-ante games of cards and dominoes for hours on end over beer. When men drink they tell jokes, usually randy ones, with themes emphasizing penis size, unfaithful women, and especially anal sex between men. Men also joke around in a homoerotic manner.

In addition, men form both informal and formal sports teams, especially soccer teams, and may also play volleyball or basketball. Sometimes groups of men go out womanizing or visit bordellos or strip-tease bars. While together, men talk about sports and women and tell sexual jokes. Good friends genially insult each other and endow each other with nicknames.

My real name is Jõao Batista, but my friends call me "Adrião." It doesn't mean anything, it's only to show that we are men and we won't use the name that that woman my mother gave. Every man has to have a nickname. In my group we have Pipoca ("Popcorn"), Branco ("Whitey"), Negão ("Big Negro"), Pé de Quenga ("Clubfoot"), Tschau ("Good-bye").[30]

Some nicknames are given in childhood, others are acquired when men enter friendship groups. There are both nicknames of address, used to a man's face, and nicknames of reference, used behind his back. Any individual may have two or more nicknames.

Men who try to change insulting or childish nicknames usually fail. For example, one teenager was addressed by his family as Anjo Baroque ("Baroque Angel"), which he found infuriating. The story was that after his first six children turned out to be girls, this boy's father was very anxious for a son. As soon as the midwife called him he rushed into the room, demanding to see the child naked so he could make sure it really was a boy. When the midwife showed the tiny child to him, dismayed at the small size of the baby's genitals, he exclaimed, "That's not a boy, that's a baroque angel!" The name stuck, although the boy quite naturally hated it and tried to get people to call him "Kid Cá-cá" (because his best friend, André, was called "Kid Dé-dé"), but his efforts only further entrenched the nickname.

Drinking, womanizing, skinny-dipping, and joke-telling reinforce common identity among men (cf. Robben 1989), since a basic tenet of masculinity is exemption from women's moral rules. Nicknames declare men's independence from women. Generally, nicknames are used to integrate members of societies and show moral cohesiveness (Massolo 1990, 290). The use of childhood nicknames reflects men's view of themselves as mischievous boys, and nicknames with sexual connotations reflect both their self-asserted sexual potency and their exemption from feminine strictures against sexual references in speech. In this context, nicknames emphasize amoral cohesiveness.

Going out to bars to drink and pick up women and skinny-dipping also speak to men's identity as sexually free together. Otherwise prohibited attractions among them are also addressed.

I call Moises "Mosé" because I love my friends, but as I am a man and not a fag [bicha], I neither hug nor kiss them. I call them by their nicknames, go out with them, insult them, and tease them. (Beno)

Men's friendships are also economically useful because men can sometimes dar um jeitinho to find jobs and other resources for their friends, or perform reciprocal professional favors. For example, electrician Beno fixed the lights in Jõao Batista's house in return for Jõao Batista's painting Beno's refrigerator. In addition, men will stick up for each other in conflicts, and, if necessary, get into fights in each other's behalf. Men's associations, such as sports teams, can gain money, playing fields, and uniforms by pledging to vote in blocs for political candidates.

Female Friendships

Groups of female friends, relatives, and neighbors borrow both raw and cooked food from one another, as well as handing down clothes from older to younger children, sharing household chores, doing favors of various types, and watching over one another's children. Women who have credit accounts at stores allow their friends to use them, and women employ each other for services such as sewing, embroidering, baking, washing clothes, hairdressing, manicuring, and making decorations. They may also seek clients for friends who supplement their incomes with these activities. And women who have vertical contacts with wealthier patrons sometimes obtain the services of these patrons for their friends.

For example, one Caruaruense laundress who worked for a physician obtained prescriptions from him for her friends, saving them the trouble of a difficult-to-obtain doctor's visit.[31] Another woman, who was literate, not only allowed friends to charge items on her credit accounts but also kept track of credit debts for other friends who did the same thing, helping them to collect their debts. In addition she wrote letters for people, receiving in return gifts of food and clothing. In many neighborhoods, women participate in anonymous Christmas exchanges in which they buy or make small presents, giving them to neighbors whose names are drawn from a hat. Then they make the rounds of each other's houses, eating Christmas delicacies. The anonymity of the exchanges increases mutual interdependence by emphasizing that all are indebted to all.

Women also exchange small gifts as part of the building and maintenance of friendships. These gifts are romantic in form: They include the kinds of things boyfriends might give to girlfriends, such as perfume, makeup, and jewelry—especially silver chain bracelets. In addition, women may exchange notes on printed stationery decorated with drawings of flowers or kittens and puppies wearing big pink bows. Preprinted sentiments such as "Our friendship is delicate like a flower and solid as the old trees" are common.

Another such gift is a photographic portrait, wallet-sized and formal, of a woman's child, with sentimental verses handwritten on the back. Writing these rhymes is another service some women perform for other women. Fátima, who is literate, wrote such verses for all her neighbors. For example, she gave me a photograph of her son inscribed in this way:

A friendship like ours, so beautiful and so delicious [*gostoso*] to feel. For all that happened I would like that our friendship never end. Signed: your friend of yesterday, today, tomorrow, and always Fátima greetings from my son Uáxintô.

Whereas men tend to make friends in groups, women's friendships have a more one-to-one character, although women do accumulate as many friendship dyads as possible to make extensive networks. Women spend time sitting and gossiping with their friends, rehashing events in the neighborhood, comparing medical symptoms, and discussing *telenovelas*. Many women have one or more close friends in whom they confide their fears, angers, and tensions.

Although nicknames are usually thought of as a masculine phenomenon, women too have them (cf. Massolo 1990, 285). Many of these are bestowed by children. One woman, for example, was addressed as Ia because it was her nephew's pronunciation of *Tia* ("Aunt"). Another, named Graça, was called Dazza after her young cousin's pronunciation of her name. And many women are given nicknames like Mãezinha ("little mother") or simply append *mãe* ("mother") to their first name, as in Mae Ida or Mae Cecilia, when they have their first child. Other nicknames are references to physical characteristics. In one neighborhood I was called Titia Brincos ("Auntie Earrings") by the children because of my hearing aids; the children enjoyed running up to clap their hands over my ears and make feedback squeals. Two sisters were called Maria Xoxinha ("Skinny Mary") and Maria Gorda ("Fat Mary") in reference to their contrasting girths; other women had nicknames such as Branquinha ("Little Whitey"), Lourinha ("Blondie"), and Pretinha ("Little Blacky"). One was called Bolinha de Sabão ("Little Soapball") because she had been chubby as a child.

Friends also share material resources with one another. For example, a woman who has received a large load of beans will sit shelling and drying them with her friends, each of whom will be offered a portion. On Fátima's street, Dona Francinha likes the way Fátima makes beans and always exchanges her special recipe rice for some of Fátima's beans. Geixa lets Dona Francinha use her credit account at a local store to buy clothes; in return Dona Francinha's nephew, a farmer, sells his fresh corn exclusively through Geixa's food stall in the market. Women baby-sit each other's children, pass on hand-me-down clothes, sew, cook, and help clean for each other, make hospital visits, and accompany each other on trips outside the home. Female friendships emphasize displays of sentimentality and the exchange of small items to symbolize affection. Their nicknames, like their common status as mothers, are given by their children. Often their conversations emphasize feminine interests in suffering and proper behavior within the community.

Whereas men address sexuality by sexual acting out in groups, women attempt to control it by verbal disapproval in gossip and by asking each other's advice on specific issues. While women know most of the sexual jokes that men tell, they whisper them to individual friends rather than shout them out to groups. Women's joking is different in form from men's. Unlike the stories with punch lines that men favor, women prefer teasing, joking exchanges, sarcasm, and clever phrasings.[32] Often they find bitter humor in the details of their suffering; this humor helps sustain them in painful situations. One similarity between men's and women's joking is that women like to insult each other sexually. Men insult by implication that their target is a passive-receptive homosexual or effeminate, whereas women joke that their friend is a slut (*rapariga, quenga*).[33]

For example, the *telenovela* "Tieta" inspired several rounds of joking.[34]

The *telenovela*'s story focused on the struggle between the free-spirited Tieta and her dried-up, widowed sister Perpétua, whose life ambition was to expose Tieta, the heroine, as a slut. (Tieta in fact was one of Amado's favorite types of characters: the prostitute with the heart of gold.) In several episodes, the black-garbed Perpétua, played as an exaggerated parody, waved her umbrella and hissed:

A que se DIZ a minha irma, é quenga SIM! ["She who CALLS herself my sister is a whore, YES!"]

The women on Fátima's street gleefully took up the expression, delighting in leaning into each other's doorways and hissing with Perpétua's exact intonation:

She who CALLS herself my neighbor is a whore, YES!

and giggling madly.[35]

Insult is often an index of closeness. Taking liberties by ridiculing in well-established relationships serves to "stretch" social affinities, affirming solidarity by playing with its denial (cf. Basso 1979, 68–69). One can joke so only with close friends: The ability to insult without insult being taken is a marker of affection. Joking insults are used to affirm solidarity, because only close friends have a strong enough relationship to withstand the joking abuse. By using a sarcastic or exaggerated tone of voice, or alternatively by displaying a playful facial expression or friendly smile at odds with their words, speakers negate the insult they speak. The effect is a statement opposite in meaning to the words. In the reversible world of play, sarcastically calling a woman a whore affirms her chaste honorability while emphasizing communal approval of it, and insulting a friend marks the depth of affection toward that friend.[36]

It is deviant for women to drink heavily, and most women either never drink alcohol or drink sparingly of mild beverages (like beer) and only at coed gatherings or while out on dates. It is not the custom for groups of women to get together and share drinks as men do. Groups of women may share cigarettes, however, although smoking has vulgar connotations. Women often share snacks, candy, and soft drinks when they get together.

Love in Network Relations

Both men and women speak of their network relations as characterized by love. Patrons aid clients because of their altruistic love. Female neighbors form loving friendships. Men love the members of their *turmas*. Family members are said to love one another and share because of that love. Through love men and women marry, gaining their own house and economic interdependence. Love also inspires parents to support their children, and a loving son or daughter will support his parents in their old age. People who love one another share their resources because they are morally bound to do so—and friends and relatives are constrained to love one another, or at least behave as if they do.

Sharing resources is not only consequence but also marker and seal of love. The economic interest underlying loving relationships in families and networks does not automatically diminish the sentiment people feel toward their associates: Indeed, it may intensify it (cf. Thompson 1977). In working-class Caruaruense families, economic sharing is part of the metaphorical communication code in which a verbal declaration of tender feelings is more frightening than demonstration of loyal devotion in practice. Working in behalf of one's dependents is a sign of love for them.

For men especially, supporting one's family economically is a sign of love, and men may be forgiven other transgressions if they are good providers, especially in comparison with the many men who abandon their families:

My brother-in-law has made my sister suffer so much, with his womanizing, my sister, her children, the other woman, the other woman's children, who knows how many other women. But for all his sins he is a good father who always buys groceries [*bota feira*] for his sons, which not all fathers do. No one can say he doesn't love his children. They don't go hungry. (Joselma)

Here, *botando feira* (lit. "putting market": buying a week's worth of groceries in the *feira*) is not only a paternal duty but also a sign of redeeming love. Economics also figure into power dynamics within the family, because those who *bota feira* can impose their will on dependent family members.

Whether you want to or not, the financial factor always influences. Because of the fact that I work and have responsibility and help sustain my parents and sister, I began to be respected. It is partly personalities, partly age. But when my father retired and I started to earn more, I started to be able to order people around more. And now that my sister has a job and is earning a little money, she doesn't do what people tell her to any more. (Agostinho)

The complex dynamics of family economic relations, protestations of love, and economically influenced power dynamics give many opportunities for the *jeitoso* to maneuver. Despite widespread cynicism about relatives' sincerity, people are more bitterly disappointed by relatives who cheat or use them than they are by friends or neighbors because the betrayal is deeper.[37]

Friendship with nonrelatives, such as neighbors, is an urban phenomenon. In small towns everyone is a parent, brother, sister, aunt, uncle, cousin, or in-law, and if by some mischance they are not, adoption, godparenthood, or some other social fiction can remedy the situation. Relatives are supposed to stick together and treat each other well, while friends behave like pseudo-cousins as a matter of personal choice rather than obligation. Relationships with them are presumed to be shallower. Caruaruenses use a sarcastic Spanish-language expression to describe false friends:

Look, there are friends and there are FRIENDS. It's like, there are people who you think are your friends, but in truth they are not. We say *muito amigo* ["very much a friend"] for a true friend. A false friend is a *muy amigo, né,* in the Spanish language. "He's a *muy amigo*" means he's fooling you, using you, giving a *jeitinho* in you.[38]

It is easier to get away with cheating people in the city than in small towns because of the greater mobility people have in cities: If you so foul your nest in a city that there is no one left to trust you, and thus be susceptible to being cheated, you can move on to another neighborhood or, if need be, to another city. If, however, you have to live your whole life in the same town, you have to be very clever to get away with cheating. A woman in a small town deep in the Sertão explained the dynamics of small town life this way: "We don't always say things here, *né?* Maybe nobody talks about it. But everyone knows, whatever it is, everyone knows, and nobody forgets. Not never. Small town life, you know?" Everybody knows but nobody says: This common knowledge is what allows everybody to understand the references in metaphorical folk speech, to understand what is being communicated without having to risk saying it, to get the jokes. Restricted communication codes are characteristic of face-to-face, long-term, intimate relations, such as family life in small-scale societies, because they work only where people intimately know each other and each other's history. They allow people to convey what they need to communicate while being able to deny that anything at all upsetting was said.

Emotion as Service and Commodity

Emotional style may vary with the type of economy. In addition, an emotional service may be given as a gift or exchanged as a commodity. Caring, worrying about, or any of a number of emotions in behalf of others are services given as gifts or exchanged, or sometimes given as accompaniments to other forms of exchange. Many female-dominated occupations include emotional labor (cf. Hochschild 1983, 1985) as part of their performance throughout the world. Female social roles like that of wife, mother, girlfriend, sister, aunt, or female cousin also require a certain level of worrying and emotional caretaking for the benefit of others. While to attempt to place an economic value on emotional services in female social roles is generally regarded as offensive, these roles have strong economic importance.

In an ambiguous economy like Caruaru's, whether an emotional interaction is a gift or a commodity is both a highly charged moral question and a matter of point of view. For many impoverished women, services such as friendship, love, marriage, and sexuality are the only commodities they have to offer.[39] Just as laborers may become alienated from their labor in a commodity exchange market, producers of such services as emotional labor may become alienated where their labor has an unrecognized but real economic exchange value. This process of alienation is complex and painful because it involves a separation from an experience regarded as a part of the self—and not just any part of the self but that part most closely related to the moral worth of the individual: her sentiments and, in particular, her ability to love.

In the United States, nineteenth-century feminists sought to improve the condition of women and the dignity of the family by extending into the public realm the values of the domestic: love, respect, cleanliness. By elevating feminine values and feminizing the heretofore masculine public realm, they hoped to create a more caring society in which women and children could live better lives and in which women and men could more easily find "true love and perfect union" (Leach 1980). Similarly, Caruaruense women spoke of public institutions and economic conditions in terms of love rather than of impersonal societal rights or forces.[40] For example, the mother of a teenage son crippled by polio, after telling me the long story of how she had been unable to find a state vaccination post or to afford a private doctor to protect him from the disease, which eventually paralyzed him, remarked, "If Brazil had love, my son would walk."

Another woman, who worked in a secretarial capacity in city hall, was frustrated by her inability to obtain help for the mother of a moribund infant sick with diarrheal dehydration. The mother had come to city hall in search of a free bus ticket to Recife, where she could obtain better medical care than in Caruaru. The secretary was able to obtain neither the bus ticket nor a *ficha* ("token") for free treatment at a Caruaru hospital, because the official in charge of such things was out of town and no one else had the authority to give them out. She instructed the infant's mother in how to make oral rehydration solution and took up a collection among the secretaries so that the destitute woman would be able to buy bottled water, sugar, and salt. Discussing it later, the secretary expressed her opinion that the sorry fate of too many tiny infants is due to "lack of love—not on the part of the mothers, of course, but on the part of the doctors and politicians who don't care about the lives of the poor little critters [*bichinhos*]."

Here the entire complex interplay of socioeconomic forces on the infant is reduced to the single emotion of love—or its absence. The impersonal indifference of the medical bureaucracy is contrasted to the warm, individualized concern of a mother, and it is found morally lacking. The secretary's solution to the problems of Brazil: *Tem que ter mais amor* ("There has to be more love") finds redemption not in the cold indignation of demands for contractual rights but rather in pleas for love. It is a nostalgic lament for the romanticized emotional warmth of the world of patronage, in which the wealthy owed loyalty to those who had so long served them. Laments for love in public life contrast the emotional morality of a stratified gift economy with that of a contractual, commodity-based economy—and find modern capitalist relations wanting.

Shadowing the official version of events in modern Brazil is a parallel reality in which legal and illegal are not distinct; friends may be enemies and yet again friends; charity can hurt more than it helps; faith is both a shield and a prison; and love is both a deeply felt sentiment and a cynical verbal mask thrown over exploitation. A disorganized economy leads to moral murk and conflicting emotional pressures. To survive in this confusing milieu, women must exploit their love to build necessary friendship networks and supplement their meager incomes. Paradoxically, they must trust enough to make friends, but be wary enough to avoid exploitation by the *jeitoso*.

Top: Rural house. *Bottom:* The mouth of the Sertão.

Top: Village in the Agreste. *Bottom: Jangadas* (fishing rafts) on a beach.

Top: Street in Caruaru. *Bottom:* Pigs in an open sewer in a Pernambuco town.

Top: Women do laundry in a river. *Bottom:* Transporting rush mats to market by donkey.

Top: Couple making piecework blue jeans at their home. *Bottom:* Clay pots for sale in Caruaru market.

Top: Figurines for sale in Caruaru market. *Bottom:* Food for sale in Caruaru market.

Top: A woman speaks with a holy figure in a church. *Bottom:* Two women visit in a doorway in Caruaru.

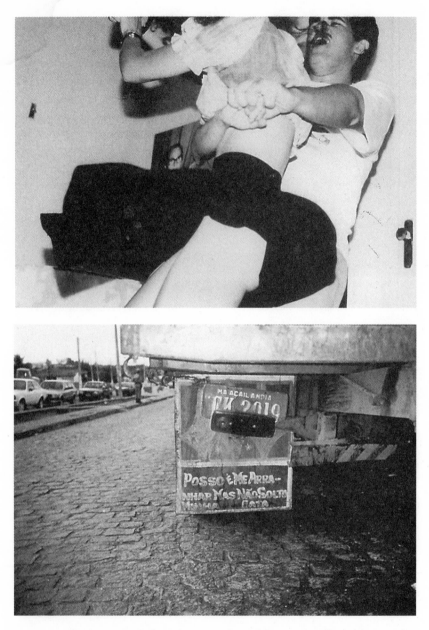

Top: A couple dances *lambada*. *Bottom:* Truck mud flap reads, "She might scratch me, but I won't let my (female) cat go."

Killing a pig with a *marra* (sledgehammer).

A couple.

Part II

⌒ Romantic Love in a Changing Economy

Heretofore I have been concerned with discussing love in the sense of affiliation: friendship, kinship, customership, patronage, public responsibilities. The word *love* (*amor*) is also used to describe romantic attractions: courtship, sexual relationships, marriage, cohabitation. This kind of love has similarities to other forms of affiliation but also displays striking differences, most particularly in its gendered nature and tie to sexuality. Like other kinds of love it is intertwined with economic relationships, and its nature and role are affected by changes in the economic system.

Love seems an ironic topic to pursue in a country where violence (both informal and as part of governmental policy) has structured so much of life and politics, where the extremity of poverty makes sentiment a seemingly unaffordable luxury, and where a ruthlessly casual indifference toward human dignity causes so much suffering. Compassion, affection, mercy, appreciation, idealization, passionate desire—all the forms of human connection seem out of place when viewed from the perspective of health statistics, class structure, and governmental policy.

Love, however, is always a fundamentally ironic topic, as deeply comic as it is profoundly serious, as mysteriously enigmatic as it is transparently obvious. Romantic love was as much a topic of casual conversations as was violence during my fieldwork, both its presence and its absence. People often expressed concepts of love in terms of temperature, describing themselves as hot-blooded (*de sangue quente*) and therefore passionate, both emotionally and sexually. This concept is heir to a lengthy history shaped by the impressions of Europeans encountering first Africans (including North Africans) and later the native peoples of the Pacific Islands and the Americas. It encompasses humoral theories on the sensual effects of tropical climates, racialized concepts of the variety of human sexuality, and eroticized versions of the rape that accompanies pillage during conquest. As used in Northeast Brazil, it is also a commentary on a perceived lack of both sensuality and compassion in the cultural styles of "cold-blooded" Northern Europe.

The ideology of hot-bloodedness contains both racialized notions of greater sensuality among dark-skinned populations living where the heat and humidity of the tropics encourages nudity, indolence, and passion (cf. Parker 1991), and the idea of a greater tendency toward compassionate human connection than is to be found, for example, among Northern Europeans and North Americans. Thoroughly intertwined with pernicious stereotypes of race, the concept of hot blood finds its origin in exoticized images of the sensual Moor (cf. Said 1978), applied to Spain and Portugal during their incorporation into the Moorish empire from the eighth to the fifteenth centuries. In Iberian America, orientalism met tropicalism to create a sexualized image portraying the Latin American as passionate: hypersexual, overly prideful, prone to anger, violently jealous, exaggeratedly sentimental—in short, displaying all the metaphorical qualities associated with the concept of heat.

Theories of race, in the colonial context, were simultaneously theories of sexuality. Robert Young has called them "covert theories of desire" because of the explicit concern with hybridity as the result of sexual congress between Europeans and their darker-skinned subjects in colonial areas that permeates Victorian theories of race (Young 1995).[1] Although the stereotype may be applied to any Latino, it is more commonly applied to the lower classes and the darker-skinned, revealing its classist and racist nature.

While some Caruaruenses I spoke to decried the hot-blooded stereotype as racist, others took a certain pride in what they saw as their own hot-blooded capacity for passion. People describe hot-bloodedness as both a physical and a temperamental quality, as is its opposite, cold-bloodedness. Cold-bloodedness may be as much a racist stereotype as hot-bloodedness, but there was little awareness of its pernicious character among Caruaruenses. That I, as a North American of European descent, was cold-blooded was presented as simply a fact of nature. Cold-bloodedness on my part was as likely to be put forward as an explanation for why I couldn't dance like a Brazilian as it was for why I suffered so many fevers, sores, and rashes.

The metaphor spans social classes. My upper-class doctor told me that the reason I had developed a persistent low-grade fever was that, as a descendant of Northern Europeans, my body temperature was lower than that of a Brazilian: I was essentially melting in the tropical heat. He amused himself by speculating about what he thought must be numerous Eskimo words for ice that would describe the exact shades of blue and white found in my eyes and skin.

Similarly, my working-class friends used my presumed cold-blooded-ness to explain why I could drink milk while eating mangos and not die, or why I could consume lemonade during my menstrual period and not get sick. They themselves could not combine substances and conditions meta-phorically hot with those metaphorically cold and survive, they said, be-cause they were hot-blooded and therefore delicately balanced in terms of temperature. My slower, colder blood, on the other hand, could better withstand otherwise explosive combinations.[2]

Hot-bloodedness also explains a self-described greater presence of human warmth among Brazilians: a greater tendency toward "hot" emo-tions such as anger, jealousy, and desire, a greater capacity for the tender sentiments that make up compassion on the one hand and hurt feelings on the other. As hot-blooded people, my Caruaruense friends explained, Brazilians were experts on romantic love. It was their intrinsic heat that made them so sexy, so good looking, such good dancers, such great flirts, gave them such exciting music, made them so generally passionate about human contact.

Yet despite this self-image as the most excitingly sexy people on earth, Caruaruenses were also relatively conservative about sexual mores, at least on the surface, struggling with issues of propriety, morality, honor, and shame, and wrestling with how far they thought sexual liberation should go. Romantic passion, while hardly a new idea, was newly central to considerations of marriage among young people in urban areas, and people were concerned to figure out the proper relationships between romantic passion, sexual intimacy, sentimental affiliation, economic obli-gation, and marriage in what seemed to them a rapidly changing moral landscape.

4 ⪻ Romance and Modernization

I do [love her] / But to find / a wife at dawn / at noon a wife / a wife
also at dinner / and afterward in bed / and to always have to
protect / my family and my honor / drives me crazy, by God!
                    Lope de Vega, *La Bella Malmaridada,* 1596[1]

Arthur Danto has characterized philosophical investigations of love as
"braying to the lute," a process in which scholars too often set up "a
ghostly effigy of an important subject and then . . . wrestle their readers into believing that they have gotten to the heart of things" (1991:
ix–xii). The literature on the history of love in European traditions is
replete with such ghostly effigies, with historians arguing over not
only the meanings of historical events but also the details of the events
themselves. Danto's criticism of philosophy of love as "incorrigibly
stiff . . . when it undertakes to lay its icy fingers" on a subject as "raucous," "farcical," and "tragic" as love (1991: xii) may also be applied
to histories (and anthropologies)—a fault not so much of scholars as of
the contradictory nature of love itself.

"Love," of course, refers not only to the positive sentiments that
hold together kinship and friendship networks but also to the complex
of fervent infatuation and physical desire that make up sexual passion,
and further, to the comfortable intimacy ideally enjoyed by long-mar-
ried couples for whom the memory of youthful lust's intensity warms
today's more sober affections. Histories of love, or at least of erotic
love, tend to focus on love in relation to marriage, either looking for
love within marriage or examining it as extramarital.

Marriage does not concern love alone; its base includes membership in families and rights over property, legal parentage and custody
of children, individuals' place in the social structure, their obligations
and the obligations of others to them—subjects that form the bulk of
anthropological investigations of marriage. All of these questions com-

plicate people's ideas of the place of love in conjugal relations, their ability to love, their ideas of how best to express love, and their problems in sustaining loving attachments.

A relationship like marriage works better if the couple like one another, or at least do not hate one another too much. But whether they must love one another, what shape marital love must take, and whether love is a prior condition for marriage, its result, or properly in the sphere of extramarital attractions varies widely.[2]

My Caruaruense friends would be amazed to know that most scholarly research on romantic love has focused on cold-blooded Northern Europeans of the past and the contemporary British and U.S. middle classes. While a few anthropologists ruminate on the nature of romance cross-culturally (cf. Jankowiak 1995; Sarsby 1983), they have largely left the field to psychologists concerned with biophysiological and psychosocial aspects of sexual attraction (Fisher 1992; Money 1980; Sternberg and Barnes 1980) and historians, who have largely discussed love in the context of marriage.

Numerous historians associate romantic marriage with modernization, and Alan MacFarlane goes so far as to describe it as "a central feature of modern industrial societies" (1987, 123), although there is spirited debate on exactly when in history it assumed its current importance (Borscheid 1986; Burguière 1987; Gillis 1988; MacFarlane 1987; Stone 1977). This literature offers insights into issues in contemporary love and love-marriage in Caruaru. While there are significant differences between the centuries-long demographic, cultural, and economic transformation of early modern Western Europe and the rapid, recent changes in Brazil, the unfolding of shifts in romance in Northeast Brazil has followed a path similar to that described in historical Europe.[3] Although a simple declaration that a certain situation existed in historical Europe and therefore must also exist in modern Brazil is not sufficient, examination of the historical literature helps to explain the dynamics of contemporary situations.

Approaches to the History of Romance:
Love and Modernization

For the Mehinaku [indigenous Brazilians], the idea of romantic love
is absurd. Nothing is more ridiculous to the young men who
understand some Portuguese than the love songs they hear on their
transistor radios. "What is this 'I love you, I love you,'" Amiri
asked me, "I don't understand it, I don't like it. Why does the white
man make himself a fool?"

(Gregor 1985)

Sérvulo Figueira describes an "invisible dimension" of retained archaism
in the contemporary Brazilian family, the "subtle and complex" ways that
"the modern cohabits with the archaic in the Brazilian family" (1986, 29;
my translation). The history of love, romance, and marriage sheds light
not only on how the patterns of contemporary life came to be but also on
how current family practices reflect Canclini's multitemporal heterogeneity (1995). Modern concepts and practices build on older forms more re-
constructed than discarded.

Just as emotion vocabularies vary by language, a single language's vocabulary may change over time so that particular constructions of emotions may become old-fashioned or obsolete.[4] Certainly, concepts of ideal
love have changed through European history: from the ancient Greek
reverence for men's passion for adolescent boys, to the medieval troubadour's adulterous veneration of married lady-loves, to the Victorian idealization of a mother's chaste devotion to her children, to the modern association of romance with companionate peer-marriage (Cancian 1986,
693). In each of these situations, true love varies in its idealized object, its
relation to sexuality, and its place within or outside of marriage.

Here I will outline only a few of the more important debates in the vast
and contentious historical literature on love, arguments that influence interpretations of modern romance. Historians disagree on whether romantic love has existed from early times in Europe, or whether as an early
modern invention it was unknown earlier in any meaningfully recognizable form.[5] Both historical demography, which seeks clues to emotional
life in the structures of household composition, and psychohistory, with a
more psychodynamic approach, have been influential (Behar and Frye
1988), as have economic theories. Phillipe Ariès's claims about the effects
of falling mortality rates on people's ability to form loving attachments to

spouses and children (1962) has strongly impacted theorizing on love in history, as has Frederick Engels's 1902 declaration that capitalism promotes love-marriage but ultimately destroys love itself.

Engels's influential model posits that wage labor affords young people economic independence. No longer beholden to their parents, they resist arranged marriages, instead making matches on the basis of personal attraction. This creates a marriage market in which love itself becomes the commodity, lovers become alienated from the product of their emotional labor, and the authenticity of love itself is devastated.[6] Here, marital true love is more characteristic of proletariat relations, because bourgeois couples have more property concerns.

Edward Shorter (1975) also locates love-based marriage first among the working class, adding to Engels a particular concern with how women's extradomestic wage labor frees them from arranged marriage. Lawrence Stone (1977), while agreeing with Engels and Shorter that familial sentimentalization began in eighteenth-century Northern Europe, places it in the upper classes, claiming that, without the high mortality rates of the lower classes, bourgeois families could form loving attachments not only between parents and children but also between spouses.[7] According to Stone, in combination with the invention of private property, the increased importance of subjectivity, and the Romantic movement, with its emphasis on imagination, emotion, and rebellion against authority, economic and demographic change allowed for the emergence of ideologies of happiness and relations of love within the family.

These theorists have been critiqued on both factual and conceptual grounds. Other historians have found evidence of market economies, concepts of individuality, love-marriage, and affection for children centuries before Engels, Shorter, Stone, and Ariès claim they first appeared.[8] In addition, critics disparage the naturalistic model of sentiment implicit in their models, as well as the idea that arranged marriages are necessarily loveless (see especially Borscheid 1986; Gillis 1988; Goody 1983; MacFarlane 1987; Mount 1982; and Sarsby 1983).[9]

Shorter, Stone, and Ariès also do not consider the strong interrelationships among religion, emotionality, and family life in European history. As Jack Goody points out, Christianity not only contained a theology of love; it also incorporated kinship terms into its religious structure.[10] The work of Alan MacFarlane (1987), John Gillis (1988), and Jack Goody (1983) indicates that a European emphasis on the romantic beauty of frustrated longing is related to the Christian belief in the virtue of celibacy and the theological importance of *agapé*, or altruistic self-sacrifice,[11] combined with a very old demographic pattern of late age at first marriage, neolocality, and nuclear family structure (see also Laslett and Wall 1972 on historical demography).[12]

Finally, these analyses depend on naturalistic models of emotion, treating love as an organic condition influenced by social and economic forces rather than a socially constructed phenomenon in itself. Certainly in the Marxist model, love takes on a moral character: Its posited destruction is used to condemn capitalism. The idea that love flourishes more naturally among proletariats can be seen as a political romanticization, whereas Stone's confinement of love to the Northern European upper classes reflects a general trend of attributing to the lower classes, Southern Europeans, and North Africans a lesser refinement of character (cf. Said 1978) that prevents the experiencing of anything more sophisticated than lust. Rather than an accurate description of how love plays out in the different social classes, these theories constitute data about long-standing prejudices.

Hans Medick and David Warren Sabean (1984), in combination with John Gillis (1988), attempt a less naturalized view of emotion in their search for the antiquity of love. They claim that apparent differences in the emotional lives of modern families are due not to the introduction of a new sentiment (love) but rather to changes in forms of expression. The tender sensibilities and intimate sharing expected in loving relationships today are a style of expression rather than the creation of a new type of emotion. Changes in forms of expression do not indicate, as Stone would have it, that family affection was "both ambiguous and rare" in the distant past (1977, 88). What changed about love after the mid-eighteenth century was not the capacity or inclination for tender feelings but rather the details of the proper role of parent or lover, the importance of love as a prior condition for marriage, and the propriety of various actions as public declarations of love, whether marital or parental (Gillis 1988). Love has been privatized, but not invented, in the modern era.[13] And yet the insights of Shorter, Stone, and Ariès that something about both conjugal and familial love changed in the eighteenth century and that this change was related to economic and demographic shift cannot be entirely dismissed.

The task of the historian is difficult: It is hard to distinguish in the historical record those who married for love from those who married with love, or hoping to love, or willing to love, or trying to love, or determined not to be ensnared by love. Divorce and separation suits give some indication of how people were disillusioned by love, and poetry and literature what they may have hoped for or dreamed of in love. In general, the historical record shows great diversity and complexity in human relations, and a close association between economic and emotional ties among family members, including conjugal couples.

The Church and Family Forms in Iberia and Colonial Brazil

The history of modern Brazil begins in the colonial period, that very period from the sixteenth to the eighteenth century that so interests historians of love. Colonial life was influenced by the structure of Portuguese society but also by the exigencies of life in the New World, with its different opportunities and constraints and its very different ethnic mix. In particular, the enslavement first of the native inhabitants and then of Africans, and the eventual creation of racial stratification interlaced with the social, economic, and political hierarchy imported from Portugal (Schwartz 1985, 245), strongly affected patterns of marriage, love affairs, and family structure in Brazil.

The history of love-marriage in Latin America parallels that of Southern Europe, modified by racial and class politics unique to the New World. Seven hundred years of Moorish control (from 711 to 1492) left the family form in Iberian cultures different from those of Northern Europe in several ways, including an earlier age at first marriage for girls; a greater emphasis on the necessity of female premarital virginity for the maintenance of family honor, combined with sexual freedom for young men; and strong paternal authority (Goody 1983, 29).[14]

Differences between Moorish and European family forms included the tendency toward endogamy (marriage within the family) among Moors (Goody 1983, 31). The marriage of cousins, prohibited by the medieval Catholic Church,[15] was common in Moorish Spain and Portugal, common in New Spain and colonial Brazil,[16] and continues to be common in Brazil today. Maria Imaculada and her husband were first cousins, and, in addition, the woman with whom he was having his affair had significant ties to yet another female cousin who had been Maria Imaculada's rival for his affections in their youth.

The leaders of the Latin Catholic Church took different positions on a number of theological issues than did their Northern colleagues, especially in terms of the theology of the Virgin Mary,[17] whose increasing

semideification was strongly supported by Latin clerics,[18] with implications both for the attitude of the Church toward women and for the attrac-
tiveness of Catholic theology to women. In particular, images of the Virgin
emphasize both sexual purity and selfless giving as ideals for women.

Catholic theology, while closely associating sexuality with sin, recognized marriage as a corrective for concupiscence. That is, it was better to
have sex with one's spouse than to fornicate, and "better to marry than to
burn" (1 Corinthians 7:9). To be valid, a marriage had to be not only monogamous but also sexually satisfying, in moderation. Physical love properly expressed marital love, and the Church saw the satisfaction of the
physical desires of a spouse as a duty of conjugals—as long as it was tied
to reproduction and did not include any prohibited acts (Lavrin 1989,
53).[19] This attitude also entered into the Church's opinion that sexual attraction could be a sign of spiritual connection and its support of allowing
young people attracted to one another to marry.

In Spanish America, the Church frequently intervened in behalf of beleaguered couples against parents trying to break up their unions. Local
priests abetted couples in eloping, removing young women from parental
custody, hiding couples from angry parents, and waiving the publication
of engagement and banns in order to perform quick weddings.[20] The
Church encouraged laws prohibiting parents from disinheriting daughters or mistreating their children in disputes over marriages; however,
civil authorities did not always go along with Church directives (Seed
1985, 288–91).[21]

Sexuality, Power, and Medical Hygiene

Brazil differs from much of the rest of South America in that it was colonized not by the Spanish but by the Portuguese, who had a unique political relationship with their colony. In 1808, threatened by war, the royal
government fled Portugal for Brazil, bringing with it such benefits of civilization as open ports, universities, medical schools, printing presses, and
libraries, heretofore prohibited. In addition, the king appointed a chief
surgeon, a chief physician, and a committee on public hygiene, and set up
laws regulating public health, alcohol sales, and sanitation (Stepan 1976,
23–25).

When political conditions permitted, the court returned to Portugal,
leaving the King's son on Brazil's throne. He immediately declared Brazil
an independent empire, which lasted from 1822 to 1889, followed after-

ward by a secular republic. Political independence from Portugal did not
result in a change in governmental form or class structure and did not
have much of an impact on the lives of most Brazilians.

In the nineteenth century, laws and norms regulating sexual behavior,
family relations, and women's behavior became more strict (Costa 1989).
The final abolition of slavery in 1888 accelerated the formation of economically based classes.[22] Popular images increasingly celebrated such
feminine virtues as self-sacrifice, submission, dedication, and abdication
of personal desire as proofs of love (Trigo 1989, 90), and love as the glue
holding marriage, family, and society itself together (Costa 1989, 62).

The idea of love as sweet, sweet pain, of the object of desire as incom-
parable, of love as a form of madness, can be traced back far beyond the
eighteenth century. However, in the eighteenth century the theme of love-
as-passion began to supersede love-as-sufferance, love-as-constancy, or
love-as-caretaking as the definition of true love, and the idea that true love
properly culminates in happy marriage rather than tragedy became more
widespread.

Attempts to add the prestige of medical definition to long-standing
Church condemnations of nonreproductive sexual behavior were bol-
stered by the emerging Brazilian state, which enacted antiperversion laws
and more closely defined the sexual rights of conjugals within marriage.
Although much of the theorizing on sexuality occurred in literature not
widely read by the people (many of whom were illiterate), the concepts of
normality, deviance, and propriety were incorporated into medical practice, religious confessionals, and laws regulating sexual behavior. Paradoxically, while the supposedly value-neutral language of science increasingly bound sexual practices into tight definitions of normality and
deviance, an increasing liberality allowed these same practices to become
a basis for self-knowledge and an expression of connection to others
(Giddens 1992, 28–31).[23]

Love, Power, and the Legacy of Slavery

The history of love is also a history of kissing, cuddling, lovemaking, and
desire, a history as much of power as of pleasure, as those in power sought
to guarantee their control of access to pleasure. Struggles over pleasure
and power have extended through religious, medical, and political domains. The containment of desire within moral categories, already elaborated by Christian churches, expanded in the eighteenth century as early

scientists distinguished varieties of what they called "sexuality" in the eighteenth century. Medical scientists, and especially the early hygienists, focused on the importance of physical and moral cleanliness, defined in largely sexual terms (Foucault 1978).

Two major factors structured political struggles over pleasure and power in colonial Brazil: slavery and the marked shortage of women eligible to marry. Popular and intellectual concepts of the nature of Brazilian slavery have been heavily influenced by Recife native Gilberto Freyre's 1933 seminal work *Casa grande e senzala* (published in English as *The Masters and the Slaves*). Although more recent researchers dispute almost every aspect of Freyre's depiction of slavery, his insistence on its centrality to Brazilian culture remains an influential and brilliant insight (Schwartz 1992, 2).

The stories told today about Portuguese men and their relationships with African and Native women serve current political purposes, often functioning as just-so stories about racial identity and class status. The Freyre-influenced historical stories my Caruaruense friends learned in school, in which Portuguese *conquistadores* found themselves in a sensual paradise of lustful dark women, engendering mixed-race Brazilians under the sway of tropical heat, serve as a romance not only about the past but also about contemporary men's treatment of women poorer and darker than themselves (see also Parker 1991, 7–29), transforming conquest, slavery, and rape through the idiom of romance into a story about love.

In addition to enslaving Native Brazilians in the early years of the colony, Brazil participated in the Atlantic slave trade, which brought millions of enslaved Africans to the country.[24] Today Brazil has more people of African descent than any other country of the world but Nigeria; many live in the Northeast, especially the state of Bahia. Clothing, cookery, language, religion, music, and art have all been heavily influenced by the sensibilities of slaves and their descendants. Popular imagery as well as intellectual discourse depict master-slave relations as largely benign, describing enslaved wet nurses lovingly giving their breasts to white children just as enslaved women gave their bodies to white men (Freyre 1963, 278).[25] Freyre's vision of benevolent slavery and relaxed race relations has not been sustained by more recent historical research, which has uncovered the particular brutality of Caribbean and Brazilian slavery on sugar plantations and the persistence of racism in contemporary Brazil (Conrad 1986; Degler 1971; Schwartz 1992).

Slavery intensified the already deeply felt divisions among social classes, creating both new categories at the lower ends of society (slaves, freedmen) and a new racial take on class relations. It created a class of women who, because of their condition of indenture, were not able to refuse sexual advances by more powerful men, and whose romances with men closer to their own station were unprotected by the legalities of marriage. Although it was not legally prohibited for slaves to marry, as it was in some other areas of the Americas, owners could and often did discourage or disregard slave marriages. In addition, not concerned with property or inheritance and coming from African societies where patterns of marriage and especially of divorce were very different, slaves may have preferred their own arrangements to Catholic marriage (Schwartz 1985, 387–88).

It was also difficult for men to marry women below them in station, computed on the basis of a combination of factors including legal status (such as slave, freed, freeborn, and the condition of legitimacy), economic resources, the social reputation of the family, and indications of racial "purity" such as skin color (Nazzari 1996).[26] In general, conventional wisdom dictated marriage among social, racial, and economic equals (da Silva 1984, 66). Interracial (and interclass) marriage was not legally prohibited in Brazil, as it was in the United States, but there were serious legal, religious, and social impediments to it.

A shortage of women existed in the early years of colonial Brazil, occasioned both by the small number of Portuguese women who immigrated (Figueiredo 1993; Russell-Wood 1978; Soeiro 1978) and the small number of female slaves imported (Conrad 1986; Schwartz 1985, 346). The Portuguese crown penalized white men for marrying any but legitimately freeborn white women of Old Christian stock (Russell-Wood 1978, 64).[27] In response to these concerns, the Portuguese king, beginning in 1726, restricted political offices, honorary posts, and military commissions to Old Christian white men legally married to, or widowers of, white women. Other inducements such as land grants followed, to encourage white men to marry white women (Russell-Wood 1978, 64). In addition, the Portuguese delayed until 1677 permission to create convents in Brazil and even then gave only few permits. (In contrast, Spanish America had convents from the 1500s.) It also prohibited travel out of the colony by white women without royal permission, making it difficult for white women to avoid marriage (Russell-Wood 1978, 63; Soeiro 1978, 178–79).

The marriage policies of the Catholic Church and of the Portuguese crown were in conflict with the realities of sexual power in racially stratified and slavery-based colonial society. Whereas in Portugal the upper reaches of society were in the hands of a small number of families in possession of titles of nobility, these titles were in very short supply in Brazil. To reach the upper strata of Brazilian society, a family had to be in possession of land, own slaves, and be white. Whiteness in and of itself became an important attribute of social status and a major line of demarcation between elites and the lower classes. As Stuart Schwartz has pointed out, first Indians and then African and mixed-race people became a "surrogate peasantry," and every European man, no matter his family's status in Portugal, became a "potential gentleman" in the colony (1985, 249–51).

Originally, Africans and Natives were seen as "prohibited" or "infected" races because of their pagan religions (Nazzari 1996, 109), but soon the concept of race began to focus on such visible biological qualities as hair color and form, eye color, skin color, and facial morphology. The bodily locus of race shifted from the blood—interior, largely invisible, and not noticeably different from one religious race to another—to the surface of the body: exterior, visible, and with noticeable differences between peoples.[28]

Colonists were able to attain a status recognized locally as akin to nobility by living on large estates, keeping many slaves and servants, consuming and displaying imported luxuries, maintaining private militias, and ostentatiously giving charitable gifts, especially to the Church (Schwartz 1985, 273; Soeiro 1978, 177–78). The show of high status also included the adoption of sexual habits and marital customs associated with the nobility, such as male authoritarianism, sexual access to low-status women, and the confinement of high-status females to the nuclear family dwelling (Bruschini 1990, 61–62). The Moorish-influenced Portuguese tendency toward seclusion of high-status women intensified in Brazil. Ideally, the white woman was supposed to leave her home only three times: for baptism, marriage, and burial (Russell-Wood 1978, 66). Although this ideal was rarely achieved in practice, it was then, and remains today, an important image of how high-status women ought to behave.

In the upper classes, family and property were fused: The continuity of a family's lineage depended on passing down the family estate intact to descendants. Practices such as having a set of brothers marry a set of sisters, or of marrying cousins to one another, constituted common strategies for keeping property within the same extended family (Schwartz 1985, 289–91). The choice of conjugals was of paramount importance. Sons-in-

law, for example, had to be well chosen to manage the family property reliably and not to alienate it to heirs from previous liaisons or subsequent
marriages.[29] Creating such matches on the whims of naive young girls'
fantasies would have been the height of folly.

Despite the importance of the image of the stereotypical plantation
family, such families were in fact quite rare. Plantation owners and their
families constituted only a tiny minority of the population, even in the
Northeast (Corrêa 1982; Samara 1983), and few such families lived up to
the ideal of complete sequestration for women, although the sexual license of white men was very real. Plantation owners' ability to chaperon
their women varied according to a number of factors, including the size of
the plantation, the personalities of the individuals involved, and the particular circumstances.

Women of all classes took active roles in the extradomestic world.
Many lower-class women supported themselves and their children as
heads of household (Diaz and Stewart 1991; Ramos 1991; Russell-Wood
1978), and widows could and did manage plantations, sometimes quite
successfully (Russell-Wood 1978, 88–90). Convents, once they were finally
established, also offered opportunities;[30] they often managed land and
held slaves, and they provided education and shelter for secular women.
An ambitious woman, especially if she were intellectually inclined, might
find more opportunities in a convent than in marriage (Soeiro 1978).
However, except in extraordinary cases, only after outliving their reproductive usefulness did elite women take on roles in business. Lower-class
women had to juggle economic and reproductive roles during their youth.

Brazilian historians differ on the importance of virginity in Brazil of
the late nineteenth to early twentieth century. Boris Fausto (1984) argues
that virginity was important in São Paulo of that time, but other authors
find high rates of unwed motherhood indicative of a continuing division
between women who married and sexually active women who did not—
often because they could not (Ramos 1991). Kátia de Queiros Mattoso
(1988) calculates that 52.2 percent of couples living in the city of Salvador,
Bahia, in 1855 were unmarried. She argues that most births to unmarried
women were among poor women and women of mixed race, a contention
disputed by Elizabeth Kuznesof (1991), who finds that white unmarried
women also had high rates of illegitimate births, especially in urban areas.[31]

I suspect that the importance of virginity has long been in contention,
and that its significance has varied throughout Brazilian history depend-

ing on the social class and color of the woman. It is not so much that in the past people used to value virginity and now modern sensibilities have moved beyond that, but rather that virginity at first marriage has historically been more respectable than premarital defloration or nonlegalized cohabitation for those with middle- and upper-class aspirations. Chastity continued as a virtue of the patriarchal family's women, whereas sexual availability was the hallmark of low social status. Historically and currently, a significant portion of the population has not been able to achieve the ideal in practice.

Despite its rarity, the image of the patriarchal family forms a major part of popular conceptions of marital and sexual relations in Brazil. Upper-class female sexuality became a commodity associated with inheritance and succession and was confined to marriage, while male sexuality remained a source of both pleasure and power (Bruschini 1990, 62). Lower-class and dark-skinned women were so widely regarded as legitimate targets of upper-class male lust that Brazilians thought their chastity inconceivable (Russell-Wood 1978, 68). Today, a similar color hierarchy of female sexual honor remains. In addition, the pattern of institutionalized male infidelity constituting a functional polygyny, especially in the upper classes, also persists.

It would be an error to regard such relationships as simply the result of powerful men preying upon vulnerable women, for poor women have their own sentiments, aspirations, and desires, and their own uses for such alliances. Ligia Bellini, for example, in a study of Brazilian letters of manumission, has described "spaces of invention" (1988, 74) between master and slave created by the complex of power and emotion involved in engendering and bearing children. She describes them as "singular games of power and seduction" in which some slave women sought opportunities to better their own situations and those of their children through alliances with their owners (p. 75; my translation).

Muriel Nazzari suggests that powerful Brazilian men may have loved their lower-status concubines precisely because the status difference gave them so much more freedom of action with them than with their wives (1996, 119), offering the possibility of being cherished to poor women who keep their place. Similarly, Donna Goldstein (forthcoming) has described the contemporary Cinderella fantasies that poor, black domestic workers have of seducing their white employers as a way out of poverty. The complexity of the interplay of desire, affection, and power in a society as marked by legal, economic, and social inequality as Brazil (both historically and currently) confounds even more the already multiple intricacies of sexual love: The line between seduction and rape becomes ever blurrier, and who is screwing over whom shifts continually.[32]

Stereotypes deriving from the racism incorporated in the discourse on hot-bloodedness powerfully affect not only racialized concepts of what makes a person sexually attractive but also the issues of which women have the right to say no to sexual advances and women's potential to marry honorably or to claim injury when sexually assaulted. Racist stereotypes also affect the life chances of men, both in the labor market and in the marriage market.

Love in the Modern Hygienic Family

Brazilian historian Jurandir Freire Costa has provided a detailed study of the impact of the Brazilian hygiene movement on family forms and concepts of love in Brazil. As he shows, in the 1880s ideas of hygiene contributed to a newly medicalized view of the nature of the family, which was then codified into law. The nineteenth century saw the rise of the Brazilian medical profession, flourishing under royal patronage. Originally concerned with the profusion of serious infectious diseases, only just beginning to hint of vulnerability to human control through the then-novel techniques of antibacterial medicines, statistically based epidemiological description, and general sanitary reform, nineteenth-century medicine turned its attention to moral issues, convinced that moral cleanliness could prove as revolutionary as had physical hygiene. Although today the United States and Western European countries have taken over the leadership in medical research, nineteenth-century Brazil was in the forefront of academic medicine, its French-trained physicians identifying and combating such scourges as Chagas' disease, smallpox, and yellow fever.[33]

Brazilian medical hygienists, following trends in Europe, proposed that moral and social cleanliness could prevent and correct disease. While this was not a new idea, it was newly scientized: Tied to dramatically effective new methods of infection control and promulgated by a medical profession increasingly supported by state agencies, it took on an authoritative character. Doctors defined moral cleanliness largely in sexual terms, campaigning against sodomy and masturbation, male homosexuality, prostitution, sexual libertinism, and other forms of sexual behavior long condemned religiously and newly classed as medical deviancy (Parker 1991, 78–83).

Brazilian hygienists promoted the love-based, monogamous, nuclear family as conducive to social order. Following a vogue for breast-feeding among European elites, they condemned wet-nursing by slaves in particular,[34] denouncing as cruel the practice of abandoning slave infants in foundling homes in order to free their lactating mothers for rental as wet nurses. But they were even more concerned with what they saw as the negative effects of wet-nursing on white children, positing that a healthy family could exist only if white women reared their own children, maintained by a protective father (Costa 1989, 168–71; see also Schwartz 1985, 275).

Hygienists also condemned slavery as destructive of love-based marriage because it encouraged adulterous miscegenation, destroying both marital unity and white racial purity (Costa 1989, 166). Although most whites, including abolitionists, thought true love a sentiment too refined for "savage" races such as Africans to comprehend, they did note loyalty and affection among slaves, remarking on the willingness of some slaves to brave punishments in order to spend time with loved ones. Some advocated encouraging marriage among slaves in order to foster a sense of responsibility that would pay off for the owner in harder work and fewer acts of defiance (Schwartz 1985, 380–81).[35]

Here, marital love was portrayed as integral to progress: an important part of the modern, hygienic, healthy family. Marriage was increasingly redefined as a relationship of love licensed by the state, and the formation and maintenance of a loving, hygienic nuclear family became an act of patriotism within that state (Costa 1989, 63). Love shifted from a religious to a medical concept. Tied to the body through its definition as sexual passion, it came under the purview of doctors as managers of the body; as a psychological experience it entered the jurisdiction of psychiatrists; in its domesticated form it became the province of hygienists (Costa 1989, 64–65).[36] Deeply racist, these discourses of domesticated love in the hygienic family developed in the context of the abolition of slavery not as part of any attempt to improve the lives of former slaves but as part of attempts to improve the domestic lives of slave owners by separating them from their human property. The racism of colonial slave holders and nineteenth-century hygienists remains an integral part of concepts of love-marriage in Brazil, to the extent that chastity and whiteness remain intertwined in judgments of women's sexual virtue and therefore eligibility for legitimate marriage.

By the middle of the nineteenth century, upper-class Brazilians were contracting what Muriel Nazzari has called a "new marriage bargain" (1991, 131). The decline of the dowry both in Portugal and in Brazil accompanied the spread of the expectation that the husband would support his family economically. Nazzari points out that while prior to the mid-1800s, women either retained their father's family name after marriage or used no name, and children frequently were given the mother's rather than the father's family name, by 1917 the Brazilian Civil Code required a woman to take her husband's surname and made the presumption that he would support her as well as her children. The proportion of children with their father's family name increased throughout the nineteenth and twentieth centuries (1991, 141, 168).[37] Economically, men were more powerful than women in marriage, and increasingly the woman was incorporated into the man's family, rather than the earlier system in which young men took their place in the wife's family as manager of her dowry (1991, 148).

Although the 1831 criminal code of Brazil made it illegal for clergy to carry out their age-old practice of marrying couples without paternal consent, legal cases from the nineteenth century show an increasing concern with obtaining explicit consent to marriage on the part of the conjugals (Nazzari 1991, 140). This suggests that women, or at least young women, were gaining in power because they were no longer easily forced into marriages with strangers in order to support family economic schemes. Yet, as Nazzari points out, the rise of romantic ideology and concern with consent accompanied a sharp decline in women's ownership of conjugal property, ownership of their own family names and ability to pass those on to children, and a rise in marriage contracts in which wives were prohibited from inheriting their husband's property should he predecease them (1991, 145).

As families shifted from units of production to units of consumption, men, as the major public producers and managers of family consumption, gained in economic power over their wives (1991, 148). The shift to a capitalist economy, the decline in the hegemony of propertied families, did give young people a greater ability to contract their own marriages. However, men had the advantage in this; families still largely controlled whom their daughters met, in some cases deliberately manipulating situations so that they would indeed fall in love with the man their father had chosen, since he was virtually the only young man with whom they spent time. The advent of love-marriage did not mean that women were necessarily marrying for love, although men may have had greater freedom to do so than before, nor did it mean that women had greater power within marriage. In many ways they had less.

The image of the patriarchal plantation family as an idealized norm owes as much to the postabolition creation of the hygienic family as to romanticized images of plantation life. Couples today judge the state of their relationships in the context of their images of the past and of what they believe to be eternal norms of human behavior. When Maria Imaculada's doctor told her husband that his sexual infidelity was harmful to the health of his wife and daughters, he was reacting not only to the physical evidence of her nervous debility but also to his own intellectual heritage of seeing monogamous marriage as a healthful norm and marital infidelity, however common, as an unhealthy, dysfunctional abnormality.

Love begins to show its varied facets—as an internal personal experience, an obligation of states toward their citizens, an aspect of passionate sexual attraction, an obligation of patriotic and properly married spouses, a gift of patrons to clients, and a source of power over patrons by clients—as it threads through discourse and practice in Northeast Brazil. Although love is often portrayed as the opposite of economic interest, love and interest are intertwined. A marriage is not only a relationship of physical and emotional intimacy; it is also a relationship of economic intimacy, and social status similarly shows an intertwining of economic and sexual factors.

Throughout history, concepts of love have responded to women's status. Verbally elaborated codes to express love tend to arise as much when changes in women's economic and social status make men's power over them less certain as when close-knit, small-scale societies give way to larger, less intimate communities. Medieval European troubadours struggled in poetic words with their desire for women they could not be sure of possessing, and early modern Europeans struggled to express in words what actions could no longer say at a time when elite men and women were increasingly segregated into separate economic spheres.[38] Contemporary Caruaruenses similarly contend with changes in women's economic role and in the balance of power between the sexes, and with shifts in both emotional and sexual mores around gender relations.

5 ⌇ Ideals of Masculinity and Femininity

Love in a Divided Society

> But don't ask me to be Vadinho and Teodoro at one and the same
> time, for I can't. I can only be Vadinho and I have only love to give
> you. Everything else you need, he gives you: your own house,
> conjugal fidelity, respect, order, consideration and security. . . . His
> love is made up of these noble (and tiresome) things, and you need
> all of them to be happy. You also need my love to be happy, this
> impure, wrong, crooked love, dissolute and fiery, which makes you
> suffer. . . . I am the husband of poor Dona Flor, the one who comes
> to stir up your longing and provoke your desire. . . . He is the
> husband of Madame Dona Flor, who protects your virtue, your
> honor, your respect among people. . . . We are your two husbands.
> . . . To be happy you need both of us.
>
> Jorge Amado (1969, 505–6)

In *Dona Flor and Her Two Husbands: A Moral and Amorous Tale*, Brazilian novelist Jorge Amado presents a fantasy of widow Dona Flor, who, re-married to the reliable but dull pharmacist Teodoro, experiences visits from the ghost of her ne'er-do-well scalawag of a first husband, Vadinho. The ghost, nude and visible only to her, makes the ardent love to her that her new husband cannot. With the security of the boring husband enlivened by the excitement of the rascal, and freed by her social and economic circumstances to relish ghostly Vadinho's erotic antics, she enjoys the perfect marital situation. Most people, alas, lack supernatural help to negotiate the tension between excitement and propriety inherent to the difficulties of sustaining relationships of long-term intimacy.

These difficulties include misunderstandings derived from the different perspectives held by men and women, perspectives shaped by culturally constructed notions of masculinity and femininity. Men and women inhabit different social worlds, even in the same society, and have different stakes in issues of propriety, sexuality, and family responsibility. Anthropologists in Latin America, in similar Caribbean societies, and in contemporary Mediterranean societies have tried with varying success to characterize the different perspectives and stakes men and women have in their sexual lives, the bases of their status, and their concepts of propriety.

Latin and Caribbean Gendered Propriety

Scholars trying to characterize constructions of sexual propriety in Mediterranean, Latin American, and Caribbean societies have written a portrait of cultures divided by gender into complementary but conflicting segments. In particular, theorists have noted the far-reaching consequences to gender roles of the shift from agrarian to urban economies created by the impact of the agrarian transformation on the gendered basis of economic cooperation (Browner and Lewin 1982; Bustos 1980; Ehlers 1991; Fox 1973; Kelly and Sassen 1995; Pearlman 1984; Roldan 1988; Rothstein 1983; Stern 1995; Stevens 1973).

These theories have salience to my fieldwork because Northeast Brazil was undergoing a major rural-to-urban migration at the time of my study, in which Caruaru was the first major urban stop for many formerly rural people on their way to eventual resettlement in Rio de Janeiro or São Paulo. In addition, it was also subject to the shifts in gender roles then galvanizing the country as a whole, the result not only of an organized feminist movement but also of political and economic changes following the First World War, and the consequent impact on both the legal and popular concepts of marriage, the family, and the role of women (Besse 1996).

Although conservative compared with larger cities and located in the Northeast—itself conservative compared with the South—Caruaru experienced the challenge to customary patriarchy spearheaded by middle-class Southern women, and the transformations that challenge wrought. Nonetheless, it remains conservative, an area where, in the words of Brazilian psychoanalyst Sérvulo A. Figueira, the "modern and the archaic" coexist uneasily in the "new family" of modern Brazil (1986).

Even when not living in societies in the throes of rapid change, women and men view one another through the filter of stereotypes fed by social separation, differences in point of view, and the misleading perceptions of desire itself. Ideas on the propriety of sexual behavior figure among the factors that structure each gender's perceptions of and responses to the other.[1] In addition, a number of literary stereotypes have attained great influence, both popularly and academically, Among them are those based on theories of honor developed from study of Mediterranean societies.

These stereotypes have come under increasing critical scrutiny, not only as applied to New World cultures but also as used in the Mediterranean societies for which they were developed. According to the literature, honor, defined as both personal virtue and high status, preoccupies Mediterranean—and by extension—Latin American men. As described, the Mediterranean honor complex centers on men's right to respect and on the relationship of each gender to sexual intercourse and its proprieties. Masculine signifiers of honor include the use of styles of esteem, a virile forcefulness expressed both in sexual aggression and personal willpower, and the ability to sustain and protect a family while inspiring devotion and submission from subordinates of both sexes. Important attributes include protection of legitimate wives and daughters from any contact with other men's sexuality, and a readiness to use deadly force to obliterate any disrespectful implication about the honor of any member of the household, no matter how slight the provocation (Gilmore 1987; Greenberg 1996; Miller 1993; Pitt-Rivers 1966; Schneider 1971; Stewart 1994).

Critics have delineated a number of problems with the model, including its rigidity, its disregard of women's point of view,[2] and what some have seen as its ethnocentric nature (Brandes 1987; Cole 1991; de Alameida 1996; Hertzfeld 1980, 1984).[3] Some have also questioned its applicability to Latin American societies, where the formula tends to be discussed in the literature on machismo.[4] Nonetheless, the model remains influential.

In an attempt to create a model more applicable to the American societies of the African Diaspora, Peter Wilson suggested the substitution of the terms "reputation" and "respectability" (1969, 1973). Basing his opinion on a study undertaken on the Caribbean island of Providencia, Wilson posited that lower-class men gain status by building individual reputations that emphasize their right to respect through demonstration of a personally adventuresome spirit as shown by successful travels,[5] the right to demand courtesy from other men and obedience from women, and the ability to bed many women, father many children (especially boys), drink prodigious amounts of alcohol without obvious inebriation, tell dramatic and entertaining stories of their personal exploits, and spend money openly and generously. Also included is the possession of a nickname, especially if it includes a title of some sort. Men further enhance their reputations by owning land, displaying entrepreneurial skills, and participating in certain religious observances (1969, 73–76).

In contrast, women tend to pursue respectability in an opposite fashion. A respectable woman stays at home, does not drink alcohol, behaves in a modest and chaste manner, and, above all, marries legally. Wilson points out that men are more likely to attain the goal of reputation than women are to achieve respectability. Although the patterns of behavior that mark respectability are the same in all social classes, most of the actions that lower-class men employ to build their reputations connote vulgarity to the upper classes (1969, 76–79): swaggering, wearing a mustache and pompadour hairstyle, aggressive flirting and womanizing, touchiness, and a propensity for violence.

While agreeing that the terms "reputation" and "respectability" come closer to the mark than the use of concepts such as "honor" and "shame" for Caribbean and Latin American cultures, feminist scholars interested in the lives of lower-class and dark-skinned women have criticized Wilson's model on both ethnographic and political grounds. For example, Jean Besson, while praising Wilson for illuminating issues in the lives of Caribbean men, decries the inaccuracies of his views on Caribbean women. She points out that women as well as men may pursue reputations in the extradomestic world through the ownership of land, through business dealings, and through religious participation, as well as by mothering children, holding titles, and using nicknames.

In addition, she reprimands Wilson on political grounds, because his theory suggests that while men resist the domination of the largely light-skinned middle classes, women are complicit with their own oppression through their acceptance of respectability as a value. On the contrary, women have a long history of resistance, both in slavery and in freedom, often using poisoned food or venomous words to assault their masters or patrons, as demonstrated in the many records of flogging and other punishments for such crimes. She also points out that in the Jamaican village she studied, women tended to bear children young and marry middle aged, suggesting that much may be missing from Wilson's discussion of the place of marriage in women's lives (Besson 1993).

Shame and Notoriety in Caruaru

During the time I lived in Caruaru I frequently heard the word *honra* ("honor") from social scientists, especially in connection with discussions of male self-identity in the lower classes (it was often in combination with the word *machismo*). I also came across the term in newspapers in relation to changes in legal opinions on domestic violence. The customary male right to use deadly force to defend personal honor, especially in cases of actual or suspected female infidelity ("legitimate defense of honor") was in contention in the Brazilian supreme court at the time, occasioning much discussion.

However, I rarely heard the word *honra* from lower-class people, except in discussions of ongoing trials for wife-murder, although I did hear *honrado* ("honorable"), especially in reference to older, rural men. More common was *fama*, referring to a negative reputation, especially in the sense of a woman's notoriety for sexual impropriety. The common form of usage, *Ela já tem fama de ser* ("She's already well known for being") was a staple of gossip. I heard the word *vergonha* ("shame") constantly, along with its complement *semvergonha* ("shameless"), especially to describe women who drank, smoked, or acted out sexually, children who disobeyed their mothers, and men who embarrassed their womenfolk. Applied to a woman, *semvergonha* was a serious insult; applied to men it could take on playful connotations.[6]

The word *honra* seemed more an intellectual and legal concept than an everyday idea. *Vergonha* was a much more constantly present notion, at least among women. Yet many men did use the styles of respect described in both the literature on honor and Wilson's characterization of "reputation," even if they did not have a specific word for it, apart from the word *homem* ("man") itself. There were, however, a wealth of words to describe men lacking in masculinity. These (*bicha, fruta, veado, vinte-e-quatro*, and the English word *gay*) also connoted both effeminacy and willingness to engage in passive anal intercourse.[7]

"Honor" and "reputation" may best be seen as theoretical constructions rather than indigenous concepts, referring to a set of social ideas about the relationships among masculinity, power, and respect. They are subject to contingent interpretations, creating a structure of possibilities within which people negotiate status. As a system of ideal proprieties, concepts of masculinity work not so much as blueprints for practice as symbolic vocabularies through which to judge status—and in that judgment to determine how to treat a man. Perhaps more useful than either "honor" or "reputation" is Miguel de Alameida's term "hegemonic male," elaborated in his study of men in Portugal. He defines the term as "the central model that attempts to subordinate alternative masculinities ... and which is the model of male domination," including "compulsive heterosexuality and reproduction" (1996, 3).

This clarifies the male dilemma depicted in Wilson's descriptions of reputation: how to accommodate the desire of lower-class men to assert their right to respect in highly stratified societies like those of the postslavery Americas. While some aspects of reputation, such as landholding, correspond to upper-class bases of economic and political power, albeit on a lesser scale, others, such as heavy drinking, substitute for political and economic power a variety of phallocentric privileges, hence connoting vulgarity to the upper classes.

I agree with Besson that Wilson's flawed but nonetheless illuminating model better illustrates issues in men's than women's lives. His insight that legal marriage ties in to women's status, while important, does not take into account many complexities in women's involvement with concepts of sexual propriety. And his implication of greater female complicity with oppression does not well describe a reality in which women have frequently been in the forefront of both active and passive resistance. However, it is undeniable that legal marriage, domesticity, and both the physical structure of the house and the conceptual realm of the home all figure in the social construction of an idealized or hegemonic femininity in terms, or in defiance, of which women define themselves, or find themselves defined.

House and Street

Roberto da Matta first formalized the discussion of house and street as complementary gendered spheres in Brazil, with "house" (*casa*) being the domain of women and "street" (*rua*) that of men (1985). Of course men live in houses and women move about on streets, so the two spheres overlap. But he described conceptual differences partly contiguous with the physical architecture of buildings and roads, and especially intertwined with ideas of how properly to be a man or a woman. Here, the *casa*, characterized by familiarity, hospitality, love, and honorable dealing, becomes the realm of women, children, and domestic servants (da Matta 1985, 41–42). The *rua* is where individuals fight for dominance, the realm of men, violence, and exploitation where the rule "every man for himself" prevails. The relationships of individual couples form a microcosm of the dynamic complementarity of house and street in the broader society. The division between *casa* and *rua* may be seen as a distinction between that area where love structures actions and judges morality, and that area where love is lacking (da Matta 1985, 47). This distinction is best seen as a conceptual tendency rather than a description of the behavior of men and women. Nonetheless, it remains an important insight, at least in the description of urban areas.

Marking masculine and feminine social worlds through architecture reflects urban practice. On small farms, ideal male and female realms revolve around task and species, not buildings and roads. Men generally identify with the larger fields and with animals such as horses, goats, sheep, and cattle, which wander in pasture or are ridden or driven, as well as with dogs, which help manage herds and hunt game. Women's realm includes the house, food preparation, the care of children, and cleaning, as well as the tending of chickens, cats, pigs, and other animals that stay close to home, the kitchen garden, and sources of water. While both men and women may work the fields, ideally men take tasks that require standing up and using tools, women those associated with bending, such as planting and gathering.

In practice, men and women often do similar agricultural work, although tending to the house, children, and home animals remains a female responsibility. The lower the status of the workers, the more likely that women will work alongside the men. Rather than the emancipation of women workers, this fact reflects their poverty, their inability to lighten the work that comes on top of family responsibilities.

In cities, however, gender difference conceptually overlaps architecture, a fact reflected in Caruaruense women's frequent description of themselves as married to their houses, and their discussion of housing when asked about conjugal love: "Oh my God I don't love him, he's so ugly! I like him but I don't love from the heart. But I want to have my house. I think that the dream of every woman is to have a house and a husband, *né?*" (Maria da Conceição).

The verb *casar*, "to marry," derives from *casa*, "house": To marry is to house. Though neither illegal nor socially impossible, a woman's buying her own house in Caruaru would be scandalous. Properly men buy and build houses, and fathers may demand possession of a house by a suitor as a customary condition for the release of a daughter for marriage. Unmarried or never paired women generally obtain houses by inheritance, and only very rarely do women buy and maintain their own houses.[8] Marriage and cohabitation are the main ways by which women obtain a house, and even though men legally own the houses, when they leave a relationship they leave the house for the woman and her children.[9]

Most lower-class Brazilian houses follow the basic pattern mandated by colonial Portuguese law: two bedrooms, a front or living room, a kitchen, and a *quintal*, or "fifth area," in the back of the house (cf. Robben 1989). The *quintal* usually consists of an uncovered, walled area.[10] In most houses, the only piped water is in the *quintal*, and many houses have water tanks or jars there as well. Economic status can be measured by whether a house has access to piped water, if so how many water outlets it has (toilet, sink, shower, etc.), and the extent to which it has water outlets outside the *quintal*.[11]

People mark their transition from street to house with small ceremonies. Polite visitors ask permission to enter by hand-clapping and calling out: Õ *de casa!* ("Oh, of the house!")[12] Upon being invited in, they wipe their feet and say *Licença* ("With your permission"), as they pass through the door. Family members usually offer water or coffee to guests and serve it in a ceremonious manner, followed by offers of crackers, cake, or other food.[13] Upon leaving the house and entering the street, family members request a blessing from relatives. A boy might call out *Bença, mãe!* ("Blessing, mother!"), and his mother respond *Deus te bençoa, meu fi'o* ("God bless you, my son"). Some families also kiss hands upon giving the blessing (which is also given to children before they sleep).[14] Being accepted into the friendship network of a family means gaining the right to enter the house without saying *Licença*. At mealtimes, guests are pressed to eat. Only after the refreshment is consumed and the stress of the street dissipated do people address their business. All of these customs serve to emphasize the difference between the realms of *casa* and *rua* and to protect the family from the dangers of the street.[15]

The realm of *casa* extends beyond the walls of the house, to the area directly in front of the door. Women frequently congregate on front stoops, and they may take over a small area of the street in front of their door. Men spend their nonwork hours at bars or restaurants or on road trips with their buddies, returning home only to eat and sleep. Although impatient teenage girls may daydream about the freedom they will enjoy when they have their own house, after elopement, marriage, or cohabitation many find that while the *casa* shelters a woman in her own domain it can also imprison. Girls who think that once married they will be free from the constant chaperonage of fathers and brothers find that husbands press them to demonstrate by action that they are, if not virgin, at least chaste. One way to demonstrate this is to avoid leaving the house.

I only live inside the house, taking care of my house. . . . I don't hardly have any time to go out to visit, only sometimes a sick neighbor nearby, I visit that sick person, I go to church, sometimes I visit my mother, only this. (Maria do Carmo)

Decent women rarely walk about unaccompanied, and never alone to remote areas. This practice, increasingly old-fashioned, characterizes rural areas and small cities like Caruaru more than the large coastal cities. Women go out in groups with other married women, sometimes accompanied by male relatives, or at the very least accompanied by their children.

My husband was complaining that I go out with Maria because she's still single, and he said that I was flirting over there with a single girl. He said married women only go out with other respectable women or with their son or husband. His nonsense! (Severina)

As Severina's comment shows, men may demand ostentatious displays of chastity by their women, who may resist what they see as unreasonable restrictions on their freedom. Men vary in how much they want or are able to isolate their wives: For some men this is not much of an issue, but for others any attempt to go out could facilitate infidelity. Since most people have only one key to the front door, possession of the key becomes an important aspect of conjugal power struggles.

If a man returns to the house to find no wife at home and no food ready to be served, he may respond with outrage.

The other day he returned and I wasn't in the house because I went to visit Glória. So he got angry, said I was after males [atrás de macho], so when he left for work he locked the door and left with the key. So I stayed locked inside. But after some three days his mother kept talking to him about how a fire could happen, so he let me out. But I can't go far away from the house nor be outside when he returns or it's trouble. (Inaia)

Confinement of women to the house is strongest among the working classes. In favelas, the house may not be enough of a structure to confine a woman, many women work outside the home, and a high percentage of households are headed by women. Middle-class and wealthy women may have both professions and cars, and many attend universities or engage in volunteer charitable activities that take them out of the house. But for the working class, among which the tension between men's actual and presumed power is greatest, shutting the woman away in the home in imitation of popular images of the white plantation wife of old becomes symbolically important, a pattern not unfamiliar to scholars of working-class conjugal relations in other parts of the world (cf. Komarovsky 1967; Rubin 1976).

If marriage, formal or informal, is the way for a woman to get a house, it also identifies her with that house. *Dona-de-casa* ("housewife") literally means "mistress of the house." Women belong to their homes more than do men.

My husband doesn't live here, you know? He resides here but he doesn't live. It's his house, he doesn't have another. But he visits here. He neither works here nor preoccupies himself with how it looks. He sleeps here but works outside. I send my boy with his lunch to eat outside; weekends he goes with his friends. I'm here day, night, day, night, the whole week. Him, no. (Emília)

The identification of women with houses, and the attempt by some men to confine them at home, does not, however, mean that the distinction women/house versus men/street adequately describes social practice. While women, houses, the domestic realm, virtue, the family, and love all intertwine conceptually, as do men, streets, the public realm, immorality, solitude, and cruel indifference, confinement of women to the home and dominance of men over the streets is not absolute. Brazilian anthropologist Klaas Woortman describes the Bahian *favelados* of his study as holding simultaneously an ideal model of the proper family and what he calls a *modelo da práxis*, or a practice-model, adapted to the exigencies of poverty (1987, 59). I observed a similar situation in Caruaru.

Like Woortman's Bahians, Caruaruenses I knew emphasized the family as a moral realm, contrasting decent *moças da família* ["family girls"] with indecent *meninas da rua* ["street girls"], and using the term *família* in general to denote virtue, stability, and loving relationships associated with the home (cf. Woortman 1987, 58). However, in practice women often worked outside the home, traveled on streets to go shopping and do errands, and participated in extradomestic duties in churches, labor unions, and other public arenas. Like other politically active women studied in Latin America (cf. Cubitt and Greenslade 1997), some Caruaruense women had joined political movements as an extension of their domestic concerns, organizing to obtain better housing, food, schooling, and medical care for their children. They also organized to oppose conjugal violence, trying to rescue women from prostitution or working to prevent rape. Often, women active in labor unions portrayed their interest as an extension of their desire to feed their families. Indeed, connection to family interest served as a potent moral justification for women's political activity outside the home.

While in the ideal model of the family, women stay home while men rule the streets, in the practice-model adopted by most working-class families the boundaries between house and street blur, and some women adroitly manipulate concepts of domestic virtue to justify and lend moral weight to their political and economic activities outside the family home. Here we can see that Wilson's model is correct in its delineation of the association between respectability and legal marriage. However, as Besson (1993) points out, he fails to capture the complexity of women's involvement with respectability, and he fails to recognize the clever ways that some women have managed to manipulate images of family decency and feminine respectability to gain a foothold in and influence over the "masculine" realm of the streets.

Marriage as Economic Partnership

Marriage legally creates an economic partnership in which men and women have different, complementary roles. Ideally, at the time of wedding men are responsible for providing and furnishing a house, women for a trousseau of household items such as sheets, towels, and dishes, in a remnant of the dowry of old. Throughout the marriage, custom designates the man as provider of major necessities, such as food and clothing, whereas women, to the extent that they have money, buy extras such as toys or candy for the children. These ideals tend to be realized in most couples' practice models, modified only by the necessity for women to contribute more to major expenses in cases where men do not allocate sufficiently.

I am speaking here of households based around a conjugal couple. There are also many households in which a man does not reside regularly and in which a woman or several women carry the economic responsibility. In addition, some households are composed of more than one couple, or a combination of a couple or couples and one or more single adults and their children. Often in these cases the adults are close relatives who may all contribute to family expenses. Even in households in which, as a common expression has it, "the cock does not crow" (*o galo não canta*), the gendered arrangements tend to apply.

In most households women are completely responsible for cooking, cleaning the house, laundry, and the care of children.[16] These tasks involve constant, heavy labor, and women rise earlier, work longer, and go to sleep later than men.

Have you ever thought how it nauseates to take care of a house? You do the same things, the same things. Put the children in to take a bath, make *café* [breakfast], put them out for school, put out *café* for your husband, wash dishes, make lunch, put out lunch for the children, put it out for your husband, wash again the same plates, wash the clothes, sweep the house, set the children down to study, make dinner, wash the same dishes again, put the children to bed, put your husband to bed, do his "service" [have sexual intercourse], sleep, wake at dawn, make *café*. There are days when I have pains in every part of my body from the work I do—never marry, Linda-Anne! Never, never, never! Oh my God, what horror! (Fátima)

Some women taught their sons to cook, especially if there were no daughters in the family or if the boy was the oldest son, and there were also some fostered boys who did household labor. In addition, where the family business involved cooking, boys sometimes helped, especially if there were strenuous lifting, carrying, or stirring involved. But teaching boys to do household labor was controversial, with some people claiming that such an incorrectly gendered activity would make them grow up to be homosexual. Older men sometimes helped with tasks such as shelling beans, and some men helped their wives to prepare special foods for festivals, especially with tasks that require some strength. Barbecuing meat was the one male food specialty, although restaurant cooks are frequently male. Although small boys may accompany their mothers to rivers to do laundry, the lifting, pounding, and scrubbing required to wash often heavy sheets, hammocks, and clothing in cold water was a female responsibility.

In most working-class families, when a man is hungry he sits at the table, calling for food, and his wife or daughter ladles it into his bowl for him and clears and cleans his utensils when he is done. When his clothes are dirty, he takes them off and drops them on the floor, and his wife or daughter picks them up and washes, dries, and then irons them, folds them, and puts them away, While men often play affectionately with their children, major care for children is women's work.

Show a kid to him, he runs screaming. He buys groceries for them and *pronto*, he's done his part. To make a child, all a man has to do is come [*chega lá*]. It's the woman who suffers to have [the child]. And the woman, she has to be pregnant [*buchuda*],[17] then she has to have labor to have the child, then she has to feed that child and clean that child and discipline that child and raise [*educar*] that child, and then eighteen years later the father comes back and says with all the pride, "That's my son!" And it's the same with everything, that the man does the little part and goes away and the woman does all the rest and the man takes the credit. (Maria das Dores)

Most people I spoke with told me that men ought to earn sufficient money to supply the house itself, all the food, and clothing for all household members. However, only a few men were able to do this. More were either unemployed or occasionally employed in the informal, or parallel, economy (*parallelo*), which comprises the unregulated economic activities of the poor. Here nonlicensed electricians, plumbers, and mechanics negotiate fees on a job-by-job basis, housewives bake and sew, unregistered workers are hired at less than the minimum wage, and small children are *agregado* (adopted as domestic servants).[18] Jobs in the informal economy are occasional, unregulated, and untaxed. As such, they are less expensive for employers than jobs in the formal economy. They are also a significant part of the economy. A 1987 study in Fortaleza, the capital of the Northeastern state of Ceará, showed that 29 percent of the economically active population of the city functioned exclusively within the informal sector (Cavalcanti 1987, 70).

The informal sector is largely composed of women because the market for female domestic servants is so large and because factory owners tend to prefer female workers, who are lower paid and more likely to be sober than men (cf. Driessen 1983, 126). Women also may create their own employment, often by door-to-door selling of food they prepare, by designing and sewing clothing for neighbors, or by opening beauty salons, small shops, or other businesses in their homes. Only such jobs as construction and the trades remain mostly male.

All in all it is easier for a woman to work. She can wash clothes, can be a maid, can make and sell cake, can babysit, sew, can do a lot of things. And the man, no. Also woman is a more responsible being than the man. The woman with a son works to sustain him; the man, he can abandon his own son and his woman. (Rosabela)

Women and men do not earn equal wages. Although women are generally lower paid than men, a study published in 1989 showed that while

college-educated women earned only 36 percent of what similarly educated men earned, illiterate women earned as much as 96 percent of what
illiterate men earned (Neuhouser 1989, 689). This means that the poorer
the woman, the less economically dependent she may be on men. Among
the lower classes, women's earning potential is actually greater than
men's because, while they earn slightly less when employed, they are
more frequently employed than are men.

In addition, women's networks are more economically important for
family maintenance than are men's (cf. Neuhouser 1989, 669–670). Some
households are maintained mostly on income from networks. Employed
lower-class women frequently have access to and control over a greater
portion of resources than do men, not only bringing it in but, in their role
as cook, server, and launderer, also controlling the distribution of resources inside the household (cf. Neuhouser 1989, 691–93). Today's urban, lower-class women have economic power both inside and outside
the home, despite the cultural ideal of female economic dependency.

Lower-class women's potential comparative economic advantage
over men does not, however, mean that they are well off. From the 1950s
through the 1990s, Brazilian national administrations unsuccessfully
made control of inflation the priority of one failed economic plan after another. Starting in 1964, wages were indexed to inflation, responding to
concerns over an increase in strikes by labor unions. Indexing wages
served to hide the extent of inflation, helping to attract foreign investment
as part of the government's interest in keeping up the rapid economic
growth of the Miracle. However, real wages, or the actual buying power
of the wage, declined sharply during the first decade of indexing (Wood
and de Carvalho 1988, 112–14).

This decline most strongly affected the lower classes. A Brazilian government study in 1974–75 showed that, whereas in families earning 30 or
more times the basic minimum wage, food expenditures totaled 6 percent
of the household budget, in families earning 3.5 or fewer minimum
wages, food expenditure consumed as much as 50 percent of household
expenses: Poor people were thus much more vulnerable to fluctuations in
food prices. Disjuncture between the economic indicators used as the basis for indexing and the actual cost of food to poor families meant that inflation continued to erode their ability to feed their family members. Infant mortality among the lower classes, especially in the Northeast, rose in
tandem with the decline in real wages from 1964 to 1974, reflecting both

the importance of nutrition for child survival and the failure of national economic policies to relieve poverty (Wood and de Carvalho 1988, 116–26).

The poor in Brazil have not simply accepted their fate. They have responded to economic inequality with attempts at labor organization, strikes, occasional outbursts of violence (often aimed at public transportation or supermarkets), and the creation of neighborhood organizations, frequently religiously based, that work to lobby politicians, educate and support their members, and redistribute resources to sustain the poorest.[19] Poor people have also engaged in a massive and growing migration from rural areas to cities, from small cities to larger cities, from Northeastern cities to Southern megalopolises, and into the Amazon in search of land, work, and an escape from crushing poverty. Women have been especially active in community organizations, both women from the upper classes who take on charitable activities and women from the lower classes who organize to demand higher wages, better nutrition, an end to violence, and other necessities of family survival.

Women's increasing economic importance in poor families is the result not so much of feminist desires for self-actualization through economic independence as of a growing inability on the part of men to support their families. Women, more closely tied to the family, more involved in the care of children and the provision of food, are more likely than men to use their money to maintain their families. In general, men continue to spend money on alcohol for themselves and their buddies, on women, gambling, and other diversions, even as their children go hungry.

It doesn't matter how much he earns, he buys the groceries and that's it. The rest he drinks or uses with his *turma*. What I earn I use for my children and for the house and to help my mother, or sometimes I have friends who helped me in the past. (Assunção)

While economic dislocations have given women access to and control over a significant portion of family resources so that male dominance is no longer an absolute reality, women cannot easily function independently from men because of their social subordination. The disjuncture between the social ideal of male dominance buttressed by economic power and the reality of male demands for obedience from those they can no longer sustain is painful. Putting up with a man's requirements for time, attention, and affection may not be worth the trouble.

Thank God I have my independence. My husband thinks he dominates me, but he's mistaken. I let him think it but I do what I want. God save me from having to live asking for money from him. I have my money and do what I want. It was different when I married. But I looked, thought, and saw how it is. Now I work. (Joselma)

Although theories of love based on European history tend to suggest that wage labor generally increases young people's opportunities to manage their own marital affairs, in Caruaru wage labor frees men more than it does women. The ability to leave the family or defy the parents because of the independence of wage labor remains a largely male liberty. Unmarried girls or women cannot live alone, not only because the state of being unchaperoned would reflect badly on them and their families but also because a woman not clearly protected by a father, brother, or son is considered fair sexual game. Women living alone are subject to sexual harassment, including both verbal and physical assaults. Even once a match has been made, women remain socially subordinate to their husbands or boyfriends, facing greater possible social sanctions should they leave the relationship. Even more than a widow, a divorced or separated woman faces the possibility of sexual harassment as a nonvirginal but nonattached and therefore unprotected woman.

Economic Relations among Working-Class Couples

Couples can choose among several methods of handling family finances. Where the husband is the major breadwinner, he may either make all purchases himself, giving money to his wife only upon request, or give his wife a weekly allowance. Because shopping involves walking some distance and mixing with crowds in the marketplace, some men prefer to do it themselves, keeping their wives more confined at home. In addition, some regard money as part of the world of the *rua*, inappropriate to women's domain: "He gives me money when there's necessity. I know that he earns one [minimum] wage only because he said that he earns one wage, but I have never seen money in his hand, no" (Sebastiana).

If such a wife wants to buy any extra item, she must convince her husband that it is necessary. He may have a different point of view:

He gives forced [*a pulso*]. For food, he himself makes the market, but to buy, like, a little extra thing, it's a little difficult to get anything from him. You see, he is tight [*arramadinho*], his hand is like a parrot on wire, always closed.[20] (Assunçao)

Another method by which a man can keep control of money is to give his wife or girlfriend an allowance from his wages for making purchases. Especially during periods of rapid inflation, couples may argue over the size of the allowance, with the man accusing the woman of injudicious buying and the woman accusing the man of selfishness. In a few cases I encountered, the man turned his entire paycheck over to his wife, receiving in return an allowance from her. Where the woman earns a significant portion of the family income, the couple may divide major purchases, but this is similarly rare. It is more common for one partner, usually the man, to be responsible for food purchases. Men typically spend any extra money on drink, women, gambling, barbecues with male friends, and such extravagances as radios; women typically use their extra earnings buy children's clothing, candy, toys, household items, and supplementary necessities. Women and men frequently disagree on what portion of a man's income can legitimately be considered "extra," as well as on the depth of his necessity to participate in expensive male friendship-building activities such as drinking.[21]

Economic Independence and Love

In a study of rural women in the Northeast Brazilian state of Maranhão, psychoanalyst Elisabeth Bittencourt found that women's concepts of themselves, their legal rights, and particularly their sexual lives had been changed by feminist ideas, even among illiterate women (1989). The women she interviewed told her that ideally young women should be virgins until they marry; every girl of thirteen to fifteen, however, passes through a "crazy-dog phase" (fase de cachorro doido) in which she can think of nothing but boys, they said, and most girls elope with a boy during that time. By age fifteen they discover themselves pregnant and living a very different life than they had imagined (1989, 20). While I never heard the specific phrase "crazy-dog phase" in Caruaru, women did describe doidice ("craziness") during their early teen years, and many young women lost their virginity when they eloped.

Some women eloped with comparative strangers, more in the hope of excitement and independence from parents than because of any deep emotion for the man with whom they ran away. Other women absconded with a man who had been carrying on a clandestine courtship with them for some time. In either case, they soon discovered that courtship and marriage (or cohabitation) call forth different behavior patterns from men.

Instead of a life of independence with a loving man, often they found themselves responsible for even more household chores than before and living with a man as distant and demanding as their father, and expected to put out sexually as well.

Younger women in Caruaru, especially young married women who worked outside the home, told me of their increasing anger at what they saw as men's laziness and lack of consideration. Older and more rural women also complained about having sole responsibility for housework and children. They stated that men were generally insensitive to women but did not go as far as younger, urban women in expressing a belief that helping out around the house is part of the obligation of a loving husband and father.

Because you see it isn't only house and food that makes a woman happy. . . . So what is his obligation? To help me, to take the children, put them in the *quintal*, tell the older children to take a bath so I can make dinner, to do something, to show he even notices, to help me. . . . That is to say, this would captivate me each day more. But no, it stays all for me. (Damiana)

Whereas the historical division of society into complementary male and female spheres allowed men and women to lead parallel lives, mutually interdependent but encompassing separate tasks and responsibilities, today the paths of men and women are increasingly asymptotic: now approaching, now diverging, never quite meeting, and no longer parallel. Emotional expectations designed for a different social arrangement no longer work as well. The domestic chores of housework and child-rearing have become a "second shift" (Hochschild 1989) that women must perform on top of their extradomestic labor. Supporting his family is no longer enough to show a man's love, and the privileges of masculinity, important for men whose sense of self is undercut by their inability to earn, seem increasingly intolerable to women who suffer the loss of each *cruzeiro* spent on male recreation.

Despite liberalizations of marriage law and extensions of women's rights, marriage remains an unequal relationship. Working outside the home for cash gives women a measure of independence but makes housework and care for children an even more onerous burden. The logic of men's exemption from domestic duty is eroded when outside-the-home labor is no longer their sole domain. From the point of view of a man who defines his masculinity in terms of his ability to control and maintain his wife and family, the economic opportunities now available to women seem like an attack on masculine roles, masculine prerogatives, and, in some ways, masculinity itself. With increasingly divergent interests, men and women find it even more difficult than it used to be to achieve the consonance of understanding and interests necessary for affectionate cooperation.

Women's Emotional Role

Historically, women's main avenue of power in the broader society has been through their men. Maria Imaculada, for example, used her greater knowledge of emotional heuristics to control her husband's philandering. Similarly, other women spoke of *arrumando* ("arranging") their men to bring them around to the woman's *jeito* of thinking. For example, one day I overheard Laurinha instructing her daughter-in-law about how a woman ought to handle male misbehavior:

Just today when I went there above to buy bread, I saw an argument, a horrible thing. The woman saying: "But you did such and such, spent the night out and so on and so forth." . . . This was wrong. What was the woman's obligation? To stay at home, *né*, taking care of her kids, waiting. . . . When he arrives at home, arrange him [*arrumá-lo*]. Talk to him, stroke him [*alisá-lo*], not scold him, no. Make him see how much he causes suffering, hurts his family, but gently, gently. Men don't respond well to insults, you have to *dar um jeitinho*, gently, gently. That way she will reap much more than to stay in the street jawing [*batendo papo*].

Emotional manipulation, a major source of female influence, can be quite effective, but it depends for its efficacy on the cooperation of its object. One of women's biggest complaints about men is that they do not cooperate. "Men! They only do what they want, not what you tell them to! What useless creatures!" (Maria da Paz). It is very difficult for women to control their men if the men refuse to feel guilty. For example, once when Nauma was quarreling with her husband over her questions about his fidelity, she exclaimed: "You make me so mad!" (*Você me faz tanta raiva!*). He replied:

I don't make you angry. I do what I do and you decide to be angry about it. Maybe you should calm down. We could talk to Dr. N——, get you some tranquilizers. You are too nervous.

Like that of Maria da Paz, Nauma's anger was coopted by its identification as *nervos*, diminishing her ability to use it to control her husband. Women are most successful at controlling their husbands when, like

Maria Imaculada, they succeed in portraying themselves as blameless victims of male misbehavior rather than as scolding shrews. Frequently this involves evoking religiously based ideas about the nature of suffering.

Although when a woman is good at such manipulation and her men are vulnerable (generally because they have been properly raised by women who were good at it!) she can amass a great deal of influence over her social world, emotional manipulation is an unstable basis for power. Whereas women are empowered by social norms, men are empowered by social norms, laws, and physical force. Men's power is ascribed, but women must achieve power through the force of their personalities, the authority of age, their positions as mother or mother-in-law, and their own personal skills at emotional manipulation. Women's power depends on the participation of its objects. If a husband refuses to feel guilty, a daughter-in-law to feel intimidated, or a son to be devoted, woman's power is circumvented. In addition, men can get away with violence toward family members that women cannot as easily employ.

Love and its attendant guilt are more important to women's position in their social worlds than to men's for those reasons. People said that those who love are in the power of their beloveds.

When I said that I didn't want to marry because I didn't like the guy, Mama said, "It's good that the guy likes you more than you like him because he will do everything you want and live well with you. And if you like him more, he'll know that you are incapable of leaving him, so he will play with you the way he wants to." And so it was. (Severina)

Women experience contradictory pressures to love those with whom they interact, and to interact with people for whom they do not feel too much love. The importance of social networks and the emotional role of women within networks place greater emotional constraints on women. The friendlier a woman is, the more resources she has access to; the more unfriendly she is, the more she is cut off from resources that might make the difference between survival and economic failure. The constraints on women to be pleasant, generous, and accommodating are very strong, and their sanction is economic extinction. On the other hand, some distance is required for the emotional manipulations upon which women's traditional power is based. In addition to being wary of the *jeitoso*, a prudent woman must police her own feelings in order to maintain the control over herself she needs to efficiently control those around her.

Dona Flor had the magic of her author's imagination to help her resolve the conflicts among propriety, respectability, desire, and love, but nonfictional women do not have that luxury. The best they can come up with in most cases is an uneasy compromise, hemmed in on all sides by the expectations, behavior, and judgments of the men and women with whom they interact.

6 ☞ Courtship, Marriage, and Cohabitation

The Practice of Conjugal Love

> There are three kinds of marriage: [for economic] interests, intelligence, and sentiment. So in the first, the person wants to gain by way of the other person. In the second, the people have some rational reason to stay together. And in the third, the two are in love. It's the third the worst of all because sentiment, it keeps diminishing and diminishing and so it goes away and there's no more reason to stay together. Interests you don't know because who is rich today is poor later. It is only intelligence that lasts, that the man and the girl recognize that they need to stay together because it is only together that they will build a home and have children. And it is building a home and raising children together that the two love.
>
> Natalino

Caruaruenses I spoke with frequently decried what they described as the decline of marriage, and with it of morality. Although popularly portrayed as consequences of the moral failings of modernization, the practices of cohabitation without marriage, single motherhood, unstable and short-term sexual relationships, bigamy, and female heading of households extend far back into the past of Brazil and its colonial founders. Indeed, cohabitation without marriage, and what Brazilian law calls concubinage (*concubinato*), or the creation of a secondary household by a married man, is so well established as to require a whole section of family law to regulate it. Such laws attempt to delineate and protect the rights of legitimate wives, concubines, and all a man's "children of the body," whatever the legal status of their mothers (Dias 1975).

Nonetheless, while I discuss cohabitation and concubinage in this and the following chapters, I focus on marriage because it is the perceived norm in terms of which people judge other types of relationships. Folk speech labels the *concubina,* or secondary wife, *a outra* ("the other") in distinction to *a legítima* ("the legitimate wife"). Women refer to live-in boyfriends as *o meu marido* ("my husband"), not *namorado* ("boyfriend") or *companheiro* ("live-in boyfriend"), making cohabitation a sort of as-if marriage rather than a legitimate alternative. I will begin with a discussion of courtship and marriage as people told me they used to be or ought to be practiced, and as some people did and still do practice them. Following that will be a consideration of the varieties of nonmarital, pseudo-marital, and semimarital relationships commonly practiced.

Marriage extends beyond personal experience to create alliances in the broader society, constructing the channels by which rights over property, loyalty, and services will flow among groups. Courtship sets up the who and when of alliances, testing for the fit of individuals to the roles they will have to play as adult members of society, as well as probing (as openly or cautiously as the principals can get away with) for information on what it will be like to live the alliance. Will the couple have the skill and maturity to make a prosperous living under difficult circumstances? Will the man's ability to provide and the woman's cooking skills enable them to eat well? Will they be able to develop a warm, comfortable cooperation, or will their resentments mount until they can bear neither sight nor sound of one another? What will their days together be like, and—oh, most terrifying and intriguing—what will their nights?

Namoro and Noivado

According both to scholars and Caruaruenses I interviewed, when done properly and according to custom, Northeast Brazilian marriage takes place in three stages: *namoro* ("courtship"), *noivado* ("engagement"), and *casamento* ("wedding") (cf. de Azevedo 1986, 5). This pattern is rarely followed today, but it remains the model of propriety and the language in which courtship, marriage, and cohabitation are described. In older times (and presently in rural areas), a couple would *namorar* ("court") on the verandah of the woman's house, often with her parents sitting between them. One fortyish woman described it:

He arrived, sat over there, and I sat here [pointing to two spots some distance apart]. My father sat between us. From that what needed to be said, everyone was listening. When my father went inside, so we spoke a little bit; he returned, the conversation ended.

Physical contact between *namorados* was strongly discouraged. A woman who was raised in a small village reminisced:

My father thought that *namoro* was like this: You there and me here! Nothing of kisses nor hugs! I'm not so very old [thirty-four], but when I was a girl, if the girl and the guy, if she hugged him, kissed him, the people already incriminated her, already thought that she didn't have any respect. . . . My father did not permit it.

It was not the case, although some Caruaruenses insisted it was, that in the past all girls were decent and chaperoned; nor is it the case today that sexual morality has disappeared. Today, as in the past, some women follow the chaperoned-maidenhood-to-decent-marriage route; others run away from parental control with a man they hope will be their true love; others lose (or never had) the ability to present themselves as decent and end up in a series of short-term and low-quality relationships; and some hire out their bodies either in their own behalf or in the service of whoever controls them. What route a woman takes, or what route takes her, is only partly a matter of her choice: It is also influenced by her family, her class and ethnicity, and the details of her personal situation. It was difficult for parents to chaperon their daughters in the past; it is more difficult today, and it is harder in cities than in small towns.

Despite liberalization, a couple alone together still run the risk of moderate scandal in Caruaru. However, young people today have more chance for conversation and varying degrees of physical intimacy than their parents did; supervision of young people varies widely among economic classes and from family to family. In the small towns and rural farms of the recent past, the *namoro* consisted mostly of glances, facial expressions, covert gestures, stolen whispers, and messages passed through intermediaries, rather than hand-holding, hugs, kisses, or intense conversations. This style of courtship continues in some places and has left its mark on definitions of love even in more loosely structured urban situations. Many, when asked to define love, quoted a verse, *O amor nasce num olhar, cresce num sorriso, e amaduresce numa paixão* ("Love is born in a glance, grows in a smile, and matures in a passion"), reflecting both the Christian idea that the eyes are the window to the soul and the constraints young lovers faced as they explored their attractions.

According to descriptions of old-fashioned courtship, couples could meet at community celebrations like the June saints' days festivals,[1] or they might pass each other in the town's central plaza and exchange glances, notes, or a few whispered words (cf. de Azevedo 1986, 4). Young men sometimes congregated in groups in the plaza so they could flirt with young women out walking with their families on a Saturday night. *Namoro* was usually kept a secret from the woman's father and brothers in its early stages. But friends, neighbors, and servants could always be found to help perpetuate a secret love affair. After a period of covert exchanges the man's formal request for the father's permission to court initiated a public *namoro*. Often fathers demanded proof of serious intent and financial means. A man in his fifties explained:

My father-in-law told me that marriage is a serious commitment, and asked me if I had a house. . . . She was very young [twelve], so we arrived at an accord about her age and how the *namoro* would be. So it was once a week, on Saturday or Sunday, that we met . . . everyone conversing in the living room, very serious conversations, about the future, like the old-time people used to talk, different from today. So after a while her father would start to tell ghost stories, which was the signal for me to leave. So I got on my bicycle and left "raining" [very fast].

Once a man had proven his serious intent in *namoro* and could show he was well on his way to establishing the financial and social maturity required to acquire a house, he formally asked the young woman's father for permission to *noivar*. In the past, *noivado* ("engagement") could last anywhere from one to twelve or more years. Today, it averages one to two years. Many young men still ask for formal permission to marry, and a courtship is considered serious if the man has visited the woman at home, meeting her parents.

Although sexual mores have loosened in cities, and the larger the city the greater the tendency, the idea that a woman's sexuality belongs to her father and brothers until they decide to give it to her husband or husband-to-be remains strong, at least among men. Secret courtships are still common, for many men do not want their daughters or sisters to court anyone, and because young people find them exciting. In these *namoros da esquina* ("street-corner romances"), couples sneak around corners to gain a few minutes of whispered togetherness before watchful family members catch up. If you wander around Caruaru neighborhoods at night, you will stumble over many such couples huddled in dark niches.[2]

Today, while people still practice the traditional *namoro* in some Northeastern rural areas, city dwellers have adopted more liberal practices, allowing young lovers greater freedom. The larger the city, the more liberal; in addition, Southern cities are more liberal than those of the

Northeast. Although *namorados* still tend to go out to entertainments in the company of siblings, cousins, and other couples, today's Caruaru *noivos* can go out alone together. Indeed, becoming officially engaged provides one *jeitinho* for a couple to get rid of their chaperoning entourage. A teenager explained:

To get engaged is just for the two to be able to go out alone, not necessarily to actually marry. Then you drop that one and get engaged to the next girlfriend or boyfriend, so people will leave you alone.

Namorados who are not engaged go out in groups with other young people. Sometimes they manage to combine with their companions to let them slip away for a little private getting to know one another. Although other young people may be sympathetic to the frustrations of chaperonage, they may also have interests in controlling young women (especially if they are the woman's brothers or rival potential suitors).

When couples slip away they might just go somewhere secluded for a private conversation. There are however establishments known as *motels* designed for the facilitation of sexual intercourse without public scrutiny. In Brazilian Portuguese, the English word *motel* is used exclusively to refer to these establishments,[3] where rooms can be rented by the hour and which often provide (at extra charge) such amenities as soft drinks, alcoholic beverages, and pornographic videos. The better quality establishments will have witticisms such as round beds and conveniences such as showers; the most expensive will have elaborate procedures of entrance and payment, including sliding panels and dumbwaiters, that allow the couple to avoid face-to-face interaction with the staff. Agostinho offered to enlighten me about these places:

Do you really want to know about *motels?* I can take you to one. We'll call it research. What is research without a little experimentation, hmm? In fact, to let you know what a great informant I am, I know all of them. We can take a grand tour. We'll visit every *motel* in Caruaru, and a few in the rural zone. And in exchange, well, we can work something out. In this one I know, you'll find this really interesting, so when you want to order a Coca-Cola or a video, write this down, or when you want to pay your tab and leave, there is a little cabinet in the room, built into the wall. And you open the cabinet and there are order forms and a plate, and you put your order and your money and ring a bell and slide the door closed, and then on the other side they open their little sliding door and take the money and all and then when they ring their bell you can open the door and there's your change and what you ordered or whatever. And it's a drive-in place where you go in in the car, and you ring this bell and it lights up showing you where to go and you drive there and go directly to the room from parking in front of it so they don't see you or anything. It's very classy. Most of them you have to check in with a clerk and they bring you whatever you want to the door, but the better ones are more private.

Parents of adolescent girls have good cause to worry about suitors' intentions. That, of course, is not unique to Brazil, as horny, callow youth are a legitimate worry for parents of nubile girls everywhere. But as we have seen, Brazilian men are often encouraged to be, and certainly can get away with being, sexually aggressive, and they derive status within their *turmas* from multiple sexual conquests. It is not uncommon for a young man to see how far he can get with the greatest number of girls, limited only by his skills at romancing them, their fathers' and brothers' skills at discouraging him, and his nerve—and not by any respect or affection for the targets of his attentions. This game is facilitated by the romantic illusions of young girls. One twenty-one-year-old man told me:

I arrived at the point of having five girlfriends at the same time. I felt pleasure in *namorando* with many women; I courted just to *namorar*. . . . I would be with a girl without even liking her, and when I saw that their love for me was very high, I simply abandoned them, went away. Today I see that this is a very wrong thing, because you shouldn't play with other people's feelings. But at the time, it was a lot of fun.

Moral accountability for sexual behavior still resides with women, and theirs is the responsibility to say no to sexual advances (cf. Goldstein 1994). A woman in her thirties explained:

It isn't enough for a girl who doesn't want to screw [*transar*] just to say no. Here in Brazil, especially in the Northeast, there is a very big division between good girls and sluts [*meninas bonitinhas e raparigas*]. So you have to be a chaste person, don't go to certain locales, don't dress in an indiscreet manner, don't say certain words, be easily embarrassed. You have to be the type of girl that everyone thinks will say no. You can't go showing yourself all around, flirting too much, and escape the boys.[4]

Many men adopt an ardent, insistent style of courtship, filled with dramatic declarations of adoration and romantic flourishes such as gift-giving (usually perfume or flowers) combined with smoldering appreciation of the hair, fingernails, clothing, and other physical attributes of the woman. But the pursuit's the thing, and a woman who allows herself to be taken in by impassioned appeals will soon be alone and dishonored. A man in his thirties reminisced:

When I saw a woman I liked, I had to have her. I worked at it and I worked at it until she went out with me. I talked with her, tried to know the things she liked, act as if I liked them. . . . I tried to encounter her by deliberate accident. I went gaining her confidence until I could *namorar* with her. So we courted hidden. Sometimes I saw her father watching, so I ended it, you know, fear of commitment. . . . In Brazil, the game of the Brazilian is *namoro*, he is with someone without commitment. . . . If a problem of commitment came up, I ended the relationship, I didn't go there anymore. . . . I simply abandoned her until she eventually understood that it had ended. . . . If I managed to score with her, so I screwed and screwed her as much as I could, and then I abandoned her because *namorada* and *rapariga* aren't the same thing.

Today young people have opportunities to mingle at public dances, dance halls, and cafés. Caruaru's central plaza, lined with open-air cafés, is sometimes called *Rua quem-me-quer* ("Who-wants-me Street") because of the groups of young people eyeing each other from table to table. Young people generally go out in groups and flirt across the tables. Occasionally a young man, egged on by wisecracking colleagues, will get up the courage to approach a woman and her giggling friends. A teenager explained his technique:

They say, "Go, go! Are you a man or a *frango* ["fag"; lit., "chicken"]?" So I go, and I say, it's called an ice-breaker [*quebra-gelo*]. I say: "I think I know you from somewhere." "What time is it?" or so I arrive saying, "How's it going? What's your name? Shall we dance?" Or, "Very pretty, your dress." You have to be very straight-faced [*cara-de-pau*, lit. "face-of-wood"], go right away arriving and talking. My eyes talk a lot, I am playing with the girl, and I use a subtle smile. . . . Generally here the man approaches the woman.

Some scholars believe that in Brazil the traditional *namoro* has been replaced by the *paquera* (which means both "flirt" and "brief, nonserious courtship"), but in the Northeast and especially in the interior, the traditional *namoro* persists (de Azevedo 1986, 2), although the *paquera* is gaining ground, especially in the cities.

Public dances afford young people some proximity. Caruaru calls itself the capital of *forró*, a couples' two-step. *Forró* is danced in a waltz position, but the couple are positioned much closer together than in the waltz, often with chests touching or nearly touching, and sometimes with the man's knee between the woman's knees. Watchful chaperones and gossipy neighbors pay close attention to how closely the dancers clutch and which arm position they choose, because the dance affords young people many chances for physical closeness. A teenage man explained:

Generally the man puts one hand on her waist and takes the other hand extended. But there are variations. If she likes him, she can put her arms around his neck. And he has both arms around her waist. So it's very delicious [*gostoso*] because she, leaning, has to stay with her breasts pushing on the man's chest. And the mothers, "Have shame!" There's another that doesn't use the hands at all. Both keep their hands behind their backs, and the man dances forward looking into her eyes, and her looking into his eyes, him advancing, her retreating. It's the sexiest thing. You don't have to actually make love in order to make love.

Dancers may try to *tirar uma sarra*, embracing closely and wiggling to the music so as to rub chests and crotches together in an exaggeration of the *forró*.[5] Couples may seek shadows at the periphery of the dance area or hide in the midst of the dancers, sometimes taking turns with collaborating couples in hiding one another's indiscretions from the watching crowd. If they are bold enough they may *tirar uma sarra* in the middle of the floor and say they were just dancing. With the introduction of the sexy *lambada, tirando uma sarra* in public is easier than ever.[6]

Especially in larger cities such as Recife, where the practice is associated with teenage use of shopping malls, today's young people have perfected the brief *namoro* or *paquera*, speaking of *ficando com* ("staying with") a partner rather than full-scale courtship. They spend afternoons or evenings hanging out in groups, hugging, and behaving like *namorados*, but the relationship does not necessarily last longer than a few days. A teenage woman told me: "A little kiss here or there doesn't mean anything serious. It's *ficando com* him only." Teenagers tend to go out in groups of ten or twelve, *ficando com* one group member one night, another the next, before settling on one for a serious *namoro*. This practice is very new and more common in Recife than in Caruaru (which had no shopping mall in 1990), and more common in Caruaru than in smaller towns.[7]

While some women marry their first *namorado*, especially in the smaller towns and rural areas, many women and most men today have a series of flirtations and *namoros* of varying intensity before settling on one that lasts longer and is more exclusive than previous ones. People consider a *namoro* serious from the moment it is made public, by the man's being introduced to the woman's parents as a suitor. While men may go through several *namoros*, they rarely break up once and for all with any given woman. Catrina, after watching a U.S. movie in which the boyfriend gave a lengthy and awkward breakup speech to his girlfriend, complained to me:

Men here in Brazil don't break up with women. They accumulate ex-*namoradas* is what they do, you know? At the time they break up, they disappear,
stay gone for some time, some months, because they are waiting for you to
stop being angry, for your broken heart to mend, as they say, you know?
Then they come back, hanging around. Maybe they have some *namorada* and
then they have some problem with her, *né*, so they leave her a little and come
back to you, not really serious, you know, but they forget the trouble and remember what they liked and they come around for a little comfort until they
feel like going back to her, *né*. That's why women don't like their *namorado's*
old *namoradas*, because he can always go back to them.

From a male point of view, revisiting a once-possessed woman is morally
different from a new conquest, in terms of their fidelity to their primary
relationship. Welingon, a married man in his late twenties, explained:

I'm faithful to my wife, yes. I've never been with any other woman since I met
her. Well, not counting Teresa, but that's another story. . . . I am and I'm not,
to tell the truth, because I married but I didn't die, as they say, you know. Because, she was my *namorada* before I met my wife, Teresa, so sometimes, if I
have a quarrel or something, because the woman, she has an intuition, you
know? She knows if I'm after someone else. So if she's mad at me, I can go
and visit Teresa, and it all starts, you know? Her friends tell her, my wife's,
maybe she sees something, hears something, smells something, so she wants
more closeness to me, you know, she comes back. Because even if you don't
like someone, then if you think you are going to lose them, then all of a sudden you have to have them. But it's not really cheating on her because it's not
like I'm looking for some new woman who I never, you know, before. It's just
Teresa, and I had Teresa before I even met my wife. Teresa has nothing to do
with my wife. She's not "the other woman." She's just Teresa.

While Welington's statement may be a self-serving rationalization,
part of a scheme to cheat on his wife without "really" cheating on her
while using his infidelity to manipulate her, it is also more than simply
that. Although marriage or cohabitation are the public markers of a permanent sexual relationship, *namoro*, however brief, creates a link between
people, however tenuous. This relationship can be resumed, intensified,
temporarily ignored, calmed down, heated up, modified in many ways,
but it is rarely entirely or permanently abandoned. An officially recognized *namoro* can also create relationships among women that may outlast
the sexual relationship, as when an ex-*namorada* maintains ties with her
ex-*namorado's* mother, sisters, or other female relatives.

Many lower-class romances do not culminate in formal engagement or
marriage. But some *namoros* move on to *noivado*. In the upper classes and
in popular mass media such as soap operas and movies, *noivado* is marked

by the man's giving a ring, especially one with a diamond or other pre-
cious stone, to the woman as a down payment on the promise to wed.
However, among the poor, the working class, and the lower middle
classes, such an extravagance is extremely rare. There, *noivado* is marked
by the couple's telling people that they are now engaged, often after a
formal request for permission to become engaged has been accepted by
the *noiva*'s father. Once a couple are formally engaged, they have some
years to plan how they are going to get married, if in fact that is their intent.

Marriage

Marriage may be described as a legal relationship between two (or more)
people who, by the rituals prescribed in their cultures, gain rights over one
another, including rights to sexual access and economic sharing, and
rights over children resulting from their sexual union. In Brazil, as in
similar areas of the Caribbean and other parts of the world, many couples
who live together and refer to one another by kinship terms usually re-
served for spouses are not, in fact, legally married. These types of cohabitation may reflect an ideological resistance to state or church control over
sexual alliances. But often such cohabitation indicates a desire to marry on
the part of one partner combined with a failure to convince the other.
Couples may cohabit to see if *se vai dar* ("it will work out"), or at least pretend to one another that there are intentions in the union nobler than those
of convenience, sexual attraction, or the need to get one's laundry done.

Legal marriage forms the model for cohabitation, which in Brazil is a
form of "as if" marriage, lower in status than legal matrimony. The lesser
status of cohabitation, the definition of female-headed households as deviant, the moral condemnation of men who float among the houses of
various girlfriends but marry none—all reflect the higher status of legal
marriage and cannot be understood without reference to it.

It is possible, and certainly commonly done, to discuss marriage without reference to sentiment. It is also possible, and commonly done, to
transact marriages as seals of alliance, forms of property transfer, and legal transactions. The personal experiences of the conjugals, especially the
woman, in terms of their sexuality and sentiment may be officially irrelevant except as they relate to legal obligations such as rights over sexual access or the production and rearing of children. But sentiment and sexual
practice make up the day-to-day lived experience of marriage and strong-

ly influence the success or failure of particular marriages. While it is possible to discuss social, legal, and economic aspects of marriage without reference to sentiment, it is not possible to discuss sentimental aspects of marriage without the broader context to which the sentiments respond. We begin, therefore, with legal technicalities.

Civil and Religious Regulation of Marriage

Marriage is more than a formal charter of a sexual union, involving also the creation of kinship ties among families, recognition of filiation of children, and rights over property and labor. Marriage brings together two genders, attempting to fuse their differing roles and perspectives into a complementary whole. Marriage also makes kin of the unrelated, or reformulates the kinship relationships of already related people. In Western cultures, marriage forms an economic and social partnership with specific rights and obligations laid out in a legal code.

In Brazil, these rights and obligations have changed over time, as one legal code has replaced another. Love has historically been an expectation of marriage, although increasingly its timing has shifted from after marriage to prior to it. People speak of love even in arranged marriages because, by creating legal kinship, marriage endows erstwhile strangers with affective obligations. Gender and economic relations, emotion roles, and sexuality come together in marriage under the gloss of love.

Current legal and customary aspects of marriage in Brazil have grown out of and continue to be influenced by the history of religious and civil regulation. Laws delineate how marriage may be initiated and dissolved, and regulate spousal responsibilities. Often, marriage is regulated by religious as well as civil authorities. In Brazil, Catholic doctrines have had a strong influence on marriage, even though current Brazilian law does not recognize religious marriage as legally binding.

Current Catholic doctrine on marriage originates in the proclamations of the Council of Trent (1545–63), which reformulated Catholic doctrinal rules on marriage in a series of controversial proclamations, not all of which were accepted by the Portuguese civil authorities. Portuguese interpretation of Tridentine rules became the law in colonial Brazil, formalized in 1707 in the *Constituções primeiras do Arcebispado da Bahia* (Lavrin 1989, 7). Under these rules, betrothal publicly announced constituted an unconsummated marriage, and if it became publicly known that the couple had had sexual intercourse while engaged but before a formal public marriage ceremony had taken place, the marriage was considered consummated and permanent. Breaking an unconsummated engagement seriously compromised a woman's ability to contract further marriages. No divorce was permitted, although there were forms of juridical separation with no possibility of legitimate remarriage while the spouse remained living.

In addition, Tridentine rules mandated mutual consent for marriage: No one could be forced to marry against his or her will (Lavrin 1989, 5–6). This idea was very controversial and widely resisted or ignored by civil authorities. The concept of will was a theological point in contention between Catholics and Protestants at the time of the Council of Trent. Affirming the necessity of consent to marriage was part of the Catholic Church's insistence that marriage is a sacrament, best adjudicated by the Church; it also affirmed the Church's position that free will, and therefore personal behavior, are more important to salvation than predestination and faith, as Protestants claimed (Seed 1988, 33).[8]

Through its insistence on consent, the Church recognized the right of conjugals to defy parental edicts, and in some cases local priests sheltered runaway lovers, protecting them from their parents until they could be formally married. The consent edict privileged the desires of young people over the social and economic interests of parents in their offspring's alliances. The Church's reasoning came from its philosophy on the nature of free will as part of salvation, not from any sentimentality over the beauty of romantic passion or from approval of sexual attraction. That Tridentine rules had the effect of empowering young women and men to act on sexual attractions represents a side effect of Church fathers' broader interest in the nature of human moral being.

The idea that a young person, especially a young woman, would defy her parents' wishes in as important a matter as marriage was difficult to swallow. Parents acted to constrain defiance, often abetted by civil regulation. For example, Portuguese king Don Manuel, in defiance of Tridentine edicts, permitted parents to disinherit a daughter who married against their will (Lavrin 1989, 5–6), and parents also used chaperonage, confinement, and in some cases the threat or application of physical punishment to keep young lovers in line.[9] Brazilian law followed the example of Portuguese law, both in the matter of marital choice and in the status of women within marriage.

Until the mid-twentieth century, Brazilian law viewed women as subsidiary to their husbands both socially and economically. However, in

1962, Law 4.121 abolished a married woman's need for her husband's permission to inherit property or use a bank account. For the first time, women could own property in their own names, rather than relying on fathers, brothers, or husbands. The language of description was also changed, and women became economic "collaborators" (*colaboradoras*) instead of merely "auxiliaries" (*auxiliárias*) of their husbands, as under earlier legal codes.

This was a necessary first step toward an even more revolutionary change. On December 26, 1977, Law 6.515, known as the "divorce law," permitted civil divorce for the first time in Brazilian history.[10] The divorce law also set up possible variations in the economic relationship of man and wife, adding to *comunhão universál de bens* ["universal union of property"], by which all property held by conjugals was held jointly and under the jurisdiction of the man, *comunhão parcial de bens* ["partial union of property"], in which conjugals could hold property separately under specified circumstances, as well as *separação de bens,* in which property was held separately.[11] In addition, the new law provided inheritance rights for all offspring of the man, whether conceived within the current marriage, from previous marriages, or outside of marriage (Varela 1980, 1–3). Laws continue to regard men as the head of household, responsible for the material sustenance of the family, and women as the family's moral center and secondary leader.

The woman, with marriage, assumes the condition of companion, consort, and collaborator of the husband in the responsibilities of family, fulfilling them by overseeing the material and moral direction of it. (Brazilian Civil Code, Article 240; my translation)

The minimum age for marriage is sixteen years for women and eighteen years for men, with parental consent, or twenty-one years without consent (Rocha 1980, 23). This law is not enforced, however, and neither is birth registry, making legal age manipulable. That fact became clear to me when I set out to determine the average age at marriage in Caruaru by examining the records in local civil registries. My findings were very peculiar. An examination of the 1984 civil marriage registers showed that 50.7 percent of men and 67.2 percent of women were officially less than fifteen years old at the time of marriage. Moreover, 10.8 percent of women were officially only seven years old at marriage.

This finding does not reflect any widespread practice of child marriage in the region. Rather, it reflects the bureaucratic opinion that a person's age is the amount of time lapsed since the birth registration, com-

bined with lax enforcement of birth registries. Many parents do not register children until there is some need to do so, such as entry into school or
the extension of a parent's work benefits to the child.[12] If a child is six or
seven years old at the time of registration, his or her official age will be six
or seven years less than his or her chronological age.

Although the registrars take their duties seriously, carefully maintaining records of births, marriages, and deaths in voluminous and dusty
files, civil registries do not reveal who was born when, who is living with
whom, who is having sexual relations with whom, who is the father of
whose child, or who is supporting whom economically. In fact, they reveal
very little about familial, sexual, and economic relations in Brazil. Once
again, official story and lived experience diverge.

Civil laws and religious authorities support the legally married, monogamous nuclear family in modern Brazil. This does not mean, however,
that such pairings are the norm in all classes. Fornication and adulterous
unions are not protected by law,[13] nor are they praised by religious
authorities, encouraged by doctors, or used as markers of status by parents—although they are both common and important in determining
membership in social networks. Sometimes elopements, illicit love affairs,
adulterous unions, and common-law alliances are the result of human
weakness, sexual exploitation, or economic necessity. Sometimes they are
rebellions against authority, a way of expressing lust, independence, or
love in a repressive society. Some people prefer illicit to legal unions because they regard them as freer or less troublesome. Always such unions
are strongly marked by class and history.

Marriage in Caruaru: The Official Story

Marriage customs and sexual mores have changed in Caruaru, especially
in the urban area, although it is more a change in frequency among types
of conjugal alliances than a massive social innovation. People said that, in
the recent past and still in rural areas, marriage most commonly took
place between young women of twelve to eighteen years of age and men
in their mid to late twenties or early thirties. The couple were engaged for
four or more years before marriage and frequently were first cousins.[14] A
man needed a woman's father's permission to court and marry her. The
marriage was celebrated when the couple had accumulated the material
requirements: The man provided a house and furnishings, the woman,
pots, dishes, and sheets. Occasionally a couple were forced by economic

circumstances to live with one set of parents after marriage, but the ideal and norm was neolocality.

A husband's responsibilities included maintaining the house, providing food, and protecting his family from physical and social harm. A wife cleaned house and washed laundry, cooked, bore and raised children, and upheld the family honor through her monogamous chastity. While men did not need to be sexually faithful, they were expected to be discreet. Courtesy was the rule between husband and wife, and many older couples still address each other as *senhor* and *senhora* after decades of marriage. One elderly farmer summed up marital courtesy:

A woman is like a cow. If you want the cow's milk, you can't beat her, yell at her, no. You have to treat her with tenderness and care for her to give you her milk. With a woman it is the same thing. ... You have to choose a good woman, respectable, and treat her well. That way it works out.[15]

To say that marriages in the past were arranged is not to say that all parents had control over marital choice, and to say that young people today arrange their own marriages is not to say that young men and women have equal say in deciding whom they will marry. In some cases in the past, especially in the upper classes, where property concerns were important, parents, especially fathers, preferred to choose their sons-in-law, and careful chaperonage of young upper-class women gave them few opportunities to meet inappropriate young men. Lower-class parents, however, were less able to maintain their daughters in near total seclusion, and issues such as dowries and inheritances were less likely to intrude. In some cases in the past, and in some cases today, young people choose while relying on their parents' advice. In many cases young men have greater freedom both to meet prospective brides and to contract engagements with the fathers of their fiancées. When a young man arranges with a father to marry his daughter, it is not clear whether the marriage is a love match or an arranged marriage: From the point of view of the bride, there may be little difference.

In the past, resistance to parental control over marital choice could take the form of elopement and attempted elopement, as well as legal cases in which young people sued for the right to marry. Resistance could also take the form of covert courtships (whether consummated or not), even after dutiful marriage to a parent's choice (de Azevedo 1986, 7). This option was more open to men than to women.

Age at Marriage

While they do not marry as shockingly young as official records would seem to indicate, Caruaruenses do tend to marry or pair off young. Girls start to be considered marriageable at about twelve years of age, and a never-paired woman of twenty-five may consider herself an old maid. Age at marriage is slightly lower in small towns than in Caruaru. In addition, my older respondents had married at a younger age than had my younger ones.

In these little towns, like Toritama, girls of twelve years are all women already,[16] all already married or *amigado* [cohabiting with a man]. I myself started living together at thirteen years, had my son at fourteen. (Fátima)

Older unmarried women are called *titias* ("aunties"), *moças velhas* ("old maids"), or *coroas* ("crowns").[17] It is not a coveted status, and some women grasp at any chance to get married to avoid it.

The woman carries a fantasy, that "if I don't marry him, I will be [nothing but] an auntie, I will be a *coroa*," isn't it? So whoever appears and says, "Do you want to marry me?" she immediately says, "I want to." (Bárbara)

Old maid status, or the fear of it, can lead some women to make otherwise unattractive matches. One man, adopted by a family of German descent but himself very dark in complexion, married a woman of much less African appearance than himself. He told me that he felt very lucky to be marrying such a woman, whose light skin color made her beautiful in his eyes, saying he knew that she did not love him and was afraid that he would give her dark children. However, the minister of their Seventh-Day Adventist congregation had spoken to them, pointing out that each had good points and bad points. The strikes against her in the marriage market: She was already twenty-five, and, having been orphaned as a child and adopted as a maid,[18] had a compromised honor and few material resources to bring into a match. If the man would overlook her age and status, and she would overlook his color, they could make a good match, because both were hard working and God fearing. Indeed, the man, although not highly educated, was fluent in English, Spanish, German, and French, as well as his native Portuguese.[19] They did eventually marry, not with love, but with the hope of eventually attaining it. Sometimes such couples do learn to love one another, but often they do not.

I don't know what love is. I never felt love. Because I was twenty-four years old and I thought that I was very old, that no one would want me anymore, that I was "on the cart" [*na caroça*, "an old maid"] and it would be a long time for me to find another . . . and I never was impassioned for anyone, nor for him. What I felt was pity [*pena*], pity for him because he wanted me so much and pity for myself because I was becoming a *coroa*. (Emília)

Husbands are properly older than wives, and many men are several years older than their young brides. Some men deliberately seek out much younger women to marry.

When I was a young man, I traveled a lot. I was handsome, and there were lots of girls wanting to marry me. But I married Dona Maria, do you know why? Because she was very young, twelve years old, very young, very naive, and very stupid. So I thought that I could train her to be the wife I wanted. So with patience, I raised her, so today even though she's not a pretty woman, she is a faithful wife, works well, and is the mother of my children, takes good care of them. So I'm content. (Natalino)

Not all women prove as tractable as Dona Maria, however. Women's status increases with age and motherhood. In addition, as they weather their husbands' infidelities, rudeness, petty cruelties, or in some cases emotional or physical abuse, any idealization they might have once felt fades.

When I completed twenty years I wanted to give my shout of liberty, because from fourteen to twenty, I had learned many things. . . . I wasn't anymore that idiot who put up with everything, you know? Everything the others wanted to do to me I thought was right. Afterward I learned that it isn't like that, that you don't live by love, that love is an illusion. (Fátima)

While some couples still follow the script of *namoro-noivado-casamento*, many engage in other forms of union. Cohabitation without formal marriage is especially common among the lower classes. In addition, particular matches may meet resistance from various quarters. Where parents resist a match, couples may use elopement to obtain independence. Where a couple (or one member of it) resists formalizing their union, parents and other family members try to find a way to bring about a legal marriage if they suspect a sexual relationship already exists or is imminent. As one young man joked, men in small towns marry *por seu livre espontânea pressão social* ("of their free and spontaneous social pressure").

Religious Wedding Ceremonies

There are a variety of ways to get married in modern Brazil. Wedding customs tend to be retained when they give economic advantages to newlyweds or increase family status (Brandes 1973, 74). Religious wedding ceremonies are a status item in Brazil but have no legal effect because, since the promulgation of Decree 181 in the 1890s, religious leaders have not been endowed with the legal right to form such unions. In 1934, Article 146 of the new national constitution softened the law: Marriage remained civil, but religious ceremonies were allowed as gratuitous celebrations, provided that the couple fulfilled civil requirements. Law Number 1.110 of 1950 allowed religious marriage ceremonies to be registered civilly. The couple still had to fill out civil forms and pay civil fees, but linking religious and civil records meant that men could no longer marry one woman in a religious ceremony and another in a legal ceremony. The Divorce Law of 1977, by allowing divorce, which is not permitted in Catholic religious marriage, firmly established that religious ceremonies merely celebrate a civilly defined and regulated marriage (Varela 1980, 32–33). Some older couples from rural areas were married in religious ceremonies without civil registration, but today's young people do not have that option.

Older, rural couples described simple religious ceremonies. The couple and guests dressed in their Sunday best, but there was no strong tradition of special wedding garb for the couple. The bride was picked up at her father's house by an ox-cart (the expression "the ox-cart is coming" still means a wedding is imminent). At the church the union was blessed during a special Mass, and the whole event was followed by a meal sponsored by the parents of the bride. Afterward the couple retired together to their new home and began their life as married people.

Members of the community often gave presents to the bride and groom, usually useful items such as dishes or towels for the home. Contributions to the new couple also included services, such as labor for building their house, but in hard times or modest circumstances gifts were not required. One woman, celebrating her fiftieth wedding anniversary in 1989,[20] told me, as she stood looking at a bed full of gifts from her children and grandchildren: "When I married half a century ago, the only gift I got was the groom!"

Today religious wedding ceremonies are more elaborate, reflecting their nature as more a status item than a sacrament.[21] Religious wedding ceremonies vary by denomination but generally follow the pattern of the Victorian white wedding. Formal clothing may be specially made for the occasion, but both male and female wedding attire can be rented from wedding emporiums. This includes the bride's wedding gown and groom's tuxedo, attendant dresses and suits, and clothing for the flower girl and ring bearer as well as dresses for the mother of the bride and mother of the groom.

The status-conscious bride arrives late, in a rented limousine, and waits outside while the godparents (*madrinhas e padrinhos*), witnesses (*testemunhos*—the equivalent would be called bridesmaids and ushers in English), and flower girl parade down the church's main aisle and take their places either in parallel rows lining the aisle or on either side of the altar.[22] The later the arrival of the bride the more status she gains, partly because her reluctance to wed bespeaks a properly timorous and maidenly spirit and partly because her lateness shows her power to make everyone wait.

My friend was very chic. She was almost an hour late, everyone waiting. Everyone there waiting, waiting, so she enters with a beautiful dress, all done up, flowers in her hair, all made up [*pintado*]. It was the max [*o máximo*]! You have to do it just that way. (Bárbara)

The guests rise when the bride makes her dramatic entrance, escorted by her father. Rented bridal gowns are very elaborate, often featuring beading, embroidery, lace, and flounces with accompanying beaded headdresses with attached veils. The father hands the bride to the groom, the priest or minister makes a speech, usually about the saving power of love and the necessity for the couple to be sexually faithful, after which the couple take their wedding vows to love and honor one another. They place wedding rings on each other's ring finger and sign the marriage contract along with the godparents, the witnesses, and the priest or minister. The priest or minister does not proclaim the couple husband and wife, because he lacks the legal authority to do so. If the couple can afford it, they can pay a civil registrar to come to the religious ceremony and legalize it; otherwise they have to go to a civil ceremony whenever it is scheduled, along with all other couples marrying that day, to register their union.

A party follows the ceremony, featuring food (usually hors d'oeuvres but in wealthier families and older times a meal). Some weddings are followed by music and dancing, but many are not. Protestants regard dancing as sinful, and many couples cannot afford to hire a band or play records.[23] At the reception a professional photographer takes pictures of the couple and participants. Standard pictures include shots with family members and attendants as well as scenes of the couple cutting the cake,[24] drinking out of champagne glasses with linked arms, and sitting among their gifts, which are displayed on a bed or couch in a nearby home. Gifts usually include household items such as dishes, pots and pans, towels, decorative items, and clothing, especially sexy underwear and sleep wear for brides. Some better-off urban couples hold a *chá de panela* ("wedding shower," literally "pan tea") at which the bride's friends give her gifts while the groom is entertained by his *turma* at a raucous party. These events are recent innovations and very rare among the lower classes.

The importance of wedding photos cannot be overestimated. Even Protestants, who don't drink, will pose with empty champagne glasses or with glasses filled with soda pop. At one wedding I attended the photographer never showed up, and the bride refused to leave the rental car or enter the church. When I mentioned the camera in my pocket, I was pressed into service. The batteries were low, but the minister paused in the service after each photograph until the ready light on the flash attachment came on and they could proceed, secure in the knowledge that the proper images were being preserved for posterity.[25] The emphasis on photographs derives from the importance of the wedding as a status event.[26] People proudly frame wedding photos and display them in the houses of the couple and their parents.[27]

I wanted to marry only in the church. . . . "Never," I said to Mama, "will I marry in the civil," because my dream was in the church. If I marry in the civil I would prefer to *amigar* ["live together"] because it's a graceless thing, isn't it? . . . I think that if I had eloped with him before, I think that I would have regretted it. . . . And he agreed. He said, "I'm going to show everyone in my family that I am a man, and I am going to marry only as a bridegroom." . . . My mother was very happy because my sister eloped, and my brother didn't marry, he lives together [*amigou*], so she really wanted that a daughter of hers marry, so it was I, the youngest, who gave this to her as a present. (Araruna)

A religious wedding, properly performed after a publicly announced and parent-approved engagement, may be an ideal, but few live up to it. Among those legally married, a civil ceremony unaccompanied by religious blessing is much more common.

Civil Marriage

Because of the cost of religious wedding ceremonies, and the fact that they are not legally binding, many couples opt for the less expensive civil ceremony, which is very simple. Couples in and around Caruaru first apply for licenses at civil registries and have their witnesses approved. They are then assigned a wedding date and appear with all other couples marrying that day, usually in ordinary street clothes. Weddings are usually performed twice a month. Each couple lines up with the other couples, their two official witnesses lining up with the other witnesses, and they all go into the designated room as a group. The judge appears, asks them as a group if they consent, and, raising their right hands, they all say, "Yes," in unison. At one civil wedding I attended the judge said, "Okay. You all know the question and it is just to say yes or no in accordance with your case."[28] Everyone laughed, said yes, and were married. At another, he said, "Okay. Let's go, yes or no?" In neither case was the legally required consent question actually stated in the official words. After the question and response the judge leaves and the registrar calls each couple in turn to sign the register, along with their witnesses, and to pay the fee.

Although legally more important than religious marriage, civil marriage does not convey the status of a religious ceremony.

So his family always said that I was a poor *nega*,[29] that I was no good. They always tormented me a lot, thinking themselves better. So, when we married, so when the judge was calling the people, I found out that my sister-in-law was marrying at the same time. . . . I thought it was great that she was marrying like she married, and not even her family accompanied her to the wedding. She was always saying that she was so chic, so superior, but she had to marry in the civil like poor people. I greeted her politely but inside I was laughing. (Fátima)

Some people dress up civil ceremonies, either by wearing formal clothing during the brief ceremony or by holding a small party at home afterward. Some Protestant sects do not permit their members to marry without a religious ceremony, although the Catholic Church is more lenient.

Marrying by Sledgehammer or by Theft

In the interior, butchers slaughter large animals with blows to the head from a sledgehammer. Men who have sex with virgins they do not intend to marry may find themselves threatened with a similar fate.

Everyone in the interior uses "sledgehammer wedding" [*casamento na marra*], *né*, if the guy [*rapaz*] messes with the virgin [*moça*], takes her virginity before she's old enough to marry, or if they "steal" [*rouba*] her, *né*, like they say, the girl's parents obligate the guy to marry by whatever manner. Take the virginity, have to marry. (Severina)

Marriage *na marra* ("by the sledgehammer") is the customary salve for family honor when faced with loss of a daughter's virginity. Although it forms part of the stereotype of the hillbilly (*matuto*), it is not confined to rural areas. Today, reluctant bridegrooms less commonly face threats of physical violence than they did in the past, but their girlfriend's parents or interested others may try to shame them into formalizing their union, and they may face social ostracism or loss of economic opportunities if disappointed prospective in-laws have enough pull to arrange such sanctions.

Occasionally parents can engage civil authorities to pressure a reluctant bridegroom, especially if the girl is underage. In one forced marriage of this type that I witnessed in Caruaru, the police chief sent out his officers to arrest the man and bring him in with his girlfriend and his parents to meet the girl's parents, who were already at the station. The chief then stood the accused man in front of everybody and let the girl's parents present their case, which the man's parents did not dispute. The chief then delivered a lecture on respect, honor, and the importance of love in a Christian society. He repeatedly told the blushing accused to stop hanging his head and stammering, and to answer like a man: "Had he or had he not courted this girl? Was she or was she not a virgin when the courtship started, and was she or was she not a virgin now?" Since the man was not already married, the chief told him there was a choice. He could look his girlfriend in the eyes and, in front of everybody, say that he did not love her and had been interested only in sex, that his promises had been lies, and that he was a dishonorable lout, and then go to jail for statutory rape. Or he could wait in a holding cell while papers were processed at a civil registry and then be escorted by police guard to a civil wedding ceremony.

In this particular case, the man, a skinny, cross-eyed fellow in his midthirties, agreed to marry his fifteen-year-old paramour. The chief told me that if the man had already been married, he would have been fined and probably jailed for some time on charges of statutory rape.

This kind of personal justice can be obtained only in cases where the local police chief happens to be interested in pursuing it on behalf of the outraged parents.[30] Forced marriage may satisfy the requirements of family honor, but it can also lead to great pain.

Before we married . . . I had relations with her before time, I shouldn't have done this, she was a virgin. . . . So I explained to her that it wouldn't work out . . . that I didn't love her, that we wouldn't be happy . . . but even so she didn't want to understand. . . . She liked me too much. . . . She was a virgin and her father insisted, *casamento na marra*, but I don't accept this marriage because . . . one mistake doesn't fix another. So I live the same life I always led, courting here, courting there. . . . Do you know when I kiss my wife? New Year's Day only. . . . It's that climate, I passed two days at home without speaking to the woman, little house, me and the woman, a four-month-old boy and a two-year-old girl. So what she wants to tell me she sends by way of the girl, my God in heaven! I wanted to marry for love and be faithful but it did not work out that way. (Donizete)

Although stereotypically the pressure to perform a *casamento na marra* comes from the bride's parents, in practice a young woman can use her father's outrage to force her boyfriend to marry her while acting as though she were passively carried along by events. Alternatively, a man rejected by a particular family may use rape to force both parents and reluctant bride to perform a marriage so as to retain their honor, while the man pretends that it is he who is being forced. Or a couple may conspire to reveal the loss of virginity and oblige parents to accept their wedding in what may be called a *fuga* ("elopement") or *rouba* ("theft"), depending on one's point of view. Pregnancy typically spurs marriage.[31]

In some areas, nearly all marriages and cohabitations begin with a *fuga*. A *fuga* sometimes literally involves running away together, but more commonly it consists of making the bride's loss of virginity public, often by the couple's going to some friend's or relative's house and sleeping there (not necessarily together), after which the parents supposedly cannot refuse the union. They may, however, refuse to speak to the couple for several years. It is also possible to *fugir* ("elope") in one's own home. For example, Fátima, who had been adopted by Maria do Rosário, infuriated her mother by carrying on a courtship with a man whom Maria do Rosário regarded as not good enough for her daughter. Fátima told me that she had eloped with Jõao Batista, although she never left her mother's house to do so:

He was eighteen, I was thirteen. . . . I was engaged to some guy that Mama arranged, but I wanted Jõao Batista. So, Mama didn't want him, *né:* "You won't marry him, he doesn't have anything to give you." Because my fiancé was hard working, a good man, deathly boring. And Jõao Batista already had a reputation, he was exciting. And my fiancé was in Rio working to earn money for our wedding, an older man, in his twenties. . . . Mama always prayed the Ave Maria at six in the evening when it comes on the radio. And me in the kitchen doing my school homework. So she started to pray in the bedroom and he entered by the kitchen window, and I lifted my skirt, and well, we went screwing [*transando*] here on the table and her praying there inside. There's no doors inside this house, no! Just a curtain. She was very deaf, saying, "Fátima! What's that noise!" Me saying, "Mama, I'm studying! I'm studying!" I didn't say what I was studying! . . . So everyone commented, *né*, that they thought we were "husband and wife" . . . but she didn't pay any attention. The people said: "If you ambush them, *Senhora*, you'll catch them there." So she said that she was going to the *sítio* to visit my sister. . . . I put on the record player very loud, and I sent him a message at his work where he was. So then he arrived, and we went to bed. Finally, a real bed, not a table! All of a sudden, she was right there at the door! She saw him come here and us shut the door. *Ô minha nossa Senhora!*[32] She beat on the door, beat on it. I didn't open it. I told him to hide himself but he was going to confront her, come what God wanted.

So Mama ordered a boy to jump over the *quintal* wall and see who was here inside. And everybody outside there on the street . . . so, when he entered, he shouted, "She's with her boyfriend and she's only wearing underpants!" What shame [*que vergonha!*]. . . . So that way I got pregnant with Uáxintô. My fiancé said he was willing to overlook the affair and marry me anyway, but I did not want to marry him. I loved Jõao Batista. Then when my brother-in-law was murdered soon after that, Mama went to live with my sister and Jõao Batista moved in here. And we stayed living here until we married seven years later. Oh, but Mama was angry! That's how I eloped without ever leaving my mother's house. (Fátima)

Couples may *fugir* to avoid the cost of legal marriage (cf. Gnaccarini 1989). In some areas, elopement is more common than any other form of marriage.

I fell in the nonsense and eloped. He took me to another house, you know? And from the other house, we left to go marry. . . . My parents wanted us to marry regular but the majority of the girls of this world elope. I think it's because they don't have conditions to make a marriage like it's supposed to be made, *né*? So I think you elope to marry, like, you don't have to have all the preparations that a bride needs. Because of poverty. (Branquinha)

Some couples elope to escape controlling parents, or because a father refuses to give his daughter's hand.

I was twelve years old . . . he asked to marry me, my father did not consent. . . . He went to Rio de Janeiro. Sometimes he wrote to a friend of his here, who spoke to me. . . . So by way of the friend, we combined to elope. It was 11:30

at night, he came back, communicated with the friend ... and we prepared and we eloped. I climbed out a window, just like in the stories.

We went ... to São Paulo, lived eight years there. ... If it had depended on Mama we would have married correctly. But my father ... he wasn't very affectionate with me, but he was very jealous with me. ... He didn't want me to marry because of the jealousy he felt. ... I was his only girl, the youngest. I never saw Papa again. He died angry with me, and my father-in-law never spoke to me as long as he lived. I came back only when they were dead, and even then it took so much work for his mother and my own mother to speak to me. I had to sneak to the back door to speak to her, and she wouldn't open it, only whisper through it. She wouldn't look at me or see my children. I cannot tell you the pain I felt and still feel about this. My father never saw my children and died with anger in his heart for me, who had been his favorite. (Sílvia)

Some *fugas* result in happy marriages. But often, when a young girl elopes with a man after a brief acquaintance, she is not acting on the basis of a realistic evaluation of her situation but rather on a combination of youthful resentment of parental constraints and romantic fantasies. She may find to her horror that her new situation is much worse than her old, but she can never go back.

I had never seen this man ... and when we saw each other, I don't know what it was that happened, ... if it was love at first sight or what it was ... but after one week I eloped with him, went to live with him. ... It was bad because I didn't know him, it was, like, a sudden thing. We didn't even *namorar*. It was horrible for me. ... It was like a prison, because I didn't even know the guy ... didn't know his inside. ... At home I didn't live imprisoned, I had other boyfriends who invited me to elope, and I didn't elope, no, I had to elope with a married man separated from his wife, but he didn't tell me until later. ... My mother didn't like it, her dream and my father's was that we children would leave in wedding dress from home, like poor people but well married, with legal papers. But I had to do this, and have his children besides! (Flávia)

Men know that teenage and preteenage girls are vulnerable to the glamour of attention from an older man. If a man is unscrupulous he may stage a *fuga* as a *jeitinho* to get a young woman into bed and then abandon her. If he is not local, she may not know that he is already married somewhere else.

You see that girl over there? That one is an idiot woman who ran away with a guy. He slept with her for two days, later said that he was already married. So pronto, disgrace. It happens a lot. (Maria da Paz)

Or a man may simply be unwilling to legalize a relationship, and once a

young woman is already publicly known to be living with him, she has
little leverage to force a *casamento na marra*.

The use of a *fuga* to force parents to accede to a marriage works only if
the parents have strong feelings about a daughter's honor and if the
daughter's public reputation is intact. If the parents do not feel that way,
they may still oppose a marriage after a *fuga* has taken place. This is easier
in Caruaru and larger cities than in smaller towns, where virginity is still
very important. One Caruaruense woman, whose underage daughter had
run away with an unemployed man and had then tried to get her mother
(who was a widow) to pay for an apartment, told me:

It won't work. I am not going to marry her to him. . . . Never, a lazy man like
that, for me to have to sustain the both of them. If tomorrow it doesn't work
out, she will be alone and will confront her life. Work. I don't care about her
virginity if I have to pay for it. (Toinha)

But more frequently a *fuga* ends in marriage or cohabitation.

Separation

Under the 1977 Divorce Law, divorcing couples must have been married
at least two years and must undergo legal separation, either by mutual
consent or court order (Rocha 1980, 122). Legally recognized reasons for
judicial separation include dishonorable conduct; violation of the obligations of marriage, including infidelity, abandonment of the home, and
physical or verbal aggression; noncohabitation for five consecutive years;
and incurable mental illness. After three years of legal separation, a couple
may apply for a divorce (Rocha 1980, 130–32). The law also allows annul-
ment of marriages if one of the partners was legally ineligible to marry at
the time the marriage was performed (Varela 1980, 20).

Lower-class couples, with less property to divide, are unlikely to get
official separations or divorces unless one of the partners wishes to marry
again. After a failed marriage the former spouses may return to live with
relatives or live *amigado* with a new partner. This arrangement is very
common; in taking life histories I had to ask not only whether people were
married but also whether the person they presently lived with was their
legal spouse. No data on the rate of divorce and separation are available,
but from my sample it appears to be very high. Certainly many people believed that the rate of broken marriages is higher nowadays than in the
past. Not all thought this a bad thing.

Separation is better than our mothers' suffering life of putting up with stuff. (Rosabela)

Without easy access to divorce, separated individuals may start new relationships without the ability to legalize them. This is only one of several reasons why cohabitation without formal ceremony is also common. Cohabitation is similar to marriage; it may follow a courtship or *fuga*, but it is neither religiously blessed nor legally protected. The reasons why couples may opt to cohabit without marrying are complex.

O Amasiamento, or Living Together

The term *o amasiamento* refers to living together maritally but without legalizing the union.[33] In some neighborhoods, such unions are the norm. Indeed, in the countryside of the recent past many couples' unions were socially recognized as marriage, culminated a formal courtship, or marked the initiation of a formal courtship, including such ceremonies as a fetching by ox-cart or a party at the new house, but were not licensed or ritually marked by either church or state. The prevalence of nonlegalized unions reflects both historical and contemporary conditions. Among the legacies of slavery is the exclusion of large portions of the population from legal marriage. In addition, the history of popular resistance to church and state regulation of sexual behavior goes far back in European popular practice, a resistance continued by the American offspring of European settlers. In addition, contemporary social and economic conditions discourage men from marrying. Those poor women who wish to legalize or bless their unions often find it difficult to convince their men to acquiesce in a milieu in which legal marriage holds little status for men—indeed in which legal marriage may appear to be a submission to feminine wiles harmful to a man's independent reputation. And both men and women may find social and economic reasons to eschew legal marriage.

In newspaper accounts, a cohabiting man is called the *companheiro* ["companion"] of his female *companheira*, but in speech, unmarried couples tend to refer to each other as *o meu marido* ["my husband"] or *a minha mulher* ["my woman"], just as married couples do. But the marriage is a social fiction, and as such more vulnerable to challenge than a legal marriage. It is harder to be *amigado* without social ostracism in small towns than in larger cities. In general, the larger the city, the more *favela* the neighborhood, the higher the percentage of *amigado* couples and the less social challenge to their legitimacy.

It is very difficult to tell which couples are legally married and which
are not, unless a couple has wedding pictures displayed. And many legally married couples, having had a civil wedding, do not have photos.
While some openly admit that they are not married, more find it a source
of shame. When I would ask to see a wedding certificate, interviewees
would sometimes make a show of searching for it in drawers and cabinets,
behaving as if they expected to find one. I believe that most interviewees
who could not produce one were legally unmarried.

The moral status of *amasiamento* is murky. In many cases *amigado* couples are treated exactly like married couples by their neighbors and relatives. But the as-if character of the relationship allows moral condemnation when it is socially convenient. For example, Nezinha was *amigado* for
fifteen years, during which time her brother treated her *companheiro* as a
brother-in-law. But when the relationship broke up, Nezinha went to live
with her parents, bringing along her children, her maid, and her maid's
children. The addition of so many people seriously strained relationships
in the new household and forced Nezinha's brother to delay his plans to
marry and bring his fiancée to live in an addition to his parents' house
(now occupied by Nezinha's household). The brother expressed his anger
by recasting his sister's relationship.

I lived fifteen years with António, but I never married. My maid went out
some two times with José and had that boy over there. So my brother said to
me that I was as big a whore (*quenga*) as she because I had three kids without
being married. Before it was okay, but now suddenly fifteen years is like going to bed on the first date, not that he has ever denied himself, but he's a
man. (Nezinha)

In Caruaru, *amasiamento* and concubinage are neither entirely identical
nor entirely distinct. They are more of a continuum, with the couple more
likely to be considered *amigado* if they reside together. Designation as *amasiamento*, *concubinato* ("concubinage"), *chamego* ("having an affair"), or
prostituição ("prostitution") depends on the attitude of the speaker toward
the union. A woman may describe herself as *amigado*, while her neighbors
whisper that she is a concubine, her boyfriend's wife calls her a whore,
and he boasts to his friends about his *chamego*.

Reasons for *amigando* instead of marrying vary. Some couples do not
have the money for a wedding; for others, one or both partners are already
legally married and cannot or will not obtain a divorce.[34] Others are waiting to see *se vai dar* ("if it will work out"), in a version of the Caribbean

practice of bearing children when young and unmarried, reserving legal marriage for middle age (cf. Besson 1993).

O amasiamento also permits unions between men and women of differing social status, just as concubinage with slaves did in the past (Ribeiro 1982, 67–68; cf. Alexander 1984). It is not uncommon for a wealthy man to have a legal wife and family in a good neighborhood while *amigando* with an impoverished woman or two in a poor one. In the more stable of these types of relationships, the man follows a regular schedule of visitation to his secondary wife/wives and their children, which may include daily visits, and he maintains the household as would a husband. Lower-class men who can afford it may maintain more than one *companheira* in different towns, especially men whose work involves travel, as was the case for Maria Imaculada's husband.

Amasiamento may have advantages over marriage to the extent that it gives partners more room to maneuver. Men can use the accumulation of bonds with past and present *namoradas* to create a network of households among which to float as circumstances warrant. If they do not legally marry, they retain the promise of eventual marriage as a lure. It is more difficult for a woman to have multiple *namorados* openly, but if she is socially skilled it is not impossible, again especially in larger cities and poorer neighborhoods. Sequential or multiple boyfriends give her a network of men to ask for food, money, or favors, and also allow her to form networks with their female relatives, especially if she can convince people that one or another of her children were fathered by the man.

In some cases, one or the other partner is simply unwilling to commit to legal marriage. Sometimes men refuse to marry because they want to keep their options open, because the woman was not a virgin at the beginning of the relationship, or because they are biding their time until some fantasized true love shows up. Both men and women may believe that cohabitation affords them more freedom to leave the relationship if it does not work out. They may also fear their companion's gaining legal control over their incomes.

The worst thing in the world is to marry. To screw [*trepar*] is one thing, but marriage, why would a woman want to give so much to a man? You're already giving your body, which is very important, it's you yourself. And after that to live with him, give him your money, your things, and stay legally tied to him too. Bad idea. (Oneida)

Some people professed a general objection to marriage as an infringement on their freedom, proclaiming that their alliances were nobody's business.

Men were more likely to fear being trapped in a marriage by a gold-digging woman, but many women as well were opposed to marriage.

In my opinion, marriage is prostitution without being paid. For what marry? To sign a paper? Only for example, in my brother's case, his fiancée's parents think she is a virgin and they will permit her to have relations with him only if they're married. Little do they know! Her sister had a daughter without being married. So she has to marry to recuperate the family honor. Marriage is only this, for family reasons or to divide wealth, if there is a lot to divide. I never wanted to marry, nor do I want to marry, nor would I marry. (Nezinha)

People expect *amigado* women, like wives, to remain sexually faithful while doing domestic labor, and the man to maintain and govern the woman and children. In the lower classes marriage is not economically necessary, because there is little family wealth to protect. Legal marriage is, however, valuable as a status item, more important for some families than others.[35]

People may also consider marriage a religious duty, especially among Protestants. Many Protestant churches offer economic benefits to members, either through direct handouts or through the side effects of their required sobriety, education, thrift, and hard work. *Amasiamento* can threaten membership in the group. Among Catholics, some priests require proof of legitimate birth before they will perform a baptism. And some women believe that extramarital sex is indecent and therefore want marriage or at least engagement as a precondition for sex or as a proof of love.

One advantage of legal marriage is that a husband is the presumptive father of his wife's children and can extend health care or other benefits to them. This was a major factor in João Batista's eventual decision to marry Fátima after seven years of cohabitation. As she tells the story:

We married because of a nonsense [*besteirinha*]. João Batista wanted to make a card for Uáxintô to go to the pool. Because of his work he can use the pool, him and his family. So the delegate asked for the marriage registry to prove that Uáxintô really is his son. So he had to say he wasn't married. So he [the delegate] said, "But how is it that your boy's mother is no good? What are you doing, man [*cara*, lit. "face"], good enough to screw but not to marry? Who are you waiting for, some girl to appear and you leave the mother of your children?" . . . So suddenly João Batista arrived here, saying, "I passed such shame today!" . . . Later he arrived with a paper, said, "Sign here, fast, I'm going to take it!" So I signed and didn't even know what it was. So later he arrived quickly from work, me washing clothes, and he said, "Listen, Fátima, get dressed in a hurry, real fast because we are going to marry today! Two o'clock!" I was big-bellied [*buchuda*] with my younger boy, in my washday clothes with a belly this big! So pronto. We went to the registry, so we married. I never expected it. I never asked for it. Then we came back home and I finished washing the clothes. That's why I say, where did I spend my honeymoon? In the *quintal!*[36] (Fátima)

Here, Jõao Batista decided to marry partly because he felt shamed by the delegate's pointed questions and partly to allow his son to use the swimming pool. By legally marrying he not only extended his work-related benefits to Fátima and Uáxintô but also proved how seriously he took his commitment to living with Fátima: that he wasn't, as the delegate suggested, simply waiting around with her until someone better came along. By this time both his mother and hers had stopped opposing the union. He also told me that at twenty-five he felt more ready to take on the role of *um homem* ("a man") than he had at eighteen, and that he wanted his second child to be legitimate.

Neither marriage nor *amasiamento* guarantees that a woman will remain paired with the same man for the rest of her life. After she has gained independence from her parents through her relationship with a man, a woman may find herself the head of household because of the death or desertion of her man. Or he may do something so unacceptable to her that she kicks him out of the house. The incidence of female-headed households increases with poverty and is greater in larger cities and *favelas* than in small towns or rural areas, although it is rare for women to live entirely alone.[37] Uncoupled women live with their children, sisters, mothers, brothers, cousins, nephews, or other relatives. Glória, who never married, lives with her widowed mother, nephew, and a cousin. She explained:

No one lives alone, alone. I don't think of living alone. In the future, when my nephew grows up, I think I'll get a girl to raise, so I will always have someone with me. Adopt a child for me.

Occasionally a woman who never married or cohabited will become, upon the death of her father, head of the household she lived in all her life. It is common for Catholic faith healers to be widows or never-married heads of household, whose reputations for blessedness preserve them from nasty gossip. Widows and other unmarried women must take even more ostentatious care never to be alone than married women. For divorcées who do not remarry the problem is worse, because divorce is new and still scandalous. Divorcées and separated or abandoned women are often suspected of having been left alone because they were adulterous; because they are neither virgins nor coupled, they are sexually suspect. In general, nonvirgins who are not seen as governed by a man have a hard time with gossip.

My neighbor keeps talking, sent me an anonymous letter, keeps saying that I'm having an affair with her husband. I'm [doing] nothing! It's because I'm a widow. The people keep saying, "A widow is like green wood, weeps, but catches fire," *né*? So they keep talking about me.[38] (Teresa)

Often, related widows will live together. For example, when Fátima's brother-in-law was murdered, her long-widowed mother moved in with Fátima's newly widowed sister. By combining the households, the two women were able to provide child care for Fátima's nine nieces and nephews while also bringing in an outside income until the boys were old enough to support the family. Previously, Fátima's mother had lived with Fátima in Caruaru, but after the murder João Batista moved in with Fátima and they took up life as an *amigado* couple until they married.

Some women were terrified of being the object of gossip.

I live with him only to live, really, so as not to be alone, for no one to be talking. Because here any little thing the people keep talking about us, if we don't keep living with that person until the end. So I put up with a lot of his stuff. (Sebastiana)

Being the object of negative gossip can lead to ostracism. Being cut off from female social networks, especially for a single woman, can be economically devastating, as well as terrifyingly lonely in a society where solitude is both rare and frightening. In addition, being gossiped about can also be physically dangerous: Women may mount physical attacks against those they believe are having affairs with their men. And a woman who is neither a virgin nor protected by a man may be subject to sexual harassment if she is unlucky enough to know a particularly aggressive man.[39]

While some women may stay in bad relationships to avoid single motherhood and gossip, other female heads of households very much want to arrange for a man to take over their responsibilities and protect them from gossip. Still others relish their independence and ignore gossip.

People talk about me, so what? People like to talk, that's all. They talk about everyone regardless. I used to be afraid of people talking, but then I learned it is worse to live with him, afraid to leave, afraid of gossip, than it is to leave and at least be free of him. Freedom! What a freedom it was, free of him, free of fear of neighbors talking, free to fight my own battles and live my own life. (Ifigênia)

The difference lies partly in differences in personality and personal situation. Ifigênia, for example, had been married to a truck driver who was rarely home. Like many women whose husbands or *companheiros* travel or work far away, she was subject to nasty gossip when he was out of town. She learned from experience that despite the suspicion of some of her neighbors, she retained some friendships and was able to survive. As she matured from a preteen bride to a young mother in her twenties, earning cash by making frozen fruit juice treats and selling them door to door, her outlook and confidence also matured, and eventually she made her break from her abusive husband.

Sebastiana, on the other hand, had married relatively late, moving from her father's house to her husband's while in her twenties, relieved to be able to marry and escape the fate of being a *coroa*. She considered herself lucky to have a husband, any husband. Her husband managed a stall in the marketplace and had never left her alone. With his help she ran a small clothing business from their home, but she was dependent on him to bring her wholesale what she retailed in the store and to help her keep track of her books. Her outlook did not include any experience of what it might be like to go it alone.

A tendency toward cohabitation rather than marriage in the lower classes is not unique to Northeast Brazil. In general, in the Northeast as elsewhere, nonmarried cohabitation is more characteristic of the poor than of the middle class, less honorable than marriage, intertwined in both past and present with concubinage, and seen as less civilized and less hygienic than marriage by both Church and state.[40]

7 ⬌ The Language of Love in Northeast Brazil

O que é amor? É uma doença e grave!
("What is love? It is a sickness, and serious!")
Fátima

In his novel *The Unbearable Lightness of Being*, Milan Kundera describes his Czech characters as feeling what he calls an *es muss sein:* "it must be," an overriding necessity or passionate determination that some dramatic theme about their lives must be played out, no matter the cost (1984, 193–97). In Kundera's description, these determinations give a melodramatic intensity to lives that are not imbued with sufficient significance to live up to the characters' feelings of personal importance: the "unbearable lightness" of the title.[1] In many ways, social constructions of emotions are *es muss sein*'s as people push themselves and those around them to live out theatrical emotional predicaments. This is perhaps especially true of the complications of romance.

Kundera's *Unbearable Lightness* is a novel, a story that works out a philosophical theme by means of events in the lives of fictional characters. In Portuguese, such a narrative would be called a *romance*, and the term can also be so used in Spanish, French, English, and German. The word "romance" first appeared in England and France in the seventeenth century to describe medieval epics such as the Arthurian cycle, *El Cid, Don Quixote*, and some of what is today called "troubadour poetry." It was later extended to styles of literature and art displaying sentimental and fanciful aspects (Wellek 1973, 187), especially in the nineteenth century.[2]

In religion and philosophy, romantic approaches emphasized individuality, passion as opposed to reason, the primacy of the human will (Baumer 1973, 200–202), spirituality, and an opposition to the rationalism of the Enlightenment (Kirschner 1996, 152). Applied to personal stories of sexual passion, it reflected a newly individualized concept of love as the intertwining of two personal narratives (Giddens 1992, 40), with overlays of religiously derived concepts of the mystical union of souls. To Romantics, love resulted from the union of soul mates, two individuals who share a spiritual likeness. Women were the spiritual and intellectual equals of men in the romantic endeavor, and as much as did men, they chose their path through life. In contrast to earlier conceptions of human beings as puppets of fate, Romantics emphasized personal choice in human destiny (Branden 1980, 39–40).

Romance as a Narrative

Romantic love, then, is a story, or a type of story, about passionate involvement of an idealized sort. Certainly in its medieval form, the romance revealed deep-seated ambivalence about the nature of passion, especially sexual passion, in the context of idealized virtue. This ambivalence, and these types of idealized stories, resonate today in the lives of people I interviewed in Caruaru and neighboring communities, as deeply felt and unresolved as they are in any literary representation.

One of the standard questions that I asked during both formal interviews and informal conversations was "What is love?" (*O que é amor?*), or, "What does 'love' mean?" (*O que significa 'amor'?*) People's answers to these questions varied, falling broadly into patterns influenced by gender, age, or rural/urban residence, but also displaying wide individual diversity. In their answers I heard echoes of the definitions and interpretations of historians who have studied romance, both as a literary form and as a social practice, in European history as well as in the history of Brazil.

Although they dealt with similar issues in similar language, men and women had distinct ideas about the constitution of a proper love story— especially younger men and women. To say that for men a proper love story ends up in bed whereas for women it ends up in church (or at least at the civil registrar) would not be completely accurate as an absolute statement, but it is worth thinking about as a tendency. The varied pressures of gendered propriety play a part in this difference, as does the historical expectation that a man will provide economically. There are material advantages in marriage and cohabitation for both sexes, but women more than men define themselves and find themselves defined by others in terms of their conjugal and familial relationships. Even as children, little girls carry dolls, when they have them, and often care for infant siblings,

while they play games of "house" and "mommy and daddy." Their brothers shoot marbles, make trucks and wagons from scrap, and play soccer.
While pubescent girls gossip about reputed budding relationships, giggling together about who is still a virgin, who will marry whom, and what
everybody will wear, their brothers ogle the pornographic magazines
freely available at newsstands, practice standing and combing their hair
and smoking seductively, and often get treated to a prostitute by an uncle
or older cousin.

Girls and women frequently told me of the *príncipe encantado* ("enchanted prince") who was supposed to love, honor, and above all, take
care of them. The contrast between the fairy-tale Prince Charming and the
actuality of a real husband or boyfriend can be jarring.

I always thought this enchanted prince would come for me, fall in love, go to
live in a castle. And I would stay in the castle, and him out in the world
fighting the dragons to protect me. But as it turned out, who has to fight the
dragons is me, here in this [sarcastically] castle of mine, him out there in the
world chasing whores [*raparigas*]. I think what I married is the mistake, not
the prince, but the frog. (Sebastiana)

Like the Spanish villagers of James Taggart's description, who use folktales to communicate differing male and female ideas of gender relations
(1990, 200), Caruarense women use folktale imagery to comment on the
fantasies and realities of heterosexual love. But in Caruaru, folktale imagery sharpens the contrast between idealization and reality, leaving
women waiting for a Prince Charming who never comes.

Given men's historical role as family provider, dreaming of an economically fulfilling love makes sense for a young girl, but not for a boy.
This came out once when I was photographing some children. A boy of
about seven pointed at my camera and yelled, "I've got to get me one of
those!" At the same time an eight-year-old girl remarked:

When I'm a grown woman I want to marry a rich man to have my own camera!

This expectation of the male providing partially explains why respectable marriage appeals more to women than men: Their economic status
historically has depended more on making a good match.[3] Although a
dashing rake may exude seductive charm, conventional wisdom has it
that choosing a sober, hard-working man has a greater chance of leading
to lasting satisfaction than choosing a husband on the basis of passionate

attraction. As the proverb tartly advises: *Pai pobre é destino, marido pobre é burrice* ("A poor father is destiny, a poor husband is idiocy").

Why? Marry some poor man for you, him, and the children to suffer? What is important is *moh-nee* [money].[4] I would want to marry only if it were a man with a steady job. . . . It's bad to be alone—and it's worse yet to be with a poor man. (Lourdinha)

However, conventional wisdom may be exactly the kind of story a young woman of thirteen or fourteen, embarking on her first exciting flirtations, does not want to hear. Flush with the power of her newfound ability to attract male attention, dazzled by her own sensations and the ardently whispered promises of her suitors, a young woman may want to live a different kind of story, one in which she takes the role of gorgeous princess to his enchanted prince and the two go off to live happily, if vaguely, ever after in a favorable economic situation. Such young teenage women may be imprudent, foolish, and naive, but they are also the targets of many men's desires. If they are so foolhardy as to make a reckless choice, they run the risk of ruining forever any possibility of intact reputation and therefore the marriageability they may unfortunately and incorrectly believe to be the inevitable outcome of a great love story.

Such heedless daydreaming may be particularly characteristic of inexperienced young women, but older women, and even women with lengthy and painful education in the school of sweet, passionate lies, sometimes repeatedly try to act out the *es muss sein* of passion-is-love, love-is-marriage, marriage-is-forever, trying to make the story come true this time. Their male counterparts, caught in the *es muss sein* of "if you loved me you would have sex with me," equally ardently try to make their stories come true, albeit with a strong subtext of "if you have sex with me I can't marry you." Some people are more foolish than others, some outgrow youthful naiveté, others never have the chance to make their own choices because of situations forced on them by circumstance. And there are some individual women who, because of a favorable combination of circumstance and personality, manage to break all the rules and get away with it. But at some point, everyone wrestles with the difficulties of reconciling preconceived notions about the nature and consequences of true love with the actual way events unfold in the real world.

True Love: Parental Love as Model

Caruaruenses I spoke with frequently tried to distinguish between what they called "true love" (*amor verdadeiro*) and various forms of false (*falso*) love. Here, *falso*, like the English "false," refers to mistaken beliefs and lies as well as to disloyalty in the form of infidelity. Although Caruaruenses frequently used duration as a determinant of the "trueness" of love, some speakers, especially men, saw a kind of tragic beauty in short-lived but intense attractions. For many, a love was true to the extent that it conformed to their ideas of the proper nature of a beautiful story. The beauty of the beloved, either physical or spiritual loveliness, and the magnificent nature of the lover's sentiment together create an exquisite story. The splendor of a love can be enhanced, for example, if the beloved is extraordinarily lovely, or alternatively if the selfless love of the lover transcends some defect in the beloved. The proverb *o amor embeleza* ("love beautifies") is as much a commentary on the proprieties of love stories as it is a statement of experience.

In Northeast Brazil, several different points of view on the nature of love coexist, overlap, and generally stir up trouble, not only from one person to another but often also in the opinions expressed by a single individual. The idea that true love falls outside the realm of sexual relationships remains powerful: The phrase *amor só de mãe* ("mother love only") frequently decorates trucks and T-shirts. I heard various versions of the idea that the only true love is mother love from both men and women. Women tended to bring up mother love in contrast to what they described as an intrinsic male inability to love, and men in the context of discussions of the relative merits of different types of women. People discussed mother love in religious terms, as a kind of *agapé*.

There exist only two types of love: first the love that we feel for God, true love, and second the love that we feel for our mother and for our children . . . the truest love there is. (Rosabela)

For many women, their mothers were their protectors as children and remain their friends and advocates as adults.

We have lots of acquaintances [*colegas*], but true friend, we only have mother. You can trust your mother in everything. You can confide in her. She will help you, you can depend on her. Without my mother I could not have survived to now, not only when I was a baby and she raised me, but now, advising me on how to manage my husband, helping me raise my children, nursing me when I am sick, lending me money when I'm broke [*liso*]. (Maria da Paz)

For many men, their mothers were the standard by which they judged all other relationships, both with women and with men.

I trust my mother ten times. Only my mother. Not my sister, not my wife, not my friends. Look, once I had a friend, he was such a good friend, if one of us had on a pair of pants the other one liked we would switch. We shared our money, everything. What was mine was his, what was his was mine. That close. Then I discovered that he thought this extended to my wife. I heard him talking to her, trying to get her to leave me and go with him. I confronted him and he attacked me with a knife. He almost killed me! And if it had gone a little differently, I might have killed him. We could have been both dead. Imagine if one of us were carrying a pistol! You can't trust anyone. And the closer you are to them, the less you can trust them. Except your mother. (João Batista)

In practice, mother-child relations are often fraught with as much conflict, ambivalence, and guilt as affection. Some mothers are puzzled when their actual feelings do not live up to their ideals, although most agree that there is something very special in maternal relationships:

I used to think that when I had children, the maternal instinct would fall and I would turn into a good mother. But it never fell, and so, here I am, the same person I always was. But even so, I would give my arm for my children. I can't stand them, but I would give my arm. And for my mother I would give one of my kidneys, a piece of my liver. And not for another person. . . . I still can't stand children. And I don't get along very well with my mother. But I would give my arm. I would give a kidney. It's a thing more profound and stronger than love. There is no word for this thing. (Catrina)

Despite the nearly universal veneration of mother love, or perhaps because of it, many people I spoke with, after praising mothers' trustworthiness in general, discussed their conflicts and disappointments with their own mothers. Mothers, in turn, expressed disillusion with children who defied, disobeyed, and otherwise disappointed them. Both mothers and children expressed feelings of guilt toward one another for failing to live up to superhuman ideals of love.

We never succeed at liberating ourselves from our mothers. They are always "grabbing our foot" [*pegando o pé*] for something. Even after they die, they stay there inside us, making us feel guilty. (Agostinho)

We never liberate ourselves from our children. They are always "grabbing our foot," wanting something, never letting go of our skirts. Until the day we die, we have to manage them. (Agostinho's mother)

For all their complaints, women with children generally recognize the power of their position and frequently act to make sure that they do not lose a son's love to a younger woman.

My mother always told me that I have only one mother, one mother who loves me. I can always find some whore [*rapariga*] there in the street, but I can never replace my mother. (Donizete)

By far the most powerful tactic a mother can use is manipulation through guilt.

The old story, how my mother suffered to have me, suffered to bear me, suffered to raise me. But I can say to you, "That old story," sarcastically, you know, and yet inside me, I feel guilty. How she suffered for me! And how I can't escape her suffering. Nothing I can do will ever pay the debt I owe her. (Beno)

Guilt manipulation, while it can be a powerful source of influence, works only if its object participates by feeling guilty.

My mother tries a lot to control me by guilt. "But you did it, but Jesus doesn't want you to act like that, but you know it's wrong!" So, I lower my head, "Forgive me, Mother, I was wrong. I'll try to be better in the future." Then I continue the same way I always was. She doesn't know. For her I'm one person. For the world I'm another person. For example, my mother doesn't know that I smoke.[5] I never smoke in her presence, nor do I let her see me with a cigarette. I think it is the greatest disrespect to smoke in front of her. My mother does not sleep until I come in; she waits, she thinks that I can't sleep around if I come home early. I think maybe I've been to bed with two hundred women, before ten o'clock at night. Maybe that's an exaggeration. One hundred ninety-nine. No, really, counting, thinking how I live—I've lost count. Every weekend, picking up girls in bars, not to mention the ones whose names I knew before I screwed them. But at home I'm still her virgin baby boy. (Cleiton)

Smother love may be part of a mother's deliberate strategy to control her son. It may also be a desperate grab for a son seen by his mother as her last best chance for love. Just as sons and daughters depend on mothers for true love, women disillusioned by their husbands' and boyfriends' physical or emotional abandonment depend on their children for true love.

I raised these boys almost alone because my husband was young, beautiful, a lover of women, a truck driver, never home. When I saw how he really was, I dedicated myself to my son. Then my second son was born dying, screaming, black in the face, child sickness [*doença de criança*]. I fought, I fought for him to live, to raise him. Everyone said he would die, but I sustained him, I think, by the force of my will, and he lived. Oh, I fought! To have a child is a terrible sacrifice, and I worked for them. I fought for them, my daughter! He never grew up, that younger one. He stayed a baby inside even as he grew.[6] But it doesn't matter, I love him. I saw that my husband was a little disorganized and so I dedicated myself to my sons. I love them, and they love me. (Joselma)

Fathers also may feel a quasi-romantic, fiercely possessive love toward daughters. Siring a son may prove that a man's virility is strong enough to increase the quotient of maleness in the universe, but a daughter calls forth even deeper passions. Many fathers delight in decorating infant daughters with bows and frilly "Daddy's Princess" dresses.[7] A father's protective jealousy of daughters often prevents them from having any open courtships. When a girl reaches courting age, her father's friends begin to tease that soon boys will be *mijando na porta* ("peeing at the door") of his house. The phrase reflects the view that young men's sexual interest in a girl dirties a father's home.[8] Some men are afraid to have daughters for fear of dishonor.

I never wanted a daughter. Because my sister gave herself to a comrade [*camarada*] who was no good, dishonored completely, it was a shame, and my father suffered a lot. So I was afraid. But now that Renata was born I like her better than my two sons, she is my little princess, pretty little one. (Renato)

Fathers' feelings about daughters' sexual conduct go deeper than simply concern for family honor. Many daughters describe their fathers as jealous (*ciumento*).

My father wasn't very affectionate with me. But he was very jealous with me [*tinha muita ciume comigo*] because I was the only virgin daughter [*filha moça*] at home. I had five other sisters, my mother had three, the other woman had two. But they were grown and married, so I felt that distance that he had, he didn't want me to *namorar*, nor to marry because of the jealousy that he felt. (Sílvia)

Although some fathers are demonstratively affectionate with their children, many show their concern by being good providers but without physical or verbal expressions of fondness. Or, as in the case of Sílvia's father, they show concern through jealousy.

While caring for the children remains primarily a female responsibility, it is not uncommon to see fathers playing with or carrying infants and small children. Father love is not as central a cultural value as mother love, but many men feel a deep connection with their children.

My son is everything for me. . . . It's like my mother told me, tomorrow I could arrange twenty women, but mother, I have only one. Son is the same way. . . . If, God defend me, my woman were to die, I would be sad, pass one year, two, and marry again. But if I lost my son I would be destroyed. I live for the moment I arrive at home and he is there waiting for me, "Papa!" (Cleiton)

However, because of women's greater responsibility for the children, men's access to their children depends on their relationship with their children's mother(s). For some men, loving a child is an outgrowth of loving the child's mother, and when the relationship with the woman ends, so does the relationship with the child.

In addition to my legitimate children, I also have a daughter from an affair I had. I know she is my daughter, but when I see her, I see her like any other child. It's different: I never lived with her. If I were to leave my wife and have another family, of course I would have more tenderness with the children with whom I would live. . . . Of course, I have already lived with these of my present wife; they are older. I've already seen these children sick, already played with these children, already beat [disciplined] these children, certain things that imprison the heart, so I won't totally forget them like with my bastard daughter. (Donizete)

Because men's relationships with their children extend from their affiliation with the children's mothers they find it easier to abandon the children together with the mothers. In addition, the easy availability of multiple women to satisfy a man's housework and sexual demands means that men can abandon any woman who becomes too burdensome without depriving themselves of food, shelter, or sexual release. All too often, the woman becomes burdensome precisely because she has borne the man so many children.

Being a woman is really more difficult. To give an example, the woman marries, has five, six kids. The man, he's free, he can go away in the hour he wants to. Like lots of cases that I know, he leaves the woman, says he's going to work and never more returns. Doesn't want to give food anymore to so many children. Or maybe they're all girls and he wanted sons. How is she going to live, has to battle [lutar], work, and never rest. The man no, arranges another woman, so pronto. Therefore it is harder to be a woman than a man in my opinion. (Vagner)

Whereas people spoke of mother love as a natural instinct that "falls," as Catrina put it, father love was more formally defined and practiced. Most couples divided their emotional responsibilities toward children, delegating indulgence to the mother and discipline to the father. Although many mothers used verbal threats and slaps with a sandal (chineladas) to discipline children, severe physical punishment was more likely to be administered by fathers, who might use a fist, belt, or hairbrush to deliver a spanking, or to act in a randomly violent way while drunk.

Although individual fathers may behave in an affectionate way with their children, formally, sons and daughters owe respect and obedience to their father. While men and boys engage in erotically tinged joking with uncles and cousins, they feel uncomfortable addressing sexual themes with fathers. A man should not smoke in his father's presence, discuss women or sexual topics, drink alcohol casually, or openly defy his father no matter what the provocation. When one teenage boy complained to me that his father repeatedly beat him with a strap, I asked why he did not hit back, since he was larger than his father. Shocked, he exclaimed, *Mi'a mão cairá!* ("My hand would fall off!") He opted to stay away from home when his father was in so as to avoid conflict.[9]

Historically, parental love was the model for conjugal love. Couples became emotionally close only after long cohabitation, when both had lost their mothers to death and their virility or fertility to age; when increasing age and the status of motherhood had increased a woman's power, and physical decline decreased a man's, so that the couple were more equal (cf. Símic 1983). The long-term dynamics of family relations created complementary life trajectories for men and women, increasing emotional intermeshing over the life span. With age, women become more like the mothers men were raised to love and obey, and men become more like the passionately beloved fathers of a young girl's imagination.

Companionate Love, or *Consideração*

Companionate love, based on the restricted communicative codes of face-to-face communities, valuing the perspective of maturity over the impetuosity of youth, takes shape in day-to-day interaction, labor, cooperation, and the proper fulfillment of gender roles, rather than the verbally expressed internal experience of individuals. One typical rural housewife responded to the question "What does the word *amor* mean?" in this way:

Because I love my husband, because I cook his food, because I wash his clothes, because I clean his house, because I do his service [have sex with him], because I bear his children, the people say, love and faith in actions you see, in these actions that I do, in my work is my love. And my husband, he works in a factory in the city, and he brings his paycheck home, and he pays the costs of the household and he shows his love for me. (Assunção)

This is love as practice, the accumulation of presence; the kind of becoming-used-to that leads to pain when the loved one is gone, the love that Gillis (1988) describes as typical of precapitalist Europe. In marriage, this kind of love includes respect and friendship within the performance of traditional gender roles. The physical labor the partners perform as part of their assigned roles not only reflects but also constitutes their love. Marital love, like familial love, is expressed as cooperation and mutual economic support. Sex is simply part of the daily round of housework, not a transformative intimate experience.

Many quoted the proverb *amor 'tá na convivência* ("love is in familiarity"), stating that love consists of long-term cooperative association within the framework of trust.

Love is trusting in that person, having refuge, being honest with that person, making a home together, working together, raising children together, supporting each other. (Samara)

The religious underpinnings of this kind of companionate love are explicit: Love is a form of keeping faith with the beloved.

Both academic writers and lay Caruaruenses identify this concept as an old-fashioned, rural style of thinking about marriage, although age and rurality alone did not in fact predict which individuals used this definition in Caruaru. Some young women and urban women also described their marriages in companionate terms. A good companionate marriage depends more on honesty and courtesy than affection as such, although affection can improve a marriage. People spoke of *obrigação* ("obligation") and *consideração* ("consideration") (cf. Robben 1989, 577), saying that married couples have obligations to fulfill to one another, the husband to provide and support a house, the wife to do housework and raise children. They can simply perform these obligations dutifully, or they can also add little flourishes of *consideração*, or actions beyond simple responsibility. If a woman not only cooks but also cooks her husband's favorite foods the way he likes them, she is acting with *consideração*. While *consideração* is not strictly necessary in a marriage, its lack can lead to bad treatment. Agostinho described it in this way:

When a couple do not have *consideração*, they treat each other badly. What a man does bad to a woman is to not value her, not listen to her; he betrays her [sexually]; he doesn't let her take part in decisions, he only communicates them to her; he mistreats her, even physically. What a woman does bad to a man is to try to dominate him, to impede him from having her physically, to try to manipulate the man.

While everyone has obligations and is free to act with consideration, obligation and consideration operate differently for men and for women. Men are forgiven for lacking consideration: They can even get out of some obligations without too much social consequence. But women are held to their obligations and expected to show consideration as well, because they are responsible for nurturing and worrying about others.

For many women, true love requires renouncing one's own interests in favor of those of the beloved.

For me, love is the renunciation of I [*a renúncia de eu*]. When you like another person, when you love, understand, you give yourself totally to that person, you forget yourself and remember to love the other person. (Saxa)

Here, love between women and men has taken on some of the qualities of mother love: self-abnegating, suffering, generous. While several women spoke to me of their obligation to self-abnegation in love, not a single man saw self-abnegation as something he was required to do. This attitude contributes to women's cynical idea that men are incapable of true love.

Women's personal identities are submerged in their families and social networks to a much greater extent than are men's, and they sustain the emotional relationships that hold networks and families together. While most men and some women said that supporting a wife economically is sufficient proof of love, most women wanted *consideração* in the form of emotional intimacy as well.

I feel needy. . . . He gives me material things that I don't need. I need more a friendly word from him. I wish that he was more my friend than my husband, but he isn't like that. (Fátima)

Sometimes men and women differ in their ideas of what constitutes *consideração*. For example, women stated that talking over problems together was part of *consideração* and a sign of affection.

What upsets me is that he's a cold, shut-up man, has a problem and doesn't talk. . . . That is to say, he doesn't have confidence in me. He doesn't love me. (Assunção)

However, men tended to say that they avoided speaking of personal problems to their wives out of consideration, sparing their wives worry or sheltering them from subjects not proper to decent women.

Amor versus Paixão

People said that the emotions roused by marriage, cohabitation, and short-term physical relations are both similar and distinct. In general, young men found the difference between what they called *amor* ("love") and *paixão* ("passion, infatuation") deeply confusing. They debated which, if either, is true love and struggled to fit these concepts to their experiences. While some women, especially younger urban women, struggled with the ideas of *amor* and *paixão*, it was a greater problem for men.

Really, it doesn't make sense. Sometimes we know that we like someone only when it ends. Sometimes we think we hate someone and it turns out we love them and didn't know it, or we didn't want to admit it. And *amor* is so good and yet people are so scared of it, because it can really hurt a person. But the thing is, sometimes we are so afraid of being hurt that we go push the other person away and get hurt just so as not to get hurt. I told you, no sense! (Agostinho)

Ideally, *amor* differs from *paixão* in its duration and selflessness. Another young man, Leonel, quoted a religiously derived popular image to differentiate them:

Now, *amor* and *paixão*, they walk together, but before the end of the road, *paixão*, it stops walking. But *amor* goes the whole distance, no matter how difficult the road. *Amor* walks with you, and if you fall, *amor* carries you.[10]

Men saw *paixão* as characterized by more idealizing than *amor*, and some said it was therefore less satisfying. Edilson explained:

Paixão is that fantasy, that you see the person and start to imagine how they are. But with time the impression changes and one becomes disillusioned, and goes looking for another person to idealize, always thinking, "This is her! This is the only one!" But it never is, because it is imaginary.

But the subjective experience of *amor* and *paixão* are very similar, especially in the early stages of a relationship, when the two sentiments are nearly indistinguishable.

Paixão is a temporary sentiment. It doesn't last forever. It is only something that we beautify [*embeleza*] about someone; we idealize them, but that is temporary. At times *paixão* is the deceiver because it seems like *amor*. But *paixão* is rapid, it is also very greedy, it only wants for itself. *Paixão* is where jealousy exists. *Amor* does not have jealousy, it lasts forever. It is certain. But *paixão* is unsure, and uncertainty is what breeds jealousy. The people say, *Bem ama quem nunca esquece* ["Who loves well never forgets"]. That is, love never forgets, it endures. (Vagner)

Even when men tried to distinguish their descriptions of the two, they ended up saying very similar things about *amor* and *paixão*.

Amor is when you feel a desire to always be with her, you breathe her, eat her, drink her, you are always thinking of her, you don't manage to live without her. There are moments when you will adore staying with her, and there will be moments when you will hate to stay with her. And about *paixão*, you feel an attraction as if it were a rocket: I want to hug you, to squeeze you, to kiss you. But this is not love, it's horniness [*tesão*], a very strong sexual attraction for a person. (Agostinho)

Lovers must ask themselves constantly whether what they are feeling is true love or merely *paixão*:

Sometimes I keep thinking, could it be that what we feel is really love? We become infatuated thinking it is love, but from one hour to the next all that ends. Except that what we feel does not end, but the relationship ends; we stay with that stored inside of us, hurting, injuring us. I don't understand it. Is it only love if the two both love? Sometimes I think back about some old girlfriend, and I remember some little thing about her with great pleasure, still all this time later. Does that mean I loved her? Or did I just love that one little thing and the rest was *paixão*? (Francisco de Assis)

While men were more likely to puzzle over *amor* and *paixão*, women also experienced them as different, seeing *paixão* as youthful and *amor* as enduring and mature. Many women stated that their feelings toward their husbands had changed over the course of the marriage.

I like him, I love him. I won't say it's that LOOO-OOO-OOVE of before, love of a bride . . . but if, God defend me, if I became a widow, I wouldn't want another man. I'm his wife until the end. (Maria da Adoração)

Other women saw this change as caused not only by the maturation of *paixão* but also by their own personal maturation. It is quite common for young women to marry at age fourteen or fifteen, and not unheard-of for brides to be as young as twelve. But with the passing years, and especially with the increasing status and responsibility of child-rearing, once submissive young women begin to develop a different perspective.

When I married, I was very dumb because I was only fourteen years old. I thought that I could eat an egg only when he brought it to me. . . . But, maturing, nowadays I have courage to work, and I don't have fear of dying of hunger anymore. Once I put up with hunger and beatings. But never again. Now I have three kids and am no longer afraid to confront life by any means. . . . If I want an egg, *I* buy that egg. When we marry very young what happens is crazy jealousy, dependence, a sad ignorance. (Damiana)

As women learn that they can support themselves through work or network-building, as they supervise their children and later their daughters-in-law, as they grow into the increased status of maturity, they gain confidence.

Women's changing attitudes about love over the course of a marriage are also influenced by the difference between the way most men treat a girlfriend and the way they treat a wife.

After we married, our love changed with marriage. Because in *namoro* you always walk hugging, holding hands, *né?* But afterward, you don't hold hands, nor hug. It's him over there, me over here. Strange—we sleep together, you know, husband and wife, but it's like, before it's everything but, you know? And after it's the main dish and nothing else. I ask him, Why don't you hold my hand? He says he's embarrassed [*tem vergonha*], the boys tease him. (Imelda)

When a man courts a woman, his actions are influenced by his desire to prove his sincerity to her and to overcome the social restrictions on his access to her. But once a couple marries or begins cohabiting, his actions are directed toward another audience, his *turma* of male buddies, to whom he must prove he is not controlled by his wife. Women do not undergo a similar shift in audience upon marriage. They may experience this shift as a cooling of their man's love.

When we were *namorando*, I was his princess, you know? Nothing was too much, nothing was too good, everything was passion, everything was desperation. He spoke, he said pretty things, my hair, my eyes, oh, how he loved me! Then we married, and—*pum!*—like that, all of a sudden, where did the princess go? Suddenly I'm his slave, that's it, you know? It was "How pretty are your eyes!" and then suddenly just "Where's my lunch, woman? Hurry!" (Damiana)

Catering to a *namorada* does not diminish manhood because being passion's slave enhances virility. In addition, a man can portray his ardency to his girlfriend as true love while laughing with the guys about how he is managing his *namorada* with his irresistible courtship technique. But once he marries, his possession of the woman is complete, and he can no longer justify enticing her with sweetness. New husbands frequently make a show of not being controlled by their wives, by coming home late, bossing, spending little time at home, drinking, and, in may cases, openly carrying on extramarital affairs or engaging in violence against their wives (cf. Robben 1989, 182). A man's actual emotional attitude toward his wife may not change with marriage. Indeed, his affection and dependency may deepen. But it is difficult for him to show that without losing face, and he may react to feelings of dependency with ever more desperate attempts to show independence.

Also, folklore provides more explicit instruction in how to conduct courtship than in how to maintain a romantic marriage. Romantic gestures such as gifts of flowers, jewelry, or perfume; romantic statements like "your lips are like cherries, your eyes like dark pools"; romantic behavior such as serenading under a window—these result not from individual men's personal imaginations but rather the store of romantic folk-lore available to a courting man. Techniques for gaining a woman's attention while evading her father's have a similarly long history in folklore: sending notes by way of a domestic servant or child of the household, for example, is a customary dodge of great antiquity (de Azevedo 1986, 27–28). But customary marriage is companionate, not romantic, and romance within marriage is at odds with male concepts in which women are game pieces that, once won, need no more courting. The standard compliments of courtship come ready-made and are easier to deliver than honest sentiments.

It is not surprising that women so often become disillusioned with conjugal love, freeing themselves from their own feelings of obligatory consideration for their husbands. While, ideally, cohabitation itself creates and sustains love, for some women too much familiarity destroys love.

It is so difficult, so very difficult, to live with a person. It's like a drop of water dripping, dripping, and eventually you can't stand it anymore. There is no love capable of surviving cohabitation. (Catrina)

To Catrina, cohabitation destroys the idealization necessary for love. But for others that very idealization is not love but *paixão*, and its fading is part of the development of true love.

In general, men and women differed on these issues, young, single people differing more than older, married ones. It is not surprising that the sexes would have very different points of view on love in a culture where men and women socialize separately, have different moral constraints on their sexual behavior, and are affected differently by economic change. In addition to being more confused than women over how to distinguish *amor* from *paixão*, many men stated that it is possible to feel true *amor* for more than one woman at a time, whereas women emphatically rejected this idea, seeing true *amor* as monogamous. Other men said that their infidelities did not threaten their marriages, precisely because what the husband felt for the "other woman" (*a outra*) was *paixão*, whereas what he felt for his wife was *amor*. For many women, this male attitude is part of men's inability to love truly, as women do. An elderly rural woman rejected my question about love entirely:

Love between men and women? Is that what you asked me, my daughter? I can't tell you what means a thing that does not exist. You hear? It doesn't exist. It's a lie. It's deception. It's just a word men use to get women into bed and women use to get men to pay their bills. That's all. (Elzeneide)

This statement forms part of a well-developed discourse of female skepticism about men; many women denied that men were capable of feeling love, and some that sexual love exists at all. There is a constant back and forth between women's role as lovers vis-à-vis men and their role as mothers. In both roles women are expected to behave like the Virgin Mary, self-abnegating and suffering in behalf of their men. A woman who is particularly skilled can turn this suffering into guilt in both husbands and children.

Once, when I went to interview a woman in her twenties, her mother-in-law, with whom she lived, interrupted so frequently that I ended up interviewing the older woman instead. She boasted of how she was able to use her ability to make men love her into a source of wealth:

My husband and all of my sons give a part of what they earn to me. I worked a lot for them; today I'm harvesting what I planted! Thanks to my Jesus Christ ... I adopted one, brought him here, he's already six years in my power. I saw him quarreling with his mother so I began, little by little. Calling him over, give a little food, listen with total sympathy to his problems, encourage him, give advice. Sooner or later he's here all the time, living here like my own son. So the boy doesn't like his mother, he likes me. He's a good boy, hard worker. He gives me money to help me market. ... Who lost out was his mother. She didn't know how to handle men. ... This house is full of men-ô! [makes gesture with forefinger and thumb signifying money]. I've got a little one, a child, his mother wasn't taking good care of him, a very poor woman. I convinced her to give him to me, and I'm raising him with care, to work hard and love his mother. These young women nowadays, they don't know what is the best part of a man, they have the wrong idea about what a man can do to give you pleasure [repeating gesture]. We women have to know how to deal with men because if not, we will starve. (Laurinha)

Wage Labor and True Love

In the past, marriage could be contracted between a father and a suitor without much input from the barely pubescent girl involved. According to Marxist theory, expanded wage-labor opportunities should free women from such oppressive arrangements. If Engels (1942) is correct that wage labor's financial independence gives young people the freedom to choose spouses they love, then the shift to an urban capitalist economy should increase the incidence of love-marriage among the urban proletariat in Caruaru. He nonetheless warns, however, that the continuing economic importance of conjugal ties should also create a marriage market, constraining choice through the impersonal forces of the marketplace rather than through the historically earlier personalized authority of parents. This prediction, while insightful, does not adequately describe the situation in contemporary Caruaru.

Although people increasingly hold up romance within marriage as an ideal, the customary definition of companionate marriage as simply the union of a typical good man and a typical good woman without regard to personality remains common. Even when young people arrange their own marriages, they may do so on a basis other than that of passionate love. In some cases that is a matter of conviction; some people, more commonly women than men, believe that not loving one's conjugal partner allows for necessary emotional distance. Or it may result from infortuitous circumstance.

I wanted very much to love, you know, but unfortunately I don't love my husband, nor do I plan to. . . . But there are many out there who keep saying, "I love so-and-so, I'd die for so-and-so, he's the man of my life, and then afterward they're betraying him without a thought. . . . So I think now that the way I am is better, understand me? It's to respect him as much as I can, right? . . . Thanks to God I live well with him, and I cannot ask for more. (Samira)

In other cases, women end up in relationships that start out (and frequently continue) loveless for reasons beyond their control. Some women I interviewed, emancipated from their fathers by age, income, abandonment, or other circumstances, contracted their own marriages to men who were nearly strangers. These relationships only occasionally led to legal marriage because of the compromised status of emancipated women, but they could become long-term, stable cohabitation. However, they were not necessarily love matches—or better, they were not necessarily preceded by love—and were sometimes contracted between couples who were virtually strangers.

In addition, many poor women become *concubinas* of married men or *companheiras* of unmarried men as an extension of their duties as domestic servants. Here wage labor, rather than freeing them from sexual servitude, puts them at even greater risk, because unlike their chaperoned sisters, the relationships they end up with carry neither legal nor social protections. Engels's prediction that economic emancipation through wage labor leads to a greater availability of love marriage for proletariat women must be modified to recognize, first, the existence of lower-status alternatives to legal marriage, and second, sexually conservative mores that constrain poor women's choices.

Verbally Elaborated Romance and
New Economic Gender Deals

Urban capitalization differently affects men and women, increasing the already existing divergences in their perspectives and roles. Urban working-class men in Caruaru find it difficult to achieve the expected status of breadwinner; the social privileges of manhood increasingly rest on empty economic foundations. The material bargain of male-female co-operation at the basis of companionate love can no longer easily be made.

Historical research focusing on the growth of verbally elaborated romantic traditions in Europe suggests that they have arisen in times when the relative social and economic power of men and women has changed. In the courts in which troubadour poetry celebrated tragically frustrated passion, elite women used their inherited wealth and position to gain unprecedented political influence. Similarly, the early modern period, upon which so many historians focus their search for the origins of family affection in the Western tradition, saw dramatic shifts in men's and women's economic and social relationships. That discussion of verbally professed passionate love as the basis of marital and mari-form relationships should proliferate during the current socioeconomic shifts in Northeast Brazil is not surprising, given this history. It does not mean that prior to socioeconomic change people did not or could not love one another, but rather that how they define and what they expect from love changes in response to social and economic transformations.

This change is both imperfect and painful. Allowing young people to make their own conjugal choices corrects some of the problems that can lead to excruciating mismatches but opens the terrible possibilities of making one's own mistakes. The elaboration of passionate imagery in the story of romantic love owes more to feverish adolescent fantasies and the desires of teenagers to heal the wounds of their childhood disappointments through sexual union with a soul mate than it does to adult needs for solace, support, and assistance. Add to that the difficulties of negotiating relationships in which men and women have different points of view on and social stakes in sexuality, can no longer count on one another's support under difficult physical and economic conditions, and have more demanding emotional expectations of one another than ever before, and the stage is set for emotional disaster.

It is no wonder that both men and women express such bitter disappointment in one another and in love itself. Brazilian anthropologist Tania

Salem coined the term *dupla indeterminação* ("double indeterminacy") to interpret what the *favela* women she studied in Rio de Janeiro reported as persistent feelings of abandonment (1980, 64). Lower-class Brazilian women, she explains, suffer from a lack of power over their destiny in two distinct ways. The first is the common lot of the poor and the powerless, from which lower-class men suffer as well. The second has to do with the way women and men interact. Women see men as their supporter, protector, and agent in the world. But men consistently refuse or fail this role, leaving the woman adrift to confront both the powerlessness of poverty and the unreliability of men.

The women that Salem interviewed felt themselves sequentially abandoned, first by father, then by husband or lover, and finally by son. When asked about their poverty, they tended to blame not impersonal socioeconomic forces but rather the personal failings of their men, interpreting the weakness of class as a failure of the individual men upon whom they felt such dependence (Salem 1980, 65–77). And yet, paradoxically, women felt their situation worse when abandoned even by abusive men, because of the loss of the opportunity to manipulate men that constitutes women's one small source of power over their lives (1980, 98–99).

Although Salem studied *favela* women in Rio rather than the Northeastern interior working class of my study, many of her observations are true for those I studied as well. In practical terms, the difference between working class and *favela* is more a matter of the degree of poverty than a difference in kind. And many inhabitants of *favelas* in large Southern Brazilian cities are migrant workers from the Northeast who bring Northeast interaction patterns with them.

Like Salem, I found that many women felt outraged at what they saw as emotional abandonment and personal weakness in their men. The difference between actual and expected male power disturbs both men and women. But whereas men tend either to deny problems through adoption of compensatory hypermasculine mannerisms or to blame their troubles on poverty caused by the corrupt machinations of more powerful men, women tend to blame male powerlessness on the individual weaknesses of particular men as well as on male irresponsibility in general.

As discussed in chapter one, emotions, rather than being simply biological states, linguistic categories, elements of self-presentation, or interior states, are amalgams of all of these and more. While often experienced as passions, emotions can be actively manipulated or used to manipulate others as part of the play of social interaction. Frequently there is a gap between the transitory nature of emotional states and the regularizing tendencies of linguistic descriptions and role expectations. Thus while a wife may say she loves her husband, in daily experience she feels a variety of sentiments in connection with him. Her love, rather than a singular brain-body state, becomes something more like an attitude, or a theme in the story of her relationship to that man. She may experience the gap between what she thinks her attitude ought to be and what she is feeling at the moment as ambivalence, or interpret it to mean that her entire attitude is incorrect, the man is not worthy of love, or love itself is a lie.

Love as Suffering

Did you see the end of the *novela* where they die and are reunited in Heaven? Only in a *novela*, my daughter, only in fiction is love stronger than death. I'll tell you, love changes nothing in this world: anger, hatred, sex are what motivate people and death is stronger than all of them.

Regina

Love would be fraught with difficulties enough, even if social and economic pressures were absent. Attractions are not always mutual or of equal strength; partners may not be sufficiently mature, empathic, or generous enough to know their own hearts, much less their partners'; or appeal may lack sufficient depth to survive the fading of passion's fires. If these personal difficulties were not enough to derail romance, conflicting economic and social pressures on lovers and the different perspectives of the two genders combine to ruin romances.

Disillusionment and customary expectations of suffering in behalf of loved ones combine in many women's description of love as a form of suffering. Proverbs declare *A mulher brasileira é feito de amor* ("The Brazilian woman is made of love"), *Ser mulher é sofrer* ("To be a woman is to suffer"), and *Amar é sofrer* ("To love is to suffer"). Love can cause suffering by being unrequited or by failing to endure.

Oh, don't ask me this, I don't know. I only know that love is a sadness that goes away. The heart still cries. But we have to have it, don't we? We have to suffer it. It doesn't do any good to run away from it because it will come after us, hurting. . . . Now all I ask my sweet Jesus is to send me strength to raise my children. And don't send any more men my way. I loved him a lot, I thought that he loved me, but after everything that happened, I think that, that— because never does anyone know the heart of another! Never! It's a deception [*engano*]. (Bel)

Love can be painful simply because it is such a powerful passion that it overcomes the lover's ability to ignore it.

I think that love is a little thing, a little teeny tiny beastie [*bichinho bem pequenininho*], you know? That gnaws away a lot inside and goes on gnawing, gnawing. That if we aren't careful he kills us. . . . There is only one love, that true love we kill and die for.[11] (Engrácia)

Or love can be painful because it calls upon the lover to sacrifice self for beloved. For men, love causes suffering when unrequited.

I think all men carry with them the memory of that one girl who did not want them. Women say that women suffer with love and men do not suffer, but this is not true. Men suffer with love because always there is the girl you can't have. The one you love desperately, and she does not love you. And you end up with a broken heart. Just because men don't cry all the time like women do doesn't mean they don't get broken hearts too. (Edilson)

For women, unrequited love is also painful. Even more painful is the disillusion brought on by women's interpretation of men's behavior toward them.

So you've been asking people about love, huh? I know what the men say to you. They say that they suffer because of the one girl they loved and she didn't love them. They say men suffer from the women they can't have. Well, my daughter, women suffer from the men they *do* have. It is much better to have a broken heart and live your life dreaming of how it might have been than it is to get your heart's desire, marry, and find out that it is hopeless, what you thought was love is not. . . . We live fooled, thinking we are doing things right until one fine day something terrible happens and everything falls on top of us. What is the hardest to survive isn't the thing itself, it's that we have to recognize all the errors we made thinking we were right. The human being is a foolish being. (Dafne)

Here, far from being a sublime and beautiful experience, love is a powerfully painful imperative that calls upon people to make sacrifices, endure pain, and suffer disillusion and rejection, an alluring but frightening mix of passions that while seeming to sweep over an ego from outside also reach deep within, dragging up everything so carefully hidden from oneself—frightening not only for the chance of rejection but perhaps more for the possibility of success. In a culture in which suffering is both one's lot in life and one's defense against it, the prospect of enduring happiness is as frighteningly unfamiliar as it is alluring. And yet, for all its pain, love can give life an energy that makes it worth living.

Have you ever been in love [*apaixonada*]? I have been so many times, and been hurt so many times. And when it ends it is the worst pain in the world. But even so, all the pain is worth it for those few minutes. Because love is the most delicious dish there is to eat in the world, it is what makes life worth living, those moments of love. (Zaira)

Love, with all its drama, is after all more interesting than any other story we might make of our lives. In its pursuit people can reach out not only for what is best in human character but also taste titillatingly of what is worst.

The question of love doesn't have to be useful; love is good in itself. Love is so good, so good, that even loving a person and she doesn't love you, even hurting, hurting, you don't want it to end, because love is good, is delicious, is a sentiment that God left for the world. (Donizete)

Lóvi, or Love as a Foreign Import

While watching the popular prime time Brazilian soap operas (*telenovelas*), I was sometimes startled to see fictional couples look deep into each other's eyes and declare, *Ai lóvi iú*. This English phrase is also written on T-shirts, notebooks, truck bumpers, and stickers. Both academics and laypeople describe *lóvi*, also called *amor da novela* (soap opera love), or in academic writing *amor-paixão*, as a U.S. import, although it might more accurately be described as the outcome of economic and social changes in Brazil that have been influenced by the United States.

Lóvi is characterized by mutual economic and emotional interdependence, expressed in verbal tenderness and declarations of love; it constitutes as much a merging of souls as of bodies. The configuration of *amor-paixão* mixes various types of love, combining the romantization of *paixão* with the merging of souls and the self-abnegating devotion promised by Christian theological *agapé*, and adding the hygienists' veneration of marriage as the basis of stable society, trying to base steady marriage on the exciting whirlwinds of desire.

In both *telenovelas* and the *photonovela* comic book magazines that appeal to teenage girls, male characters' declarations of *lóvi* are portrayed as painfully achieved catharses that free them to experience the unbounded true love heretofore denied them by male inarticulateness. Columns in Brazilian fashion and lifestyle magazines advise women to get their men to verbalize *lóvi* in order to free them to plumb the depths of intimacy while scaling the heights of passion. The promise of these representations of love, although targeted at a middle-class audience, strike a chord with working-class women disillusioned by what they see as the unloving abandonment of their economically faltering men.

Amor-paixão, or *lóvi*, fits urban lifestyles because it emphasizes the importance of the couple as a social unit, the primacy of personal emotional experience, and the dependency of women on men. The companionate love of *obrigação* and *consideração* fit a system in which men and women were economically, socially, and personally interdependent, since neither could live without the work performed by the other. But *lóvi* emphasizes the expressive side of love while downplaying its economic and instrumental aspects.

The emphasis on *lóvi* as the basis for marriage conceals the economic interdependence of the sexes (cf. Cancian 1986, 258), and furthers the process of redefining obligations as voluntary forms of consideration. Since consideration is more obligatory for women than for men, it has the effect of rendering male obligations voluntary while keeping women obligated to perform not only duties but also favors. *Lóvi* takes its place as a tactic in the struggle for control between men and women.

Lóvi's emphasis on emotional intimacy is very difficult for men to accept, what with their concerns over power and independence from women. In addition, its insistence on monogamy conflicts with men's need to prove their virility and independence from female control. Some men reject *lóvi* outright as feminine frippery. Others are torn between *machista* views of sexual relations and the modern expectation of a more equal sharing:

I like women who please me, stroke me, do things for me. . . . But generally they are very empty people and I don't manage to stay with them. . . . I try to be open-minded, but it is impossible to liberate yourself from the remnants of machismo . . . so we keep always wanting that there exist women who live their lives as a function of ours, but this doesn't satisfy us. It's impossible, the situation. (Agostinho)

Some men like the idealization and tenderness of *lóvi* but find it hard to take seriously enough to commit permanently to one woman. A common saying goes: *Ser carinhoso é fácil, difícil é ser sincero* ("It is easy to be tender, difficult to be sincere"). Other men want to enjoy the union of *lóvi* but find it difficult to attain, either because they do not know how or because the problems of daily life interfere.

The human being is incomplete, and the man completes the woman, and the woman the man. A couple shouldn't lack anything. But for the two to get along well you have to understand the other's problems in detail, each point.

There are times when you don't have a head to secure even your own problems, much less those of others. (Donizete)

Problems in communication between the genders, disappointments over ruptured love affairs, the disillusionment of long acquaintance all combine to leave many feeling very cynical indeed about love.

Modern Love, or a Difficult Road to Travel

Amor é uma rua que nem sabemos andar mais.
("Love is a road we don't know how to walk on any more.")
                                                    Branquinha

The romance of sexual passion, bounded by social proscriptions, confined to relationships weighted with economic interests and occurring between genders with differing investments and viewpoints, has a difficult path indeed. Customary marriage, with its emphasis on decency, courtesy, cooperation, and the performance of custom-bounded roles, makes little demand on the personalities of the conjugals. They do not have to like one another; the interests they have in common are their shared economic status and their children, and their strongest emotional bonds are with parents, children, siblings, and cousins, not one another.

In romantic marriage, the emphasis is on personality, on habits, interests, likes, and dislikes. The strongest emotional bond is the conjugal bond, and sex becomes not just another household duty for the wife but an expression of deep intimacy. Tragically, for many couples the promise of, the desire for, the demand to have this kind of intimacy comes when shifting social and economic patterns push men and women further apart in their interests, their outlooks, and their ability to comprehend, appreciate, and depend upon one another. Romantic marriage demands a kind of love that is increasingly impossible in modern Brazilian cities.

Under the changes of rapid urbanization, love shifts from a sentiment expressed in the practice of cohabitation to one expressed in discourse on the tender sensibilities of individuals. But socioeconomic changes affect men and women differently, pushing them away from each other with the same force with which they are pushed together. In our theories of emotion we need to pay attention to the often contradictory social and economic pressures that shape the experience and expression of sentiment. In addition, we need to recognize the role of human error in emotional interactions. As Northeast Brazilian men and women strive to gain shelter, food, and affection from one another, they often miscalculate, misunderstand, and misconstrue. Their perspectives are shaped by very different economic and moral pressures, so that mutual understanding and affection are extremely difficult to achieve.

Their sentiments come out not only in the form of verbal statements but also in Desjarlais's "gut feelings": powerful but inarticulate passions experienced as embodied distress (1992). The emotional folk syndromes of *susto, nervos, peito aberto*, and so forth, from which so many Caruaruense women (and some men) suffer, have their origins in the gap between what people believe they ought to feel, desperately try to feel, and what they actually manage to bring themselves to feel. They also take their place as tactics in the dramas that people create as attempts to ensure their access to and control over the emotional resources upon which access to economic resources depends.

Caruaruenses find love confusing; they do not always know what they feel, they change their minds, fool themselves, and make mistakes. Our theories need to make room for the playful nature of sentiment: the constant emotional manipulation in the micropolitics of gender relations, and the very human errors people make as they try their best to love one another under very difficult circumstances. For many Caruaruenses, modern society is a chaotic, confusing milieu in which mutual misunderstandings are rife and in which what they see as the solid, understandable love of olden times has been replaced by dishonest sentiments.

Love is falling, every day it's falling more. Out of one hundred marriages, I think five last. People confuse love and liberty. The way I was raised, the children divided their earnings with their parents and paid the rent, but today the kids think they know everything and that their earnings are their own to do with what they want. Disobedience of children to parents and wives to husbands is on the rise. Too many marriages are based on lies, that she promises him or he promises her what he or she will not really do, and this is the cause of so many weak marriages. Sometimes it is not really a promise, it is that she thinks that he promised or he thinks that she promised, but the other one has a different idea. Then each one ends up betrayed, but there was no real promise to start. Just a lot of hope and a little delusion. (Natalino)

Social and economic change has made it easier for young people to act on their feelings in the formation of marriages. However, economic considerations and traditional gender roles remain important forces in shaping marital relations. Men remain freer than women to satisfy their physical and emotional desires, and both sexes must negotiate complex situa-

tions as they try to figure out what they feel, how they can act, and what
the consequences of their actions may turn out to be. The choices they
make are not necessarily the best or most rational ones. Frequently they
mistake each other's or their own motivations and miscalculate the consequences of their actions. While many are disillusioned by their experiences, others hold on to the hope that one day they will achieve true love
and perfect union.

I think that there still exist people in the middle of a thousand, there are two
or three who still love truly. And we all watch them, and envy them, and try
to be like them, and cause ourselves and those we love so much pain trying so
hard to love, and failing, because we are human, we err, we are imperfect,
and love is a sublime thing that comes from God, and can get so lost inside of
us. And yet every once in a while, there it is, a flower blooming in a desert,
surviving against all the odds. (Josefa)

People couple for love, with love, foolishly deceived about love, in
hopes of future love, willing to love, trying to love, determined not to be
ensnared by love, convinced that to love would be senseless, desperate
over the necessity of a loveless match. Love forms the idiom in which people discuss courtship and marriage, the underlying theme of the story of a
relationship.

Urbanization and capitalization have changed both the content of
gender roles and the relationships of men and women; men and women
continue to inhabit interdependent but largely separate spheres in today's
Caruaru, as they did in the past. But unlike the rural past, today these
separate spheres are increasingly disconnected from one another, while at
the same time urban society expects a degree of emotional intimacy between men and women that is unprecedented.

8 ∜ Infidelity in Companionate and Romantic Marriage

> I can say that I lack for nothing, I'm doing well. But my husband is *safado*, a womanizer, shameless. So I have a car, I have a house, I have money, but this is not what a woman wants. I want love. Like the people's saying: Without love you don't live.
>
> Sarita

Why was Maria Imaculada so upset when she heard that her husband was having an affair? A perusal of the literature on Latin America gives the impression that male infidelity is so common as to be an expected part of marriage. To understand the depths of Maria Imaculada's rage, we need to examine more closely the meaning of her husband's infidelity.

As we have seen in previous chapters, the intensity of romantic passion contradicts the routinization of marital relations and the calmness of ideal companionate love. Marital relations, always complex and multilayered, have become even more than ever a thicket of conflicting obligations, interpretations, and levels of meaning, as rapid change modifies social relations in Northeast Brazil. In marriages increasingly described as based on romantic love, customary sexual infidelity threatens the basis of the marital relationship as never before. Like Sarita, quoted above, working-class Northeast Brazilian women increasingly demand that their husbands not only support but also love them, and see fidelity as one of love's major constituents.

It is not surprising that Caruaruenses, so highly interdependent, place a high value on loyalty. They not only worry about unfaithful spouses but also judge the loyalty of friends and relatives. The same terms are used for disloyalty by spouse, relative, or friend. The word "infidelity" (*infidelidade*) is rare; people prefer the stronger *traição* ("betrayal") or *covardia* ("cowardliness"). People I spoke with generally agreed that fidelity, honesty, and respect are all aspects of the same phenomenon.

Fidelity is to respect the other, don't speak ill of him behind his back, be honest. . . . Don't make *safadeza* ("mischief") with him. (Margarida)

In the past, and continuing in some rural areas today, a man showed respect for his wife by sparing her anything but *sexo papai e mamãe*,[1] being discreet about his extramarital sexual adventures, and treating her with courtesy. Women showed respect for their husbands through courtesy, obedience, and sexual fidelity. In this system, the wife tolerated her husband's infidelities as long as they did not become serious enough to constitute an economic threat. This does not mean that the wife had no emotional reaction to infidelity, just that her possible jealous anger was not socially recognized as serious enough to warrant a change in male behavior.

Jealousy

> *Ciúme* is when you like a woman and can't have her, and *inveja* is
> when a person is angry because another has something that the
> first wants and can't have. So if my girlfriend is betraying me I can
> have *ciúme* for her, and if my friend has a beautiful car and me here
> with only this ugly little VW Bug, I can have *inveja* for him.
>
>   Chico

Emotion ideologies do not only define individual sentiments; they also demarcate the relations among different sentiments and assign them moral values. Since love is ideally supposed to be self-sacrificing, Northeast Brazilians tend to consider jealousy, as a selfish sentiment, more part of *paixão* than of love.

Folklore portrays envy, so destructive of social harmony in small-scale societies, as poisonous in itself, not only harming the group but also damaging personal health: In the form of the evil eye, it can cause sickness, kill plants, and even crack stones and bricks (Rebhun 1995). However, although jealousy may also be condemned as harmful, unlike envy it can be exciting; the degree to which a woman is jealous is said to indicate her sexual fire; to which a man is jealous his virility. As the proverb says, *Mulher sem ciume é como flor sem perfume* ("A woman without jealousy is like a flower without scent"). And while many generally associate *ciúme* with *paixão*, others see it as an indicator of *amor*, although this is controversial:

I have a friend who has a husband, he leaves her at will; she does what she wants, she goes where she wants, understand, so she said that he doesn't love her. So I said, "Oh, creature, he loves you, he trusts you." But she says no. (Samira)

Here, Samira defines love as mutual trust, and thus the husband's liberality as a marker of love. Her friend sees the liberality as marking lack of interest.

A Outra: Male Adultery

In 1990, a character in the hit *telenovela Rainha da Sucata* decided that it was better to be *a outra* ("the other woman") than to be a wife, not only because *a outra* is more powerful but also because she has more fun.[2] Slinking up to her rival's fiancé, she purred:

I will be that one who will disturb your home, ruin your family, destroy your relation little by little. . . . I will not give you one minute of relief.[3]

The character was played as a comic figure, but her adventures sparked a flurry of interest, inspiring television talk shows, newspaper and magazine articles, and even a best-selling anthropological study on the phenomenon of *a outra* in Brazilian life (Goldenberg 1990).

Adultery, a federal offense, is legally defined as a "crime against the family" (Rocha 1980, 81). Popularly, people define adultery as sexual relations between a married woman and a man not her husband, or the maintenance of a woman as a mistress by a man (de Azevedo 1968, 295). Laws, however, define adultery as a state of *namoro* between a married person and any individual not his or her spouse. Sexual intercourse is not necessary for a legal finding of adultery (Rocha 1980, 82; Varela 1980). Any material goods a married man gives to his mistress can be legally repossessed by his legitimate wife, at which point they become her private property, excluded from the joint property administered by husbands (Rocha 1980, 101). Nonetheless, Brazilian men's reputation for marital infidelity is too often well deserved.

The North Americans have only one woman, and the Brazilians also have one—one on every street! (Glória)

For some men, sex is an issue separate from love and marriage.

I have a great fault. I have an irresistible attraction for infidelity. I am faithful, at times. I like my wife, but this doesn't mean that I don't get interested in other people. According to the normal moral standards this is wrong. But inside of me I don't think this is wrong, understand? . . . Betrayal is a very relative thing. . . . The fact that you like one person doesn't mean that you don't get horny for another person, you know how it is? (Welington)

For men like Welington, to be a man is to have license, and they feel free to take any sexual opportunity offered to them. Jõaozinho was only half joking when he told me:

All men like to "jump the fence." It is because everyone says that a woman's heart is big because there is always room for one more. A man's heart is also big. It's in the Bible, you have to share with those who don't have any. Really, an adventure adds interest to life, renews. I don't go seeking after, but if a little girlfriend appears offering herself I won't say no, saying I'm married, go away, no. My wife knows. Sometimes I go out at night and return the next day, and I tell her right away, I arranged another. A little flirt here or there never hurt anyone.[4]

Men generally do not define occasional one-night stands or brief affairs as adulterous, reserving the word *adultéria* for long-term affairs. Keeping a mistress is disloyal to one's wife, but bedding an easy conquest a few times is a simple *aventura* ("adventure") and none of a wife's business. Women are more divided on the topic; while some regard *aventuras* as insulting irritations and long-term affairs as infuriating, others call any sexual contact outside of marriage *traição* ("betrayal"). Although most women would prefer that their husbands remain faithful, a brief fling can be dismissed with *Usou, lavou, enxugou, 'ta limpo* ("He used it, he washed it, he dried it, it's clean"),[5] but a long-term affair is deeply troubling for many wives.

Casual infidelity is often an integral part of male friendship formation, especially in the working class (cf. Robben 1989). Working-class men go drinking and womanizing together, and much of their conversation involves telling sexual jokes and boasting about sexual conquests. Such men regard a faithful husband as *manso* ("tame, domesticated") because he lets his wife's jealousies control rather than excite him.

A woman has to hide her infidelities, but the man, he shows it to the world. The man gains status by way of affairs. But the woman stays dirty. (Bárbara)

A man who refuses to betray his wife may lose out not only on personal status but also on economic opportunities available through social networks.[6]

As proverbs indicate, all women are fair game for sexual attempts under the *machista* ethos: *Não desejas a mulher do próximo quando ele estiver perto* ("Thou shalt not covet thy neighbor's wife when he is nearby"), and *Só canto mulher de alguém quando o alguém não tá perto* ("Flirt with someone's wife only when that someone isn't nearby"). Jokes constantly play with men's fear of their neighbors' sexual aggressions and their wives' disloyalties.

It happened that in a small town a baby was born. So it was born in the morning and that very afternoon it spoke. It said, "Three days from now my father dies." So everyone was shocked, the newspaper came, the television came, and the infant said, "Three days from now my father dies." And the mother was crying, her husband was crying, *né*, one day passed, two days passed. "Tomorrow my father dies!" He cried more, three days passed. "Today my father dies!" He was crying constantly, it was the afternoon of the third day, crying uncontrollably, and the neighbor died!

Sometimes infidelity takes the form of a series of brief affairs or one-night stands. But often it develops into a long-term, stable relationship, with the man living maritally with more than one woman.

A Teuda e Manteuda: Concubinage

Caruaruenses distinguish between two types of *outras*: the sexually loose woman who has brief flings with married men, and *a teuda e manteuda* ("the had and kept woman") who maintains a long-term affair with a married man, often bearing him children and being supported by him. Such a man lives between his *casa civil* ("civil house") with his wife and his *casa militar* ("military house") with his concubine, often residing with the wife and visiting the concubine regularly.[7]

Papa visits Mommy every day, only not on Sunday. He lunches here every weekday [lunch is the major meal of the day] and spends Saturday here also. It's Mommy who goes with him to do the shopping for the two families. Papa eats dinner with his wife. If it happens that he does not arrive at their house on time, his wife sends one of my half-brothers to call him here. (Arnoldo, age eight)

It is easy for men to arrange adulterous liaisons, in part because many men travel in connection with their work as traveling salesmen, migrant workers, or truck drivers. Maintaining auxiliary "wives" in homes along a route, as Maria Imaculada's husband did, or at two poles of a labor migration, serves as much as a convenience as a pleasure for many men. Two "wives" provide more than one location at which to get laundry done and food prepared, as well as sexual variety. More than one woman also means maintaining more than one relationship, more than one set of responsibilities, more than one set of lies, more than one source of guilt.

The Brazilian man makes a point of betraying his wife. There are some who go out, screw a slut in a motel, return home, and screw their legal wife the same day. Make a point of it. I don't know why. There was a time when I was very much a *namorador*. I courted three, four women at the same time. Seems

good, doesn't it? It was an inferno. Sometimes two appeared here and fought.
I decided to choose one woman and be loyal to her to demonstrate my love
for her. So I married. But it's really difficult. I try, I try, but actually to be honest I don't manage to. At the beginning of my relationship as fiancé and later
as husband, I was doing everything to be faithful. But an old girlfriend of
mine appeared. So, now it makes two years that I am having an affair with
her. Now I don't know. I don't love her, but I will say, sex with her is the best
in my life. I can't say why, what is different; she doesn't do anything that others haven't already done for me. I can only say that I won't let her go. But
there comes the guilt, there comes—my head is all, I am totally confused, and
I don't have any ideas about how I'm going to resolve all this. I feel that I'm
waiting for something to happen, just that I don't know what is going to happen nor how the situation is going to be resolved, nor if there exists a resolu-
tion. (Robson)

Sometimes concubinage results from a breakdown in the original marriage or liàison. Until recently, in the absence of divorce, a man might
leave his wife and move in with another woman without legalizing their
new status. A responsible man will continue to support and occasionally
visit his legitimate wife and children even after starting a new relationship. Here concubinage is more a form of serial semimonogamy than informal polygyny. Of course, there do also exist men who maintain more
than one concubine at a time, although this is rare. Often men abandon a
woman during her pregnancy because of sexual prohibitions on pregnant
and lactating women, or tensions about being sexual with a woman defined as a mother, or for other reasons. Men with several families can always maintain one or more "wives" pregnant while not being sexually
deprived. As the saying goes: *Melhor ter duas porque quando uma não pode, a
outra quer* ("It's better to have two because when one can't, the other one
wants to"). Occasionally men take a concubine if their marriage is infertile
or produces only daughters.

My uncle got mad at my aunt because she had four daughters. So she got
pregnant, and he went and also knocked up four other women. He said he
would live with the one who had a son, would give a new car to the woman
who had a son. So all five had girls and he became the father of nine daughters, dying of rage. When my aunt finally had a son it was this kind that looks
like a Chinese baby and stays foolish, very fat with little, short fingers, and
the tongue hanging out all the time.[8] But it is only this one that the father
loves. (Emília)

Very rarely a man lives in one house with more than one woman and set of
children. I knew of three cases: In two, the women were twin sisters; in the
other the two "wives" had been maintained in separate houses until the

man suffered an economic downturn and consolidated his households. The two women in that case fought both with fisticuffs and verbal abuse until a hierarchy was established. The blended family lived together in a state of constant conflict. I knew of one case where a woman lived maritally with two men. This was regarded as a perverse, immoral aberration by the neighbors.

The motivation for concubinage is not entirely masculine. Some women pursue married men because they do not know the man is married, because they do not care whether he is married, because they derive a sense of status from "stealing" other women's men, or because they prefer liaisons with married men.

The blame for these shameless men of three wives, I think it's the women's fault. Because there are lots of women who want a man for economic interests and don't care if he is married. (Rubí)

Since association with a man is so important for a woman who wants a house and children, many women seek out relations regardless of whether the man is married. As long as they like the man and can get the economic support they need, they do not feel any necessity to marry legally or to worry about previous or current relationships. Other women have personal or ideological aversions to marriage. For such women, a married man is the perfect partner: There is no danger that he will want the relationship to turn more serious. Other women would prefer to be the legitimate spouse but do not manage to arrange that. In some cases they do not discover that their boyfriend is married until they are already involved with him:

A friend of mine knew a man and was going out with him and so on and so forth. She discovered that he was married, that he had never told her. So she confronted the man and said, "You're thinking what? You're going to do what with me?" So he said, "I can go so far as to get engaged. But I can't marry, no." And she was already sleeping with him. (Catrina)

In other cases, they decide that they love the man, married or not.

I knew that he was married when I started with him, but I liked him. I never thought about his wife. I didn't want him to leave his wife for me. I wasn't upset with her. . . . He went to ask my father to court me. So Dad said, "No, because you are already married." So he said, "But I'll *dar um jeitinho*." . . . There are many women who marry and it's only to have the status [lit. "name"] of a married woman. . . . . They want to have their home, their house, their husband. Not me . . . I erred, but I'm sorry. . . . I suffered a lot under his fingernails. For a woman to love a womanizer, it's for the person to really suffer. . . . Men already are no good, so it's neither better to be the wife nor better to be the other woman.[9] I know from my own experience that the other woman suffers a lot, but I think that a *legítima* ("the legitimate wife") suffers more. (Quitéria)

In the past, a man might pursue a *concubina* in order to spare his wife the demands of his appetite for sexual diversity and frequency. Transgressive sexual acts (especially anal sodomy) might dishonor a wife, and a concubine could better accommodate a man's desire for sexual frequency. Here, adultery, rather than being a crime of betrayal against a wife, reflects a lack of male refinement.

Because men are dogs. They belch. They fart. They chew with their mouths open. They like to fuck asses. And they love to screw around. They are not ashamed of anything. They do it all in public. (Maria das Prazeres)

It is not surprising that so many women believe that they cannot trust any man, that even the seemingly best husband could be concealing an affair. They are right. This fear is reflected in a joke told to me by a housewife:

There was a married woman, and she kept watching her husband. He was a hard worker. He left home every day at six A.M. and returned at seven P.M. And she always watched to see that he returned at the right time. One day he died. So she went every day to his grave and stayed there crying and praying. One day she met another lady also praying at the same grave. So she asked, "Do you know who is buried here, ma'am?" The other lady said, "It's my husband, the father of my seven children." So the wife said, "You are deceived, ma'am. Here is buried *my* husband and the father of *my* seven children. And I know that he never had another woman because I was watching him and noted that he left at 6 A.M. and returned at 7 P.M. I know he was at work or at home every hour of every day." So the other lady said, "It is you who are deceived, *senhora*. You forgot the lunch hour!"

Wives on Adultery

Women vary widely in their response to adultery. Some women regard any infidelity as destructive to marital love.

A man who truly loves doesn't have any reason to "jump the fence" because he doesn't have anything to look for outside. (Emília)

Others believe that if they show trust in their husband he will respond by being faithful.

I think that if a woman gives liberty to the man, even if he wants to practice something wrong there outside, because man is a damned beast . . . he will remember that she's there, that the woman didn't fight with him, he doesn't have a motive to do such nonsense, to arrange women. (Josefa)

One reason women give for their men's infidelity is the search for sexual adventure, especially the desire to engage in anal sex. But housewives contrast the fleeting pleasures of sexual adventure with the lasting value of housework:

They arrange other women outside to make a different love, but at base they like the maid-servant they have at home. Because there outside they encounter sex. But at home they have washed clothes, they have food, they have the . children, they have a lot of things. And if one day he comes to lose all of this, so, what will he do? (Severina)

While some wives put up with their husband's infidelities, many do not. Some refuse to remain with a philanderer. Others stay with their husbands but attack the other woman, especially when they view her as a financial threat.

He bought a good house for her. If I had a proof I would have taken her house because I had minor children of his. . . . I went out with my daughter, I saw her. . . . I kept talking very sarcastically with her. . . . I opened her purse, took her money . . . she had a little knife in her purse, I would have given a stab in her belly, but my daughter held me and she left town. (Marilú)

Generally a woman may attack any rival who appears after herself in her man's life, but previously established or legalized relationships have precedence. The legitimate wife can go after *as outras*, and *outra* number one can attack subsequent girlfriends, as long as she leaves *a legítima* alone.

The legitimate wife I leave over there, but when he arranged this third woman, I broke the wood of her house and she locked herself in. I was small but fierce, *ooxe!* He advanced on me to take me out forcefully, that hell. He moved her to another place; I went and broke her door. He moved her again to there; I discovered her house. . . . I gave a punch that threw her teeth out. She only lived with broken teeth, that rat-fever.[10] So when the other woman died, his wife came here to say to me, "One already damned, one to go!" (Zeferina)

Neighbors told me that one reason relations between little Arnoldo's mother and his father's legitimate wife were so calm was that she was so good at keeping him from his other girlfriends. She also had more children with him (six) than any of his other girlfriends. The children knew who their legitimate half-siblings were, and knew that other illegitimate half-siblings existed, although they could not identify those.

The legitimate wife needs to be careful in how she responds to *as outras,* because contact with a nonvirtuous rival pollutes a virtuous woman.

Once I learned that he was there with her. . . . I went there, broke the window, climbed on top of the two, on top of the bed. So he grabbed me, covering my mouth for me not to yell. She ran away, but he kept fighting, me hitting him. . . . He kept saying not to do this at all, it's ugly for me because a married woman crosses paths with a slut there outside. He didn't want this at all. (Samara)

Men's sexual escapades belong to the amoral *rua,* and for a wife to come into contact with them pollutes the sanctity of the *casa* (cf. Robben 1989, 198). Men's Teflon character allows them to wash off the moral pollution of the *rua,* but women are permanently degraded by publicly acknowledging awareness of or contact with it. Some women play on this contrast, responding to adultery by increasing their moral sanctity through exaggerated piety, as when Dona Magdalena, Glória's mother, eschewed new clothing upon learning of her husband's long-term infidelity (chapter three). In so doing, she made her life into a moral contrast with her husband's, and that contrast into an accusation.

Despite the pain of betrayal, women often stay with their adulterous husbands because of financial dependence, fear of gossip, or fear of returning to their paternal home:

He's a big womanizer, skirt chaser, an arranger of women. He never arranges for keeps, but he always prepares one. . . . We already separated, but the *jeito* is, I think that if I separate from him, for me to return to my family's house with my children will be worse. I will suffer even more. So I have to put up with it. (Damiana)

The emotional control required to stay in a bad marriage can be arduous.

The people say that he has another woman, already so many times I'm used to it. . . . I ask, he says it's because man is really shameless, leaves the good in *casa* and goes after the bad on the *rua.* . . . But I can't leave because I have three kids and don't work at anything. . . . I'm trying to see if I manage to not care anymore, stay calm, only try to live with him like this, because if I care a lot I will separate from him. I try to forget, to take the thought out of my head. Oh, but it's so hard! (Samara)

Even when a woman believes that she has forgiven her husband for a past infidelity, the hurt may continue to haunt a marriage.

I don't have any more anger. I pardoned him, pardoned her; it's all right. But there are times when I stay thinking. We go to sleep, him sleeping, and me there thinking. I touch the subject, he says, "I'm going to sleep." He doesn't want to talk at all. But I keep thinking. I almost don't sleep anymore. My nerves are shot. (Maria Consolata)

This is a different kind of inarticulate communication than the companionably unstated understanding of a restricted communicative code. There love goes without speaking, expressed through practices, but here silence smothers resentment as fear of open conflict prevents open discussion.

It's not like we were, no, it stays with that coldness inside the house. We perceive it, *né*, in the speech, in the look, in everything. . . . Before we shared everything, but not now. (Assunção)

When the infidelity is on the part of the woman, the situation is even more difficult.

Female Adultery and the *Corno*

Female adultery is popularly seen as very different from male adultery. Men's honor is dependent on their women's chastity; their masculinity on their ability to control their women. While a straying husband may wound a wife's feelings and steal from joint property to support a mistress, a straying wife diminishes a man's masculinity and insults his authority. A woman who stays with an adulterous husband will be praised for her long-suffering loyalty, whereas a man who stays with an adulterous wife is considered a weak fool. Thus while male adultery is a mere indiscretion, female adultery can end the marriage. That is why one day, when I arrived at the end of a marital spat, I heard a housewife shouting at her husband's retreating back:

If you want it this way, fine! Go away, really go away and see what I'll do! I'll get the first dog [I meet] and take him to bed. This marriage bed right here, oh! Just for you to know that you can never more return. Never more!

Had she made good on her threat, her husband would in fact not have been able to return to her without serious loss of social status. Her threat, however, was idle; she would have lost more status by adultery than he would have lost by abandoning an unfaithful wife.

An adulterous wife "puts horns" on her husband, a *corno* ("cuckold"). Any man might be cuckolded without knowing it, but a man who knows it and stays with his wife nonetheless is utterly contemptible (cf. Brandes 1980, 88). Such a man is derided as a *corno convencido* ("a convinced cuck-

old") who likes his status, a *corno manso* ("tame cuckold"), who is too controlled by his wife, or a *corno papai-noel* ("Santa Claus cuckold"), who gives
gifts to other men's children as if they were his own. A *corno ateu* ("atheist
cuckold"), who does not believe the evidence of his wife's infidelity, is as
foolish as the one who does believe and does nothing. People pun that *cornos* belong to the *Irmandade de São Cornélio* (Brotherhood of St. Cornelius):
de-sexed, like monks.

In general, while women regard male infidelity as destructive of love,
men regard female infidelity as destructive of masculinity, as indicated by
the folk saying *O pau mais mole é o do meu marido porque o do vizinho endure-
ceu* ("The softest prick is my husband's because my neighbor's got hard").
The *corno* is seen as sexually penetrated by his rival; his wife's infidelity
symbolically feminizes him (Brandes 1980, 95; Parker 1991, 48). Significantly, a *corno* is "horned" not by his rival but by his wife (Brandes 1980,
90; Parker 1991, 48), a consequence of the idea that women bear the moral
responsibility and stain of sexuality. While the rival bests and betrays the
corno, the wife's treachery is considered the greater disgrace.

Disrespected *cornos* cannot protect members of their household from
other men's sexual aggression. The stigma of his weakness and his wife's
misbehavior spreads to all members of the household, dishonoring
daughters.

Everyone said that my brother wasn't Papa's son, and truthfully, he looks a
lot like the man who is Mama's friend. She always had, let us say, strange
friendships with men. It is difficult for a girl to have a whore [*rapariga*]
mother and a weak father who puts up with anything. One day I went to ask
five cents from a friend of Mama's, and he said only if I grab his "stick." So I
told Papa, and he, convinced *corno* that he is, did nothing. All my little friends
from school went saying that Mama was a whore and him a *corno*. So when I
had my first boyfriend, his mother said, "No, that one is the daughter of a
whore." So we couldn't date. But he thought we could screw, because of my
mother. (Catrina)

The stigma of *corno* status intensifies male sexual jealousy. Proverbs
warn not to trust women: *Em mulher e freio de carro não se deve confiar* ("In
woman and car brakes you shouldn't have confidence") says one; another
sneers *A única mulher que andou na linha o trem matou* ("The only woman
who walked the line was killed by the train").[11] Many men forbid their
women from social intercourse with unrelated men and from dressing or
acting in any way to attract male sexual interest; they also may accuse
their wives and girlfriends of inviting men's sexual interest.

He is very jealous. When we go to a dance, the guys look at me . . . so he already starts to fight with me. "But you've already started to look at so and so!" and me, "I'm not looking." He says, "You are, because he is looking at you." So the argument already starts. It was because of this that I stopped going to dances. (Araruna)

Given the importance of controlling their women, men are often exaggeratedly jealous of their womenfolk, accusing them of having affairs with every man they meet.

He said that I arranged men. Every man that arrived here he said was my male until it was disgusting. (Maria das Dores)

Male sexual jealousy is a major factor not only in widespread conjugal violence but also in what Brazilians call the crime of passion (*crime da paixão*): the murder of an adulterous wife, and often her lover, by an outraged husband. This has been legally permitted for most of Brazil's history as the "legitimate defense of honor" (*legítima defesa de honra*). Given the prevalence of suspicion, betrayal, and violence in sexual relations, disillusion with love is common, especially among women.

Disillusion

Love doesn't exist, no. Only the word exists.

Maria da Paz

Some informants, disillusioned by their own experiences, stated that there is no such thing as love, that it is simply a story told to mislead the naive. Women are often disillusioned by the fading of infatuation in the dailiness of marriage, and by infidelity.

I learned that it's not like that, that you don't live for love, that love is an illusion. . . . I made a marriage for love. . . . But today I have respect, I like him, I don't want anything bad ever to happen to him, but I don't feel love because I already passed so much bitterness. . . . Our love is divided every day that we pass; we love our parents, don't we love them? Isn't it the only thing we love? So a man appears that takes us away from our parents. Why did he take us? Because we didn't feel so much love that we could stay with them. Afterward he disillusions you, so you have a son and that love already divides itself. There ahead he thinks another woman better than you, so what love is this? (Fátima)

Here, Fátima describes love as a zero-sum game, so that love for a man diminishes love for parents, love for children robs from love for husband, and a husband's infidelity detracts from his love for his wife (cf. Foster

1965). Others see love as an illusion for the young, disbelieved by wise elders.

At the time that I married, I thought everything was love, but it wasn't. . . . At times people said, "But Damiana, you are so young and to marry now! You look at marriage as good, but that is not all there is to life. Think of the salt [bitterness]!" I would say, "Salt is to put in the beans!" So pronto, it ended that the salt is what I am living now, you know? . . . Life two-by-two, when the two like each other, it's marvelous. But when you don't understand each other, it is a purgative like the worst you can drink (laughing). . . . But marriage is made like a lottery, isn't it? Not everyone has to be lucky. (Damiana)

Others see love as fleeting or momentary.

True love does not exist, no. I think that what exists are moments of happiness. But love the whole life I don't believe in it, no. There doesn't exist happiness in marriage. There exist moments of happiness, but not the whole life happy. If I was a maiden [moça] again, I wouldn't marry again, no way. The maidens are full of imagination, but it isn't a happy life, no. (Severina)

In some cases disbelief in love results from the conflict between the companionate and the romantic love models.

Love between men and women doesn't exist, no. The people keep talking of love because there are people who get too accustomed to each other. . . . This love is the greatest illusion of the world. (Rosabela)

Paradoxically, happiness flees the more you seek it.

Love is a grand lie. It doesn't exist, no. We idealize everything. When we are children we only want to be big to have liberty. When we are big we keep saying, "Where did my youth go?" When single, we only want to marry to be happy. When married, we only want to separate. When separated we only want to marry again. Always happiness is one step there ahead of us, but step there and it has already fled. (Catrina)

Love and Infidelity

Men's customary sexual freedom threatens romantic marriage and increases women's resentment of infidelity, as sexual intercourse shifts to its modern definition as an expression of love in the form of perfect union.

I don't like my husband. I loved him before, but nowadays I don't like him anymore, from the moment that I discovered him with the other woman. I don't feel any more confidence in him. . . . It's a relief when he's not in the house. It's difficult when he's in the house, we fight. I complain; he goes: "Get lost!" so I cry. In the past I loved him a lot. For me love means to be faithful, one to the other, *né:* If he liked me he would be faithful. But I discovered and so the love ended, everything ended. (Sebastiana)

Some women manage to turn infidelity into an affirmation of love by contrasting the fleeting nature of affairs with the endurance of true love.

There are women who don't accept girlfriends, no way. If he has another woman, I go after. Fight. Order him to choose. Either he leaves her or he leaves home. As he himself says, he would never disdain neither me nor the kids for no woman on the street. I've already gone after many times; I've already caught him with them . . . but he chooses me and leaves the girlfriend. I think that's why we are still living together, because he always chooses me. (Nilza)

But the idea that a man who truly loves does not commit adultery is gaining ground.

If the man likes the woman he doesn't do that role. He doesn't betray the woman, no way. . . . It's to respect one another because that's what's important. . . . It's an irresponsibility of the man; he isn't much of a man, no, if he does that. Not nowadays. (Clorinda)

The joys of love are tempered by the pain of betrayal, as much for men as for women:

Love generally hurts more than it pleases. When I feel I lost a person it hurts a lot, and the pain that I have already felt from this was a thousand times greater than all the love I have already felt. . . . Generally, in love, women suffer more than men because of husbands' infidelity. When a man knows of his wife's betrayal he separates from her, but the women continue with them because of security or for love. (Agostinho)

Daughters, Sons, Love, and Adultery

In the *telenovela Tieta*, based on Jorge Amado's novel of the same name, a male character's long-term infidelity is tolerated by his wife, at least on the surface. But when his teenage daughter finds out about it, she feels so betrayed that she cannot stand the sight of her father, throwing him out of the house and accepting him back only after he has dropped the affair and been publicly humiliated. During this plot segment the mother continues to speak and even sleep with her husband, and she befriends the other woman.[12] The story, and the fictional daughter's anguish, rang true with many women.

In my family it's the same as in the *novela*. The history of my grandfather is the following: He left Grandma and went to live with the other woman. He left her with nine children. So she always remained his friend, sent food to him, everything. But Aunt Maria, who was a teenager at the time, never accepted it. No way. She kept crying, saying he was no good, everything.

So the other woman died. He's already old, returned to live with Grandma. It's all right with her. But Aunt Maria, who never married, who still lives at home, she doesn't talk to him, no. Doesn't even look in his face. For her, she doesn't have a father. There was no way. He had to leave there. Daughters never accept the other woman. It has to be either the mother or her. He can't love anyone else. (Catrina)

Men have two competing attitudes toward their daughters. On the one hand, daughters may feel more loyal to them than wives, almost as loyal and loving as mothers. On the other, father-daughter relations often display great tensions. Four older, unmarried women each told me that they had never married because *P'ra mim, homem, só existe o meu pai* ("For me, man, there exists only my father"). Discovery of a father's infidelity can be shattering to a young girl, causing a hurt that haunts her even as an adult. Glória told me about the impact of her discovery of her father's long-term affair:

I discovered the situation when I was about seven years old. I was playing with my dolls. I was wearing a lilac and rose princess dress, and my little friend there was wearing green. So then a woman who was there made some sarcastic comment that I did not understand: if I was the daughter of the man who was with so-and-so. So I went to my mother and asked what it meant, and she began crying. That's when she started to wear old clothes, but before she had been very fashionable. It was the biggest shock of my life because I really adored my father until the moment I found out. You have to understand that I was his little princess, and he was so handsome, so very. . . . So today I love to sew, I love to make princess style dresses for girls, the prettiest thing in the world. But I can't use these colors, lilac, rose, green, without getting dizzy, nauseated, chest pains. I never keep my money; I spend it soon, so no one will marry me just for money. I'm not going to suffer as my mother suffered, as I saw her suffer. I'm not going to marry just for him to die in the other woman's bed as my father did with my mother. It won't happen to me.

Relations between fathers and daughters are often fraught with tension. Loving fathers want to indulge their daughters, dress them in princess dresses with bows and flounces, taking pride in their daughters' beauty. However, their very beauty attracts suitors who may take them away. While many daughters describe their fathers' attempts to seclude and control them as cruel, fathers describe their actions as protective. As with mothers and sons, the relationships between fathers and daughters often have the intensity of courtship, and equally intense conflicts.

Boys tend to regard their fathers' infidelities more in terms of the effect on their mothers than in terms of a hurt to themselves. One son of an adulterous union complained:

My father is a "jerk in boots" [*chato de galoxa*], a real shameless one. He is married over there but he lives courting. He met my mother, kept screwing and all, and look at the result [pointing to himself]. . . . I keep thinking, I'm never going to do this, make a woman suffer as my mother suffers—and I don't know how many others. But to be a man you have to do it. (Sebastião)

The frustrations of young lovers who discover that they are half-siblings because of a father's adultery are a staple of *telenovelas*. It also occurs in real life.

My friend had a big problem. She was courting a cousin, was ready to marry. So her mother, who is a widow, found a letter at home, a love letter that showed that her husband had had an affair with her sister, the mother's sister. It was exactly with the mother of the cousin fiancé that the father was sleeping, and it was more or less in the time that the fiancé was born, nine months before, that year. So pronto, it's a thing from a *novela* because it might be that the two are siblings. So now the mother hates the sister, prohibited the marriage, what terrible suffering! (Samara)

Sometimes adultery extends to stepdaughters, and when it is discovered it can tear families apart. One teenage man told me about the impact of his father's affair with his half-sister:

What happened was that my mother was a widow with two children. So she started with my father, he's married. So my half-sister from Mama's marriage, she was about sixteen years old at the time. So she lived with Grandpa. So she hated us. . . . She was angry because Mama began to live with Papa. And she felt abandoned. . . . Now my father is very *safado* ["mischievous"]. And she was pretty, and to tell the truth, she was flirting with him. And the two were seeing each other, Papa and my sister. Mama did not know. Isn't it the most horrible thing?

A maid named Maria lived with us, that she knew everything, just not how to tell Mama. I was at Grandpa's house. I remember as if it were today. I didn't know it was going to be the last time I lunched with Grandpa. So my adorable sister stayed in the bedroom with Papa, so Maria couldn't stand it and called Mama. So my mother kept beating her and spilling all she felt, yelling. And the worst was that my grandfather knew everything but he didn't say because Papa was giving money to them. So he expelled my mother and with her all the years of happiness that I might have had. Today, Mama doesn't even speak Grandpa's name, nor that of my sister; for her, they don't exist. I hate that whore [*puta*] my sister. I hate my grandfather; I hate Mama who stayed with the *safado* and threw her family away in order to have money for those little pests my brothers. About my father, not even hate covers what I feel. I swear to you that I will avenge myself of him yet. I will kill him from the heart, like he killed me.

Female infidelity has always threatened marriages, and it continues to do so. Increased pressures on men because of their economic weakness may intensify their horror of losing control of their women. Male infidelity, never easy for women to live with, more than ever threatens marital love. With romantic passion increasingly held up as a prior condition for, and emotional basis of, marriage, infidelity threatens the foundations of modern relationships. While wage labor does not completely free women to choose their mates, it does open possibilities for escape from untenable relationships. Not every woman has the necessary vision, courage, or life circumstances to enable her to leave an unfaithful mate, but the new emphasis on romantic marriage increases many women's desire to do so. The different pressures that economic change brings to bear on men and on women make infidelity even more painful for both genders than ever before.

9 ⌒ Considerations of Love in Caruaru

The discovery of a palimpsest, or old document upon whose parchment some ancient hand wrote, erased imperfectly, and wrote again, pleases scholars, who can see in both writing and erasure the layered history of the ideas that went into the creation of the written record. From the Greek for "rubbed again," the word *palimpsest* can also be used in an extended, metaphoric sense to refer to the layers of confused, partial memories experienced after an alcoholic bender (Jellinek 1952), as well as to the thicket of competing discourses fragmented and superimposed in today's multitemporally heterogeneous cultures (cf. Alarcón 1997).

Contemporary discourses of love in Caruaru display this palimpsestic quality. Deeply marked by their history among the European ancestors of New World settlers, and within the mixed cultural matrix of the Brazilian experience, they respond to contemporary pressures as well. Considerations of the history of love illuminate contemporary situations not only as a scene-setting device or story of origins but also because they reveal situations in which various pressures and solutions were brought to bear on comparable emotional paradoxes.

Love-Marriage and Economic Change

In the 1980s, Jane Fishburne Collier returned to the Andalusian village where she had conducted fieldwork twenty years earlier, to find marked changes in how people spoke about marriage. The children of people who had carried out long, formal courtships and spoke of marriage in terms of social obligations were marrying after short courtships and speaking of marriage in terms of romance (1997). Laurel Kendall (1996) found "new style" marriages on the rise in the Korea of the 1980s; Vassos Argyrou (1996) traced the development of new ways of making matches and holding wedding ceremonies in Cyprus in the early 1990s; Homa Hoodfar (1997) found Egyptians debating the relative virtues of love matches and arranged marriages in 1983; and Simon Charsley (1991) presents details of the elaboration of the wedding industry in Scotland in the 1980s. In many settings, anthropologists have noted a general tendency toward elaborate white wedding ceremonies, shorter courtships, and more discussion of marriage as an outcome of romance occurring at about the same time as greater integration into the world economy. I have found a similar process at work in Caruaru.

Like these other theorists, I believe that economic changes and changes in marriage practices are related. In addition, I see *amor* not only as a vocabulary item that, like so many other words studied by anthropologists, encapsulates philosophies in shorthand but also as a set of stories in terms of which people describe themselves and their experiences to themselves and to others. I agree with Jane Collier that the shift, as she so poetically puts it, "from duty to desire" has a lot to do with how people talk about love and marriage, how they represent the relationship between the two to each other and themselves, and how they rationalize their decisions (1997). Charsley points out that people decide to marry for "perhaps typically tangled reasons," giving "standard justifications" for their decision. Love, he says, "will motivate or at least provide a language in which the complexities and idiosyncrasies of personal relationships can be expressed and presented in immediately acceptable form" (1991, 27–28).

Here we return to sentiment as language, with *amor* constituting a vocabulary in which to discuss a complex series of experiences and motivations. Like other sentiments, *amor* encompasses not only the words used to describe it, each with an attached set of expected scripts and correspondences, but also the series of viscerally felt, imperfect performances that people use as they attempt to convince themselves and others of their sincere feelings. *Amor* may describe a sense of delight experienced in the presence of the beloved, the joy of tender intimacy with a cherished friend, the ecstasy of passionate engagement. It also encompasses loyalty, compassion, generosity, forgiveness: labor on behalf of and suffering for the sake of another, and altruistic sacrifice as benevolent gift.

Collier theorizes that a change from property ownership to wage labor underlies the shift in discourse on love and marriage in Andalusia, because it alters the economic basis of marriage, changing spouses from co-owners to coworkers (1997, 113). In addition, she notes that while Andalusian villagers in the 1960s spoke of the necessity for endurance to maintain marriage, couples in the 1980s spoke of "working" on their relationships, a declaration she attributes to the need to produce an individual self in modern society (1997, 134), and which is reminiscent of Arlie Hochschild's descriptions of "emotion work" in the contemporary United States (1985).

Land ownership among European peasants has a deeper history than among the Brazilian peasantariat: In the Northeast Brazilian Agreste, farmers are more likely to squat, rent, or sharecrop than to own outright and legally. However, the move into the cities has created a process similar to Collier's shift to coworkers, as spouses turn to wage labor paid in cash and women increasingly bring in a larger share of income. I also find a similar shift from endurance or resignation (*conformação* in Portuguese) to emotion work in how women discuss the maintenance of their relationships, reflecting perhaps some of the difficulties of sustaining sentiment in the self. When people represent marriage as underpinned by love, then love needs to be maintained in order to continue the marriage, and that requires introspection, discussion, and effort. Where the marriage is based on duty (as Collier has it), or *obrigação* and *consideração* (as Caruaruenses described it), spouses must endure physical or emotional challenges as their responsibility; they can feel however they choose and discuss it or not as they see fit. But love, now that is hard work.

Love's Contradictions

As described in English and in Portuguese, the performance of *amor* is at once the most natural and the most difficult of human tasks. Upon *amor* and the cooperation, sharing, and protection it elicits depends our ability to sustain our corporeal lives in material and social worlds fraught with danger. To love is to experience the most acute of vulnerabilities: risking both rejection by the beloved and the hazards of loss in a world without guarantees of survival. People described themselves as loving helplessly, dangerously, and against their better judgment, or characterized *amor* as a willful act requiring constant effort to sustain. To do *amor* well requires strength of character, generosity, forgiveness, and maturity. The demands of *amor* often conflict, not only with personal human frailties but also with important cultural ideas and social patterns.

Ideas about love, its nature, course, and significance, its relationship to sexuality, its morality, its place in the family and in conjugal relationships, have changed over European and Brazilian history in response to the differing needs of changing economic and social arrangements. Change, however, has not been absolute; each new idea nests itself among existing ideas. Contemporary ideas of love incorporate the echoes of all that went before, giving modern love its palimsestic qualities. Always an idealization more virtuous than actual practice, love threads through theological concepts, social obligations, gender definitions, and economic ties: Discourses of love structure social roles, duties, and relationships. Although Christian theology ranks love morally opposite to economic stake, economic interest and emotional tie work in concert to create and sustain social relationships.

Kinship, friendship, and partnership all combine economic and emotional aspects as people demonstrate love through sharing, and through sharing obtain the goods and services upon which their lives depend. Sharing may be accomplished fairly and equally, or it may be coerced, unfair, unequal, and exploitative. Love itself can be as selfish as it can be generous. I have described love as a sort of emotional glue that can help societies to cohere. While considerations of love do not begin and end with exclusively functionalist considerations, it unfortunately must nonetheless be pointed out that unequal, exploitative sharing and selfish love can cohere societies as well as, if not better than, equality and generosity. Love is no guarantee of considerate treatment or equitable allotment, even from a functionalist point of view; it is no panacea.

Particularly in its sense as sexual desire, love lends itself to exploitation, control, and abuse. Sexual partners structure their relationships in accordance with notions of proper masculinity and femininity: behavioral rather than strictly physical qualities. A biological male may behave effeminately, a female behave in a masculine fashion. In Brazil, interpretations of sexual intercourse between two males or two females are as structured by notions of masculine and feminine as is heterosexual congress: All that is passive, receptive, and giving is styled feminine; all that is active, acquisitive, and devouring masculine (cf. Parker 1991). This division encourages people to react to one another not as individuals but as members of opposing groups, each with its stereotypical behavior. Ideally, given the complementarity of customary roles, as long as each partner plays his or her part properly, the couple can achieve smooth cooperation. Practical exigencies, however, wreak havoc. Social and economic change nibbles away at people's ability to live according to set roles, and even when things are relatively stable some find expected roles too confining, too different from their own preferences, too hard to live up to.

The idea of marrying on the basis of romantic attachment seems to offer a way out of stultifying role requirements, of tragic mismatches, of the lifelong misery a bad match can bring. Yet creating stable, long-term relationships centered on desire demands much of participants. Marriage and similar conjugal arrangements are about emotional and physical intimacy, yes, but they are also about economic intimacy: about dividing and sharing the labor of sustaining and running a household, about bearing and caring for children, and about facing and overcoming hardships, about accepting shortcomings, irritating habits, and failures in one's partner. These demand very different emotional skills than does ecstatic union.

The emotional requirements of sustaining long-term relationships have historically fallen more on women than on men. Women more than men have been told to subordinate their own desires to those of their families, to act generously, forgivingly, and affectionately regardless of their private sentiments, to work as hard as possible to convince not only others but also themselves of the depth and purity of the love they must feel. Historically, women in the areas I have discussed have had fewer escapes from partner and children than have men. There is no equivalent of the *concubina* for women: If they do not get their emotional needs met by their husband they cannot easily take a boyfriend on the side. Friendship with women, relations with female kin, and relations with children have provided greater emotional support for women than sexual relationships with men.

The sexual nature of passionate attraction has also presented difficulties for the women of Northeast Brazil, both historically and today. The legacy of Christian squeamishness about the body, especially the sexuality of the female body, strongly affects practices of sexual love in this region. Ironically, throughout Christian history, liberation from the demand to love has come for women in the form of asceticism: The rejection of the body, its sexuality, hunger, and desires, has allowed a rejection of the need to take care of others (Bloch 1991, 86–88). Until very recently, only by devoting themselves to a bodiless ideal of holiness through adoption of religious vocations have Christian women managed to escape being given in marriage and been allowed to compete in realms of intellect and spirituality defined as masculine. Women who cannot or will not submit to austerity must participate in sexuality, but largely on terms imposed in a masculocentric order, balancing between the contradictory ideas applied to sexual intimacy: A generous sharing of bodies and pleasures contrasts with a degrading besmirchment of virtue that characterizes the same acts.[1]

The shift, from seeing sexual intercourse as a right of husbands and highborn men toward wives and low-status women, to seeing it as an expression and proof of deep personal regard in all social classes is recent, imperfect, and incomplete. Sex-as-love competes ineffectively with sex-as-debauchery, sex-as-obligation, sex-as-right, sex-as-degradation. As long as impersonal sources of sexual satisfaction remain popular, sex-as-love will characterize only a portion of acts of sexual intercourse. The very different stakes and consequences for men and for women in sexual intercourse militate against achievement of sex-as-intimate-love for a large portion of the population. To the extent that emotional intimacy requires comprehension of the perspectives and experiences of the beloved, men's and women's customarily different social positions and correspondingly different viewpoints interfere with love-as-intimacy.

The concept of love as verbally elaborated emotional intimacy is not a recent innovation in the history of European and Europeanate cultures. Rather, it becomes more widespread and socially important at certain points in history, responding to changes in economic and social relationships and the relative power of men and women. The medieval troubadours wrote their elaborate love poetry in those European courts in which women had newly become most powerful. Similarly, the rise of the Romantic movement came at a time of shift in women's economic and social power, and, particularly, the decline of the use of dowries in upper-class marriages.[2]

As historian Howard Bloch points out, romantic love glorifies not individual women but Woman as category, a category thoroughly permeated by misogynistic ambivalence. The troubadour's lady love was lovable to the extent that she maintained her virtuous discretion; the Church's Bride of Christ was beloved of God at the expense of her sexuality (1991, 195–97). Similarly, the Romantic movement's attempt to conflate deep personal regard and sexual pleasure also idealized objectification of women, insisting that women passively accept male adoration, and basing itself in the division of the world into the two spheres of the virtuous, dependent, loving feminine and the amoral, independent, nonemotional masculine (Leach 1980, 112). This is reflected in contemporary Brazilian discourses on house and street.

While social change suggests the possibility of breaking out of stultifying conventions, of satisfying personal needs in ways not available to one's parents, dreams of love falter not only on the exigencies of daily practice but also on the complications of human frailty and difficulties in the concept of love itself. As long as love remains a female specialty demanding self-sacrifice, forgiveness, and self-renunciation, it keeps women socially and emotionally dependent on men, even when increasing economic power might give them the upper hand. When the customary balance of social and emotional power between men and women is disrupted, historically parallel role systems no longer work, and the trajectory of men's and women's lives becomes increasingly asymptotic, approaching, never meeting, separating, perhaps to attempt approach again.

Men and women have regarded one another through lenses shaped by need: the demands of desire, the exigencies of status, the search for affection's solace, the requirements of independence from parents, the wish for children, the coveting of property. Concepts such as the nineteenth-century feminists' "rational love," customary Brazilian companionate marriage, or the attempts at peer marriage now fashionable in the U.S. middle class constitute attempts to meet these needs calmly. Such realistic arrangements lack passion's ability to stir the soul's depths. However, creating a balance between the need for security and the need for passionate excitement is quite difficult. Some people never achieve it; others achieve it for brief periods only. And a few lucky souls manage to love passionately, securely, and for the long term, inspiring everyone else's jealous scrutiny. But since things are easier for everyone when most people are not having their passionate depths stirred, in often socially disruptive ways, sexual and emotional satisfaction constitute luxuries whose pursuit is more characteristic of those whose status gives them the leisure to indulge: the highborn, the wealthy, men. Those of low status, the poor, and women have rarely set the parameters of the search for love, and historically, definitions of true love reflect their exclusion.

Maria Imaculada: The Rest of the Story

As we have seen, Northeast Brazilians have historically placed more emotional emphasis on the mother-child bond than the husband-wife dyad as a relationship likely to yield satisfaction. With the exception of female religious, women of all classes looked to men for protection and influence in the world. Whether using sex to form alliances with powerful men or combining affection with guilt to manage sons, women could manipulate the varied meanings of love to gain a little breathing space in a

masculocentric world. Customary definitions of the nature of love may
have been male creations, but individual women have managed to play
upon love's contradictions to get what they cannot take directly.

We can see these processes at work in the story of Maria Imaculada
and her straying husband. Although on the surface this is a story about
love—his adulterous love for another woman, the hurt his betrayal cost
her loving heart, and so on—it also displays many characteristics that
have nothing to do with idealized concepts of love.

To fully understand the story, we need first to return to the beginnings
of their relationship, how they met, and why they decided to marry. Maria
Imaculada and her husband were first cousins. Her father wanted her to
marry his brother's son, but there were other brothers who thought their
daughters might also make a good match for the boy. He had begun to
namorar with another cousin, one Olívia, but Maria Imaculada's older,
married sister encouraged him to come visit and check out the possibilities. Upon meeting Maria Imaculada he became enthusiastic about the
match, but she took longer to make up her mind.

I didn't want to marry him, but my sister arranged it so he wanted to court
me. . . . I thought it was ugly to court your cousin. . . . I didn't like the idea,
but he did . . . and later I created a little friendship in my heart for him, and
we married.

Olívia also eventually married, and lived close to her brother in a small
town. When Maria Imaculada's husband began to travel the blue jeans
circuit, he would often stay at his cousins' houses, trading blue jeans in the
market and doing a little labor for his cousins on the side.

Then my husband went to the house of my father's brother's son, his cousin
too, Olívia's brother, who had never forgiven the slight when he didn't marry
her. . . . He used to work there a little bit for them, and they wanted him to
stay living there, working for them.

Olívia and her brother decided to make it more comfortable for their
cousin to visit, and perhaps stay longer.

They arranged a little house for my husband to live in so he would stay near
them. . . . They gave him a bed and arranged a woman to lie in it with him.
That is, her job was to cook for him and to clean, but you know how that is.

Maria Imaculada's husband's behavior had little to do with love for
his *concubina*, and much to do with his cousins' economic interest in him
and their hurt pride in his rejection of them in the past. I did not get a

chance to meet his *concubina*, but I did meet many women in a similar position: unable because of their family's social and economic condition to refuse sexual advances, having no nondomestic employable skills, and being forced to live as a kind of wife for hire, sometimes from a very young age. For some women, putting out sexually is a small price to pay for a house and part-time husband, since they never expected any fate but to have a stranger to husband anyway. But other women experience such a situation as a kind of interminably slow-motion rape. Whether the *concubina* had any affection or sexual desire for Maria Imaculada's husband is irrelevant to how their affair came to be. It is possible that their relationship eventually became a kind of love story for one or the other of them, or for both, but it did not start that way.

Maria Imaculada may have felt friendship, affection, or desire for her husband; she also was dependent on him to market the jeans she made. Further, she had two daughters whose ability to make a legitimate marriage, to refuse sexual advances, and to aspire to a middle-class lifestyle would have been seriously injured by their father's abandonment. Getting her husband out of the clutches of the scheming cousins was vital to her own and her daughters' social and economic well-being. That she and they also had feelings about the situation was important but not central to the reasons why the affair was so threatening.

We can see that while sexual relations are discussed in the idiom of the gloss *amor*, they take place under intense economic pressure. Many women like Maria Imaculada, and perhaps like her husband's *concubina*, "create friendship" in their hearts for the lovers they are given by circumstance, rather than choosing lovers freely on emotional grounds. Similarly, men may find lovers by circumstance, creating friendship as a matter of convenience. Sexual services here take their place in the round of chores a woman owes her man, rather than reflecting intimacy. Indeed, many men might very well not really want to know any inconvenient intimate truths about how the women they use feel.

Women may feel emotionally wounded by their husbands' infidelities; they are also economically hurt. If Maria Imaculada's husband had eventually moved over to the *concubina*'s house permanently, she would have had to arrange with another man to sell her jeans and bring her the denim pieces, a man who might have cheated her or placed sexual demands on her. Abandonment by her husband would have put both her and her daughters at risk for sexual harassment, since they would have been without a man to protect them, and the daughters would have been in a less favorable position to make a legitimate marriage, since their virginity could not be ensured without a father's chaperonage.

Although the situation of the affair was not brought about by emotion, Maria Imaculada used emotion as her tool to end it. Her distress, her daughter's anguish, and the community's outrage became instruments she could use against her husband, and, by extension, against the cousins who had betrayed her through their machinations. Her husband may have had scheming cousins on his side; Maria Imaculada enlisted her daughters, and by making the affair public, the community at large.

Not only could her daughters' hurt, pain, and *ataques de nervos* be added to hers to put greater emotional pressure on her husband, but in addition the public nature of their knowledge of his sexual behavior was shocking. It is a parent's, and especially a father's, responsibility to keep his daughters sexually ignorant until marriage. Revealing his sexual misbehavior to his daughters meant acknowledging it in their presence, violating the father's responsibility. The community's presence at the unveiling of the father's dereliction compromised their sexual purity, shaming him. This is what Lindinalva meant when she said that it was her father's shame that had died. He had conducted the affair without concern for its effect on the family's honor or his daughters' well-being.

Maria Imaculada emphasizes how "artless" (*simples*) her younger daughter, Laura, is; the word also means "naive." Laura was virtuously *simples* until her father's shameless behavior destroyed her innocence. Revealing the infidelity to his daughters via the letter brought out the shocked betrayal that they were freer to express than was their mother, and it impressed on the husband how his sexual misbehavior endangered not only his wife's health but also his daughters', and by extension his own status.

The Importance of Personal Skill

Throughout this book I have emphasized the importance of individual skill in determining how situations turn out. This emphasis does not mean that life consequences are entirely the result of individual effort. People play the hand they are dealt, and some get better cards than others. To extend the metaphor, while some people are better players than others, there are some hands that even the best player can't do much with, just as there are some players who can lose with a winning hand. And we haven't even gotten into bluffers, cheaters, and different rules for different players. I have tried to lay out some of the structural, historical, and cultural constraints that constitute the rules of the game of love in Northeast Brazil, to show what it is that social actors are negotiating as they love, try to love, and try to use love in social interactions.

While, in general, Northeast Brazilian social forms do not permit much freedom of action for women, some individual women manage to win the respect, obedience, and contrition of those around them. Customary sources of authority for women cluster around the inspiration of guilt. Women like Maria Imaculada and Glória use their deep, intuitive understanding of emotional dynamics to gain the authority denied them by a sexist social order. Other women, like Maria da Paz, reach for that authority but fall short.

While men can lose the respect due them by failing to live up to masculine ideals, and the tension surrounding the maintenance of masculinity is palpable, women also must earn respect, but on different grounds. The contradictory combination of chastity and motherhood forms part of those grounds. Some women manage to overcome the disgrace of unmarried sexual behavior through the virtue of motherhood; other women do not. These different paths reflect different subcultural patterns within Brazil's varied society, differences in individual women's personal situations, and differences in women's characters.

To become the kind of woman who maintains respect despite what in others might be considered unforgivable conduct, who can terrify her children with a single glance, to whom neighbors and relatives turn for advice, whose husband and sons feel guilty just thinking of her, takes enormous strength of character. Some women carry it off, but others manage little more than neurotic flailing.

Verbal Love and Romantic Marriage

Sentiments of affiliation in the family and among associates are not an innovation of the modern era, nor are they entirely absent from either old-fashioned areas of the countryside or cities afflicted with urban blight. However, differences in emotional style are discernible: shifts from nonverbal to verbal forms of expression accompany the increasing impersonalization of urban residence and capitalist-contractual social systems. In addition, as other forms of support and protection for women fall away, women increasingly rely on fantasies of romance to protect them from potential abuse at the hands of husbands and lovers. However, women's position vis-à-vis men in struggles over love is weak. Women have more invested in the idea that love ought inevitably to lead to marriage than do men: more economically, socially, and emotionally. In addition, because sex degrades women and magnifies men, women have more stake in ideologies that imbue sexual conduct with moral strictures, lifting it beyond the "lower" range of physical satisfactions.

Romance, and especially romantic marriage, gives women the hope of emotional support and consideration, intimacy beyond the physical, respectability and therefore protection in the broader society, and recognition of a kind of human dignity often denied those at the lower ranks of society. It is no wonder that the promise of romantic marriage appeals more to them than to men, and that their disappointments with it can be so very bitter. Because of their greater sexual freedom, men have been able to balance among the contradictions of love, getting affectionate support and personal services at home while satisfying adventurous desires outside. Women, emotionally and sexually confined to the domestic sphere, must try to satisfy their desires, their needs, and their preferences in an emotional and sexual world largely defined and controlled by men.

Some women, like Maria Imaculada, can use their intuitive knowledge of emotional dynamics as a tool or weapon with which to manipulate those around them. What takes a book to explain, Maria Imaculada knew wordlessly. "With the powers of God I dismantled it all," she boasted. "I was clever, really clever!" Indeed she was.

Emotion as Political—or Not

Despite the obvious strategic cleverness of Maria Imaculada's ploy, Theresa O'Nell's caution that emotion is not all politics (1996, 188) remains sound. People's control over their own feelings, their ability to feel what they or others think they ought to feel, their ability to convince others and themselves that indeed they do feel a particular way is not absolute. And some social ends are too important for mere sentiment to get in their way.

The culturally constructed nature of sentiment and its social usefulness do not obviate the personal, visceral, bodily nature of feelings. Some emotion glosses encompass a variety of distinct phenomena. Under the label *amor*, for example, we can find brain-body states like desire, momentary affections, and fond satisfaction. *Amor* also glosses an attitude, when we use it to describe the feelings that members of successful conjugal pairs have for one another. Through moments of hatred, of anger, of frustration, irritation, disappointment, jealousy, through periods of boredom, dissatisfaction, disillusionment, and discontent, such love builds itself as a story based around a theme of caring, concern, and affectionately humorous acceptance of human foibles. While the momentary sentiments have clear biological components, love-as-attitude and love-as-story are social creations extended outward from their basis in these momentary experiences. There is always a gap between what the story promises and what the lover actually confronts, between the attempt to maintain the general attitude and the sentiment of the moment.

The story of romantic love promises that the fantasized ecstatic union with an idealized other who in turn idealizes oneself will last forever as a sort of permanent peak experience. In fiction, lovers can fade into a vaguely defined "happily ever after," but real life men and women do not fade out discretely,[3] nor can they successfully maintain themselves in the "crazy-dog" stage of adolescent emotionality indefinitely. Successful lovers must improvise continually in order to *dar um jeitinho* to maintain their positive attitude and write a successful love story of their lives despite all the difficult obstacles placed in their paths. Along the route they may feel and act in ways that do not look much like true love, but to the extent that the overall story of their love reflects affection, concern, interdependence, and understanding, it may be judged successful.

True love and perfect union involve physical intimacy, emotional intimacy, and economic intimacy in various measures. Not everyone seeks it and few attain it for any length of time, but its image remains a powerful vision in modern society. In a society as stratified, as sexist, as economically stressed, as dramatically transforming as that of cities like Caruaru, achieving a successful conjugal love is more difficult than ever. The strenuous path of modern love in Caruaru reflects the complexities of its history, its contemporary situation, and the personalities of its residents.

Engaging in romantic relationships, having sex as part of the complexities of love, men and woman act on the basis of hopes, fears, dreams, lusts, partial information, and faulty expectations. They do things not realizing how their partners see them. They do things they know better than to do, but they do them anyway. They do things while denying to themselves and others that they are doing them. They do things they should not do, hoping that they will not get caught. In most cases, their choices are constrained, and in some cases very constrained; knowledge is incomplete, behavior the result of a confluence of influences outside their control.

Whether voiced or unvoiced, the sentiments composing love are among the most powerful, the most important, and the most necessary in human life. They are at once the most natural and the most difficult to achieve and sustain. Societies work out their stories of love differently, and individuals within a society write their own distinctive personal stories of love. In Caruaru, rapid social and economic change has forced an acute tension around issues of love, honesty, status, and sexuality. The answers that people find to their questions on these issues reflect both their ancestors' answers to similar questions and the distinctive character of life in a modern society. The stories of love they enact reveal their human foibles and failures. They also show courage, generosity, self-sacrifice, and intelligence. They have much to tell us about the geography of the unknown country of the human heart.

REFERENCE MATTER

☞ People Cited in the Text

People are identified by pseudonym, gender, age, marital status, number of children, profession, religious affiliation, and the economic class of their neighborhood. "Married" refers to persons joined in civil or religious ceremonies, or both. "Housing developments" are government-built projects in which small dwellings are granted to impoverished people by lottery; the term includes both *cohabs* (composed of houses) and *multerões* (condominium complexes). "Lower middle class" refers to people who live in working-class neighborhoods but have a higher educational level than their neighbors. Where relevant, relationships with other people are noted. People who do not live in Caruaru are listed as living in "village," which refers to a number of different small towns.

Agostinho, male; twenty-five; engaged; no children; Baptist; brother of Catrina, cousin of Chico; lower middle class.

Araruna, female; twenty-one; recently married; no children; factory worker; devout Catholic; poor neighborhood, Caruaru.

Arnoldo, eight; working-class neighborhood; Caruaru.

Assunção, female; thirty; married; two children; housewife; Catholic; housing development.

Bárbara, female; twenty-five; married; two children; con artist; lower middle class; Seventh-Day Adventist.

Bel, female; forty-eight; *amigada* for twenty years but now separated; three children, one adopted child; storekeeper; Catholic; poor neighborhood; born in countryside.

Beno, male; twenty-four; married; no children; electrician; working class; Catholic.

Branquinha, female; thirty; separated; two children; blue jeans piecer; Catholic; cousin of Glória; lives on *sítio*.

Catrina, female; thirty-two; single; three children; college educated; secretary; nonreligious; lower middle class.

Chico, male; twenty-five; engaged; businessman; college educated; Baptist; lower middle class.

Cleiton, male; twenty-four; single; construction worker; impoverished neighborhood; Catholic.

Clorinda, female; thirty-two; *amigada*; five children; housewife; lives in housing project; Catholic.

Dafne, female; sixty-two; married; six children, three who died; housewife; Catholic; *sítio*.

Damiana, female; twenty-five; married; manicurist; three surviving children of four; lives in *favela*; Catholic.

Deana, female; twenty-eight; abandoned; shoemaker; four children; impoverished neighborhood; Catholic.

Donizete, male; thirty-four; married; two legitimate children, one illegitimate; mechanic; impoverished neighborhood; Protestant.

Edilson, male; twenty-eight; single; no children; salesclerk; lower middle class; Catholic.

Elzeneide, female; sixty; married; five children, seven stepchildren, four who died; housewife; Catholic; *sítio*.

Emília, female; thirty-five; married; three children; housewife; lives in a *favela*; oldest child lives with her mother; Catholic.

Engrácia, female; forty; widowed, remarried; two surviving children of six born to first marriage, one child from second marriage; housewife; Seventh-Day Adventist; village.

Fátima, female; twenty-nine; married; two sons; housewife; Catholic; impoverished neighborhood; born in village.

Flávia, female; twenty-three; *amigada*; two children; pregnant at time of interview; housewife; housing development; Catholic; born on *sítio*.

Francinha, seventy-two; widow; six children; Catholic; impoverished neighborhood; born in *sítio*.

Francisco de Assis, male; thirty-two; divorced; three children; bank teller; lower middle class; Catholic.

Geixa, female; twenty-eight; married; three children; shopkeeper; Catholic, impoverished neighborhood.

Glória, female; thirty-six; single; no children; seamstress; devout Catholic; working-class neighborhood; daughter of Magdalena.

Ifigênia, female; twenty-eight; separated; one child not with husband; store clerk; Catholic; impoverished neighborhood.

Imelda, female; twenty-eight; married; three children; housewife; Seventh-Day Adventist; village.

Inaia, female; twenty-nine; married; no children; housewife; Catholic; impoverished neighborhood.

Jõao Batista, male; thirty-four; married; two children; mechanic's assistant; Catholic; impoverished neighborhood.

Jõaozinho, male; thirty-one; married; three children; small shop owner; lower middle class; born on *sítio*; Catholic.

Josefa, female; twenty-seven; separated; *amigada*; one child with husband, two with boyfriend; manicurist; Catholic. At time of interview lived in *favela*; near end of fieldwork period, Josefa won a house in a housing development.

Joselma, female; forty; married; two children, one adopted child; schoolteacher; lives in housing development; Catholic.

Laurinha, female; fifty-eight; retired shoemaker; housewife; seven children, two of whom are adopted; impoverished neighborhood; Catholic.

Leonel, male; twenty-one; unmarried; unemployed; Catholic; lower middle class family.

Lourdinha, female; twenty-four; unemployed; unmarried; no children; Catholic; impoverished neighborhood.

Magdalena, female; sixty-seven; widow; two children; Catholic working-class neighborhood; mother of Glória.

Margarida, female; twenty-three; unmarried; no children; works in daycare center; lives in housing development.

Maria da Adoração, female; forty-seven; married; nine surviving children of fifteen, also suffered five miscarriages; seamstress; lives on *sítio*; Catholic.

Maria Consolata, female; twenty-five; married; two children; housewife; Seventh-Day Adventist; village.

Maria da Conceição, female; twenty-one; single; two children; manicurist; Catholic; impoverished neighborhood. About five months after the conclusion of my study, she took her youngest child and moved to São Paulo to *amigar*, leaving one child with her mother.

Maria da Paz, female; thirty-two; married; housewife; two children; lower middle class; Catholic.

Maria das Dores, female; forty-three; married; five surviving children of fifteen live births, five miscarriages; laundress; impoverished neighborhood, Caruaru; from village; Catholic.

Maria das Prazeres, female; thirty-two; separated; seamstress; one child; impoverished neighborhood; Catholic.

Maria do Carmo, fifty-seven; female; nine; surviving children of thirteen; married; seamstress; working-class neighborhood; born in the Sertão, raised in village; Catholic.

Maria do Rosário, female; sixty-eight; widow; housewife; was born and raised on a *sítio*; two children of several lived to adulthood, one died as adult; devout Catholic; village.

Maria Imaculada, female; forty-one; seamstress; two children; village; Seventh-Day Adventist. One of eleven surviving children of the twenty her mother bore.

Maria Rezadeira de São Francisco, female; fifty-eight; widow, was born in a small village; six children, one died as adult; *rezadeira*; Catholic.

Maria Xoxinha, female; sixty-one; separated; two surviving children of five; laundress; lives in a *favela*; Catholic.

Marilú, female; fifty-six; five children; never married; odd jobber; impoverished neighborhood; Catholic.

Natalino, male; sixty-three; married; five living children; one died as adult; con artist; working-class neighborhood; Seventh-Day Adventist; born on *sítio*.

Nauma, female; thirty-four; married; one child; housewife; Catholic.

Nezinha, female; thirty-five; single; no children; lives with parents; store clerk; working-class neighborhood; Catholic.

Nilza, female; thirty-one; married; three surviving children of five; housewife; Catholic; working-class neighborhood.

Oneida, female; forty-three; single; two children; hairdresser; impoverished neighborhood.

Pretinho, male, twenty-five; cousin of Glória; separated; no children; snack maker; born on *sítio*; not religious.

Quitéria, female; *concubina*; two children; boyfriend and his third girlfriend murdered by legitimate wife; unemployed; Catholic; impoverished neighborhood.

Regina, female; thirty-five; separated; one child; lawyer; Catholic; middle class.

Renato, male; thirty-one; married; three children; shop owner and spiritist healer; lower middle class; Kardecist.

Robson, male; twenty-eight; married; no children; store owner; lower middle class; Catholic.

Rosabela, female; thirty-eight; never married; three children; baker and cake vendor; Seventh-Day Adventist; village.

Rubí, female; twenty-four; daughter of Maria das Dores; married; one child; college educated; schoolteacher; Catholic; impoverished neighborhood.

Samara, female; twenty-five; married; three children; housewife; Catholic; impoverished neighborhood.

Sarita; female; thirty-six; married; one child; housewife; Catholic; Caruaru.

Saxa, female; eighteen; single; Seventh-Day Adventist. In 1991, Saxa went to São Paulo to live with a male cousin in the hope of eventually marrying him; village.

Sebastiana, female; three children; housewife with small shop in house; impoverished neighborhood; Catholic.

Sebastião, male; fourteen; student; unmarried; no children; works part-time selling cakes that his mother bakes; Catholic; working-class neighborhood.

Samira, female; thirty-one; married; two surviving children of three; housewife; impoverished neighborhood; Catholic.

Severina, female; twenty-eight; married; three children; seamstress; Catholic; working-class neighborhood.

Sílvia, female; thirty-four; married; four children; shop owner and blue jeans piece worker; Catholic; housing development.

Teresa, female; thirty-five; divorced, then remarried and widowed; two children, and raising half-brother; factory worker; Catholic; housing development.

Toinha, female; fifty-two; married; three children; seamstress; Seventh-Day Adventist; village.

Uáxintô, male; fourteen; student; unmarried; no children; works part-time as mechanic trainee; Catholic; poor neighborhood.

Vagner, male; nineteen; unmarried; no children; furniture maker; Seventh-Day Adventist; poor family; village.

Welington, male; twenty-seven; married; one child; dentist; lower middle class; Catholic.

Zaira, female; twenty-one; unmarried; no children; secretary; Catholic; impoverished neighborhood; born in small town.

Zeferina, female; twenty-five; *concubina*; two children; Catholic; lives in a *favela*.

☞ Glossary of Brazilian Terms

Agitar   prepare, adjust, adapt
Agregado   associated with a household
Agreste   rustic or rural area of the Northeast
Amasiamento   the state of living together
Amigado   describes a couple living together
Amigar   to live together unmarried
Amigo   friend
Amizade   friendship
Amor   love
Arrumando   arranging
Arrumar   to arrange for
Ataque   an attack, fit, or faint
ataque de nervos   fit of "nerves"
Boca do Sertão   border between Agreste and Sertão
Canjica   corn pudding
Casa   house
Casamento   marriage
Casamento na Marra   shotgun wedding
Casar   to marry
Chamego, de chamego   affair, having an affair
Chinela   plastic sandal
Chinelada   slap with sandal
Classe operário   working class, working poor
Comadre/Compadre   parent of one's godchild
Concubina   concubine
Concubinato   concubinage
Conquistadores   conquerors
Corno   husband of adulterous wife
Coroneis   plural of *coronel*
Coronel   plantation owner
Crente   believer, fundamentalist Protestant
Cruzado, Cruzado Novo   obsolete Brazilian money
Cruzeiro   Brazilian money current at time of fieldwork

Cuscuz   steamed corn meal
De Confiança   trustworthy
Descalço   barefoot
Descamisado   shirtless
Esposa   wife
Favela   urban shantytown
Favelado   shantytown resident
Fazenda   large farm or ranch
Feira   street market or fair
Ficando com   staying with, hanging out with
Ficar com   hang out with
Flirt, Flirte   flirtation
Forró   Northeastern two-step dance
Freguesia   customership
Fuga   elopement, rape-kidnapping
Iemanjá   Yoruba deity of the ocean
Inteira   whole, virgin, uncastrated
Interesses   economic interests
Jeito   a way or manner
Jeitinho, Jeitinho Brasileiro   resourceful rule bending
Jeitoso   resourceful
Jogo da cintura   game of social manipulation
Judiação   torment
Lambada   recent sexier version of *forró*
Lei de Gerson   rule of taking advantage
Litoral   tidewater region
Lóvi   modern romantic love
Luta   fight
Madrinha   godmother
Manguzá   corn kernals cooked in coconut milk
Marido   husband
Mariposa   slut, whore
Marra   sledgehammer
Meio-Norte   mid-north region
Menina   girl
Mil-rei   obsolete Brazilian money
Miseravel   miserable, extremely poor
Miséria   misery, extreme poverty
Moça   maiden
Mulher   women
Município   area under jurisdiction of city government
Namorada   girlfriend
Namorado   boyfriend
Namorar   to court
Namoro   courtship
Nervos   folk anxiety syndrome, "nerves"

Nervoso   nervous
Noivado   engagement
Noiva   fiancée
Noivar   to become engaged
Noivo   fiancé
(a) Outra   the other woman
Padrinho   godfather
Paquera   flirt, flirtation
Paquerar   to flirt
Paralelo   parallel; black market
pé de quenga   clubfoot
Personalismo   personal tie connection principle
Puta   whore
Quenga   slut, whore, half coconut husk
Rapariga   slut, whore
Recifes   coral reefs
Retirante   person forced off land by drought
Roça   small farm
Roçeiro   farmer
Rua   street
Sacanagem   ideology of delight in the forbidden
Salário   minimum wage unit
Segunda-feira   Monday
Senhora   Lady, Mrs.
Sertanejo   resident of *Sertão*
Sertão   backlands, semiarid region
Sexo   sex
Sexo Papai-e-Mamãe   missionary position sex
Sulanca   cheap clothing
Terça-feira   Tuesday
Terreno de Umbanda   Afro-Brazilian worship center
Testamunhos   witness
Teuda e Manteuda   had and kept woman, concubine
Tirando uma sarra   rubbing bodies together
Troca-troca   cashless exchanges
Virgem   virgin
Zona da Mata   Forest Zone, now sugar cane region

⇌ Notes

Introduction: Studying Love in Northeast Brazil

1. An ethnography constitutes a story about stories: anthropologists' interpretation of peoples' renderings of what happened and why. Any given event has multiple versions and meanings, depending on who is telling the story to whom, and varying according to the respondent's opinions and purposes. Qualitative data, narrative in form, interpretive in nature, is not amenable to rigorous testing or comparison; it is not replicable in the manner of a scientific experiment, not composed of clearly defined dependent and independent variables. It is concerned with context and meaning, not with strict definition or comparison of tightly defined phenomena.

2. I am indebted to Maria Massolo's descriptions of her research in her native Argentina for this insight (personal communication).

3. Sidney Mintz has pointed out that while early anthropologists came out of the elites of an oppressive society, they, unlike their contemporaries, took seriously the knowledge and philosophy of the peoples they studied, seeing them as intelligent, rational, and knowledgeable, worthy of contemplation and analysis (Mintz 1996).

4. My thinking here has been influenced by Vassos Argyrou's careful dissection of these issues on Cyprus (1996).

5. Caruaru is pronounced with the accent on the final syllable: *cah-roo-ah-ROO*, with a soft *r*. It can be written with an accent, Caruarú, or without. Most commonly it is written without the accent.

6. I suspect, from the size of the tip the desk clerk gave him and the general condition of the room I was given, that his statement that this hotel was better than the other was made with his interests in mind, not mine.

7. The Portuguese of Northeast Brazilian differs from that of other regions in vocabulary, grammar, and pronunciation. For example, when I first arrived in Recife I was puzzled by the number of people who came up to me and said, *Coração*, a word that means "heart." Was this some kind of endearment? It was hard enough to get used to hearing my first name all the time. I call myself Linda-Anne, which most people who do not know me attempt to shorten to Linda. Now, *linda* is not commonly used as a name in Brazil; it is a word mean-

ing "beautiful." In fact, it is the word that men are most likely to call out of their car windows to passing women whose attention they wish to attract: *Eyyy! Lii-iin-daaaah!* That makes it a good equivalent to the English, "Hey baby!" Not only was everybody calling me by some version of my first name, but in addition they were coming up and saying *Coração* too. It was not until one impatient stranger suddenly grabbed my wrist after yelling *Coração! coração!* that I finally realized what was going on. They were not saying "heart" at all. They were saying, *Que horas são?* ("What time is it?"), but in typical Northeastern fashion they were running the sounds together: *q'oras'ão*, a word indistinguishable in pronunciation from *coração*. Eventually I learned to speak and understand the Northeast Brazilian dialect and to appreciate the humor incorporated into its phrasings.

8. Other responses include critical anthropology's call for a more politically involved practice of fieldwork (Baer 1993, 1997; Scheper-Hughes 1990, 1992; Singer 1986; Singer and Baer 1995); postmodern concerns with the power inherent in contemplation, description, and definition of the "Other" (Lewis 1996; Said 1978); and increasing emphasis on doing research in one's own group, however defined. This last approach also responds to increasing entrance of nonwhite, nonmale, nonheterosexual, non–able-bodied, non-European, and non-U.S. researchers into anthropology, enriching preexisting perspectives with insiders' views, voices, and political concerns.

9. For a discussion of qualitative methods of fieldwork, see Mishler 1986; Morse 1992; Shaffir and Stebbins 1991; and Whyte 1984.

10. *Favela* refers to an urban shantytown: a neighborhood in which houses have been constructed without legal permits. *Favelas* house the poor and disenfranchised; they rarely boast sewers, running water, electricity, or the other amenities of modern life.

11. For example, it was common to reply to a query about *emoção* with a complaint that Caruaru was a really boring town; informants heard the question as, "What's exciting around here?"

12. I am indebted for this insight, and the phrase, to James C. Scott during a discussion in the Agrarian Studies Program at Yale University in 1996.

13. The men I interviewed were mostly the sons of older women interviewees, young men in their teens and twenties, or men born in the working class but currently of higher status because of their education. Some of these men were schoolteachers, worked in offices, or owned small stores or businesses related to the blue jeans industry (such as stone-washing shops). Others had moved into the lower middle class by means of university training in business, law, dentistry, or medicine (both human and veterinary). I also interviewed a few construction workers, mechanics, rural farm workers, and truck drivers, and I hired a young teenage man to help me collect jokes from men drinking in all-male groups.

14. Kardecism is a religion based on writings by "Allan Kardec." Kardec was the name of a spirit, identifying himself as a Druid, whose communications were psychographed by the Parisian Leon Rivail between 1855 and 1870. These works were translated into Portuguese and became popular in Brazil starting in

the late 1850s. Kardecism remains an important religion, especially in the urban centers of Southern Brazil (Brown 1994, 15–16).

Chapter 1: The Problem

A different version of this chapter was published as L. A. Rebhun, W. H. R. Rivers Prize Paper "Nerves and Emotional Play in Northeast Brazil," *Medical Anthropology Quarterly* 7, no. 2 (1993): 131–51.

1. A Spanish-language version of this proverb was collected in Mexico by George Foster (1970, 310): *Caras vemos, corazones no sabemos* ("Faces we see, hearts we don't know").

2. Here my discussion is influenced by Theresa O'Nell's evocative description (1996, 179–91) of how sadness and loneliness among Flathead Native People of the United States differ from similarly denominated sentiments among middle-class European-Americans, and especially by her review of the history of concepts of emotion in anthropology.

3. Many languages do not contain any word that corresponds in meaning to the English word "emotion" (Heelas 1983; Lutz 1982). The word "emotion" is a neologism in English, appearing in dictionaries for the first time near the end of the sixteenth century. In Spanish, the word *emoción* was officially accepted by the Academia de Lengua Espanola in 1843 and was not current in literature before then, although it may have been used in common speech (Crespo 1986, 210). The *Dicionario Etimológico Nova Fronteira da Lingua Portuguesa* dates the words *emotividade* and *emotivo* from 1899 but does not give a date for *emoção* itself. These dates suggest a connection between the current use of emotion/*emoción*/*emoção* to indicate sentiment and the shifts in concepts of the person in the modern era. Cross-linguistic lexicon differences bring up the question of whether emotion is an artificial category of Western theorists created by the peculiarities of vocabulary in English and other Western languages, and lumping together disparate psychological phenomena (Duffy 1941, Lutz 1988).

4. While some culturalist theorists take the strong position that emotions are entirely socially constructed (cf. Harré 1986), others take a compromise position, positing the existence of a limited series of socially elaborated but biologically based feelings (Armon-Jones 1986, 38). On problems of translation of emotion terms, see also Briggs 1970; Davitz 1969; Geertz 1959; Hiatt 1978; Leff 1977; Levy 1973; Morsbach and Tyler 1986; Myers 1979; Wallace and Carson 1973; and Wierzbicka 1986. For attempts to make lists of basic emotion terms, see Dahl and Stengel 1978; Darwin 1872; Ekman 1980; Izard and Buechler 1980; Kemper 1987; and Plutchik 1962. See also Kolenda 1987 for a critique of this approach.

5. In another example, Lutz (1988, 119) shows that the word *fago* was used by people on the Micronesian atoll she studied to mean something like the English "compassion," or then again like the English "love," with connotations of sadness. To understand the term one must understand a philosophy of the poignancy of emotional connection in a world where life is fragile and love leads inevitably to loss.

6. The word translated here is *ficava*, which could also be translated "stayed"

(and I have so translated it in earlier versions of this essay). *Ficar* ("to stay") has a broader meaning in Portuguese than in its English equivalents, as it is also used to express some of the meanings denoted by the English "to be," joining *estar* and *ser* as more finely shaded variants of to be than are denoted in English. *Ficar* can also denote "to be located at" or "to remain," "to keep [on doing something]" or "to remain [in a condition or state]." I have translated it into more idiomatic English here than elsewhere.

7. Quotations have been edited. Ellipses indicate where repetition and asides have been omitted.

8. Maria Imaculada's husband, who spent Saturdays at a bar, had not converted to Seventh-Day Adventism, which advocates abstinence from alcohol and tobacco. When I asked her if he was an Adventist (*adventista*) she replied punningly, *Não, ele é adegantista* ("No, he keeps a wine-cellar!").

9. This term refers to a woman maintained in a house by her lover, who is married to another woman.

10. Most poor neighborhoods have one or more people who will read and write for illiterates in exchange for a small consideration.

11. In Brazilian Portuguese, *nervos* is an emotion gloss; *nervoso/a* ("nervousness") the adjective describing a person who suffers from *nervos*, and *nervosismo* ("nervous-ism") or *nervosidade* is the label for the sickness of being especially susceptible to attacks of *nervos*. These are the grammatically correct terms. The most common of these words in ordinary usage are *nervos*, *ataque de nervos*, and *nervoso*. In the Northeast Brazilian accent, the *s* is sometimes left off of *nervos*. In medical anthropological writing on the subject, the folk term "nerves" is often used in quotation marks to distinguish it from the medical term referring to the physical structures.

12. I am using "folk syndrome" to describe named illnesses found primarily among one or several related cultural groups. "Nerves" has been called a culture-bound syndrome, although Setha Low has called for the term "culturally interpreted syndrome," arguing that the symptoms of "nerves" are culturally received and labeled expressions of distress responding to culturally defined theories of disease and etiology (1985, 188–89). I prefer the term "folk syndrome" because all syndromes and sicknesses are culturally interpreted. What distinguishes "nerves" from, say, anxiety is that it is part of the unofficial medical folklore rather than of the official medical canon of the countries in which the term is used. Of course, doctors may use the term "nerves," but they do not learn it in medical school except as an example of folk belief. That the physiological concepts underlying the folklore of "nerves" were at one time part of the official elite medical canon of the ancient Greeks and therefore of the colonial Iberians does not change its current status as folklore.

13. Both my male and female respondents agreed on this, although it is possible that had I interviewed a greater number or variety of men my findings would have been different.

14. Drunken men may feel free to sing sad songs of love gone wrong, em-

brace and thump one another tearfully while making dramatic declarations of male solidarity in the face of female perfidy, and generally cry in their beer while inebriated. Men also cried, often drunkenly, when their soccer teams lost important games. I was in Fortaleza during Brazil's World Cup defeat in 1986 and in Caruaru for their defeat in 1990. Both times, publicly inebriated and weeping men lined the streets. In Fortaleza in 1986 the weeping turned to anger as people burned World Cup flags, held mock funerals for important players, and roasted chickens (in response to the nickname of a player whose miss on penalty goals gave the game to the French).

15. Duarte (1993) traces the development of concepts of *nervos* as influenced by eighteenth-century notions of the nervous system, nineteenth-century ideas such as neurasthenia, and twentieth-century popular conceptions influenced by medical and hygienic campaigns. He rejects a linear evolutionary model of *nervos*, positing instead that modern concepts of *nervos* reflect various popular conceptions of these theoretical developments, as well as of earlier Greco-Arabic ideas.

16. Fátima's brother-in-law was murdered by a neighbor who had threatened him for some time and who accosted him along a path and shot him. The only witness to the murder was the man's oldest son, then a child of eight. Although the boy was able to pick the man out of a lineup and to identify the murder weapon, his testimony was not useful in a court of law because of his age, and his widowed mother (Fátima's adoptive sister), pregnant with her ninth child, was afraid to prosecute for fear of reprisals. Neither the widow nor the son (whom I interviewed when he was twenty-one) put forth any ideas as to the neighbor's motive except his general disagreeableness. The murderer had since moved away and murdered someone else in his new village, and he had not been prosecuted there, either.

17. The folk model of "nerves" is very similar to the U.S. folk model of "stress," which is often used as if it were a statistically exact, scientifically created term in medical and psychological research. Many of the same critiques that have been applied to the concept of "stress" can also be applied to "nerves" (see, for example, Allen and Cooke 1988 on "stressful life events" models of alcoholism).

18. Borrowing from biologists' increasing concern with the genetic, we can see the biology of organisms not as a series of physical givens but rather as an arrangement of possibilities coded for by the chemistry of DNA and expressed as part of an interaction with environment and event. This more flexible concept of the nature of the biological combines more easily with cultural anthropological concerns than do other models.

19. Averill's original analysis contrasts the English "emotion" with "passion." Both "emotion" and *emoção* are derived from the Latin *movere* ("to move"), as are the words "motion" and *movimento*. The root of *movere, mew* ("to push away"), underlies English words such as mobile, motor, and momentum. An overwhelming sentiment or one with an origin invisible to consciousness is called a passion (Averill 1982), from the Latin *patí*, or *passus*, "to suffer," the

same root evident in "passive," "patient," and "pathology." "Sentiment" and *sentimento* derive from the Latin *sent*, meaning "to head for" or "to go." *Sentire* means "to go mentally."

20. The idiom of "falling in" is used for love (*cair na amor*) in Portuguese as in English; the metaphor can be used to describe having one's reason fooled in general: *cair na besteira* (fall in the foolishness), for example.

21. In Portuguese, words describing emotion are different than in English. *Emoção* can mean "emotion" in the sense of sentiment, but its primary meaning is "excitement," similar to the meaning of "emotion" in English before the 1600s. *Paixão* can be translated as "passion," but it is more often used to refer to a strong sexually based attraction, more like the English "infatuation" or as a term of address to someone beloved. *Sentimento* means "sentiment" but is also used to describe sorrow, regret, or nostalgia. E. Crespo (1986), analyzing the use of the terms *emoción, sentimiento,* and *pasión* in Spanish posits that their usage implies a theory of personal action different from that of English usage. To a greater extent than English, Portuguese and Spanish treat emotion as external to the person. Whereas in English a person "is" an emotion ("He was angry"), in Portuguese and Spanish a person "is with" (Portuguese: *estar com*; Spanish: *estar con*), "stays with" (Portuguese: *ficar com*), or "has" (Portuguese: *ter*; Spanish: *tener*) an emotion. When a person "is" an emotion in Portuguese or Spanish, the expression has a strong moral connotation. For example, the phrase *estou danado da vida*, used to mean furious in colloquial Portuguese, literally translates as "I am damned of life," graphically including the moral condemnation in the description of the sentiment.

22. Duarte (1993) also critiques political reductionism in discussions of "nerves."

Chapter 2: The Setting

1. The industry is based in the village of Alto do Moura, located about five kilometers from Caruaru. In 1989 the road to Alto do Moura from Caruaru was paved. The city is steadily growing along this road, and it is likely that in the future Alto do Moura will be engulfed, becoming a neighborhood rather than a free-standing municipality. It is possible to buy figurines directly from the artists in Alto do Moura, in the market of Caruaru (especially on Wednesdays and Sundays), in the Casa de Cultura of Recife, or anywhere else in Brazil, as well as in selective shops in other countries, with prices escalating along the way. Caruaru has a small museum dedicated to the history of the figurines (which started a generation ago with the work of the artist Vitalino). In addition, the Museu do Homem do Nordeste in Recife has a large collection of figurines. Some individual figurine artists, such as Luis António, have international reputations, with examples of their work on display in museums around the world. Other artists mass produce knock-off versions of the figures invented by particularly skilled artisans.

2. Narayan Sastry (1997), in an analysis of factors in Brazilian infant mortality, found that the higher instance of infant mortality in rural than in urban

areas of Northeast Brazil was strongly correlated with socioeconomic and behavioral characteristics such as availability of piped water, sanitation, and electricity in houses, as well as the level of maternal education. In addition, the
availability of public health services, personal hygiene, and child care instruction and support were important to child survival. The availability of medical
services was not a major factor. Higher infant mortality in rural areas was due
to lack of community services, not to rural residence per se.

3. As an example, at the time of my fieldwork, Caruaru had only one telephone exchange. All numbers in the city of 210,000 started with 721, although
there were rumors that 722 was going to be added. It was nearly impossible to
get a telephone line (and there was a brisk illegal market in access to phone
lines), and even if you had a line, the system was so overextended that it was
very difficult to get a dial tone.

4. Some people repeated this rumor to me with great trepidation, others
with hope, anticipating economic opportunity under Japanese management. In
addition to the rumors of the Northeast's impending sale, some repeated another version in which the Japanese were about to buy the Amazon and cut it all
down for chopsticks, employing thousands. The largest population of Japanese
descent outside Japan lives in Brazil, and Japan has both invested in Brazilian
economic development and imported to Japan Japanese-Brazilian laborers. Near
Bonito, about forty minutes toward the coast from Caruaru, is a small *colonia Ja-
ponesa*, or Japanese settlement, that employs Japanese Brazilians and Japanese
immigrants, mostly as rose farmers.

5. See also Scheper-Hughes (1992, 82–86) for a discussion of the similar class
structure in the Zona da Mata of Pernambuco.

6. The term was coined by Robin Cohen (1991).

7. I went with some women to see *Star Trek V*, which had just come out.
After the movie, one of the women said to me, "Your country has a beautiful
future." "But," I said, "*Star Trek* is the future of the whole world." "I didn't see
any Brazilians on that star ship," she replied, "but I did see all those captains
running around in beautiful, clean, pressed uniforms. Somewhere in the Fed-
eration is a planet full of Brazilians, sewing, washing, ironing!"

8. When New Amsterdam was conquered by the British and renamed New
York, its Jewish population was allowed to stay despite laws prohibiting Jews in
England itself. Later immigrations by German and then Russian Jews swelled
New York's Jewish population. Today, New York has the largest Jewish popu-
lation of any city in the world. The first New World Jewish temple was built in
Recife. It no longer stands, although a plaque marks its site. Today there is a
small Jewish community in Recife divided between a tiny temple and a larger
Hasidic Chabad house, staffed by an American rabbi. There is no organized
Jewish community in Caruaru.

9. Contemporary immigrants from Arab countries, mostly Coptic Christians
from Lebanon, have become prominent, especially in Brazil's South, although
some live in scattered neighborhoods throughout the Northeast.

10. Outside cities in the Litoral fishing remains the major industry, using
small boats and rafts and employing fishermen either as wage workers or as a

kind of sharecroppers of the sea. Litoral rural life is heavily marked by the rhythms and concerns of harvesting the ocean (see Robben 1989a).

11. Poor systems of drainage exacerbate the problems of excess water in cities like Recife. Floods, in addition to their other damage, carry water-borne and water-washed parasitic diseases as well as chemical pollutants dumped into rivers and garbage heaps all over the city.

12. The only parts of the basic diet that need to be imported are coffee, sugar, and rice.

13. The word is of Arabic origin. Cuscuz (pronounced *coo-EES-coo-EES*), a staple of the diet, is made from flaked or grated dry corn mixed with a little manioc meal. Water is added to the limit of its absorption, and the mixture is steamed in a special pot called a *cuscuzteira*. Cuscuz is served for breakfast with milk and butter, cheese, or egg, for supper with meat or egg, or mixed with beans at lunch in place of rice. Cuscuz can also be made with other grains. A common variant is made of steamed manioc flour and grated coconut. The exact recipe varies from state to state. People told me that in neighboring Piaui, cuscuz is served with sugar, a practice they found disgusting.

14. Even those reduced by extreme want to picking through garbage dumps find more to eat in the Agreste. The by-products of agriculture in the Mata consist mainly of the fibers left over when the sugar juice is squeezed from the cane, whereas rotten fruits, vegetables, legumes, and grains (some of it edible, if barely) make up a majority of nonexcrement organic garbage in the Agreste. The Agreste is also less subject to spot shortages caused by economic instability than are regions that do not produce foodstuffs. For example, in 1986, when I was working in Fortaleza with Marilyn Nations, food retailers responded to price controls by withdrawing from the market commodities for which they believed they could not get a fair price. It became nearly impossible to find either meat or milk in stores (until the nuclear plant accident at Chernobl, that is—then we got a whole shipment of powdered milk from the irradiated region). At that time I made my first visit to Caruaru as a tourist and was amazed to see milk and meat sold openly and in abundance in the open-air market. As in other regions, these products were absent from the shelves of supermarkets, but they were available straight from the producers in the street, where prices are more negotiable, being less subject to government control. The family ties that most locals had with farming relatives also meant that people could obtain otherwise unavailable agricultural produce. Only such milk products as baby formula, sold exclusively at retail in stores, remained unobtainable for Caruaruenses.

15. She showed me the route her family walked in search of productive land or work, a path of several hundred miles through the Northeast. In charge of a wife and five small girls, her father lived in terror of the bandits that plagued the region. Had the family been accosted, the girls and wife might have been raped or carried off. After about three years of wandering the family finally settled in Caruaru, where her mother found work as a domestic and her father took odd jobs in the marketplace.

16. Aurélio's dictionary defines *retirante* as "Northeastern *Sertanejo* who emigrates, fleeing the drought" [my translation].

17. The signature song of Luís Gonzaga, popularizer of Northeastern *forró* music, "Asa Branca" ("White Wing"), describes a drought-ridden *Sertão* in which even the heartiest songbirds cannot survive. The song's chorus, *de que tamanha judiação* ("of what enormous suffering") is deeply evocative. This was the song everyone sang to me when I first arrived, and when Gonzaga died, large billboards with that phrase commemorated his contribution to the Northeast. His place in *forró* music is comparable to that of Hank Williams in U.S. country music.

18. This is the correct Portuguese plural, which was anglicized by the translator in the excerpt from the novel at the frontispiece.

19. To follow these instructions you need to go in the indicated direction, asking people all along the route. If you are going *lá embaixo*, you keep going until people start to say *lá en cima*, when you know you have gone too far and need to turn back. Unlike the United States, where we expect single individuals to be able to direct us, Brazilians require the creation of temporary alliances with large numbers of people to find their way.

20. After a pregnancy punctuated by both an eclipse of the sun and a UFO, my neighbor was relieved to give birth to a perfect little boy without a single birth mark.

21. Actually, Sairé is a charming little town with paved streets and electric lights in its downtown and a lovely central square, paved with stone block and planted with trees and flowers. The town sponsors festivals in the square at various times of the year. Many Sairenses work in Caruaru.

22. This information comes from local newspaper articles on the city's founder's day as well as from information given to me at the *Museu da Cidade de Caruaru* and at Caruaru's city hall.

23. Some farmers also have direct contracts with distributors who pick up produce for trucking directly to the capital, although even then the major paved road for trucks runs through Caruaru.

24. I divided the minimum salary by the value of the dollar on the Rio "parallel" market as reported in the newsweekly *Veja* for the first week of the month over a period of ten months in 1990 and averaged the ten monthly values. The minimum salary's value varied monthly because of inflation, and the dollar's value varied daily. The new constitution guaranteed wage indexing; however, the Collor government's two first economic plans favored wage freezes and price controls, leading to money and commodity shortages.

25. Labor unions are relatively weak. Following the 1964 military coup, labor unions were denied the right to strike until 1979. Since that time labor unions have used the strike frequently, particularly the unions of rural workers (Pereira 1997, 16–17). However, although by law workers must have a work document consisting of a small booklet in which their work history is recorded, and they must be hired and paid according to regulations laid out in the code, significant numbers of workers work off the books or informally. Many Brazilians lack even a birth certificate (da Matta 1997).

26. I took driving lessons while in Caruaru to learn how to drive a standard-shift car and to receive a Brazilian driver's license. Once, at a stop sign

near the center, my teacher asked me in a puzzled voice why I had stopped, impeding the flow of traffic. I said, "Because of the stop sign. It says in the book to stop at that kind of sign." He sighed impatiently. "You have to memorize the book to pass the test," he explained, "but that doesn't have anything to do with how to drive." He went on to explain that you have to stop only at certain stop signs and not others, and that this particular sign was not one of the ones that you had to stop at. As to how to know which were which, he said he would teach me all the signs in Caruaru. This one was put up by the government, and who knows why they put anything up. Probably some politician got some money to do it. Indeed, the entire series of lessons involved learning not only the legal requirements of interaction at signals and intersections but also the actual practices (which were quite different), as well as dual sets of meanings for such actions as using turn signals, turning on headlights, blowing the horn, and flashing brights.

27. After the royal court was rousted from Portugal by the Napoleonic wars, it settled in Brazil in 1808. When King João VI was finally able to return home in 1821, he left his son on the Brazilian throne. Dom Pedro I declared himself emperor of the independent nation of Brazil in 1822 but was forced to abdicate in favor of his underage son in 1831. In 1840, the fourteen-year-old Dom Pedro II was declared of age, reigning until 1889, when he was forced out by a new Republican government dominated by the so-called coffee barons of the Brazilian South.

28. A *cabresto* is a halter of the type used to control a horse or mule. The term may also be translated as "herd vote," which, while not literal, captures the sense of the expression.

29. One exception has been polio. Pernambuco has achieved 100 percent polio vaccination as part of the World Health Organization's push to eliminate polio worldwide, using a system of door-to-door visits by health workers distributing oral vaccines. Although polio victims can be seen everywhere, crawling and dragging themselves along in the absence of wheelchairs, the current generation of infants will be spared this particular scourge, and generations to come as well.

30. The mil-rei was a form of money, now obsolete, that replaced the colonial conto do rei.

31. Many trucks are decorated with fanciful designs, and messages are painted on the sides, back bumper, and dust flaps. These messages include advice to drivers such as *Passe-pense* ("Pass-think") or *Calma amigo* ("Calm, friend"); macho boasts like *O piloto é jovem, a maquina é quente* ("The driver is young, the engine is hot"); commercial endorsements; statements designed to ward off the evil eye, such as *O seu olho gordo é cego p'ra mim* ("Your big eye is blind to me"); proverbs; and various witticisms.

32. The parallel, or black, market in currency was only semilegal until early 1990, when President Collor decriminalized it.

33. People did not accept this quietly or calmly. Angry crowds besieged the bank's employees when the bank finally opened, not much mollified by being permitted to withdraw a small proportion of their accounts in cash. The bank

freeze affected even those who did not have the kind of accounts at which the freeze was directed (for the most part, those that paid interest based on the price of the dollar or of gold), because individuals, businesses, and governments had no money with which to pay wages for a month. After a month businesses and governments were allowed to withdraw money to pay their employees, but they could not easily get wages for those who did work off the books, in some places a large percentage of the population. A great variety of practices reflecting only loose adherence to official fiduciary regulations were caught by the tightening of the money supply. For example, a local town whose mayor had put the town treasury in a high-interest account in his own name was out of luck when money was wanted to pay municipal workers. Officially the account was personal, and like other personal accounts it remained frozen for eighteen months.

Chapter 3: Love as Connection

1. Unlike the English speakers studied by Robin Lakoff, male speakers of Brazilian Portuguese are as likely to use tag questions as are female. The tendency is greater in the Northeast and in the interior than in the South or large coastal cities, but it does not vary by gender. Lakoff attributes the use of tag questions by English-speaking women to approval-seeking (1975, 19), which may also be a factor in Northeast Brazil. It would be interesting to study how the use of tag questions varies by class in Northeast Brazil, or in the United States, for that matter.

2. I saw the U.S. movie "The Color Purple" in Fortaleza in 1986. In the film there are many scenes of reunion between tragically separated family members, scenes cleverly designed to elicit tears. They had a dramatic effect on the audience. (In Northeast Brazilian movie theaters viewing a movie is an interactive experience, and it is common for people to talk to characters on the screen and one another in loud voices.) In one scene, a mother is reunited with her daughter from whom she had been separated for years by unfair imprisonment. The daughter was an infant when her mother was imprisoned and has no memory of her mother, which is obvious from her shy and stiff formality. The audience viewing the scene began to cry and moan loudly, calling out, *Que trágico!*, *Que terrible!*, *Ay, yi, imagine!* The man with whom I went to the movie laid his head on my shoulder and began to sob loudly. At the end of the movie separated sisters are at long last reunited, which prompted another round of loud sobs from both my date and the rest of the audience, who left the theater with tears streaming copiously. Members of the audience gathered in small groups, repeating to each other the actions of these two scenes and comparing them with incidents in their own lives or the lives of people they knew.

For months afterward, my date for the movie took great pleasure in telling his friends about these scenes with much embellished detail, so they could enjoy crying together over beer. I was never able to convince my friends that the movie was about the effects of racial prejudice on African American families in the United States. They saw it as a film about ordinary people, only some of

whom looked Black to them, and emphasized the themes of loneliness, separation, and the oppression of women by men. rather than any themes of race.

3. Shkilnyk was paraphrasing an Ojibwa respondent who was discussing
the destructive power of alcohol abuse on the reservation.

4. I am indebted to James C. Scott for this insight.

5. I owe a debt here to Margaret Trawick (1990, esp. 89–93) for this formu-
lation.

6. Notice that in this interpretation love is still seen as the default interpersonal sentiment; public health conditions act as restraints on the natural sentiment among family members.

7. MacFarlane and the Stone-Ariés school differ most strongly in their ideas
about when love as an ideology first appeared or became important in European history, with MacFarlane among those scholars who see love as an idea of
great antiquity and Stone-Ariés seeing it acquiring strikingly new importance
and form in the modern era.

8. Bernstein does not mention folklore in any detail here, but considerations
of such forms as folk songs, proverbs, folk performances, folktales, and aspects
of folk speech would enrich his analysis. These offer a rich panoply of expressive media in which to couch articulations of sentiment without the necessity for
uncomfortably personal "I" statements.

9. Vendors in the art market, which appeals more to tourists than the food
or clothing markets, are more likely to accept foreign currency, checks, or credit
than other vendors.

10. There are some prestigious families who have contributed more than
one member to public service, but however advantageous it may be for a candi-
date to have prominent relatives, political office is not directly inherited the way
a status like plantation owner used to be.

11. The work of both Karl Marx and Marcel Mauss pointed to two forms of
exchange: (a) commodity exchange, in which objects or values are exchanged
between reciprocally independent transactors; and (b) gift exchange, in which
objects or values are exchanged between reciprocally dependent transactors
(Gregory 1982, 11–12). In the first case, not only are the objects or services exchanged without further obligation between the transactors, but, in addition,
they are treated as independently existing objects, obscuring the social relations
within which they are produced, in a process Marx called commodity fetishism
(Tucker 1978, 320–21). In gift exchange, the things exchanged are inalienable—
that is, they are unchangeably associated with their producers and exchangers,
who know one another. In addition, the exchange, rather than being an isolated
incident, is part of a continuing relationship involving series of exchanges between the perpetually interdependent transactors (Mauss 1974, 62).

Whereas in a commodity economy to possess is the source of power, in a
gift economy to be owed is the source of power. To give is more powerful than
to receive, because one's debtors have the obligation to repay gifts in either
goods or services when the creditor demands it (Gregory 1982, 19). Gift economies are more characteristic of small-scale societies such as tribal groups than of
large-scale urban or socially stratified groups. They also function among socie-

ties characterized by small, dense social networks, such as smaller groups within a large-scale society. Where the two types of economy overlap, an ambiguous
economy operates in which social context determines whether goods or services
are treated as commodities or as gifts (Gregory 1982, 117).

12. Of course there were those who gossiped maliciously about her, too.
One neighbor commented sarcastically to me that Dona Magdalena's holiness
was but her latest tactic in her war against her husband: "She's going to pray
that man right into heaven. Not his heaven, hers: the one with no drinks and no
women! By the time she gets there she's making sure he will be waiting there
for her, domesticated [*manso*]."

13. Dona Magdalena had for some time made food for a local high school's
lunch service, and Glória expanded this business to include new clients, bringing in a fourteen-year-old boy cousin from the countryside to work in the
kitchen in exchange for a chance to attend high school (the food was a kind of
savory pastry using chicken meat wrapped in dough). In addition she worked
on making clothing, catering parties, and baking cakes whenever she could
drum up business, and she inherited two houses from her father. One of these
she rented for cash, the other she rented to a newly married cousin from the
countryside, and he and his wife entered and helped to expand the food-mak-
ing business.

14. The men who had paid her father's debts did so out of friendship and
gratitude and may not have seen themselves as her creditors. It is possible that
they might have refused any attempt on her part to pay them back.

15. One of the dubious joys of fieldwork is that you can be annoyingly in-
trusive, blaming it on your ignorance as a foreigner and the demands of your
job rather than on your basically obnoxious personality.

16. *Quem riu de mim ontem, chora p'ra socorro hoje.*

17. For another view of the *jeitinho brasileiro* in the Mata of Pernambuco, see
Scheper-Hughes (1992, 475–79).

18. People also frequently shorten the proverb to *Quem tem boca vai arrumar.*

19. N. de Alameida Filho, personal communication.

20. Similar vocabularies exist in the slang of other Latin American countries.
For example, *juego de cintura*, associated there with soccer, serves a similar purpose as in Brazil, and the term *trepador*, or "climber," refers to someone who advances by pushing others down (Maria Massolo, personal communication). In
Brazil, because of the slang use of the verb *trepar* ("to climb") to refer to sexual
intercourse, *trepador* means something more like "fucker."

21. Lívia Barbosa finds references to the term *jeitinho* as early as the late
1940s but shows that its widespread use, especially in the nationalistic form
jeitinho brasiliero, began in the 1960s. She attributes the current use of the term to
a change in Brazilian nationalistic self-concept, from that of the "sleeping giant"
about to awaken to its rightful position in the leadership of the world, to that of
the more current perspective, in which Brazilians view their world position with
pessimistic frustration (1992, 139–47).

22. M. Massolo, personal communication.

23. There was a mob scene down at the Banco do Brasil in Caruaru, as

crowds of account holders withdrew the maximum allowed and tried to wheedle or coerce special favors out of beleaguered bank employees. I was no exception: I got the consulate to get the Fulbright commission to write a letter requesting that the balance of my grant be released—to no avail. I simply never saw it again. The money was sequestered for nine months in the form of the old cruzados novos, after which it was released according to a complex exchange rate with cruzeiros in twelve monthly increments. By that time I was back in the United States.

24. The fourteen-year-old son of the family put on a masterful show of enormous concern over the electrical and water problems. He examined all the wires and pipes and ran around as if he were trying to find someone to fix them, while offering me his sincerest insincere sympathy.

25. Brazilian Portuguese distinguishes male from female animals in common usage: A male *cão* ("dog") and a female *cadella* ("bitch"); a male *gato* ("tom") and a female *gata* ("queen"). In Northeast Brazilian Portuguese, *cachorro* ("puppy") is also used for adult dogs—*cão* can be used to refer to the Devil, and some consider it impolite. The usual form of the proverb is *Quem não tem cão caça com gato* ("Who doesn't have a [male] dog hunts with a [tom] cat"). What Glória said, however, was *Quem não tem cão caça com gata* ("Who doesn't have a [male] dog hunts with a [queen] cat").

26. Glória was determined that I master this skill of *meia-embreagem,* or "half-clutch," and insisted that we spend hours on hillsides practicing it. In general I was taught to use the clutch as much as possible rather than the brakes to control the speed of the car. My driving school teacher explained that it was necessary not only to save gas but also because it was important to be able to drive a car even if the brakes do not work. When I returned to the United States and was driving around with my father, he complained that I drove like a Brooklyn cabbie rather than a nice Virginia girl.

27. Later, being a part of Glória's network helped with another problem I had with the car. After a minor fender-bender at an intersection, the other driver, a man in a suit driving a fancy, black car, moved his car (which is illegal, and had the effect of making it look as though the accident had occurred differently than in fact it had). He began to berate me in an attempt to get me to pay him large sums of money on the spot. The woman in front of whose house the accident took place, whom I did not know, came out and informed the man that he was mistreating the famous North American anthropologist Linda-Anne, who was under her protection. "I am a lawyer," she said, and gave the man her card. She instructed me to come into the house and warned him that she had written down his license number and he had better not move because the police had already been called. In the house, to my astonishment, she told me with accuracy all about myself and my project, and then telephoned Glória. We then returned to the cars, and Glória arrived shortly with her mother, who knelt down and began praying loudly. With them were several large men, who walked around my car and discussed the minor damage as if it were more serious than it was, while fingering some frightening bulges in their pockets. The other driver politely suggested that the police really didn't have to get involved,

he could fix his own car and I could fix mine, and we could simply go our separate ways, which we did. Glória's male cousins pulled out the minor dent on the spot, and, at Glória's suggestion, I took everybody out for a nice lunch. The lawyer, it turned out, was another of Glória's many friends and therefore my friend, although a stranger. The events showed me once again how much more valuable a wealth of friends can be than a wealth of possessions.

28. William Norris's work on networks in Salvador, Bahia, (1984, 1988) helped me to understand my own similar data from Pernambuco, pointing my attention to structural differences in male and female networks.

29. There are a variety of ways in which groups of men pay for drinks at bars around the world. Each individual can take care of his own bill, or individuals can take turns treating the whole group, either alternating days or, more commonly, rounds. The structure of round-buying used in Northeast Brazil makes each man drink as much and as fast as each other (except to the extent that he is clever enough to make it look as though he's drunk more than he actually has). It is also an act of ritual gift-giving, with each man's round being his gift to the others. At the end of the evening, each man has treated and been treated by each other man in the group, and all have drunk the same amount at the same rate (cf. Robben 1989a, 212). Round-buying, more than any other form of paying for drinks, emphasizes social solidarity among a group of equals. Of course, men can manipulate this by paying for more rounds or for snacks to a greater extent than their fellows can afford, as a way of marking higher status within the group (cf. Robben 1989a, 213) if they have some reason to disrupt the fellowship of drink.

30. *Quenga* refers to a half coconut husk. *Pé de Quenga* means "clubfoot," but it also has a sexual connotation because *quenga* is also used to mean "prostitute" or "slut." *Negão* also has a sexual connotation, because Black men are thought of as especially potent, and Tschau was so called because of his reputation for lovin' 'em and leavin' 'em.

31. Most employed Brazilians and their dependents are covered by the national health insurance. However, doctor appointments are hard to get in the public health system. The line at the public health office in Caruaru often stretches around two or three city blocks. The people in line are waiting for *fichas*, or "tokens," that give them the right to wait in line at a doctor's office if a doctor happens to be available. Once I passed a group of children playing in a poor neighborhood. The difficulties of getting appointments, which they had already experienced in their short lives, were dramatized in the game of "nurse" they were playing. One little girl was dressed with a paper nurse's cap and was seated at a desk labeled with the initials of the public health service. Another girl approached carrying her baby brother.

"My baby is dying!" cried the girl. "I need to see a doctor!"

"I'm sorry," replied the pretend nurse. "We don't have any more *fichas*. Take him home, he'll just have to go ahead and die!"

Although prescription laws are not strictly enforced, tranquilizers are difficult to obtain without a prescription. It was these that the laundress sought from her patron.

32. Men also engage in joking, teasing, and sarcasm. However, men's joking focuses on stories with punch lines to a much greater extent than women's.

33. Very occasionally women will joke about lesbianism in a particular woman or pair of women (lesbian = *sapatão*, lit. "big shoe," or *lésbica*.) For example, one day when Fátima sat talking in her kitchen with a close friend, another friend stuck her head in the open door and called out, *Hein, Fátima, fazendo sabão com tua amorzinha?* ("Hey Fátima, making soap with your lovey-dovey?"). *Fazendo sabão* ("making soap") is a reference to frigging. Like other jokes of this kind, the punning reference is deniable; had she been challenged, the speaker could have said that she was asking about laundry. It is hard to say how prevalent female-female sexual relationships are or how often the romantic style of female friendships shades into physical involvement beyond the hugs, *cheirinhos*, and hand-holding of ordinary friendship. Lesbianism is not as elaborated a cultural theme as passive-receptive male homosexuality in the Brazilian Northeast. One possible message of the joke described above could have been to chide Fátima for spending too much time with one friend while neglecting another, the speaker for example.

34. The *telenovela* was loosely based on Jorge Amado's novel *Teresa Batista Cansada de Guerra*, published in English as *Tereza Batista Home from the Wars*.

35. Particular lines from *telenovelas* frequently become popular, constantly repeated. The writers know this and play up to it. In this particular *novela*, which was very popular, there were several lines that became fashionable; there were others that the writers had the characters repeat, as if to popularize them, but they did not catch on.

36. Joking also permits people to state forbidden sentiments openly while denying that that is in fact what they are doing (cf. Freud 1905). This can serve to relieve interpersonal tension as well as to send messages when a relationship is moving toward trouble.

37. Berkowitz (1984, 84) describes a similar phenomenon in Southern Italy.

38. *Muy amigo* is an exact translation of *muito amigo*. I have no idea why this Spanish phrase is used this way; I could find no one able to explain it.

39. It would be a mistake to think that what prostitutes, for example, offer is only raw sex. Exactly what transpires varies according to the type of interaction, but prostitutes provide the service of listening sympathetically to "why my wife does not understand me," and other emotional services, in addition to purely sexual acts, to a degree not generally recognized in the social science literature. This is why the prostitute with the heart of gold is such an evocative figure.

40. Tania Salem, in a study of *favela* women in Rio de Janeiro (1980, 64), showed that these women tended to personalize all their interactions, seeing such bureaucracies as INPS (the nationalized health care system) in terms of personal patronage and favor-granting rather than in terms of their own contractual, legal, or moral right to health care services. While *personalismo* is a general characteristic of social interactions in Brazil, Salem found that women emphasized love and personal contact as a factor in their interactions much more than did men. Her findings are similar to mine among working-class Caruaruense women.

Part II: Romantic Love in a Changing Economy

1. Young (1995, 6–26) also points out that the word "hybrid" refers to an animal like a mule or hinny, which is the offspring of two separate species (in this case, horse and donkey) rather than the offspring of two varieties of the same species (as in a dog with parentage in more than one breed, such as a cock-a-poo or poodle/cocker spaniel mix, for example). The use of the word "hybrid" derives from nineteenth-century debates on whether the perceived races of humans constitute different species or different varieties of a single species.

2. One of the most studied ethnomedical systems in Latin America is the so-called humoral pathology system, in which metaphorical qualities of heat and cold are attributed to substances and conditions. The basic idea of the system is that all things both material (food, medicine) and immaterial (emotion, states of illness) are either hot or cold to varying degrees, and that health is maintained by sustaining a balance between the two. This set of folk beliefs varies widely among countries, regions within countries, and individuals within a single community. The belief system has been most heavily studied in Mexico. It was not especially strongly elaborated in Caruaru. People told me that a menstruating woman cannot drink lemonade or she would die, and that the combination of mangos and milk is lethal, but they could not explain why. In trying to account for why I could drink lemonade (made with lemons, a "hot" fruit) while menstruating (a "hot" condition) without getting lethally "overheated," or why I could withstand the shock of combining very "hot" mangos with very "cold" milk, they took recourse to humoral explanations.

Humoral reasoning is not unique to Latin America and may have origins as much in Greek classical medicine as in the medical systems of native South Americans. (It is retained, for example, in the English description of mild respiratory infections as "colds," which must be heated by eating, whereas fevers are cooled by fasting.) For more on humoral pathology in the Americas, see Adams 1952; Adams and Rubel 1967; Aguirre Beltrán 1963; Colson and de Armellada 1983; Currier 1966; Foster 1987; Logan 1974; Madsen 1955.

Chapter 4: Romance and Modernization

1. Translation from Cruz (1992, 158).

2. Here I am using the term "marriage" in the loose way my informants used *casamento*: to refer to physically intimate domestic arrangements between a man and a woman without regard either for Church blessing or for state licensure. Informants referred to both legally and/or religiously married couples (the systems are largely separate), and to unmarried, cohabiting couples, with terms proper to marriage. Although newspapers used the term *companheiro*, women I knew referred to a live-in boyfriend as *marido* ("husband"). I heard the word *companheiro* only once, when the speaker was trying to denigrate the woman she was gossiping about through the implication of sexual impropriety. The slang term *urso*, or "bear," was more common if a person wanted to refer to a wom-

an's lover; it has a sexual connotation and would not be used to describe a relationship approved of by the speaker.

3. See especially the collection of essays edited by Maria Angela D'Inção for discussions of the history of romance in Brazil (1989).

4. For example, while accidie was discussed as an important emotional condition in the Middle Ages in Europe, it has fallen from the modern vocabulary. Accidie referred to spiritual lassitude, boredom, or disgust with religious obligations. It was related to melancholy, tristitia, and sloth, and was regarded as both a pathological and a sinful emotional state (Harré and Finlay-Jones 1986, 221–22).

5. General histories of love in Europe include de Rougemont 1972, 1973; Mount 1982; Murstein 1974; and Sarsby 1983. I will not review here the literature on courtly love, but interested readers might consult Benton 1968; Duby 1983; Duffy 1972; Lewis 1936; Monter 1977; Morgan 1993; Newman 1968; and Robertson 1968. Some historians claim that courtly love forms a base of European concepts of love; others claim either that it was a historical phenomenon of limited extent and influence, or that, rather than being an actual historical entity, it was the invention of the historian Gaston Paris, whose 1883 discussion of medieval poetry coined the term "courtly love."

6. Engels claimed that marriage markets do not develop in communist economies; see, however, Fisher (1980) on marriage markets in Soviet communism.

7. This claim is not necessarily supported by historical demography. Although the eighteenth-century gentry largely escaped the major causes of death of earlier and poorer populations, including sanitation-related infections, hunger, and the great plagues, they were still subject to many infectious diseases that doctors were unable to treat. Scarlet fever, for example, took a terrible toll among all classes, as did polio. And even when children survived the most vulnerable years of early childhood, they could still be cut down in early adulthood by innumerable infections, accidents, or, in the case of girls, complications during pregnancy and childbirth. M. Jeanne Peterson (1989, 110–15), for example, cites the case of the upper-class Tait family, who in 1856 lost five of their seven children in as many weeks to scarlet fever during one terrible summer. Their surviving son went on to become a minister, only to die in 1878 at the age of twenty-nine of an unidentified infection. He was quickly followed to the grave by his broken-hearted mother. Parents, even those in the upper classes, still had to contend with frequent early death among their children, and even if the statistics on mortality were somewhat less horrendous than in previous centuries, they were still not so favorable that emotional security could easily be had.

8. For example, Keith Snell (1981) describes eighteenth-century economic downturns that reduced opportunities for agricultural wage labor, especially for women, throwing doubt on the idea that newly economically empowered women were a driving force behind the "invention" of love-marriage at that time (Sarsby 1983, 35). And although infant mortality rates in some classes began to drop in the eighteenth century, parents, even upper-class parents, had good reason to fear common infections that killed and maimed children until the early

twentieth century. In addition, the idea that an eighteenth-century shift from extended families to nuclear families sparked a new emphasis on conjugal love is not supported by careful historical demography, which shows the process beginning as early as the fifth century in Byzantium and being well under way by the eleventh century in France (Goody 1983, 25).

9. Even where people say they marry for love, historical demography shows that, although the possibility of falling in love with someone completely inappropriate lends a deliciously rebellious character to romantic passion, most people's tastes are more conventional. The majority marry the kinds of people, if not the very individuals, their parents might have chosen for them. A careful analysis of marriage records in nineteenth-century Germany, for example, showed that love-matches were primarily contracted between people of nearly identical economic means. The author concluded that although marriage was discussed in the idiom of love, and couples claimed to choose one another for reasons of love, this was a "social convention," a "thin whitewash" over the material interests at the base of these marriages (Borscheid 1986, 165).

10. Not only did the deity become a father, but the pope, abbots, priests, monks, and nuns were addressed by kinship terms (father, brother, sister), and the lay faithful became brothers and sisters in Christ as well, and took godchildren (Goody 1983, 194).

11. *Agapé* is a Christian theological concept based on a quotation from I John 4:8 ("He that loveth not, knoweth not God; for God is love"). John was referring to an idealized form of generous, nonsexual, nonappetitive, utterly altruistic love considered divine (Daly 1973, 209). For an intense discussion of medieval theological concepts of passionate and divine love, including *agapé*, see the twelfth-century correspondence of Abelard and Heloise, he a noted theological philosopher, she his pupil, his wife, and later an abbess. Their lengthy correspondence, occasioned after his entrance into a monastery and hers into a convent following a tragic series of events in which her uncle, opposed to the marriage, had Abelard castrated during an assault, contains among the most cogent discussions of the nature of love, suffering, and religiosity in the literature (see translation by Betty Radice).

12. In England, France, and Germany, neolocal residence combined with a preference for similarity in age between the conjugals. This indicates, but alone does not prove, the possibility of love between conjugals much earlier than the eighteenth century. Historical demography shows no sharp structural changes in the European family for the eighteenth century, as Shorter, Stone, and Ariès imply, except for small changes in the average age at marriage and a growth in the proportion of upper-class women who never married (Sarsby 1983, 51–52). Various other forms of family life in Europe, such as the Scottish clan and the Yugoslav *zadruga*, emphasized the patrilineage over the nuclear family.

13. Stone recognizes that a change in "verbal style and cultural expression" took place from the sixteenth to the eighteenth centuries but argues that what he calls "concrete changes" were more important (1977, 89). The difference between Stone's, MacFarlane's, and Gillis's approaches includes much wrangling over the nature and timing of these "concrete" (structural) factors but also, espe-

cially in the case of Gillis, involves a deeper difference of orientation, in which each theorist dismisses as epiphenomenal that which the others hold as central.

14. Goody points out that Iberians did not adopt Moorish polygyny or patrilineality in unmodified form.

15. The Church prohibited marriage of first and second cousins and frowned on that between third and fourth cousins. In 1917 it amended its policy to prohibit only the marriage of first cousins (Goody 1983, 33–36).

16. The tendency among modern Catholics to disregard the Church's teachings on contraceptives is not part of some new skepticism toward Church teachings on sexuality, but rather the most recent form of a tradition of ignoring or defying the Church's precepts regarding sexuality that goes back to the very beginnings of the Church. Then, couples defied restrictions on marriage between cousins; today they defy restrictions on reproductive freedom.

17. Mariolatry shares similarities with courtly love, and some scholars go so far as to describe the cult of the Virgin as a religious version of the same ideas that found secular expression in troubadour poetry (cf. Warner 1976), although the beginnings of the Virgin's veneration predate troubadour poetry by half a millennium (Murstein 1974, 153).

18. Very little is said about Mary directly in Scripture. Ideas such as the Assumption (that Mary was bodily transported to Heaven) and the Immaculate Conception (that Mary was conceived without sin) were eventually adopted as mainstream theology, but each idea was vociferously debated by theologians, sometimes over a period of centuries. These ideas reflect an increasing tendency to see Mary not as an ordinary human woman selected for the extraordinary task of bearing God's son, but rather as extraordinary in her own right. Immaculate Conception theology in particular posits that Mary was without inherited original sin, and therefore different from all other humans. While on the one hand the theology satisfies a desire to see God's mother as especially qualified for her extraordinary role, on the other it tends to diminish Mary's humanity and therefore the impact of the miracle of God's birth as a human. It was adopted in December of 1854 by Pope Pius IX in a papal bull called Ineffabilis Deus. The Doctrine of the Assumption was officially declared dogma by Pope Pius XII in 1950 in a document called Munificentissimus Deus.

19. Prohibited acts included masturbation, anal sex, oral sex, or anything that could cause an ejaculation without the possibility of impregnation. Male homosexual sex was condemned for this reason: It was nonreproductive.

20. The Church did the same in Northern Europe; for example, in Shakespeare's *Romeo and Juliet* the couple are sheltered from their feuding parents and married by a sympathetic priest. Shakespeare's plot reflected realities of his day.

21. Once Protestant sects began to appear, doctrinal differences on marriage increased, along with differing reactions of local states to these disputes, which centered on who had the right to determine who would marry whom. While the Catholic Church took a position in favor of free will, Protestants favored parental control of marriage. Some civil governments opposed the Church's position; for example, France passed civil laws favoring parental control in defiance of the Church (Seed 1988, 284). But since Spain regarded itself as a leader of the

Counter Reformation, it took a position in support of couple consent, accusing France of heresy.

22. Slavery was legally abolished in stages in Brazil, starting in 1871 with the Lei do Ventre-Livre (Free Birth Law), which stated that all children of enslaved mothers were born free. A law of 1885 freed all slaves over sixty-five years of age, and the escaped slave law of early 1888 banned the return of escaped slaves (compare the Dred Scott decision in the United States). Finally, slavery was formally abolished by a law signed by Princess Isabel on May 13, 1888 (de Assis Silva and de Assis Bastos 1986, 179–80).

23. Giddens here is criticizing Foucault by emphasizing the opening up of new choices, whereas Foucault stresses the creation of new constraints as hallmarks of modernity. I suspect that each has a piece of the puzzle—in which new constraints and new liberalities accompany one another in complex ways.

24. Estimates of the numbers of slaves imported into Brazil, based on the incomplete historical records, vary from about three million to over six million. In 1817, about half of the non-Native population of Brazil were slaves (Conrad 1986, 1). Mortality rates were very high among imported slaves, the sex ratio was skewed in favor of males, and the birthrate among slaves was low. Slave populations in Brazil and the Caribbean were not self-reproducing until the late 1800s, their numbers being maintained by continued importation, even after the international illegalization of the African slave trade. In addition, for every captured slave who landed alive in Brazil several Africans died as a result of violent capture, imprisonment in Africa while awaiting sale, or the brutal Middle Passage by ship to the Americas (Conrad 1986, 26–55). The movement of enslaved Africans in the African-American Triangle Trade constitutes the largest mass movement of people in human history, a brutally deadly migration that was entirely involuntary on the part of the migrants and phenomenally profitable on the part of those who managed the trade and those who purchased the coerced labor of slaves.

25. This benign view of slavery is not unique to Brazil. I was taught something similar about slavery in the United States in the seventh grade in Charlottesville, Virginia, in 1971. Our textbooks presented a Confederate-oriented view of slavery as relatively benign. My African-American history teacher commented on the text, telling us, "You'll never understand Virginia history until you understand why the State of Virginia tells me I have to teach lies to the little children!" By the time my younger brother was in seventh grade, two years later, the textbooks had been scrapped as racist and a less benign view of slavery was being taught. Debates over racist images in textbooks are increasing in the United States but have not become an issue in Brazil.

26. Stuart Schwartz notes that among slaves and freed slaves, light-skinned women strongly preferred to marry men who were similar to or lighter in color than themselves, describing this as an example of how subjugated people frequently adopt the ideology of their oppressors, in this case the racist axiom that "lighter is better" (Schwartz 1985, 392).

27. The term "Old Christian" derives from the end of the Iberian Moorish period. Portugal and Spain had expelled or forcibly converted their Jewish and

Muslim populations in the 1490s. In addition to the Muslim Moors, sizable populations of Sephardic Jews lived in Spain and Portugal during the Moorish period. Regarded as foreigners by both Christians and Muslims, Jews found life less restricted under Muslim rule, but populations of Jews lived and worked in both Christian and Muslim areas. Many Jews and Muslims converted, at least nominally, although some continued to practice their former religions in secret. These New Christians and their descendants were considered to be of less pure blood than Old Christian families and were prohibited from receiving titles, positions, and privileges within the Portuguese empire (Nazzari 1996, 108). Although some New Christians found economic opportunity in colonial Brazil, their status was below that of Old Christians, and they were subject to investigation by the colonial office of the Inquisition (Schwartz 1985, 265). Colonials extended the concern for *sangue limpo* ("clean blood") to include concerns over what they called *mulatismo*, or "racial admixture," among Africans, Europeans, and Native Brazilians (Russell-Wood 1978, 64).

28. Ironically, contemporary physical anthropologists have moved the locus of race back into the invisible reaches of the body, emphasizing differences in tissue type, such as blood type, as being more reliably tied to the geographic origin of ancestors than any of the visible surface variations in human face and form.

29. It was more common for women to outlive than predecease their husbands, partly because women tended to live longer than men and partly because they tended to be younger than their husbands. But there were also many women who died of complications of childbirth, among other causes, so the disposal of a woman's property by her widower was a legitimate concern for families.

30. Until the late 1800s, Brazilian convents did not admit nonwhite postulants. Poor women could not enter convents because entrance required either a dowry or evidence of sufficient income to support oneself in the religious life (Soeiro 1978).

31. Kuznesof (1991, 257) argues that the importance of premarital virginity was different for different races and classes and between rural and urban areas. Although unmarried pregnancy was not necessarily a calamity for urban women, such women were more likely to be poor, marginalized, and disparaged, and their children abandoned, given up for adoption, or living in poverty. Martha de Abreu Esteves (1989) discusses contradictory pressures on lower-class women, who on the one hand desired freedom from the strictures of imposed chastity and on the other sought the legal protection accruing to honorable women. My discussion here owes much to Donna Goldstein (forthcoming), who posits that women's sexuality is more divided by the distinction between domestic and public realms than is men's, forcing lower-class women to present themselves as sexual innocents as part of impression management. See also Goldstein 1994.

32. Of course men have the ultimate advantage of legal and political power, and social permission to abandon women and children, so women start with a marked disadvantage in these "games of power and seduction." At the same time, they are not without agency or tactics of their own.

33. In 1904, one of the first large-scale vaccination campaigns against small-pox took place in Rio de Janeiro, then the Brazilian capital. It sparked riots among the poor, who were forced to submit to what they saw as bodily invasion by a government that they could not believe had their best interests at heart. Despite the violence, the campaign was one of the first to demonstrate the utility of vaccination as a population-level preventative of infectious disease, and Brazil achieved universal smallpox vaccination before other Latin American countries (Sevcenco 1984).

34. Medieval theologians condemned wet-nursing because they thought that infants could imbibe sin through milk, and some portrayed child saints as rejecting the breast (Spierenburg 1991, 255). Physicians began to condemn wet-nursing in the 1500s, and such sentiments became even more widespread in the eighteenth century.

Influenced by the writings of Jean-Jacques Rousseau, especially his 1762 *Emile*, in which he argued that breast-feeding would lead to stronger family ties, French elites began a vogue for breast-feeding by mothers instead of wet nurses (Yalom 1997, 111). There were several factors in this reasoning. First, milk was thought to be some kind of blood product. Blood metaphorically represented heredity, and mixing blood implied kinship. Thus, imbibing the milk of lesser women could possibly weaken an elite child's bloodline. Breast-feeding from the child's own mother would strengthen the elite bloodlines of a wealthy child. In addition, breast-feeding would increase the affection between mother and child. It would counter the tendency of husbands to see their wives as primarily sexual objects (among the reasons for employing wet nurses were taboos against sexual intercourse during lactation and fears that the increasingly sexualized breast might sag).

As wet-nursing increasingly became associated with the decadence of the royal courts, breast-feeding took on a political connotation. Marilyn Yalom points out that many of the images used by participants in the French Revolution portray bare-breasted women: the icon of Mother French Republic or Goddess Liberty, who opened her breasts to give nurturance to all her citizens. This figure eventually came to be called Marianne and was portrayed bare-breasted in works of art from sculptures to cartoons to the engravings on money (1997, 123). Brazilian hygienists were following the example of the republican French, several decades later. They transformed the class discourse of the French into a racial discourse in the context of slavery.

35. Portuguese laws passed in 1719 permitted the marriage of slaves. At the same time, Catholic officials urged owners to allow slaves to marry and to refrain from selling husbands and wives away from one another. However, many owners resisted slave marriages, partly because they wanted to be able to sell slaves without consideration of the slaves' own social arrangements, and partly because they feared disruption should the conjugals grow tired of one another and want to separate, or should they disregard their marital vows to form adulterous unions. Owners also feared that slaves might meet and romance slaves from other plantations, creating problems. Actually, this last was quite uncommon. In a study of slave marriages in Bahia, Stuart

Schwartz found no cases of slaves married to slaves of other plantations (1985, 383–85).

36. Costa is clearly influenced by Foucault here.

37. It is not required that all children in a family have the same surname. For example, if a couple decide to name one son after the wife's father, they can give the boy the grandfather's full name including surname. Subsequent sons may bear the father's surname, or some other family name if they are named after another relative.

38. British Victorians carried this struggle to extremes, elaborating not only verbal codes but also a great variety of communicative systems for lovers. For example, by associating particular amorous statements with specific species of flower, Victorian lovers could communicate ardently by the exchange of bouquets with combinations of significant blooms, or through notes listing flower names. Flower statements could be as elaborate as the variety of blossoms in a garland. *The Home Instructor,* published in 1886, lists the following flower conversation: Red rose—I love you. Purple pansy—You occupy my thoughts. Everlasting pea—Wilt thou go with me? Daisy—I will think of it. Shepherd's purse—I offer you my all. Laurel—Words, though sweet, may deceive. Heliotrope—I adore you. Zinnea—I mourn your absence. Jonquil and linden—I desire to marry you. Bachelor's button and red rose—Hope for love. Four-leafed clover—Be mine. Garden daisy—I share your feelings. Cedar leaf—I live for thee.

Chapter 5: Ideals of Masculinity and Femininity

1. Although usually described in heterosexual contexts, these ideas also structure same-sex attractions and figure heavily in the construction of third genders, such as the effeminate man or masculine woman.

2. For example, Cole (1991, 81) argues that in Portugal, women base their sense of self-worth not around their sexual continence but their work, both inside and outside the home.

3. These writers see the excesses of the honor-shame model as reflections of Northern European misunderstanding of Southern European emotional styles. See Cole (1991, 78) for a review of this literature.

4. The term "machismo" is derived from the Spanish and Portuguese *macho* (male). It first appeared in English-language descriptions of Spain and Latin America, although it has entered Spanish and Portuguese from the English (Gilmore and Gilmore 1979, 281). In Caruaru, people refer to *machista* men rather than use "machismo" as a noun. The word *macho* simply means "male" in Portuguese. Machismo has been described by social scientists in Mexico (Goldwert 1985; Gutmann 1996; Limón 1989; Pearlman 1984; Wiest 1983), Argentina (Suárez-Orozco 1982), Spain (Brandes 1974, 1980; Driessen 1983; Gilmore and Gilmore 1979; Gilmore and Uhl 1987; Marvin 1984; Mitchell 1990; Pratt 1960), Latin America (Kinzer 1973; Moraes-Gorechi 1988; Stevens 1973a,b; Suárez-Orozco and Dundes 1984), and Brazil (Freyre 1986; Neuhouser 1989; Oliven 1988; Robben 1988, 1989a,b; Saffioti and Ferrante 1983).

5. This may be especially important in the Caribbean Islands of his study, where travel between the various islands is quite common.

6. Sally Cole (1991, 82–83) describes a similar situation in contemporary Portugal, stating that the term *vergonha* is used without any reference to *honra* and encompasses much of what anthropologists have discussed as "honor" in the Mediterranean.

7. The word *bicha* could be loosely translated as "fag." *Fruta* means "fruit," *veado* "deer," and *vinte-e-quatro* "twenty-four," a number associated with deer because of its position in the lottery game *jogo do bicho*, in which people gamble on animal figures rather than numbers.

8. I noticed a tendency among unmarried women living alone because their parents had died, leaving them the house, to have a reputation for saintliness and to work as *rezadeiras*. I do not have a broad enough sample to tell if this is a universality or merely a tendency in Caruaru, nor do I know if this phenomenon exists elsewhere. But a reputation for piety would help protect a woman living alone against sexual harassment. Any woman reputed to be especially pious will be besieged by neighbors eager for blessing: Some *rezadeiras* I interviewed felt they had been forced into the occupation by neighborly importuning. Other women begged me to hold in confidence their skill at blessing lest the sick, the needy, and the desperate disturb them for graces at all hours of the day and night.

9. Once while I was visiting a friend I heard a commotion outside, and we went to see what was going on. One of the neighbor men had previously discovered his wife in bed with another man, and he had left her a few days earlier. He had now returned to remove everything from inside the house, including all the furniture, the refrigerator, stove, sink, toilet, dishes, clothing—everything but the walls, roof, and floor. When he and his friends had loaded everything onto a donkey cart, he turned to his weeping wife, bowed, and announced grandly that because of his great generosity he was leaving her the house. The neighbors watched silently and then broke up into little groups, discussing the case. The consensus was that the man was entirely justified in his actions.

10. Most dictionaries translate *quintal* as "backyard," although, at least in Northeastern houses, it does not resemble a U.S. backyard except in its location. Most *quintals* have cement floors and a few have roofs. A few are partially planted, with gaps in the paving for small gardens or trees. Most working-class houses in Caruaru have an open-topped cement water tank in the *quintal*, and many people keep tropical fish in this family water supply. More prosperous homes add a fiberglass-covered water tank on the roof. In this dry region water is valuable, and the more water storage capacity a house has the more valuable it is. During prolonged water rationing, during which the city simply turns off running water, poor people go begging water with buckets door to door in wealthier neighborhoods. In apartments, the term *quintal* is used to designate a back area, often a balcony, that is equipped with a washboard sink for doing laundry.

11. Many houses boast a small ceramic sink shaped like a water fountain

just outside the kitchen in the front room. The sink is designed to be absolutely useless: Its bowl is too shallow to do dishes or laundry in, it lacks a built-in scrub board, and the high faucet gives only the basic, nonpotable city tap water. It is only for show. Upper-class houses frequently boast numerous such sinks, extra bathrooms, bathtubs, and one or more built-in swimming pools. Once I was talking with a construction worker from an impoverished family who was working on a house for a wealthy family. He gave me a tour of the site, pointing out a separate water tower, two swimming pools, tennis courts, an underground gaming room and bowling alley, fully equipped kitchen with built-in sinks and stoves, and twenty-three bathrooms, each with bathtub, toilet, bidet, and sink, scattered throughout the house. In fact, each room in the house had its own separate bathroom with imported fixtures. I asked him why he thought they needed so many bathrooms, and he quipped, *Devem ser cagonas grandes!* ("They must be big shitters!").

12. Wealthy homes usually have doorbells, intercoms, and armed guards. A wall usually surrounds the estate. Some working-class houses also boast walls, varying from low constructions that mark the property line to tall, broken-glass-topped edifices seriously intended to keep people out. The higher the wall, the higher the status. During the last few months of my fieldwork I lived in one such walled house in a city-built housing development. Despite the height of the wall, with its sharp glass, neighborhood boys regularly jumped it to steal guavas from the trees in the front yard. Their sisters always came by later with guava juice and guava jam for me, often including bread and coffee as well; in fact, I never had to make breakfast. This arrangement was never discussed with me, it simply occurred. Some coordination must have taken place, because I never got more than one breakfast.

13. To serve water, a family member, usually female, comes forward holding a pitcher and a glass. She pours water into the glass, offering it to the guest, who drinks it and hands the glass back. Then the family member refills the glass and offers it again. This will continue until the guest refuses the glass, at which point the whole process starts with the next guest. Some families offer a basin of water with soap and a towel in which to wash hands before offering water to drink. Often, people working as street sweepers, construction workers, or beggars will request water at houses and be served in this manner. To refuse to give water is a severe breach of courtesy.

14. During slavery, it was customary for children and slaves to ask for a blessing from the plantation patriarch upon seeing him (Schwartz 1985, 288). The custom of asking for a blessing when leaving or entering the house may have its origins in that practice.

15. Families also emphasize the difference in the way in which they clean their houses, although here there is disagreement. Some people sweep their houses back to front in order to throw badness out of the *casa* and into the *rua*. But more think that bad luck will enter the house unless it is swept from front to back, with dirt picked up in a dust pan in the *quintal*.

16. In all-female households the harder labor tends to be performed by the lowest status women.

17. A *bucho* is a belly, and the word *bucha* can refer to a large, rounded bowl or to a particular round fruit. The proper word for pregnant is *gravida*, from the Latin, but *buchuda* ("big-bellied, round-bellied") is more common in folk speech. The word is colloquial; upper-class people find it comically vulgar.

18. The term *agregado* also refers to tenant farmers and sharecroppers, and especially those at the lowest end of access to land: people who work for share-croppers in return for room and board. In slavery times if a slave master wanted to associate a mixed race son or daughter with the household without necessarily admitting parentage, he could designate the child *agregado* and attach him to the household without either legitimizing him or giving him rights of inheritance. Today the term refers to foster parentage. *Agregado* children may be informally adopted in a pseudo-consanguineous relationship similar to formal adoption except for the lack of legalization, or they may be brought into a family as servants. The difference between beloved daughter and effective slave is entirely dependent on how the adults in the household choose to treat the *agregado* child.

19. In 1976, ten incidents of rioting on trains, involving up to five thousand workers, were recorded in São Paulo and Rio de Janeiro. Urban workers depend on the trains to get from their *favela* homes to their jobs in the enormous, sprawling southern cities, trips that can consume as much as four hours a day. Crowded conditions, frequent breakdowns, and delays that can cost hourly workers dearly (especially those at risk of being fired if they are late to work) contribute to the tensions that underlie these riots, along with awareness that the government has invested more in the roads that facilitate movement for middle- and upper-class car drivers than in the trains that move impoverished workers. In the 1980s several riots took place at supermarkets in southern cities in response to increasing layoffs caused by rising inflation and an economic recession. São Paulo lost an estimated 700,000 jobs between 1980 and 1983 (Wood and de Carvalho 1988, 131–33).

20. "A parrot on wire" is common folk speech for a tightfisted person.

21. Protestant churches explicitly require their male members to eschew such spending, investing their money instead in food, clothing, and education for their children. In this sense, although in many ways antifeminist because of their strong opinion that the male should be the head of household and the wife should not work outside the home, the family-values platforms of evangelical Protestant and Mormon churches do espouse an economic program generally consonant with the economic interests of working-class Brazilian housewives, and in that sense they are similar to U.S. nineteenth-century feminist ideals (cf. Brusco 1995), which emphasized the creation of social harmony through increasing domestication of the extradomestic sphere.

Chapter 6: Courtship, Marriage, and Cohabitation

1. The saints' days of Sts. Anthony, John, and Peter occur in a two-week period in the middle of June. These days, coinciding with the corn harvest, are celebrated with dances, feasts, and divinations to discover the identity of true

loves and future spouses. Many of the couples I interviewed who were older than thirty-five, or who resided in rural areas, had met at a June festival, gotten engaged at another, and gotten married at a June festival some years later. St. Anthony, in his role of finding lost objects and performing miracles, is the patron of courtship, marriage, and young lovers in the Iberian Church, because he finds husbands for old maids. Because St. Peter is depicted holding keys (to the Pearly Gates), he is associated with houses and therefore marriage. These associations fit well with the general excitement about fertility accompanying any harvest festival. São Jõao or Festas Juninas, as the holiday is known, is the major festival of the Northeast Agreste, and Caruaru in particular promotes itself as having the best São Jõao in the world.

2. One night one of my friends and I decided to go around and try to count couples engaged in secret romances. He drove my car while I manned the passenger-side window. This turned out to be exciting but not the safest of pursuits, since some of the men we caught kissing girls they shouldn't have been really did have pistols in their pockets.

3. A respectable room-for-the-night rental place will be called a hotel, or other term designating such variations as a bed and breakfast, for example. Couples may go to hotels for assignations, but it will cost them more, so they are less likely to go unless they are upper class or it is a special occasion.

4. Historically, Christian theology has equated thought with deed, so that a man who desired a woman not his wife was said to have committed adultery in his heart. Similarly, to be considered a virgin a woman had to be pure, not only in the technical sense that she had never had sexual intercourse and her hymen was still intact but also in that she had never had an impure thought, never had experienced desire. Further, she must never have been the object of desire, never the cause of a man's having committed adultery or fornication in his heart. Today, as in the past, women who wish to be taken for virgins must not only eschew sexual behavior but must also avoid any act, gesture, word, or situation that suggests sexual knowledge or desire. Historically, virgins had to remain secluded and covered to avoid exciting lust in men (Bloch 1991, 93–112), but in Brazil today, paradoxically, young women may dress in very revealing clothes while adopting all the mannerisms of a virgin. The idea that she who has excited lust necessarily experiences lust remains only in the jealous fantasies of possessive boyfriends and husbands.

5. A *sarra pesada* ("heavy *sarra*") is the same action unclothed or partly clothed and may form part of love-making, or what in English might be called "heavy petting."

6. There is some controversy as to the exact origins of the *lambada*, but most sources agree that it developed out of the *forró*, adding a style of music more heavily influenced by pop (perhaps especially Richie Valens's rock version of the Mexican traditional song *La Bamba*, popularized by the movie of the same name). Lambada started with Brazilian performers outside of Brazil, but at the time of my fieldwork a lambada craze was sweeping the Northeast (after it had abated in the South), and it was enormously popular in Caruaru.

7. The word for "shopping mall" in Brazilian Portuguese is *shopping center*, perhaps reflecting the U.S. origin of this kind of structure. Like U.S. middle-class urban and suburban teenagers, Brazilian urban teenagers find enclosed shopping malls an excellent arena for courtship and entertainment.

8. Not all countries accepted the Tridentine rules. Tridentine rules on consent had their strongest support in Spain but were not well accepted in Portugal. Such Catholic countries as France, for example, got around the rules by declaring marriage without the consent of the bride's father to be a form of rape. It might take place, but the husband could be condemned to death (Seed 1988, 34–35). This idea was part of the well-established tradition of male ownership of sexual access to the females in their household.

9. Killing a young man who had succeeded in seducing a virgin daughter, or killing the daughter herself, could be defended as an act of defense of masculine or family honor by father or brothers, and it was therefore permissible.

10. The Federal Constitution of 1934, article 144, reads: *A família constituida pelo casamento indissolúvel está sob a proteção especial do Estado* ("The family constituted by indissolvable marriage is under the special protection of the state"), continuing legal protection for indissolvable marriage in previous legal codes.

11. The new law modified the complete control over wifely property granted in previous legal codes. Under *comunhão universal de bens* a woman may administer all monies gained through her own employment. Women may also have their own separate pensions and gratuities and they may inherit property specifically denominated as nonjoint. Women may also designate property or monies held before marriage as nonjoint in a prenuptial agreement (Rocha 1980, 51–55). The law also provides for marriage under *separação de bens* ("separation of property") when (a) the woman is less than twenty-one years of age and does not have parental consent for the marriage; (b) the woman is less than sixteen years of age and the man less than eighteen; (c) a widow or widower with minor children marries (in order to protect the interests of the minors in the estate); (d) a woman marries less than ten months after divorce or widowhood without having given birth during those months; (e) the woman is older than fifty or the man older than sixty; (f) and under various situations in which one of the conjugals is or was at one time the legal ward or under the jurisdiction of the other (Rocha 1980, 59–61).

12. In the United States the overwhelming majority of births take place in hospitals or other medical institutions, attended by officially licensed practitioners (despite a small, vocal lay-midwife/home birth movement). This makes it relatively easy to enforce laws mandating registration of all births. But in Brazil, while many births take place in hospitals, a significant proportion, especially among the poor and in rural areas, do not. Such births are often not attended by official health personnel, and registration at birth is not enforced by hospitals.

13. Except for the interest of the children of such unions in the father's estate.

14. Either parallel or cross.

15. Cows are valuable possessions in rural households, and historically one

of the animals with which women are most associated (women being in general associated with milk, eggs, and other fertile things). The comparison of a woman to a cow is not insulting in the rural context.

16. The word used here, *mulher* ("woman"), can be used simply to designate an adult female human being. But it is also used in contrast to *moça* ("virgin") to mean a sexually experienced female. For this reason, some consider it to be a relatively rude term, preferring to use *senhoras* to describe adult, married women, in the same way that in some areas of the southeastern United States "woman" is less polite than "lady."

17. The word *coroa* can also be used to refer to an older man who could become a patron in return for sexual favors.

18. Some children are reared in families who treat them as domestic servants, forcing them to work in return for room and board in a relationship not far removed from slavery. Girls raised in such circumstances are often subject to sexual harassment by the men of the household and therefore may have trouble making a legitimate marriage. They also may have trouble gaining their freedom from their foster parents until they are relatively old for marriage.

19. He had learned Portuguese and German in his adoptive home. He had learned English and Spanish from a combination of radio broadcast lessons, public school instruction, and private lessons he paid for out of money he earned in the town museum. He learned French from a colleague. His English was absolutely fluent, with an almost native North American accent. He hoped eventually to find work in the tourist industry, although he knew he would have to move to a place with more tourists to do so. When last I saw the couple, they were managing a stand in the market that sold children's underwear.

20. This *boudas douro* ("golden anniversary") is generally properly celebrated by a renewal of vows in the church followed by a Mass, which is what this couple did.

21. There are cases where Catholic couples who have been cohabiting for some time, or who were civilly married years ago, desire to make their union right in the eyes of God before their deaths. In such cases, a simple blessing of the union by a priest, witnessed by two witnesses but without any of the expensive trappings of a status wedding, can be arranged for a modest fee.

22. The flower girl and ring bearer are generally children of five to seven years of age, dressed as miniatures of the bride and groom, who enter the church just before the couple. Sometimes the girl carries a bouquet, or in other styles she may carry a basket of flowers that she may be instructed to strew in the aisle. The boy sometimes carries the ring on a small pillow, but he functions mainly as an escort to the flower girl (the ring may either be entrusted to one of the male witnesses or held by the groom himself).

23. The most common Protestant sects in Caruaru include Seventh-Day Adventists and Jehovah's Witnesses. There is also a Baptist Church, a Church of the Reign of God, and the beginnings of evangelization by the Church of Jesus Christ of Latter Day Saints. All of these churches, despite significant theological differences, promote "clean living" and "family values."

24. It is possible to rent a mostly plaster cake for the cutting picture (it has a

little slice of actual cake for the knife to go through). Some of these display cakes are very elaborate, including such touches as electric lights. One such cake I saw was a three-tiered affair, decorated with white plaster roses and topped by a lava lamp crowned with a mop of plastic filaments with little blue lights at the tips. The couple also had an edible cake for the guests.

25. This happened right at the beginning of my fieldwork, before I was fluent in the local accent. The congregation members all seemed to have strong opinions about what I should photograph. It was sometimes hard to hear the preacher over all the *"psshht!"* sounds that would-be photography directors were aiming at me along with gestures and facial expressions pointing out good shots. At one point the proceedings came to a halt while someone gave me a ride home to get more film. My film was Kodachrome, which could not be locally developed, so the couple had to wait about a year before I was finally able to give them a slide show so that they could pick out the ones they wanted for prints. At that time I was using an old Olympus XA manual miniature camera. The flash has a little pop-up light at the top that the congregation members could see when the flash was ready for use.

26. In a history of photos of the family in Brazil, Miriam Moreira Leite (1993, 111–12) describes wedding photos as the "legitimators" of formal weddings, the "ultimate act of publicity of the union," as important a part of the ritual as the bride's white dress, veil, and ring.

27. Very rarely a couple will obtain a religious wedding for strictly religious reasons. I was pressed into service once as a witness for the religious wedding of an elderly couple who had lived together for many years and did not want to die in a state of sin. At the ceremony only the couple and the priest and I were present. For the religiously required second witness, the priest forged the signature of his deceased mother, stating that she was always with him.

28. It is possible that the judge intended a mild pun, since *caso* can be used to mean an adulterous affair.

29. This word refers to a woman of African descent. It can be used in a derogatory fashion, but it is not necessarily derogatory. It is similar in this way to the U.S. word "nigger" as it is used among African Americans. The word is derogatory only in certain circumstances, depending on who says it to whom, in what tone of voice, and in which situation. To my eye, Fátima was no more African in appearance than her husband's family. Either of these families in the United States would probably be taken for Latino rather than African American. However, Fátima had been adopted and raised by a blue-eyed, blond-haired woman of German descent and was significantly different in appearance from her adoptive family. She often referred to herself as *preto* ("black"), and so did her friends, relatives, and neighbors.

30. This particular chief of one of the civil police districts in Caruaru (there are also military police, who are much better armed and equipped and who constitute a separate force) had taken an anthropology course and took a personal interest in me when I had some legal problems with the family with which I was living when my car was stolen. He invited me to observe him in action, and that is how I was able to witness this event.

31. Collier (1997) describes a similar situation in contemporary Spain and Cole (1991) in contemporary Portugal.

32. The direct translation of this common oath is "Oh my our Lady!" It is equivalent to "Goodness gracious!" in English.

33. Verb *amigar*, adjective *amigado*, from *amigo:* "friend." The term *o amaziamento* is an academic term used in scholarly writing and occasionally in newspapers and magazines. My lower-class informants were generally unfamiliar with it, but they could figure out its meaning.

34. Such reasons include the legal spouse's refusal to cooperate, the legal spouse's whereabouts being unknown, lack of resources to pay for required legal work, lack of familiarity with how to obtain a divorce or with the legality of divorce, and a variety of personal reasons.

35. For example, youngest daughters often end up marrying legally after several older ones have eloped or *amigou,* to prove that the parents are able to control at least one daughter. Women whose mothers or sisters have a reputation for sexual misbehavior, women who for some reason have a personal reputation for sexual misbehavior, and women belonging to ethnic or racial classifications considered sensual (such as dark-skinned black women) have particular problems presenting themselves as decent, and they may be subject to sexual harassment. For such women, legal marriage may be a way to protect themselves.

36. The joke is clear to anyone familiar with lower-class house structure, since the *quintal* is the location of water and therefore of toilets and sinks. The only reason to go there is to use a toilet or wash laundry or dishes.

37. Except for your occasional foreign anthropologist, who did so many inexplicable things that this was just added to the list. For most of my fieldwork I rented a portion of a house from a family, so that I wasn't really alone in a house, although I had partial privacy (during my stay, I lived with three families, one after the other). My practice of adopting street kittens also let people say that I was not completely abandoned; that I let the kittens sleep on the bed with me was a great comfort to informants worried that I might be so strange as to sleep completely unprotected by living company. In the last four months of my fieldwork, I lived alone in a house that one man had prepared for a marriage that fell through. I did in fact live alone there except for my several cats, but people did not believe it, indulging in the most imaginative fantasies about men I was supposedly entertaining there.

38. *Viúva é como lenha, chora mas pega fogo.* Suspicion of widows, and similar proverbs expressing it, are common throughout the Mediterranean and Middle East, as well as in Latin America.

39. The term "sexual harassment" is a legal term from the United States; it does not exist except as a direct translation from American English in Brazil, much less in Northeast Brazil. However, I believe it fits this situation in its extended rather than strictly legal usage. A woman who lives alone may find that her male neighbors and acquaintances, and especially her husband's buddies, flirt with her, make sexual remarks, or otherwise test the waters to gauge how

easy she will be to bed. In some cases this does not go beyond occasional rudeness, but if a woman is unlucky enough to encounter a particularly aggressive man, or if she does not handle deftly any advances made to her, she may find herself subject to varying degrees of coercion up to and including some form of what is called acquaintance rape in the United States.

40. Jack Alexander, in a discussion of cohabitation in Jamaica (1984, 174), theorizes that one of the things that distinguishes the races and classes in Jamaica is the control of male sexuality. The more lower class and the blacker the man, the more his sexuality is regarded as socially dangerous; conversely, the more sexually uncontrolled the man, the blacker, poorer, and more dangerous he is judged to be. Legal marriage, as a container for male sexuality, becomes a marker of whiteness and middle-class status, whereas cohabitation, with its more permissive attitude toward sexuality and its play upon communal memories of concubinage during slavery, is seen as primitive, dishonorable, and lower class.

Here of course he is speaking in generalities of stereotypical images; in fact, upper-class men, however white, may have even more opportunities to indulge dangerous sexuality than men with fewer resources to attract women and less political connection with which to intimidate those who would protect their daughters from harassment. But his analysis does shed light on some of the reasons why *amaziamento* is so morally ambiguous and so closely tied to lower-class status. Even where a couple lives in a perfect "as-if" imitation of marriage, the lack of legal sanction casts doubt upon the presumed control of their sexuality in marriage. It is not only the woman's sexual purity that is compromised in *amaziamento*; the man's sexual continence is an issue as well.

Chapter 7: The Language of Love in Northeast Brazil

A different version of this chapter was previously published in William Jankowiak, ed., *Romantic Passion: A Universal Experience?* (New York: Columbia University Press, 1995).

1. Kundera also describes *es muss sein* as a "weighty duty" (1984, 96) but points out that these compulsions shift during the characters' lifetimes from heavy to light needs, from serious to tragicomic compulsions. The situations in which his characters find themselves because of their *es muss seins* are as amusing as they are pathetic.

2. Almeida Garret was the first Portuguese poet to use the term, in 1823, in his poem *Camões*, written in France (Wellek 1973, 191).

3. Of course, in the eighteenth and early nineteenth centuries, when dowries were still in use, men of the upper classes could increase their social and economic standing through marriage. Men did not as a rule marry down the socioeconomic scale in those days, although women did. For men who came from good families but for reasons of birth order or other disability did not inherit lucrative holdings, marrying into a wealthy family was an effective strategy to maintain or improve class position. From the point of view of the woman's fam-

ily, taking on a son-in-law could provide a man to manage estates in the absence of a son or could provide grandchildren whose parentage was certain. If the son-in-law were Portuguese rather than Brazilian, his whiteness was ensured, and that status could compensate for lack of wealth or family position. Some wealthy families preferred not to leave inheritances to their son's or nephew's children, for fear of the remote possibility that a daughter-in-law's secret infidelity might sneak in an unrelated heir, or that a son might marry or beget children with a nonwhite woman (Russell-Wood 1978, 90–91).

4. A number of English words, such as "okay," "bye-bye," "check-up," "cowboy," and "shopping" (to designate a mall) are so common in Brazilian Portuguese that my friends often did not realize they were not native to the language. Words like *lóvi* and *moh-nee* were conscious foreignisms, commonly used.

5. This man's clothes smelled so strongly of cigarette smoke that I doubt his mother, who washed them, was actually unaware of his smoking.

6. Brain damaged by high fevers as an infant, her younger son was significantly developmentally delayed. Although nearly twelve years old, he was unable to speak more than a few words and retained both the happy-go-lucky playful affection of a toddler and the uncontrolled temper tantrums more typical of the "terrible twos" than the early teen years.

7. A "princess" style dress has a high, round collar, an A-line shape, a bow in the back, and it is decorated with lace or ribbon rosettes. Infant girls are frequently dressed in short princess style dresses paired with frilly diaper-cover panties and a hair ribbon, stuck to bald infant pates with tape. The other prominent style of child dress is called *vovozinha* ("little granny"); it is less decorated, with a wide, often square collar and longer hem.

8. When a baby boy is born, it is customary for the father to toast the son's birth by sharing a bottle of wine with his friends. This custom is called variously *bebendo o mijo* ("drinking the urine") or *pagando o mijo* ("paying the urine"). In some areas, the term *mijo* ("urine") is used to refer to the adult man's penis, in the same way that *pipí* is used to refer to the little boy's organ. The term *mijar fora do penico* ("piss outside the pot") has a variety of meanings, including to lie and to commit adultery. To *mijar sobre a cova* ("urinate on the grave") is a strong insult (see Maior 1988, 105).

9. Nonetheless some boys do fight with their fathers. Once in Fortaleza, capital of the neighboring state of Ceará, I was sitting and chatting with vendors in the street market. One stand was being manned by a teenage boy. His father, who was (as usual) drunk, asked his son to give him some of the night's profits so he could buy more rum. The teenager refused, and the man began to insult him. The other vendors explained to me that some weeks earlier the teenager had married and soon discovered his wife in bed with another man. He had separated from the wife but had neither beaten her nor attacked her lover. His father's insults referred to the incident, disparaging the son's manhood. After enduring several minutes of verbal abuse in silence, the teenager suddenly swung around and punched his father in the nose with a loud crack, drawing

blood and causing the inebriated older man to fall down all over a table with comic exaggeration while the younger children screamed in terror.

Discussing the incident later, both male and female vendors agreed that the son's behavior was entirely unacceptable. No matter the provocation, they said, one should never strike one's father. The son should have gotten the rum even if he thought his father drank too much, even though his father was a public embarrassment to the family, and despite having endured years of drunken violence from the man. The obligation to honor one's father was the greater imperative, even though the vendors expressed compassion for what the son of an alcoholic suffers. Although the father's insults constituted "fighting words" in any other situation, words that the vendors agreed a man would be justified to use deadly force to expunge, from a father even deadly insults should be borne in silent self-control. The day after hitting his father the teenager ran away from home and did not return.

10. I believe that this image derives from a story, popularly circulated in small inspirational cards given out by proselytizing Protestants, in which a man, viewing the path of his life in the form of footsteps on the beach, chides God because His sheltering footprints are absent during the roughest passages. God corrects the man, explaining that the single set of footprints represents places where God was carrying His beloved child through difficulties.

11. These words may have been inspired by the lyrics of a popular song.

Chapter 8: Infidelity in Companionate and
Romantic Marriage

1. That is female supine, male superior, face-to-face sexual intercourse, what people in the United States tend to call the "missionary position."

2. *Rainha da Sucata* means "Queen of Scrap Metal." It was the eight o'clock *novela das oito* on network *Globo*, written by Silvio de Abreu.

3. *Veja*, October 24, 1990 (my translation).

4. Jõaozinho's wife, eight months pregnant, was present when he made this comment and nodded her head in assent as he spoke. However, later she told me, *Você não sabe como é sofrir até casa com homem machista* ("You don't know what suffering is until you marry a sexist man").

5. This expression is frequently written on truck bumpers. I also saw variants: *Usou, enxugou, 'ta limpo* and *lavou, enxugou, 'ta novo* ("He used it, he dried it, it's clean; he washed it, he dried it, it's new).

6. This is a particular handicap for *Crentes* ("Protestants"), who have a strict attitude toward drinking, smoking, and infidelity. They tend to form their own networks separate from those of Catholics, increasing distrust between the two communities.

7. The "civil house" is civil because it is legally constituted; "military house" is a pun because "military" is the opposite of "civil." *Concubina* ("concubine") is the popularly used legal term for a woman maintained in a house by another woman's husband as part of a sexual liaison.

8. I believe this is a reference to Down's Syndrome. Some Caruaruenses knew the term *sindrome de Down*, but it was more common to hear *mongoloide* or the folk term *nênê chines* (Chinese baby) to describe the condition.

9. This was in response to my question: "Is it better to be a wife or to be the other woman?"

10. Caruaruenses often used disease names like *febre do rato* ("rat fever"), *bexiga* ("smallpox"), *gota* ("gout"), *febre amarela* ("yellow fever"), and *bubónica* ("bubonic") as insults and exclamations.

11. This is a pun. "To walk the line" can mean to do the right thing or, alternatively, to walk along train tracks.

12. The character explained to her daughter that when she married she knew little of sex and was shocked and horrified by it. She did not blame her husband for taking a young mistress because he has sexual needs that she, as a decent wife, cannot fulfill. When the daughter asked about her mother's needs, the wife said, *Sou doutra geração* ("I am from another generation"). By befriending the mistress, the wife put the mistress in a bind between her obligations of loyalty to the husband and now to the wife as new friend. Eventually the wife succeeded in breaking up the affair through her friendship with the mistress, although after the marital reconciliation the husband took another mistress.

Chapter 9: Considerations of Love in Caruaru

1. Much of early Christian asceticism was addressed to women. The insistence that a marriage could not take place without the consent of the conjugals for the first time gave women the right to refuse marriage outright, to refuse remarriage if widowed, and to dispose of inheritance without offspring (by giving it to the Church) (Bloch 1991, 88). Goody (1983) suggests that this insistence allowed the Catholic Church to amass large amounts of land and other valuables because so many chose it as their heir in lieu of biological progeny, pointing out that the expansion of the Church's wealth coincided with the development of its rules on marriage, remarriage, and inheritance.

2. Under the dowry system, which first became widespread in Southern Europe in about the eleventh century, daughters received their inheritance upon marriage, sons upon the deaths of their parents. Marriage to the dowered daughter of a wealthy man was a quick way to wealth for elite young men; it is no wonder that poetry glorifying wealthy women should have arisen at this time. It is also no wonder that men should search for some way to contain the potential disruption of women's increasing economic power upon their realization of just how powerful women were becoming, with their family's wealth available during their youth and their new Church-inspired right to refuse marriage and even to choose to endow the Church with their lands and goods, rather than a husband or children.

3. Or, in the case of homosexual couples, men and men or women and women.

⌒ Bibliography

Abu-Lughod, Lila

    1987   *Veiled Sentiments: Honor and Poetry in a Bedouin Society.* Berkeley: University of California Press.

    1990   "Shifting Politics in Bedouin Love Poetry." In *Language and the Politics of Emotion*, edited by Catherine Lutz and Lila Abu-Lughod, 24–45. Cambridge: Cambridge University Press.

Abu-Lughod, Lila, and Catherine Lutz

    1990   "Introduction: Emotion, Discourse, and the Politics of Everyday Life." In *Language and the Politics of Emotion*, edited by Catherine Lutz and Lila Abu-Lughod, 1–23. Cambridge: Cambridge University Press.

Adams, R. N.

    1952   *Un Analisis de las creencias y practicias médicas en un pueblo indigenade Guatemala, con sugerencias relacionadas con la práctica de medicina en el área maya.* Guatemala City: Editorial de Ministério de Educación Pública, Públicaciones Especiales Instituto Nacionál Guatemala No. 17.

Adams, R. N., and A. J. Rubel

    1967   "Sickness and Social Relations." In *Handbook of Middle American Indians*, edited by Robert Wauchope, 633–56. Austin: University of Texas Press.

Aguirre Beltrán, Gonzalo

    1963   *Medicina y magia: El proceso de aculturación en la estructura colonial.* Colección de Alntropologia Social, no. 1. Mexico City: Instituto Nacional Indigenista.

Alarcón, Daniel Cooper

    1997   *The Aztec Palimpsest: Mexico in the Modern Imagination.* Tucson: University of Arizona Press.

Alexander, Jack

    1984   "Love, Race, Slavery, and Sexuality in Jamaican Images of the Family." In *Kinship Ideology and Practice in Latin America*, edited by Raymond T. Smith, 147–80. Chapel Hill: University of North Carolina Press.

Allen, Carole A., and D. J. Cooke

    1988   "Stressful Life Events and Alcohol Misuse in Women: A Critical Review." *Journal of Studies on Alcohol* 16, no. 2: 147–52.

Amado, Jorge
　1969　*Dona Flor and Her Two Husbands: A Moral and Amorous Tale.* Translated by Harriet de Onis. New York: Avon.
　1972　*Tereza Batista Home from the Wars.* Translated by Barbara Shelby. New York: Knopf.
Argyrou, Vassos
　1996　*Tradition and Modernity in the Mediterranean: The Wedding as Symbolic Struggle.* Cambridge: Cambridge University Press.
Ariès, Phillipe
　1962　*Centuries of Childhood.* Translated by Robert Baldick. New York: Random House.
Armon-Jones, Claire
　1986　"The Thesis of Constructionism." In *The Social Construction of Emotions,* edited by Rom Harré, 32–56. Oxford: Basil Blackwell.
Averill, James R.
　1982　*Anger and Aggression: An Essay on Emotion.* New York: Springer-Verlag.
　1983　"Studies on Anger and Aggression: Implications for Theories of Emotion." *American Psychologist* 38, no. 11: 1145–60.
　1986　"The Acquisition of Emotions during Adulthood." In *The Social Construction of Emotions,* edited by Rom Harré, 98–119. Oxford: Basil Blackwell.
Baer, Hans
　1993　"How Critical Can Clinical Anthropology Be?" *Medical Anthropology* 15: 299–317.
　1997　"The Misconstruction of Critical Medical Anthropology: A Response to a Cultural Constructivist Critique." *Social Science and Medicine* 44, no. 10: 1565–73.
Baer, Hans, M. Singer, and J. Johnsen
　1986　"Toward a Critical Medical Anthropology." *Social Science and Medicine* 23: 95–98.
Baer, Werner, and Paul Beckerman
　1988　"The Decline and Fall of Brazil's Cruzado." *Cadernos de estudos sociais* (Recife) 4, no. 1: 4–36.
Barbosa, Lívia Neves de Holanda
　1988　"O Jeitinho ou a arte de ser mais igual do que os outros." *Ciencia hoje* 7, no. 42: 50–56.
　1992　*O Jeitinho Brasileiro: A arte de ser mais igual que os outros.* Rio de Janeiro: Editora Campus.
Bard, P.
　1934　"On Emotional Expression after Decortication with Some Remarks on Certain Theoretical Views. Part I." *Psychological Review* 41, no. 4: 309–29.
Barnett, Elyse Ann
　1989　"Notes on Nervios: A Disorder of Menopause." In *Gender, Health, and Illness: The Case of Nerves,* edited by Dona L. Davis and Setha M. Low, 67–78. New York: Hemisphere Publishing Co.

Basso, Keith

1979 *Portraits of the Whiteman Linguistic Play and Cultural Symbols among the Western Apache.* Cambridge: Cambridge University Press.

Bastide, Roger, and Florestan Fernandes

1971 *Brancos e negros em São Paulo: Ensaio sociológico sobre aspectos da formação, manifestações atuais e efeitos do preconceito de cor na soceidade Paulistana.* 3d ed. São Paulo: Companhia Editora Nacional.

Baumer, Franklin L.

1973 "Romanticism (ca. 1780–ca. 1830)." In *Dictionary of the History of Ideas: Studies of Selected Pivotal Ideas,* vol. 4, edited by Philip P. Weiner, 198–204. New York: Charles Scribner's Sons.

Behar, Ruth, and David Frye

1988 "Property, Progeny, and Emotion: Family History in a Leonese Village." *Journal of Family History* 13, no. 1: 13–32.

Bellini, Ligia

1988 "Por amor e por interesse: A relação senhor-escravo em cartas de Alforria." In *Escravidão e invenção da liberdade estudos sobre o negro no Brasil,* edited by Jõao José Reis, 73–86. São Paulo: Editora Brasiliense, S.A.

Benton, John F.

1968 "Clio and Venus: An Historical View of Medieval Love." In *The Meaning of Courtly Love,* edited by F. X. Newman, 19–42. Albany: State University of New York Press.

Berkowitz, Susan G.

1984 "Familism, Kinship, and Sex Roles in Southern Italy: Contradictory Ideals and Real Contradictions." *Anthropological Quarterly* 57, no. 2: 83–91.

Bernstein, Basil

1971 *Class, Codes and Control.* Vol. 1: *Theoretical Studies Towards a Sociology of Language.* London: Routledge and Kegan Paul.

Besse, Susan K.

1996 *Restructuring Patriarchy: The Modernization of Gender Inequality in Brazil, 1914–1940.* Chapel Hill: University of North Carolina Press.

Besson, Jean

1993 "Reputation and Respectability Reconsidered: A New Perspective on Afro-Caribbean Peasant Women." In *Women and Change in the Caribbean: A Pan-Caribbean Perspective,* edited by Janet Momsen, 15–37. Bloomington: Indiana University Press.

Bittencourt, Elisabeth

1989 "Do direito de desejar: Uma leitura da fala de mulheres camponesas do Maranhao." *Cadernos do CEAS* 120: 13–20.

Bloch, R. Howard

1991 *Medieval Misogyny and the Invention of Western Romantic Love.* Chicago: University of Chicago Press.

Borscheid, Peter

1986 "Romantic Love or Material Interest: Choosing Partners in Nineteenth-Century Germany." *Journal of Family History* 11, no. 2: 157–68.

Boucher, J. D.
  1979   "Culture and Emotion." In *Perspectives on Cross-Cultural Psychology*, edited by A. J. Marsella, R. Tharp, and T. Ciborowski, 159–78. New York: Academic.
Bourdieu, Pierre
  1977, 1989   *Outline of a Theory of Practice*. Cambridge: Cambridge University Press.
Brandão, Adelino
  1971   "Influencias árabes na cultura popular do Brasil." *Revista Brasileira de folclore* 29: 65–84.
Branden, Nathaniel
  1980   *The Psychology of Romantic Love: What Love Is, Why Love Is Born, Why It Sometimes Grows, Why It Sometimes Dies*. Los Angeles: J. P. Tarcher.
Brandes, Stanley
  1973   "Wedding Ritual and Social Structure in a Castilian Peasant Village." *Anthropological Quarterly* 46, 2: 65–74.
  1974   "Crianza infantil y comportamento relativo a roles familiares en México." *Ethnica* 8: 35–47.
  1980   *Metaphors of Masculinity*. Philadelphia: University of Pennsylvania Press.
  1987   "Reflections on Honor and Shame in the Mediterranean." In *Honor and Shame and the Unity of the Mediterranean*, edited by D. Gilmore, 121–34. Washington, D.C.: American Anthropological Association (Special Publication no. 22).
Briggs, J. L.
  1970   *Never in Anger: Portrait of an Eskimo Family*. Cambridge: Harvard University Press.
Brown, Diana DeGroat
  1994   *Umbanda: Religion and Politics in Urban Brazil*. New York: Columbia University Press.
Browner, Carole, and Ellen Lewin
  1982   "Female Altruism Reconsidered: The Virgin Mary as Economic Woman." *American Ethnologist* 9, no. 1: 61–75.
Bruschini, Maria Cristina Aranha
  1990   *Mulher, casa e família cotidiano nas camadas médias paulistanas*. São Paulo: Editora Revista dos Tribunais Ltda. Edições Vértice.
Brusco, Elizabeth E.
  1995   *The Reformation of Machismo: Evangelical Conversion and Gender in Colombia*. Austin: University of Texas Press.
Burguière, Andre
  1987   "The Formation of the Couple." *Journal of Family History* 12, nos. 1–3: 39–53.
Bustos, Jorge Gissi
  1980   "Mythology about Women, with Special Reference to Chile." In *Sex and Class in Latin America: Women's Perspectives on Politics, Economics, and the*

Family in the Third World, edited by June Nash and Helen Iken Safa, 30–45. New York: J. F. Bergin Publishers.

Camino, Linda

1989 "Nerves, Worriation, and Black Women: A Community Study in the American South." In *Gender, Health, and Illness: The Case of Nerves*, edited by Dona L. Davis and Setha M. Low, 203–22. New York: Hemisphere Publishing Co.

Cancian, Francesca M.

1986 "The Feminization of Love." *Signs Journal of Women in Culture and Society* 11, no. 4: 692–709.

Canclini, Néstor García

1995 *Hybrid Cultures: Strategies for Entering and Leaving Modernity*. Minneapolis: University of Minnesota Press.

Carrier, James

1992 "Occidentalism: The World Turned Upside-Down." *American Ethnologist* 19: 195–212.

Carvalho, Rejane Vasconcelos

1987 "Coronelismo: Eternização do quadro de análise política do Nordeste?" *Cadernos de estudos sociais Recife* 3, no. 2: 193–206.

Cavalcanti, Clovis

1981 "Employment, Production, and Income Distribution in the Informal Urban Sector of the Northeast: The Case of Salvador, Bahia." *Luso-Brazilian Review* 18, no. 1: 139–54.

1987 "O mercado do pequeno e a síndrome da informalidade: Atividades informais e população de baixa renda no nordeste." *Cadernos de estudos sociais Recife* 3, no. 1: 65–74.

Charsley, Simon R.

1991 *Rites of Marrying: The Wedding Industry in Scotland*. Manchester: Manchester University Press.

Clark, Mari H.

1989 "*Nevra* in a Greek Village: Idiom, Metaphor, Symptom, or Disorder?" In *Gender, Health, and Illness: The Case of Nerves*, edited by Dona L. Davis and Setha M. Low, 103–26. New York: Hemisphere Publishing Co.

Clifford, James

1988 *The Predicament of Culture: Twentieth-Century Ethnography, Literature, and Art*. Cambridge: Harvard University Press.

Clifford, James, and J. E. Marcus, eds.

1986 *Writing Culture: The Poetics and Politics of Ethnography*. Berkeley: University of California Press.

Cohen, Robin

1991 *Contested Domains: Debates in International Labor Studies*. London: Zed Press.

Cole, Sally

1991 *Women of the Praia: Work and Lives in a Portuguese Coastal Community*. Princeton: Princeton University Press.

Collier, Jane Fishburne
  1997   *From Duty to Desire: Remaking Families in a Spanish Village*. Princeton: Princeton University Press.
Colson, Audrey Butt, and Cesareo de Armellada
  1983   "An Amerindian Derivation for Latin American Creole Illnesses and Their Treatment." *Social Science and Medicine* 17, no. 17: 1229–48.
Conrad, Robert Edgar
  1986   *World of Sorrow: The African Slave Trade to Brazil*. Baton Rouge: Louisiana State University Press.
Corrêa, Mariza
  1982   "Repensando a família patriarchal brasileira." In *Colcha de retalhos: Estudos sobre a família no Brasil*, edited by Maria Suely Kofes de Alameda, 13–38. São Paulo: Brasiliense.
Costa, Jurandir Freire
  1989   *Ordem médica e norma familiar 3ª edição*. Rio de Janeiro: Edições Graal, Ltda. (First published in 1979.)
Cowan, Jane
  1990   *Dance and the Body Politic in Northern Greece*. Princeton: Princeton University Press.
Crandon, Libbet
  1983   "Why Susto?" *Ethnology* 22, no. 2: 153–68.
Crandon-Malamud, Libbet
  1991   *From the Fat of Our Souls: Social Change, Political Process, and Medical Pluralism in Bolivia*. Berkeley: University of California Press.
Crespo, Eduardo
  1986   "A Regional Variation: Emotions in Spain." In *The Social Construction of Emotions*, edited by Rom Harré, 209–17. Oxford: Basil Blackwell.
Cruz, Anna
  1992   "La Bella Malmaridada: Lessons for the Good Wife." In *Culture and Control in Counter-Reformation Spain*, edited by Anna Cruz and Mary Elizabeth Perry, 145–70. Minneapolis: University of Minnesota Press.
Cubitt, Tessa, and Helen Greenslade
  1997   "Public and Private Spheres: The End of Dichotomy." In *Gender Politics in Latin America: Debates in Theory and Practice*, edited by Elizabeth Dore, 52–64. New York: Monthly Review Press.
Cunha, Antônio Geraldo da
  1989   *Dicionário etimológico nova fronteira da língua Portuguesa 2ª edição*. Rio de Janeiro: Nova Fronteira.
Currier, R. L.
  1966   "The Hot-Cold Syndrome and Symbolic Balance in Mexican and Spanish American Folk Medicine." *Ethnology* 5: 251–63.
Dahl, Hartvig, and B. Stengel
  1978   "A Classification of Emotion Words: A Modification and Partial Test of de Rivera's Decision Theory of Emotions." *Psychoanalysis and Contemporary Thought* 1: 269–312.

Daly, Mary

 1973 "Faith, Hope, and Charity." In *Dictionary of the History of Ideas*, vol. 2, edited by Philip P. Weiner, 209–16. New York: Charles Scribner's Sons.

Da Matta, Roberto

 1985 *A Casa e a rua*. São Paulo: Editora Brasilense, S.A.

 1997 "A vida dos documentos." Paper given at Yale University, April 26.

Daniel, E. Valentine

 1996 *Charred Lullabies: Chapters in an Anthropography of Violence*. Princeton: Princeton University Press.

Danto, Arthur C.

 1991 "Forward." In *The Philosophy of (Erotic) Love*, edited by Robert C. Solomon and Kathleen M. Higgins, ix–xii. Lawrence: University Press of Kansas.

Darwin, Charles

 1872 *The Expression of the Emotions in Man and Animals*. London: Murray.

Davis, Dona Lee

 1983 "Woman the Worrier: Confronting Feminist and Biomedical Archetypes of Stress." *Women's Studies* 10: 135–46.

 1989 "The Variable Character of Nerves in a Newfoundland Fishing Village." *Medical Anthropology* 2: 63–78.

Davis, Dona Lee, and Peter J. Guarnaccia

 1989 "Health, Culture, and the Nature of Nerves: Introduction." *Medical Anthropology* 2: 1–13.

Davis, Dona L., and Setha M. Low, eds.

 1989 *Gender, Health, and Illness: The Case of Nerves*. New York: Hemisphere Publishing Co.

Davis, Dona L., and R. G. Whitten

 1988 "Medical and Popular Traditions of Nerves." *Social Science and Medicine* 26: 1209–21.

Davitz, J. R.

 1969 *The Language of Emotion*. New York: Academic Press.

de Alameida, Miguel Vale

 1996 *The Hegemonic Male: Masculinity in a Portuguese Town*. Providence, R.I.: Berghahn Books.

de Araujo, Tânia Bacelar

 1987 "Nordeste: Diferenciais demográficas regionais e seus determinantes." *Cadernos de estudos sociais Recife* 3, no. 3: 167–92.

de Assis Silva, Francisco, and Pedro Ivo de Assis Bastos

 1986 *História do Brasil colônia, império e república 2ª ediçao*. São Paulo: Editora Moderna.

de Azevedo, Thales

 1968 "Family, Marriage, and Divorce in Brazil." In *Contemporary Cultures and Societies of Latin America*, edited by Dwight B. Heath, 288–310. New York: Random House.

 1986 *As regras do namoro à antiga*. São Paulo: Editora Atica.

Degler, Carl N.

1971 *Neither Black nor White: Slavery and Race Relations in Brazil and the United States*. Madison: University of Wisconsin Press.

Delveccio-Good, Mary-Jo, and Byron J. Good

1988 "Ritual, the State, and the Transformation of Emotional Discourse in Iranian Society." *Culture, Medicine, and Psychiatry* 12: 43–63.

de Rougemont, Denis

1972 *O Amor e o Ocidente*. Translated from the French by Paulo Brandi and Ethel Brandi Cachapuz. Rio de Janeiro: Editora Guanabara.

1973 "Love." In *Dictionary of the History of Ideas*, edited by Philip P. Weiner, 94–108. New York: Charles Scribner's Sons.

Desjarlais, Robert R.

1992 *Body and Emotion: The Aesthetics of Illness and Healing in the Nepal Himalayas*. Philadelphia: University of Pennsylvania Press.

Dias, Adahyl Lourenço

1975 *A concubina e o direito Brasileiro 2ª edição*. São Paulo: Saraiva.

Diaz, Arlene J., and Jeff Stewart

1991 "Occupational Class and Female Headed Households in Santiago Maior do Iguape, Brazil, 1835." *Journal of Family History* 16, no. 3: 299–313.

D'Inção, Maria Angela, org.

1989 *Amor e família no Brasil*. São Paulo: Editora Contexto.

Douglass, Lisa

1992 *The Power of Sentiment: Love, Hierarchy, and the Jamaican Family Elite*. Boulder: Westview Press.

Driessen, Hank

1983 "Male Sociability and Rituals of Masculinity in Rural Andalusia." *Anthropological Quarterly* 56, 3: 125–33.

Duarte, Luiz-Fernando D.

1986 *Da vida nervosa nas classes trabalhadores urbanas*. Rio de Janeiro: Jorge Zahar Editor/CNPq.

1993 "Os nervos e a antropologia médica Norte-Americana: Uma revisao crítica." *Physis revista de saúde colectiva* 3, no. 2: 43–73.

Duby, Georges

1983 *The Knight, the Lady, and the Priest: The Making of Modern Marriage in Medieval France*. Translated by Barbara Bray. New York: Pantheon Books.

Duffy, Elizabeth

1941 "The Conceptual Categories of Psychology: A Suggestion for Revision." *Psychological Review* 48: 177–203.

Duffy, Maureen

1972 *The Erotic World of Faerie*. London: Sphere Books.

Dundes, Alan

1980 *Interpreting Folklore*. Bloomington: Indiana University Press.

Dunk, Pamela

1989 "Greek Women and Broken Nerves in Montreal." *Medical Anthropology* 2: 29–45.

Ehlers, Tracy Bachrach
1991 "Debunking Marianismo: Economic Vulnerability and Survival Strategy among Guatemalan Wives." *Ethnology* 30, no. 1: 1–16.

Eisenstadt, S. N., and L. Roniger
1984 *Patrons, Clients, and Friends: Interpersonal Relations and the Structure of Trust in Society.* Cambridge: Cambridge University Press.

Ekman, Paul
1980 *The Face of Man: Universal Expression in a New Guinea Village.* New York: Garland.
1984 "Expression and the Nature of Emotion." In *Approaches to Emotion,* edited by K. Scherer and P. Ekman, 319–43. Hillsdale, N.J.: Erlbaum.

Engels, Frederick
1942 [1902] *The Origin of the Family, Private Property, and the State.* New York: International Publishers.

Erikson, Kai
1976 *Everything in Its Path.* New York: Simon and Schuster.

Esteves, Martha de Abreu
1989 *Meninas perdidas: Os populares e o cotidiano do amor no Rio de Janeiro de belle époque.* Rio de Janeiro: Paz e Terra.

Fabian, Johannes
1983 *Time and the Other: How Anthropology Makes Its Object.* New York: Columbia University Press.

Faubion, James
1993 *Modern Greek Lessons: A Primer in Historical Constructivism.* Princeton: Princeton University Press.

Fausto, Boris
1984 *Crime e cotidiano: A criminalidade em São Paulo (1800–1924).* São Paulo: Brasiliense.

Figueira, Sérvulo A.
1986 "O 'moderno' e o 'arcaico' na nova família brasileira: Notas sobre a dimensao invisível da mudança social." In *Uma nova família? O moderno e o arcaico na família de classe média Brasileira,* edited by Sérvulo A. Figueira, 11–30. Rio de Janeiro: Jorge Zahar Editor Ltda.

Figueiredo, Luciano
1993 *O avesso da memória: Cotidiano e trabalho da mulher em minas gerais no século XVIII.* Rio de Janeiro: José Olympio.

Finerman, Ruthbeth
1989 "The Burden of Responsibility: Duty, Depression, and *Nervios* in Andean Ecuador." In *Gender, Health, and Illness: The Case of Nerves,* edited by Dona L. Davis and Setha M. Low, 49–66. New York: Hemisphere Publishing Co.

Finkler, Kaja
1989 "The Universality of Nerves." In *Gender, Health, and Illness: The Case of Nerves,* edited by Dona L. Davis and Setha M. Low, 79–87. New York: Hemisphere Publishing Co.

Fisher, Helen

1992   *Anatomy of Love: The Natural History of Monogamy, Adultery, and Divorce.* New York: Norton.

Fisher, Wesley Andrew

1980   *The Soviet Marriage Market: Mate-Selection in Russia and the USSR.* New York: Praeger.

Foster, George

1953   "Relationships between Spanish and Spanish-American Folk Medicine." *Journal of American Folklore* 66: 201–17.

1965   "Peasant Society and the Image of Limited Good." *American Anthropologist* 67: 293–315.

1970   "Character and Personal Relations Seen through Proverbs in Tzintzuntzan, Mexico." *Journal of American Folklore* 83: 304–17.

1972   "The Anatomy of Envy: A Study in Symbolic Behavior." *Current Anthropology* 13: 165–202.

1987   "On the Origin of Humoral Medicine in Latin America." *Medical Anthropological Quarterly* 1: 355–93.

Foucault, Michel

1978   *The History of Sexuality.* Vol. 1, *An Introduction.* Translated by Robert Hurley. New York: Vintage Books.

1979   *Discipline and Punish: The Birth of the Prison.* Translated by Alan Sheridan. New York: Vintage Books.

Fox, Geoffrey E.

1973   "Honor, Shame, and Women's Liberation in Cuba: Views of Working Class Emigré Men." In *Female and Male in Latin America: Essays,* edited by Ann Pescatello, 273–91. Pittsburgh: University of Pittsburgh Press.

Freud, Sigmund

1960 [1905]   *Jokes and Their Relation to the Unconscious.* Translated by James Strachey. New York: Norton.

Freyre, Gilberto

1963   *Casa grande e senzala 12ª ed.* Brasília: Editora da Universidade da Brasília.

Gaines, Atwood T., and Paul E. Farmer

1986   "Visible Saints: Social Cynosures and Dysphoria in the Mediterranean Tradition." *Culture, Medicine, and Psychiatry* 10, no. 4: 295–330.

Garcia, Carlos

1986   *O que é nordeste Brasileiro 5ª ed.* São Paulo: Brasiliense.

Geertz, H.

1959   "The Vocabulary of Emotion: A Study of Javanese Socialization Practices." *Psychiatry* 22: 225–36.

Giddens, Anthony

1992   *The Transformation of Intimacy: Sexuality, Love, and Eroticism in Modern Societies.* Stanford, Calif.: Stanford University Press.

Gillis, John R.

1988   "From Ritual to Romance: Toward an Alternative History of Love." In

Emotion and Social Change: Toward a New Psychohistory, edited by C. Z. Stearns and P. N Stearns, 87–122. New York: Holms and Meier.

Gilmore, David, ed.

1987 *Honor and Shame and the Unity of the Mediterranean*. Washington, D.C.: American Anthropological Association (Special Publication no. 22).

Gilmore, David D., and Sarah C. Uhl

1987 "Further Notes on Adalusian Machismo." *Journal of Psychoanalytic Anthropology* 10, no. 4: 341–60.

Gilmore, Margaret M., and David C. Gilmore

1979 "'Machismo': A Psychodynamic Approach (Spain)." *Journal of Psychological Anthropology* 2, no. 3: 281–300.

Gnaccarini, José César

1989 "O rapto das donzelas." *Tempo social* (Revista socialógico USP São Paulo) 1, no. 1: 149–68.

Goffman, Erving

1959 *The Presentation of Self in Everyday Life*. Garden City, N.Y.: Doubleday.

Goldenberg, Miriam

1990 *A outra um estudo antropológico sobre a identidade da amante do homem casado*. Rio de Janeiro: Editora Revan.

Goldstein, Donna M.

1994 "AIDS and Women in Brazil: The Emerging Problem." *Social Science and Medicine* 39, no. 7: 919–30.

(forthcoming) "Interracial Sexuality and Racial Democracy in Brazil: Twin Concepts?" *American Anthopologist.*

Goldwert, Marvin

1985 "Mexican Machismo: The Flight from Femininity." *Psychoanalytic Review* 72, no. 1: 162–69.

Goody, Jack

1983 *The Development of the Family and Marriage in Europe*. Cambridge: Cambridge University Press.

Graham, Richard

1990 *Patronage and Politics in 19th Century Brazil*. Stanford, Calif.: Stanford University Press.

Greenberg, Kenneth S.

1996 *Honor and Slavery: Lies, Duels, Noses, Masks, Dressing as a Woman, Gifts, Strangers, Humanitarianism, Death, Slave Rebellions, the Proslavery Argument, Baseball, Hunting, and Gambling in the Old South*. Princeton: Princeton University Press.

Gregor, Thomas

1985 *Anxious Pleasures: The Sexual Lives of an Amazonian People*. Chicago: University of Chicago Press.

Gregory, C. A.

1982 *Gifts and Commodities*. London: Academic Press.

Guarnaccia, Peter, V. DeLaCancela, and Emilio Carrillo
    1989   "The Multiple Meanings of Ataques de Nervios in the Latino Commu-
            nity." *Medical Anthropology* 2: 47–62.
Gutmann, Matthew
    1996   *The Meanings of Macho: Being a Man in Mexico City.* Berkeley: University
            of California Press.
Harré, Rom, ed.
    1986   *The Social Construction of Emotions.* Oxford: Basil Blackwell.
Harré, Rom, and Robert Finlay-Jones
    1986   "Emotion Talk across Times." In *The Social Construction of Emotions,* ed-
            ited by Rom Harré, 221–33. Oxford: Basil Blackwell.
Hatfield, Elaine, John T. Cacioppo, and Richard L. Rapson
    1994   *Emotional Contagion.* Cambridge: Cambridge University Press.
Hayano, David M.
    1979   "Auto-ethnography: Paradigms, Problems, and Prospects." *Human Or-
            ganization* 38: 99–104.
Heelas, Paul
    1983   "Indigenous Representations of Emotions: The Chewong." *Journal of
            the Anthropological Society of Oxford* 14, no. 1: 87–103.
Hertzfeld, Michael
    1980   "Honour and Shame: Problems in the Comparative Analysis of Moral
            Systems." *Man* 15: 339–51.
    1984   "The Horns of the Mediterraneanist Dilemma." *American Ethnologist*
            11, no. 3: 429–54.
    1987   *Anthropology through the Looking Glass: Critical Ethnography in the Mar-
            gins of Europe.* New York: Cambridge University Press.
Hiatt, L. R.
    1978   "Classification of the Emotions." In *Australian Aboriginal Concepts,* ed-
            ited by L. R. Hiatt, 182–87. Canberra: Australian Institute of Aboriginal
            Studies.
Hochschild, Arlie Russell
    1983   *The Managed Heart: Commercialization of Human Feeling.* Berkeley: Uni-
            versity of California Press.
    1985   "Emotion Work, Feeling Rules, and Social Structure." *American Journal
            of Sociology* 85, no. 3: 551–75.
Hochschild, Arlie Russell, with Anne Machung
    1989   *The Second Shift.* New York: Avon Books.
Hoodfar, Homa
    1997   *Between Marriage and the Market: Intimate Politics and Survival in Cairo.*
            Berkeley: University of California Press.
IGBE/UNICEF
    1986   *Perfil estatistico de criancas e mães no Brasil: Aspectos socio-economicos da
            mortalidade infantil em áreas urbanas.* Rio de Janeiro: UNICEF.
Izard, C., and S. Buechler
    1980   "Aspects of Consciousness and Personality in Terms of Differential

Emotions Theory." In *Emotion: Theory, Research, and Experience,* edited by R. Plutchik and H. Kellerman, 165–87. New York: Academic Press.

Jankowiak, William, ed.

1995a *Romantic Passion: A Universal Experience?* New York: Columbia University Press.

1995b "Introduction." In *Romantic Passion: A Universal Experience?* 1–19. New York: Columbia University Press.

Jellinek, E. M.

1952 "Phases of Alcohol Addiction." *Quarterly Journal of Studies on Alcohol* 13: 673–84.

Kay, Margarita, and Carmen Portillo

1989 "*Nervios* and Dysphoria in Mexican American Widows." In *Gender, Health, and Illness: The Case of Nerves,* edited by Dona L. Davis and Setha M. Low, 181–202. New York: Hemisphere Publishing Co.

Kelly, M. Patricia Fernandez, and Saskia Sassen

1995 "Recasting Women in the Global Economy: Internationalization and Changing Definitions of Gender." In *Women in the Latin American Development Process,* edited by Christine E. Bose and Edna Acosta-Belen, 99–124. Philadelphia: Temple University Press.

Kemper, T. D.

1987 "How Many Emotions Are There? Wedding the Social and the Autonomic Components." *American Journal of Sociology* 93, no. 2: 263–89.

Kendall, Laurel

1996 *Getting Married in Korea: Of Gender, Morality, and Modernity.* Berkeley: University of California Press.

Kinzer, Nora Scott

1973 "Priests, Machos, and Babies: Or, Latin American Women and the Manichaean Heresy." *Journal of Marriage and the Family* 35, no. 2: 300–312.

Kirschner, Suzanne K.

1996 *The Religious and Romantic Origins of Psychoanalysis: Individuation and Integration in Post-Freudian Theory.* Cambridge: Cambridge University Press.

Kleinman, Arthur

1977 "Depression, Somatization, and the New 'Cross-Cultural Psychiatry.'" *Social Science and Medicine* 11: 3–10.

1980 *Patients and Healers in the Context of Culture.* Berkeley: University of California Press.

Kolenda, Konstantin

1987 "On Human Emotions." *American Anthropologist* 898: 946–47.

Komarovsky, Mirra

1967 *Blue Collar Marriage.* New York: Vintage.

Koss-Chioino, Joan D.

1989 "Experience of Nervousness and Anxiety Disorders in Puerto Rican Women: Psychiatric and Ethnopsychological Perspectives." In *Gender,*

    Health, and Illness: The Case of Nerves, edited by Dona L. Davis and Setha
    M. Low, 153–80. New York: Hemisphere Publishing Co.

Krieger, Laurie
    1989   "Nerves and Psychosomatic Illness: The Case of Um Ramadan." In
        Gender, Health, and Illness: The Case of Nerves, edited by Dona L. Davis
        and Setha M. Low, 89–102. New York: Hemisphere Publishing Co.

Kundera, Milan
    1984   *The Unbearable Lightness of Being.* Translated by Michael Henry Heim.
        New York: Harper and Row.

Kuznesof, Elizabeth Anne
    1991   "Sexual Politics, Race, and Bastard-Bearing in Nineteenth Century
        Brazil: A Question of Culture or Power?" *Journal of Family History* 16,
        no. 3: 241–60.

Lakoff, Robin
    1975   *Language and Women's Place.* New York: Harper and Row.

Lamphere, Louise, Helena Ragoné, and Patricia Zavella.
    1997   *Situated Lives: Gender and Culture in Everyday Life.* New York: Rout-
        ledge.

Laslett, Peter, and Richard Wall, eds.
    1972   *Household and Family in Past Time.* Cambridge: Cambridge University
        Press.

Lavrin, Asunción
    1989   "Sexuality in Colonial Mexico: A Church Dilemma." In *Latin American
        Women: Historical Perspectives,* edited by Asunción Lavrin, 47–92. West-
        port, Conn.: Greenwood Press.

Leach, William
    1980   *True Love and Perfect Union: The Feminist Reform of Sex and Society.* New
        York: Basic Books.

Leff, Julian
    1977   "The Cross-Cultural Study of Emotions." *Culture, Medicine, and Psy-
        chiatry* 1: 317–50.

Leff, Nathaniel H.
    1997   "Economic Development in Brazil: 1822–1913." In *How Latin America
        Fell Behind: Essays on the Economic Histories of Brazil and Mexico, 1800–
        1914,* edited by Stephen Haber, 34–64. Palo Alto, Calif.: Stanford Uni-
        versity Press.

Leite, Miriam Moreira
    1993   *Retratos de família: Leitura da fotografia histórica.* São Paulo: Editora da
        Universidade de São Paulo.

Levine, Robert M.
    1978   *Pernambuco in the Brazilian Federation 1889–1937.* Stanford, Calif.: Stan-
        ford University Press.

Levy, R. I.
    1973   *Tahitians: Mind and Experience in the Society Islands.* Chicago: University
        of Chicago Press.

Lewis, C. S.
   1936   *The Allegory of Love*. Oxford: Oxford University Press.
Lewis, Reina
   1996   *Gendering Orientalism: Race, Femininity, and Representation*. New York:
           Routledge.
Limón, José E.
   1989   "Carne, Carnales, and the Carnivalesque: Bakhtinian Batos, Disorder,
           and Narrative Discourses." *American Ethnologist* 16, no. 3: 471–86.
Lock, Margaret
   1989   "Words of Fear, Words of Power: Nerves and the Awakening of Politi-
           cal Consciousness." *Medical Anthropology* 2: 79–90.
   1990   "On Being Ethnic: The Politics of Identity Breaking and Making in Can-
           ada or *Nevra* on Sunday." *Culture, Medicine, and Psychiatry* 14: 237–54.
Logan, M. H.
   1974   "Selected References on the Hot-Cold Theory of Disease." *Medical An-
           thropology Newsletter* 6, no. 1: 8–11.
Lope de Vega, Félix
   1986   *La bella malmaridada*. Edited by Donald McGrady and Suzanne Free-
           man. Charlottesville, Va.: Biblioteca Siglo de Oro.
Low, Setha
   1981   "The Meaning of *Nervios*: A Sociocultural Analysis of Symptom Pres-
           entation in San Jose, Costa Rica." *Culture, Medicine, and Psychiatry* 5: 25–
           47.
   1985   "Culturally Interpreted Symptoms or Culture-Bound Syndromes: A
           Cross-Cultural Review of 'Nerves.'" *Social Science and Medicine* 21: 187–
           96.
   1989a   "Health, Culture, and the Nature of Nerves: A Critique." *Medical An-
           thropology* 2: 91–95.
   1989b   "Gender, Emotion, and *Nervios* in Urban Guatemala." In *Gender,
           Health, and Illness: The Case of Nerves*, edited by Dona L. Davis and Setha
           M. Low, 23–48. New York: Hemisphere Publishing Co.
Lutz, Catherine
   1982   "The Domain of Emotion Words on Ifaluk." *American Ethnology* 9: 113–
           28.
   1988   *Unnatural Emotions: Everyday Sentiments on a Micronesian Atoll and Their
           Challenge to Western Theory*. Chicago: University of Chicago Press.
Lyons, Williams
   1980   *Emotion*. Cambridge: Cambridge University Press.
MacFarlane, Alan
   1987   *The Culture of Capitalism*. Cambridge: Basil Blackwell.
McLaren, Peter
   1991   "Field Relations and the Discourse of the Other: Collaboration in Our
           Own Ruin." In *Experiencing Fieldwork: An Inside View of Qualitative Re-
           search*, edited by William B. Shaffer and Robert A. Stebbins, 149–63.
           Newbury Park, N.J.: Sage Publications.

Madsen, Claudia
    1955   "A Study of Change in Mexican Folk Medicine." In *Contemporary Latin American Culture*, edited by Munro S. Edmonson, Claudia Madsen, and Jane Fishbourne Collier, 89–138. Pub. no. 25. New Orleans: Middle American Research Institute, Tulane University.

Maior, Mário Souto
    1988   *Dicionário do palavrao e termos afins*. 5ª Edição. Rio de Janeiro: Editora Recorde.

Maloney, Clarence, ed.
    1976   *The Evil Eye*. New York: Columbia University Press.

Marcus, George E., and Michael M. J. Fischer
    1986   *Anthropology as Cultural Critique: An Experimental Moment in the Human Sciences*. Chicago: University of Chicago Press.

Martins Dias, G.
    1978   "New Patterns of Domination in Rural Brazil." *Economic Development and Cultural Change* 27, no. 1: 169–82.

Marvin, Garry
    1984   "The Cockfight in Andalusia, Spain: Images of the Truly Male." *Anthropological Quarterly* 57, no. 2: 60–70.

Massolo, Maria
    1990   "Teenage Granny: Portrayals of Women in Falkland Islands Nicknames." *Names* 38, no. 4: 283–94.

Mattoso, Kátia de Queiros
    1988   *Família e sociedade na bahia no seculo XIX*. Salvador, Bahia, Brazil: Hucitec.

Mauss, Marcel
    1974 [1925]   *The Gift*. Translated by W. D. Halls. London: Routledge and Kegan Paul.

Medick, Hans, and David Warren Sabean
    1984a   "Introduction." *Interest and Emotion Essays on the Study of Family and Kinship*, edited by H. Medick and D. W. Sabean, 1–8. Cambridge: Cambridge University Press.
    1984b   "Interest and Emotion in Family and Kinship Studies: A Critique of Social History and Anthropology." In *Interest and Emotion Essays on the Study of Family and Kinship*, edited by H. Medick and D. W. Sabean, 9–27. Cambridge: Cambridge University Press.

Messerschmidt, Donald A., ed.
    1981   *Anthropologists at Home in North America: Methods and Issues in the Study of One's Own Culture*. Cambridge: Cambridge University Press.

Miller, William Ian
    1993   *Humiliation and Other Essays on Honor, Social Discomfort, and Violence*. Ithaca, N.Y.: Cornell University Press.

Mintz, Sydney
    1996   "Sow's Ears and Silver Linings: A Backward Look at Anthropological Theory." Keynote address, American Anthropological Association Annual Meetings. San Francisco, Calif., November 23.

Mishler, Elliot G.
   1986   *Research Interviewing Context and Narrative.* Cambridge: Harvard University Press.
Mitchell, Timothy
   1990   *Passional Culture: Emotion, Religion, and Society in Southern Spain.* Philadelphia: University of Pennsylvania Press.
Money, J.
   1980   *Love and Love Sickness: The Science of Sex, Gender Difference, and Pair Bonding.* Baltimore, Md.: Johns Hopkins University Press.
Monter, E. William
   1977   "The Pedestal and the Stake: Courtly Love and Witchcraft." In *Becoming Visible: Women in European History,* edited by Renate Bridenthal and Claudia Koontz, 121–36. Boston: Houghton Mifflin Co.
Moraes-Gorechi, Vanda
   1988   "Cultural Variations on Gender: Latin American Marianismo/Machismo in Australia." *Mankind* 18, no. 1: 26–35.
Morgan, Gwendolyn A.
   1993   *Medieval Balladry and the Courtly Tradition: Literature of Revolt and Assimilation.* New York: Peter Lang.
Morley, Samuel A.
   1978   "Growth and Inequality in Brazil." *Luso-Brazilian Review* 15, no. 2: 244–71.
Morsbach, H., and W. J. Tyler
   1986   "A Japanese Emotion: *Amae.*" In *The Social Construction of Emotions,* edited by Rom Harré, 289–307. Oxford: Basil Blackwell.
Morse, Janice M.
   1992   *Qualitative Health Research.* Newbury Park, Calif.: Sage Publications.
Mount, Ferdinand
   1982   *The Subversive Family: An Alternative History of Love and Marriage.* London: Jonathan Cape.
Murstein, Bernard I.
   1974   *Love, Sex, and Marriage through the Ages.* New York: Springer Publishing Company.
Myers, F. R.
   1979   "Emotions and the Self: A Theory of Personhood and Political Order among Pintupi Aborigines." *Ethos* 7: 343–70.
Nations, Marilyn K., Linda Camino, and Frederick Walker
   1988   "Nerves: Folk Idiom for Anxiety and Depression." *Social Science and Medicine* 26, no. 12: 1245–59.
Nations, Marilyn K., and Monica Facanha Farias
   1990   "*Jeitinho Brasileiro:* Cultural Creativity and Making the Medical System Work for Poor Brazilians." In *What We Know about Health Transition: The Cultural, Social, and Behavioural Determinants of Health,* edited by John Caldwell et al., 2:756–69. Workshop proceedings, Canberra, May 1989.

Nations, Marilyn K., and L. A. Rebhun
   1988   "Angels with Wet Wings Won't Fly: Maternal Sentiment and the Im-
          age of Neglect." *Culture, Medicine, and Psychiatry* 12: 141–200.
Nazzari, Muriel
   1991   *Disappearance of the Dowry: Women, Families, and Social Change in São
          Paulo, Brazil, 1600–1900*. Stanford, Calif.: Stanford University Press.
   1996   "Concubinage in Colonial Brazil: The Inequalities of Race, Class, and
          Gender." *Journal of Family History* 21, no. 2: 107–24.
Neuhouser, Kevin
   1989   "Sources of Women's Power and Status among the Urban Poor in
          Contemporary Brazil." *Signs Journal of Women in Culture and Society* 14,
          no. 3: 685–702.
Newman, F. X., ed.
   1968   *The Meaning of Courtly Love*. Albany: State University of New York
          Press.
Noguera, Oracy
   1955   "Preconçeito de marca e preconçeito de raça de origem." In *Anais do
          XXXI: Congresso de Americanistas* (August 23–28), edited by H. Baldus,
          409–34. São Paulo: Editôra Anhembi.
Nordstrom, Carolyn, and Antonius C. G. M. Robben, eds.
   1995   *Fieldwork under Fire: Contemporary Studies of Violence and Survival*. Ber-
          keley: University of California Press.
Norris, William P.
   1988   "Household Survival in the Face of Poverty in Salvador, Brazil: To-
          wards an Integrated Model of Household Activities." *Urban Anthropol-
          ogy* 17, no. 4: 299–321.
   1984   "Patron-Client Relationships in the Urban Social Structure: A Brazilian
          Case Study." *Human Organization* 43, no. 1: 16–26.
O'Dougherty, Maureen
   1992   "Resisting 'Democratic' Fashion: Maintaining Distinctions through
          Consumption Practices in Northeast Brazil." Paper presented at Amer-
          ican Anthropological Association annual meeting. San Francisco, Calif.
   1995   "Middle Classes, Ltd.: Family Strategies in Pursuit of Symbolic Capital
          during Brazil's Economic Crisis." Paper presented at American An-
          thropological Association annual meeting. Washington, D.C.
   1996   "Consumption and Middle Class Identity: Shopping during Brazil's
          Economic Crisis." In *Anthropology for a Small Planet: Culture and Com-
          munity in a Global Environment*, edited by Anthony Marcus, 127–40. Ith-
          aca, N.Y.: Brandywine Press.
Oliven, Ruben George
   1988   "Man/Woman Relations and the Construction of Brazilian Identity in
          Popular Music." *Social Science Information* 27, no. 1: 119–38.
O'Nell, Theresa DeLeane
   1996   *Disciplined Hearts: History, Identity, and Depression in an American Indian
          Community*. Berkeley: University of California Press.

Ortner, Sherry.
1984 "Theory in Anthropology since the Sixties." *Comparative Studies in Society and History* 26, no. 2: 126–66.
1995 "Resistance and the Problem of Ethnographic Refusal." *Comparative Studies in Society and History* 37, no. 1: 173–93.
Paris, Gaston
1883 "Études sur les romans de la Table Ronde. Lancelot du Lac. II. Le Conte de la Charrette." *Romania* 12: 459–534.
Parker, Richard G.
1991 *Bodies, Pleasures, and Passions: Sexual Culture in Contemporary Brazil.* Boston: Beacon Press.
Pastore, José
1979 *Desigualdade e mobilidade social no Brasil.* São Paulo: T. A. Queiroz.
Patai, Daphne
1988 *Brazilian Women Speak Contemporary Life Stories.* New Brunswick, N.J.: Rutgers University Press.
Pearlman, Cynthia
1984 "Machismo, Marianismo, and Change from Indigenous Mexico: A Case Study from Oaxaca." *Quarterly Journal of Ideology* 8, no. 4: 53–59.
Pereira, Anthony W.
1997 *The End of the Peasantry: The Rural Labor Movement in Northeast Brazil.* Pittsburgh, Pa.: University of Pittsburgh Press.
Perlman, Janice
1976 *The Myth of Marginality.* Berkeley: University of California Press.
Peterson, M. Jeanne
1989 *Family, Love, and Work in the Lives of Victorian Gentlewomen.* Bloomington: Indiana University Press.
Pitt-Rivers, Julian
1966 "Honor and Social Status." In *Honor and Shame: The Virtues of Mediterranean Society,* edited by J. G. Peristiany, 19–78. Chicago: University of Chicago Press.
Plutchik, R.
1962 *The Emotions: Facts, Theories, and a New Model.* New York: Random House.
Powdermaker, Hortense
1966 *Stranger and Friend: The Way of an Anthropologist.* New York: W. W. Norton.
Pratt, Dallas
1960 "The Don Juan Myth." *American Imago* 17, no. 3: 321–35.
Preston, Paul
1994 *Mother Father Deaf: Living between Sound and Silence.* Cambridge: Harvard University Press.
Radice, Betty, trans.
1974 *The Letters of Abelard and Heloise.* New York: Penguin.

Ramos, Donald

1991   "Single and Married Women in Vila Rica, Brazil 1754–1838." *Journal of Family History* 16, no. 3: 261–82.

Rebhun, L. A.

1993   "Nerves and Emotional Play in Northeast Brazil." *Medical Anthropology Quarterly* 7, no. 2: 131–51.

1994   "A Heart Too Full: The Weight of Love in Northeast Brazil." *Journal of American Folklore* 104, no. 423: 167–80.

1995   "Contemporary Evil Eye in Northeast Brazil." In *Folklore Interpreted: Essays in Honor of Alan Dundes*, edited by R. Bendix and Rosemary Lévy Zumwalt, 213–33. New York: Garland.

Ribeiro, Rene

1982   "O amaziamento e outros aspectos da família no Recife." In *Antropologia da religião e outros estudos*, 59–70. Recife: Editora Massangana-Fundação Joachim Nabuco.

Robben, Antonius C. G. M.

1988   "Conflicting Gender Conceptions in a Pluriform Fishing Economy: A Hermeneutic Perspective on Conjugal Relationships in Brazil." In *To Work and to Weep: Women in Fishing Economies*, edited by Jane Nadel-Klein and Dona Lee Davis, 106–29. St. Johns, Newfoundland: Institute of Social and Economic Research.

1989a *Sons of the Sea Goddess: Economic Practice and Discursive Conflict in Brazil.* New York: Columbia University Press.

1989b "Habits of the Home: Spatial Hegemony and the Structuration of House and Society in Brazil." *American Anthropologist* 91, no. 3: 570–88.

Robertson, D. W., Jr.

1968   "The Concept of Courtly Love as an Impediment to the Understanding of Medieval Texts." In *The Meaning of Courtly Love*, edited by F. X. Newman, 1–18. Albany: State University of New York Press.

Rocha, Helina de Moura Luz

1980   *Os direitos da mulher casada.* Rio de Janeiro: Editora Technoprint.

Roldan, Martha

1988   "Renegotiating the Marital Contract: Intrahousehold Patterns of Money Allocation and Women's Subordination among Domestic Outworkers in Mexico City." In *A Home Divided: Women and Income in the Third World*, edited by Daisy Dwyer and Judith Bruce, 229–47. Stanford, Calif.: Stanford University Press.

Romão, Mauricio Costa

1988   "Estrutura produtiva e padrão de desenvolvimento no Brasil." *Cadernos de estudos sociais* 4, no. 1: 119–42.

Roniger, Luis

1987   "Coronelismo, Caciquismo, and Oyabun-kobun Bonds: Divergent Implications of Hierarchical Trust in Brazil, Mexico, and Japan." *British Journal of Sociology* 38, no. 3: 310–30.

Rosaldo, M.
  1980   *Knowledge and Passion: Ilonget Notions of Self and Social Life*. London:
          Cambridge University Press.
  1984   "Toward an Anthropology of Self and Feeling." In *Culture Theory: Es-
          says on Mind, Self and Emotion*, edited by R. A. Schweder and R. A.
          LeVine, 137–57. Cambridge: Cambridge University Press.
Rothstein, Frances
  1983   "Women and Men in the Family Economy: An Analysis of Relations
          between the Sexes in Three Peasant Communities." *Anthropological
          Quarterly* 56, no. 1: 10–23.
Rubin, Lillian Breslow
  1976   *Worlds of Pain: Life in the Working-Class Family*. New York: Basic Books.
Russell, J. A.
  1983   "Pancultural Aspects of the Human Conceptual Organization of Emo-
          tions." *Journal of Personality and Social Psychology* 45: 1281–88.
Russell-Wood, A. J. R.
  1978   "Female and Family in the Economy and Society of Colonial Brazil." In
          Latin American Women: Historical Perspectives, edited by Asunción
          Lavrin, 60–100. Westport, Conn.: Greenwood Press.
Saffioti, Heleieth, and Vera Lucia Silveira Botta Ferrante
  1983   "A mulher e as contradicoes do capitalismo agrario." *Perspectivas São
          Paulo* 6: 67–75.
Said, Edward
  1978   *Orientalism: Western Representations of the Orient*. London: Routledge
          and Kegan Paul.
  1989   "Representing the Colonized: Anthropology's Interlocutors." *Critical
          Inquiry* 15, no. 2: 205–25.
Salem, Tania
  1980   "Mulheres faveladas: 'Com a venda nos olhos.'" *Perspectivas antropo-
          lógicas da mulher* 1: 49–99.
Samara, Eni de Mesquita
  1983   *A família Brasileira*. São Paulo: Brasiliense.
Santos Filho, L. de Castro
  1966   *Pequena história da medicina Brasileira*. São Paulo: DESA.
Sarsby, Jacqueline
  1983   *Romantic Love and Society: Its Place in the Modern World*. Middlesex: Pen-
          guin Books.
Sastry, Narayan
  1997   "What Explains Rural-Urban Differentials in Child Mortality in Bra-
          zil?" *Social Science and Medicine* 44, no. 7: 989–1002.
Scheper-Hughes, Nancy
  1984   "Infant Mortality and Infant Care: Cultural and Economic Constraints
          on Nurturing in Northeast Brazil." *Social Science and Medicine* 19, no. 5:
          535–46.

1985 "Culture, Scarcity, and Maternal Thinking: Maternal Detachment and Infant Survival in a Brazilian Shantytown." *Ethos* 13, no. 4: 291–317.

1988 "The Madness of Hunger: Sickness, Delirium, and Human Needs." *Culture, Medicine and Psychiatry* 12: 429–58.

1990 "Three Propositions for a Critically Applied Medical Anthropology." *Social Science and Medicine* 30: 189–97.

1992 *Death without Weeping: The Violence of Everyday Life in Brazil.* Berkeley: University of California Press.

Scheper-Hughes, Nancy, and Margaret Lock

1987 "The Mindful Body: A Prolegomenon to Future Work in Medical Anthropology." *Medical Anthropology Quarterly* 1, no. 1: 6–41.

Schneider, J.

1971 "Of Vigilance and Virgins: Honour, Shame, and Access to Resources in Mediterranean Society." *Ethnology* 10: 1–24.

Schwartz, Stuart B.

1985 *Sugar Plantations in the Formation of Brazilian Society: Bahia, 1550–1835.* Cambridge: Cambridge University Press.

1992 *Slaves, Peasants, and Rebels: Reconsidering Brazilian Slavery.* Urbana: University of Illinois Press.

Scott, James C.

1985 *Weapons of the Weak: Everyday Forms of Peasant Resistance.* New Haven, Conn.: Yale University Press.

1990 *Domination and the Arts of Resistance: Hidden Transcripts.* New Haven, Conn.: Yale University Press.

Seed, Patricia

1988 *To Love, Honor, and Obey in Colonial Mexico: Conflicts over Marriage Choice, 1574–1821.* Stanford, Calif.: Stanford University Press.

Segalen, Martine

1983 *Love and Power in the Peasant Family: Rural France in the Nineteenth Century.* Translated by Sarah Matthews. Oxford: Basil Blackwell. (Originally published in French in 1980 under the title *Mari et femme dans la société paysanne.*)

Sevcenko, Nicolau

1984 *A revolta da vacina mentes insanas em corpos rebeldes.* Serie tudo é história. São Paulo: Brasiliense.

Shaffir, William B., and Robert A. Stebbins, eds.

1991 *Experiencing Fieldwork: An Inside View of Qualitative Research.* Newbury Park, Calif.: Sage Publications.

Shkilnyk, Anastasia M.

1985 *A Poison Stronger than Love: The Destruction of an Ojibwa Community.* New Haven, Conn.: Yale University Press.

Shorter, Edward

1975 *The Making of the Modern Family.* New York: Basic Books.

Silva, Maria Beatriz Nizza da

1984 *Sistema de casamento no Brasil colonial.* São Paulo: Editora da Universidade de São Paulo.

1993   *Vida privada e quotidiano no Brasil na época de D. Maria I e D. João VI.* Lisbon: Editorial Estampa.

Símic, Andrei

1983   "Machismo and Cryptomatriarchy." *Ethos* 11, nos. 1/2: 66–86.

Singer, Merrill

1986   "Developing a Critical Perspective in Medical Anthropology." *Medical Anthropology Quarterly* 17, no. 5: 128–29.

Singer, Merrill, and Hans Baer

1995   *Critical Medical Anthropology.* Amityville, N.Y.: Baywood Press.

Slutka, Jeffrey A.

1989   "Living on Their Nerves: Nervous Debility in Northern Ireland." In *Gender, Health, and Illness: The Case of Nerves,* edited by Dona L. Davis and Setha M. Low, 127–52. New York: Hemisphere Publishers.

Snell, Keith

1981   "Agricultural Seasonal Unemployment, the Standard of Living, and Women's Work in the South and East: 1690–1860." *Economic History Review,* Second Series, 34, no. 3: 407–37.

Soares, Gláucio Ary Dillon

1978   "After the Miracle." *Luso-Brazilian Review* 15, no. 2: 278–307.

Sobreira, Caesar

1988   "O semitismo no nordeste." *Quadra* 91: 22–25.

Soeiro, Susan A.

1978   "The Feminine Orders in Colonial Bahia, Brazil: Economic, Social, and Demographic Implications." In *Latin American Women: Historical Perspectives,* edited by Asunción Lavrin, 173–97. Westport, Conn.: Greenwood Press.

Solomon, R. C.

1984   "Getting Angry: The Jamesian Theory of Emotion in Anthropology." In *Culture Theory: Essays on Mind, Self, and Emotion,* edited by R. A. Shweder and R. A. LeVine, 238–54. Cambridge: Cambridge University Press.

Spierenburg, Peter

1991   *The Broken Spell: A Cultural and Anthropological History of Preindustrial Europe.* New Brunswick, N.J.: Rutgers University Press.

Stepan, Nancy

1976   *Beginnings of Brazilian Science: Oswaldo Cruz, Medical Research and Policy 1890–1920.* New York, N.Y.: Science History Publications.

Stern, Steve J.

1995   *The Secret History of Gender: Women, Men, and Power in Late Colonial Mexico.* Chapel Hill: University of North Carolina Press.

Sternberg, R. J., and M. L. Barnes

1980   *The Psychology of Love.* New Haven, Conn.: Yale University Press.

Stevens, Evelyn P.

1973a   "Machismo and Marianismo." *Society* 10, no. 6: 57–63.

1973b   "Marianismo: The Other Face of Machismo in Latin America." In *Fe-

male and Male in Latin America: Essays, edited by Ann Pescatello, 89–101. Pittsburgh: University of Pittsburgh Press.

Stewart, Frank Henderson

1994   *Honor.* Chicago: University of Chicago Press.

Stone, Lawrence

1977   *The Family, Sex and Marriage in England 1500–1800.* New York: Harper Colophon Books.

Suárez-Orozco, Marcelo Mario

1982   "A Study of Argentine Soccer: The Dynamics of Its Fans and Their Folklore." *Journal of Psychoanalytic Anthropology* 5, no. 1: 8–28.

Suárez-Orozco, Marcelo, and Alan Dundes

1984   "The *Piropo* and the Dual Image of Women in the Spanish-Speaking World." *Journal of Latin American Lore* 10, no. 1: 111–33.

Taggart, James

1990   *Enchanted Maidens: Gender Relations in Spanish Folktales of Courtship and Marriage.* Princeton, N.J: Princeton University Press.

Thompson, E. P.

1977   "Happy Families." *New Society* 8: 499–501.

Tousignant, Michel

1979   "*Espanto:* A Dialogue with the Gods." *Culture, Medicine, and Psychiatry* 3: 347–61.

1984   "*Pena* in the Equadorian Sierra: A Psychoanthropological Analysis of Sadness." *Culture, Medicine, and Psychiatry* 3: 381–98.

Trawick, Margaret

1990   *Notes on Love in a Tamil Family.* Berkeley: University of California Press.

Trigo, Maria Helena Bueno

1989   "Amor e casamento no seculo XX." In *Amor e família no Brasil,* edited by Maria Angela D'Incao, 88–94. São Paulo: Editora Contexto.

Tucker, Robert C.

1978   *The Marx-Engels Reader.* 2d ed. New York: W. W. Norton.

Turnbull, Colin

1972   *The Mountain People.* New York: Simon and Schuster.

Varela, Antunes

1980   *Dissolução da sociedade conjugal.* Rio de Janeiro: Forense.

Veja [news magazine]

1990   "O triunfo da outra." October 24.

Wagley, Charles

1965   "Regionalism and Cultural Unity in Brazil." In *Contemporary Cultures and Societies of Latin America,* edited by D. Heath and R. Adams, 124–36. New York: Random House.

Wallace, A. F. C., and M. T. Carson

1973   "Sharing and Diversity in Emotion Terminology." *Ethos* 1: 1–29.

Ward, J. O., and J. H. Sanders

1980   "Nutritional Determinants and Migration in the Brazilian Northeast: A Case Study of Rural and Urban Ceara." *Economic Development and Culture Change* 2, no. 1: 141–63.

Warner, Marina
  1976   *Alone of All Her Sex: The Myth and the Cult of the Virgin Mary*. New York: Alfred A. Knopf.
Wellek, René
  1973   "Romanticism in Literature." In *Dictionary of the History of Ideas: Studies of Selected Pivotal Ideas*, edited by Philip P. Weiner, 4:87–199. New York: Charles Scribner's Sons.
Whyte, William Foote
  1984   *Learning from the Field: A Guide from Experience*. Newbury Park, Calif.: Sage Publications.
Wierzbicka, Anna
  1986   "Human Emotions: Universal or Culture-Specific?" *American Anthropologist* 88, no. 3: 584–94.
Wiest, Raymond
  1983   "Male Migration Machismo and Conjugal Roles: Implications for Fertility Control in a Mexican Municipio." *Journal of Comparative Family Studies* 14, no. 2: 167–81.
Wikan, Uni
  1990   *Managing Turbulent Hearts: A Balinese Formula for Living*. Chicago: University of Chicago Press.
Williams, Raymond
  1973   *The Country and the City*. New York: Oxford University Press.
Wilson, Peter
  1969   "Reputation and Respectability: A Suggestion for Caribbean Ethnology." *Man* 4: 70–84.
  1973, 1995   *Crab Antics: A Caribbean Case Study of the Conflict between Reputation and Respectability*. Prospect Heights, Ill.: Waveland Press.
Wood, Charles H., and José Alberto Magno de Carvalho
  1988   *The Demography of Inequality in Brazil*. Cambridge: Cambridge University Press.
Woortman, Klaas
  1987   *A família das mulheres*. Rio de Janeiro: Edições Tempo Brasileiro.
Yalom, Marilyn
  1997   *A History of the Breast*. New York: Alfred A. Knopf.
Young, Robert J. C.
  1995   *Colonial Desire: Hybridity in Theory, Culture, and Race*. New York: Routledge.

⌒ Index

In this index an "f" after a number indicates a separate reference on the next page, and an "ff" indicates separate references on the next two pages. A continuous discussion over two or more pages is indicated by a span of page numbers, e.g., "57–59." *Passim* is used for a cluster of references in close but not consecutive sequence.

Library of Congress Cataloging-in-Publication Data

Rebhun, Linda-Anne
    The heart is unknown country : love in the changing economy of
northeast Brazil / L. A. Rebhun.
       p.   cm.
    Includes bibliographical references and index.
    ISBN 0-8047-3601-4 (cl. alk. paper) : ISBN 0-8047-4555-2 (pbk. alk. paper)
    1. Man-woman relationships—Brazil—Caruaru. 2. Love—Brazil—
Caruaru. 3. Marriage—Brazil—Caruaru. I. Title.

HQ594.15.C37R43   1999
306.7'0981'34—dc21   99-28657
                                                    CIP

This book is printed on acid-free, archival-quality paper.

Original printing 1999
Last figure below indicates year of this printing:
08   07   06   05   04   03   02   01

Typeset by John Feneron in 10/13 Palatino